Politics and the Migrant Poor in Mexico City

Wayne A. Cornelius

The world-wide population shift from rural to urban areas in the developing nations is especially significant in Latin America, which has surpassed all other Third World regions in urban population growth. This book, the first detailed study of political learning among rural-to-urban migrants in Mexico, examines the political attitudes and behavior of migrants and their city-born neighbors in six small low-income communities on the periphery of Mexico City.

The book addresses itself to several broad questions. How does a poor migrant form images of politics and the political system, and how does he go about becoming a participant in political activity or declining to participate? What are the most important incentives for political involvement? What effect does a large group of low-income people newly entering the political arena have on the political system, and what effect does the system have on them?

The study is both comparative and interdisciplinary: it relates its findings both to studies of the urban poor in other Third World cities and to the latest relevant research findings in political science, sociology, demography, and anthropology. It will stand as a creative model for future studies of the local community as an arena for social and political action.

Wayne A. Cornelius is Assistant Professor of Political Science at the Massachusetts Institute of Technology.

D1517798

Politics
and the Migrant Poor
in Mexico City

STANFORD, CALIFORNIA   1975

Politics
and the Migrant Poor
in Mexico City

WAYNE A. CORNELIUS

STANFORD UNIVERSITY PRESS

Stanford University Press
Stanford, California
© 1975 by the Board of Trustees of the
Leland Stanford Junior University
Printed in the United States of America
ISBN 0-8047-0880-0
LC 75-179

To Ann

Acknowledgments

M Y PRIMARY DEBT is to the residents of six *colonias proletarias* in Mexico City, who for twelve months in 1970 and two additional months in 1971 and 1972 became my extended family-away-from-home. The warmth of their welcome, their patience with seemingly endless questioning, their cooperation and active interest in every phase of the fieldwork can never be adequately acknowledged. Special thanks are owed to Bardo Fray Vela and his family, whose contributions to the conduct of the research and to my understanding of things Mexican were enormously important.

While in Mexico I also benefited greatly from my association with Luis Unikel, Agustín Porras, and their colleagues at El Colegio de México, where I was a visiting researcher during the first year of fieldwork. Robert B. Whitehouse of International Research Associates de México provided wise counsel and a superb staff of interviewers to assist me in the sample survey phase of the study. Harley Browning, Alex Inkeles, and Sidney Verba kindly granted permission for me to use a number of questionnaire items originally constructed for their survey studies of migration and political participation.

At Stanford University, where it all began, I received abundant encouragement and the best kind of substantive criticism from Richard R. Fagen, Robert A. Packenham, and Gabriel A. Almond. I am also greatly indebted to the former chairman of Latin American Studies at Stanford, John J. Johnson, and to Arlee Ellis of the Institute of Political Studies for innumerable kindnesses during my stay at Stanford.

Samuel P. Huntington made it possible for me to spend the 1971–72 academic year as a Research Fellow at Harvard University's Center for International Affairs, where much of the data processing and analysis was completed. Eugene Skolnikoff, Myron Weiner, and other colleagues in the Department of Political Science at MIT provided free time from teaching duties and a stimulating intellectual environment in which to formulate and test many of the ideas elaborated in this study.

Research assistance essential to the completion of the study was provided by Manuel V. Cisneros, Kathleen Foote, Veronica Stoddart, Merilee S. Grindle, and Elisa M. D. C. P. Reis. I also received expert typing and proofreading assistance from Sandra Leavitt, Suzanne Doherty, and Cecilia Dohrmann.

Financial support for various phases of the study was generously provided by the Danforth Foundation, the Foreign Area Fellowship Program of the Social Science Research Council and American Council of Learned Societies, the National Science Foundation (Grant GS-2738), the Center for Research in International Studies at Stanford University, and the Ford and Rockefeller Foundations' Program in Support of Social Science Research on Population Policy (Grant RF-73070). I am also grateful to the publishers of *The American Political Science Review, Urban Anthropology, Latin American Urban Research,* and *Sage Professional Papers in Comparative Politics* for permission to quote from my earlier articles on urban politics in Mexico appearing in these serial publications.

Various chapters of the study have benefited from the comments of James W. Wilkie, Joan M. Nelson, Anthony Leeds, John O. Field, Frederick W. Frey, Henry A. Dietz, Susan Eckstein, and Carlos Salinas de Gortari. However, none of these individuals, or the various funding institutions I have mentioned, should be held responsible for any remaining errors of fact or interpretation. I am also responsible for all photographs appearing in this book, most of them taken during the initial period of fieldwork in 1970.

My wife, Ann, herself a first-rate social scientist and Mexicanist, "joined" this project in its later stages, but its completion owes much to her constant encouragement and perceptive comments on earlier drafts of the study. More fundamentally, it is she who makes it all seem meaningful.

W.A.C.

Lagos de Moreno, Jal., Mexico
June 1975

Contents

8. Political System Performance   201

Dimensions of political system performance, 202. Personal contact with public officials, 208. Benefits received from government, 213. The impact of political system performance on political attitudes and behavior, 215. Symbolic outputs and support for the system, 223

9. Conclusion   226

The community as an arena of political learning, 226. Politics and urban poverty in Mexico, 228

Appendixes

Tables and Figures

FIGURES

*Photographs of the research communities and their people
appear on pp. 33, 40–46, 156, 190, 206, 211, and 212.*

Politics
and the Migrant Poor
in Mexico City

CHAPTER ONE

Introduction

THE MASSIVE population shift from rural to urban areas in developing nations is one of the great human dramas of our time. Though our attention is drawn most readily to such manifestations of societal instability in the Third World as military coups, guerrilla uprisings, and student riots, an uprising of far greater magnitude is represented by the cumulative decisions of millions of individuals—most of them peasants —to revolt against conditions of poverty, insecurity, and economic exploitation by abandoning the countryside and taking up a new life in the city.

Urban populations throughout the developing world have grown at increasing rates over the past three decades; and Latin America, already much more urbanized than Africa or Asia and somewhat more so than Southern Europe, has surpassed all other regions. From 1940 to 1960, the population in localities of 20,000 or more inhabitants in Latin America increased by about 5 percent annually, doubling in about 15 years— a rate only occasionally realized for short periods in advanced industrial nations at a much later stage of economic development. In the same period, Latin American cities of 100,000 or more grew at an annual rate of 11 percent, more than three times the rate of total population growth in the region. Although some projections indicate a slight decline in the rate of urbanization over the period 1960–80, to about 4.4 percent a year, it is expected that by the end of the 1970's some 60 percent of the Latin American population will be living in urban areas (Miller & Gakenheimer 1971: 9–10; World Bank 1972: Annex I, p. 2).

As the general dimensions of this phenomenon became evident during the late 1950's and early 1960's, social scientists and government policymakers began to wonder about its consequences for political stability in Latin America and other Third World regions. At that point virtually nothing of a concrete nature was known about the political attitudes and behavior of the newly arrived city dwellers. However, sociological theory and fragmentary empirical studies purporting to document the urbanizing experience of the United States and Western Europe offered what seemed to be relevant guideposts; and the result was a deluge of highly speculative, highly impressionistic, and highly alarmist commentary on the "probable" social and political consequences of rapid urbanization in the Third World.[1] It is now apparent that most of this preliminary effort to come to grips with what was assumed to be a "universal" process (urbanization) with a highly predictable outcome ("radical" migrant masses challenging and perhaps overturning the established sociopolitical order) was fundamentally wrongheaded. The reasons lie partly in the social scientist's tendency to generalize too widely from the experience of advanced industrial countries, but even more in the kinds of assumptions that were made about the nature of the Third World city, the life situation of cityward migrants and their perceptions of it, and the way in which residence in a city affects one's orientations toward politics and the political system. All of these assumptions will be subjected to critical scrutiny in the chapters that follow.

Are the migrant masses revolutionary? Definitely not, at least in Latin America and many other parts of the developing world. But this is by no means the only question relating to cityward migration that should concern the student of political behavior. Unfortunately, it seems to have been assumed, in the aftermath of revisionist scholarship in this area, that urban migrants who are not "radicals" must necessarily be apathetic, politically ignorant, withdrawn from the political arena, neither acting politically nor being acted on. But political learning among the migrant poor—albeit of a different sort and with different outcomes than was predicted in the writings of the 1950's and 1960's—*does* go on, and there remains a great need to specify the determinants and the consequences of that learning process.

The present work is a comparative study of migrants and their city-born neighbors living in six relatively small, predominantly low-income communities on the periphery of Mexico City, and is based on fourteen months of fieldwork in these communities during 1970, 1971, and 1972. It deals with a relatively small group of people in a limited number of localities at a particular point in time, and therefore suffers from all the restrictions on generalizability of research findings that such an approach imposes. Nevertheless, the research is also addressed to sev-

---

[1] This literature and the empirical evidence that fails to support its major contentions are summarized in Cornelius 1969 and 1971, Nelson 1969, and Schoultz 1972b.

eral broad theoretical and empirical problems. What is the process by which the individual forms images of politics and the political system, and assumes a role of participation or nonparticipation in political activity? What are the most important incentives and disincentives for political involvement? How can the individual citizen—and especially the disadvantaged citizen—manipulate the political system to satisfy his needs? What effect does a large group of people entering the political arena have on the functioning of the political system, and what effect does the system have on them? What goes on at the "grass roots" of a nation's political system, and how does political activity at that level affect system outputs? I believe that social science research bearing on these broad issues and concerns should be cumulative. Thus comparative reference has been made throughout this study to as comprehensive a body of empirical and theoretical work as possible, including research done in the United States and other advanced industrial countries.

Some have argued that in this era of huge, cross-national surveys and burgeoning data banks, case studies of the kind I have undertaken are anachronistic and contribute little to general theory-building.[2] Indeed, among social scientists who use quantitative data and research methods there appears to be a pervasive assumption that the most important contributions to our understanding of political behavior and attitude formation *must* come from studies pitched at a high level of generality —at minimum, the single nation-state; at best, a large set of countries. My research, however, was undertaken in the conviction that "micro" studies pursued within a disciplined comparative framework (see Verba 1967) and with sensitivity to the immediate sociopolitical context in which individual political behavior occurs can also make valuable contributions to our basic knowledge of political man. In fact, it could be argued that "micro" studies have been essential to progress in understanding the political attitudes and behavior of cityward migrants, since most of the relevant generalizations flowing from macroscopic comparative studies—especially those based on aggregate data—have had so little explanatory and predictive power.

It is also wrong to assume that one must cross national boundaries in order to locate appropriate contexts for testing hypotheses about political attitudes and behavior among the migrant poor. Several investigators working in Latin America have found significant differences in political culture and governmental performance between major cities

[2] See, for example, the argument made by Kaufman (1972: 378–79) with regard to the utility of case studies in Latin American urban research.

in a single country (A. Leeds 1968; Montaño 1974; Portes & Walton 1975: Chap. 4). Moreover, comparative studies of communities *within* Latin American cities have revealed equally distinctive local patterns. In some communities, residents have a strong positive identification with the community, engage in extensive formal and informal interaction with one another, and lack strong ties with the larger society and polity; in others, residents are not positively oriented to the local area, have limited contact with one another, and tie themselves into supra-local social and political structures. Some communities show no capacity for collective political action of any sort; in others, groups of residents are actively engaged in petitioning the government for land titles or urban services. Some communities seem to represent subcultures of political alienation; others appear supportive of the existing political order. Even geographically contiguous communities within a given city have been found to differ considerably in the extent and manner in which their inhabitants are integrated socially, economically, and politically into urban life.[3] The sources of these differences are numerous and complex, as will be demonstrated in subsequent chapters of this study.

The important point to be made here is that variations in the social *context* of political learning from one part of a city to another may be responsible for much of the observed diversity in political attitudes and behavior. Recent migrants to the city can be expected to differ not only in social backgrounds and personality characteristics, but also in terms of the socializing influences to which they are exposed by virtue of their residence in particular neighborhoods. This fact suggests a research strategy quite different from that employed in most research on migrant assimilation or adaptation to urban life. Usually, emphasis has been placed on the characteristics of migrants as individuals—i.e. on the set of personal attributes they exhibit before and after migration— and on how these attributes increase or decrease the migrant's life chances or opportunities for successful integration into the urban environment. The basic problem with this approach is one that has also concerned critics of excessively "individualistic" survey research in general, irrespective of subject:

As usually practiced, using random sampling of individuals, the survey is a sociological meatgrinder, tearing the individual from his social context and

---

[3] See, among others: Behrman 1971, 1972; Butterworth 1973; Collier 1971, 1973; Dietz 1974; Eckstein 1972a; Frank 1969: 281–85; Gauhan 1974: 36–39; Germani 1967: 188; Goldrich, Pratt & Schuller 1970; Lewis 1961: xii–xviii; Lutz 1970; Mercado Villar et al. 1970; Ornelas 1973; Patch 1968: 178, 219; Perlman 1971; Portes 1971a, 1971b; Roberts 1973; Rogler 1967; Stokes 1962; J. Turner 1971.

guaranteeing that nobody in the study interacts with anyone else in it. It is a little like a biologist putting his experimental animals through a hamburger machine and looking at every hundredth cell through a microscope; anatomy and physiology get lost, structure and function disappear, and one is left with cell biology. (Barton 1968: 1)

This analogy applies to much of the empirical research that has been done on cityward migrants, as well as to the more general, cross-national studies that have tried to use urban residence or migrant status as an independent variable.

To adequately explain the attitudes and behavior of migrants, we must view them as persons playing roles in ongoing social and political systems (cf. Shannon 1965; Shannon & Shannon 1968; Graves & Graves 1974). This approach focuses on the ways in which the structure and organization of a migrant's new community influence the way he adjusts to urban life. Broadly speaking, the present study is an attempt to place the low-income migrant in his social and political context. In doing so, I relied chiefly on a contextually grounded sample survey design and analytical procedure, and on a combination of data-gathering techniques drawn from both the sociological (sample survey) and anthropological (participant-observation and depth-interviewing) traditions. This eclectic approach generated an extraordinarily rich body of both quantitative and qualitative data on a relatively large number of individuals clustered in a relatively small number of communities. The communities themselves, together with their relationships to social and political institutions in the larger urban environment, were subjected to intensive ethnographic study. Throughout the research, it has been my belief that an approach enabling the investigator to focus on the interplay between individual attributes and attributes of the social and political structures in which the individual is enmeshed is likely to be the technique most productive of insights into the process of political learning.

THE LOCAL URBAN COMMUNITY AS A
SOCIALIZATION CONTEXT

The "human ecology" school of urban sociology in the United States has emphasized the residential differentiation of the city into a "mosaic of social worlds" representing territorially based subsystems of society.[4]

---

[4] This conception of urban residential differentiation is explicated most fully in Park, Burgess & McKenzie 1925, and in Park 1952: 17ff. The studies of Park and his colleagues at the University of Chicago, as well as other work stimulated by their view of the city, are summarized in Timms 1971: Chap. 1, and in Hunter 1974.

And in recent years concern over the decline of communal solidarity among city dwellers, conflicts over community control of schools and municipal services, and the problems of maximizing citizen participation in governmental programs at the local level have combined to refocus attention specifically on the low-income urban neighborhood in the United States and other advanced industrial nations as a social and political community.[5] In developing countries the emergence of hundreds of "uncontrolled" settlements formed by squatters on the peripheries of the largest cities has also led to an increased recognition of the local urban community as an arena for social and political interaction.[6]

Studies of low-income urban communities in both developing and industrialized countries provide abundant evidence that such communities represent far more than statistical aggregates of city dwellers. For one thing, they are often regarded by many of their inhabitants as identifiable segments of urban space. Among the migrants included in this study, 88 percent of those interviewed could draw a map of their community of residence that corresponded closely to the actual physical or politico-administrative boundaries of that community (see Figure 1.1).[7] Moreover, the high density of population in such areas, the greater

[5] The literature on these and other aspects of the role of the local urban community in advanced industrial societies is voluminous. The role of the neighborhood in fostering a "sense of community" among residents of large metropolitan areas is discussed most extensively in Effrat 1974; Greer & Greer 1974; Bell & Held 1969; Dennis 1968; Fellin & Litwak 1968; Keller 1968; Lenz-Romeiss 1973; Sennett 1970; and Swanson 1970. Problems of local community participation and "community control" are treated in Frederickson 1973; Greenstone & Peterson 1973; Hallman 1974; Kramer 1969; Lynch et al. 1972; Marshall 1971; Yates 1973; Zimmerman 1971, 1972. More generally, there has been a reawakening of interest in territoriality as a basis of political organization, competition, and conflict in urban settings. See especially: Cox 1973; Cox, Reynolds & Rokkan 1974; Moinat et al. 1972; Suttles 1972. Much of the renewed attention to the local urban community as a site of social and political action seems to have been inspired by detailed ethnographic studies of specific low-income neighborhoods in U.S. cities. Among the best are M. Fried 1973, Gans 1962, Suttles 1968, and Kornblum 1974.

[6] The more comprehensive studies of this pattern of urban settlement include A. Leeds 1969, Mangin 1967, Juppenlatz 1971, and Turner 1968a, 1971. Detailed case studies of specific squatter settlements have also been completed; see, for example, M. Ross 1973b, 1973c.

[7] The interviewees were asked the following question: "Now I would like to talk for a while about the *colonia* [community] in which you live. Here is a piece of paper. Could you draw me a rough map of this colonia, showing where it begins and where it ends?" Other researchers have also commented on the ability of the urban poor to visualize and describe the territorial community of which they are a part. See especially Stea 1966, 1968, Peattie 1968: 54–55, and M. Fried 1973. Fried, whose research dealt with a tenement slum in Boston, argues (1973: 63): "No matter where the slum is located and which particular types of housing the area contains . . . characteristically the slum represents a unique blending of social and physical

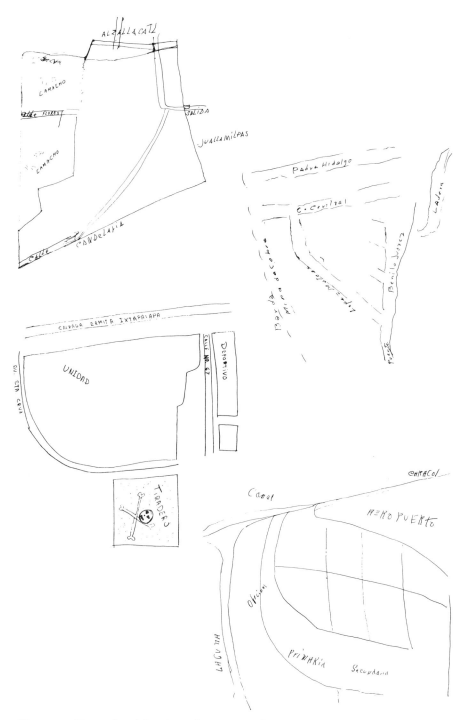

Figure 1.1. Respondents' drawings of some research communities.

amount of leisure time spent by poor people within their immediate residential environment, the use of communal facilities such as public water taps, and the existence of community-related problems such as insecurity of land tenure or lack of basic services combine to promote a high incidence of face-to-face interaction.

Residents of poor neighborhoods often exhibit a strong sense of personal identification with their community. In communities where residence is relatively stable, there may be, in addition, a substantial accumulation of shared historical experiences. Some communities have been found to possess distinctive norm structures that appear to provide important attitudinal and behavioral cues for residents in their relations with neighbors, as well as a kind of cognitive map useful for ordering perceptions of the larger urban environment. Some local norms may result primarily from internal social and political processes; others may be the product of the community's interaction with the larger social and political environment of the surrounding city.

This last point is extremely important, for it suggests that the impact of the local urban community on political learning cannot be fully appreciated or explained if the community is treated as an autonomous, isolated entity. The work of Suttles (1972: 257ff) on territoriality as a basis for social and political organization among the urban poor in the United States is particularly illuminating in this regard. He notes that the local urban community, *as a social and political grouping*, comes into being and acquires its most important socializing properties largely in response to external pressures exerted by government, big business, and other supralocal actors (cf. A. Leeds 1968). For this reason (and others discussed below), a great deal of attention has been paid in the present study to the nature and frequency of interactions between the research communities and external actors, especially political and governmental officials.

Although urban sociologists have long recognized the importance of neighborhood socialization for the learning of a wide range of social behaviors, there has been relatively little appreciation among either sociologists or political scientists of its relevance to processes of *political* learning. In fact, the apparent failure of suburban neighborhoods in U.S. cities to influence the political attitudes and behavior of incoming residents has led some sociologists to dismiss the local community altogether as an important agency of political socialization. For example,

---

space. More than other neighborhoods, the urban slum is a circumscribed and distinguishable segment of the world in the midst of the metropolis." Cf. T. Lee 1968 and L. Ross 1970.

Scott Greer (1970: 607–8) has argued: "The social products of the neighborhood *per se* are small-scale order, mutual aid, and friendship. ... The interaction of households produces a luxuriant network of neighborhoods in the suburbs but these have little direct significance for the polity."[8] For reasons that will be explored further in Chapter 5, this "noneffect" is precisely what one could expect to find in a predominantly middle- or upper-class suburb. As Marc Fried (1973: 81) has pointed out, the emphasis on localism—"a conception of the neighborhood as an extension of the home"—is much stronger among lower-class people than among those higher in the social hierarchy, whose orientation to city life is more "metropolitan" in scope and who make more selective use of their immediate residential environment.

Political scientists, too, have thought it unnecessary to devote much attention to the local community as a context or agency for political socialization. One searches in vain for even a single reference to neighborhood or place of residence in most standard treatments of the subject. It could be argued that if those pursuing empirical research on political socialization in the past decade had done more of their work among adults rather than children, and more of it outside white, middle-class neighborhoods, greater attention would have been paid to the effects of the local urban community.[9]

Particularly among low-income migrants to cities in Latin America, the local community has been an important agent of political socialization, since these people have only a minimal exposure to other socializing agents and have no other strong basis for political organization. A great many migrants to Latin American cities are not employed in large-scale enterprises, or even in small factories, offices, shops, or other stable work environments. In most cities only a very few migrants are organized in labor unions; nor are they likely to join political parties or other types of politically relevant voluntary organizations active beyond the local community. Citywide groups or movements based on class,

[8] Other sociologists who have made similar observations about the political irrelevance of residence in suburban communities include C. G. Bell (1969), Berger (1960), and Gans (1963).

[9] Studies of political socialization among adults have been rare. See Fagen 1969; Frey & Roos 1967; Krauss 1974; Maguire 1969; Roth, in progress; Uno (1972). Significantly, all but one of these studies (Uno 1972) involve non-U.S. populations. In the United States, only a small proportion of the research on political socialization among children has focused on the poor or minority groups. The major exceptions to the pattern include Hirsch 1971 (on the poor whites of Appalachia); García 1973 (on Chicanos); and the articles by Marvick and Greenberg in Greenberg 1970 (on blacks in large cities). For a rare study of neighborhood influence on political learning among children in the United States, see Gustafsson 1974.

ethnic, regional, religious, or "issue" interests are uncommon in any case, and attract only insignificant proportions of the migrant population where they do exist. People who migrate early in life are, of course, exposed to the socializing influences of the family and the school for extended periods after arrival in the city; but for those who migrate in late adolescence or later, the impact of these agents is often minimal. Finally, although exposure to mass media may be far higher in urban centers than in rural areas, most evidence indicates that attention to the political content of such communication is relatively low. Thus for a large proportion of low-income migrants to Latin American cities the local community provides the most important "cues" for political attitudes and behavior.[10]

Beyond the attitudinal and behavioral norms that the community, as a reference group, may provide for its residents, local living conditions and land-tenure situations help to determine the needs and problems they will perceive as susceptible to governmental action. As we shall see in Chapter 6, community leaders and improvement associations concerned with such problems often exercise an extremely important role in political learning by providing opportunities for participation in politically relevant activities and filtering individual perceptions of the political system.

It is often during the interaction of a local urban community with political and governmental agencies that some of the most important political learning experiences of its residents are obtained. Especially for squatter settlements and other illegally formed communities, a great deal of collective bargaining and negotiation, often extending over many years, is usually required to secure government recognition of tenure rights and a full complement of urban services and improvements. The outcomes of collective attempts to influence government decisions on these matters appear to be important determinants not only of levels and types of subsequent political participation but also of a variety of affective and evaluative orientations toward the political system.

Studies conducted in the United States, in Latin America, and in Africa have demonstrated that territorially based groups are most important as vehicles for political learning among the urban poor when their members are confronted with governmental policies or administrative actions that appear to threaten the survival or developmental prospects of the local community (Kurtz 1973; Mollenkopf 1973; Portes & Walton 1975: Chap. 3; M. Ross 1973b; Tilly 1974). Since so many low-

[10] For a general discussion of the importance of the local community as a base of political organization in Latin America, see Chalmers 1972: 110–11.

income migrants to Latin American cities eventually take up residence in squatter settlements and other neighborhoods suffering from external threats and insecurity of land tenure, the likelihood that their community will be the locus of important politicizing experiences is greatly increased.

As one student of the urban poor in the United States has argued, "If the neighborhood concept is to have utility . . . it is essential to gain a better understanding of the function of these local areas in the generation and maintenance of norms and attitudes" (Wilson 1971a: 369). It is my intention in this study to contribute to such an understanding of the kinds of communities that have been the primary receiving areas for cityward migrants in Mexico and other Latin American countries in recent decades.

POLITICAL LEARNING THROUGH THE LIFE CYCLE

Any investigation of "political learning" among adult migrants to the city necessarily assumes that whatever political orientations migrants transfer to the city are subject to modification or replacement in the postmigration period. This assumption runs counter to the dominant tradition of research on political socialization, which, as noted above, has dealt almost exclusively with political learning during childhood. The rationale for this approach rests on two basic propositions: (1) that an individual's basic orientations toward politics are learned in early childhood and adolescence; (2) that early socialization is importantly related to an adult's political attitudes and behavior (see Hirsch 1971: 2–3). According to this view of the socialization process, significant changes in political attitudes or behavior during adulthood are either anomalies that must be explained away or simply variations on the outcomes of childhood socialization.

There are at least two major objections to this view of political learning. In the first place, the direct relationship between early socialization and political behavior in later life has been assumed rather than demonstrated (see Searing, Schwartz & Lind 1973). Longitudinal studies are necessary to confirm such a relationship, and very few of these have been done; but those completed so far (Krauss 1974; Uno 1972) suggest that there may be important discontinuities in political attitudes and behavior through the life cycle.

The second major objection that must be raised concerns the *possibilities* for significant, "new" political learning or relearning among adults. As Fagen (1964: 25) has noted: "Adults in many nations now find themselves in political environments quite different from the ones in which they grew up. Once again, they must learn to participate, and furthermore, to do so they may well have to 'unlearn' many of the attitudes and skills acquired earlier." Urban migrants whose place of childhood socialization was a rural village must certainly be numbered among the adult citizens of a developing country who have to develop new orientations toward politics and the political system.

In Mexico there are important continuities in some types of political learning from rural to urban settings; but it is also clear that residence in some kinds of low-income urban communities places a premium on certain political orientations that are unlikely to have been learned in a rural community. To understand how such orientations are developed in the urban setting, it is necessary to adopt a more flexible, expansive, situational view of the political learning process than is found in most of the socialization literature. Such a view places considerable emphasis on the mechanism of situational adjustment among adults:

The person, as he moves in and out of a variety of social situations, learns the requirements of continuing in each situation and of success in it. If he has a strong desire to continue, the ability to assess accurately what is required, and can deliver the required performance, the individual turns himself into the kind of person the situation demands. (Becker 1964: 44)

This perspective is very similar to that adopted by "social learning" theorists and by those who have used social-learning models in the study of childhood political socialization (Brim 1966; Rohter 1970; Feldman 1973). In explaining why people develop the political orientations they do, it directs attention to the character of the situation (i.e. context) in which political learning occurs. It requires the investigator to specify what there is in a given situation that encourages or requires the one being socialized to hold certain beliefs or act in a certain way:

We do not ask what there is in him that requires the action or belief. All we need to know of the person is that for some reason or another he desires to continue his participation in the situation or to do well in it. From this we can deduce that he will do what he can to do what is necessary in that situation. (Becker 1964: 44)

Hopefully, as this study progresses the reader will come to appreciate the usefulness of this perspective on political learning in understanding the attitudinal and behavioral differences that may be observed among migrants in Mexico City. It helps the investigator avoid one of the major weaknesses of previous research on political socialization: the preoccupation with *what* is learned, and in what sequence, rather than with *how* it is learned.[11] One of the major concerns of this study is to specify the causal mechanisms involved in community-based political learning.

RESEARCH SETTING AND METHODS

Mexico was chosen as the site of my research because of its rapid rate of urbanization in recent decades (see Chapter 2) and because of my general interest in the evolution of Mexican politics and society since the Revolution of 1910. I had become familiar with the Mexican research environment during extended periods of travel and study in 1962 and 1964. The Mexico City urban area in 1970 seemed a particularly appropriate locale for research on the migrant poor by virtue of the almost total lack of attention to this sector of the city's population on the part of Mexican and North American social scientists. This dearth of information was all the more striking by comparison with the rich body of empirical studies that had been done on similar populations in Lima, Santiago de Chile, Rio de Janeiro, Buenos Aires, Bogotá, and other major Latin American cities.

Male heads of families aged 18 to 65 and residing in six predominantly low-income communities on the periphery of the Mexico City urban area constitute the basic universe of the study. The six communities were selected purposively; but once the selection had been made, scientific sampling procedures were employed within each community to obtain a stratified probability sample for structured, personal interviews.[12] Approximately one-third of the total respondents are nonmigrants, these being defined as individuals born or having spent most of their lives between ages 5 and 15 in the Mexico City urban area.[13] The remainder are migrants, defined as people born and having spent most of their lives between ages 5 and 15 outside the city. A subsample of eldest sons (aged 18+) of migrants was also drawn, such that in about one out of four of the migrant families represented in the total sample both the head of the family and his eldest son were interviewed separately. The sons are compared with their fathers at several points in the chapters

[11] Frey (1973) has also stressed the need for more careful specification of what it is about a given agent of socialization that affects the outcome of the socialization process. See also Cook & Scioli 1972: 957.

[12] See Appendix D, pp. 274–78, for a detailed description of the procedures employed in drawing the samples and weighting the responses for analysis. The main questionnaire used in the sample survey is reproduced, in English, in Appendix A, pp. 237–65. Copies of the Spanish version are available from the author upon request.

[13] The terms "Mexico City," "Mexico City urban area," and "Mexico City metropolitan area" will be used interchangeably in this study, except where indicated in the demographic analysis in Chapter 2.

that follow, but otherwise they have not been included in the data analysis.

Women were not included in the main sample for three principal reasons. First, time and financial constraints on sample size and the number of variables for which I wished to control in the analysis (community of residence, age, length of residence in the city, socioeconomic status) made the inclusion of sex differences highly problematic. Second, I wished to maximize the comparability of my research findings to those of other studies of low-income urban populations in Latin America, which had been limited primarily to male heads of household or family. Finally, it is an unfortunate fact of life that among most Mexicans, politics is still regarded as "men's business," and that women are, in general, less likely than men to have developed orientations toward political objects and to have participated in some forms of political activity (see Arterton 1974: Chaps. 7 and 12; Stevens 1974: 298–99).

The quantitative data gathered through the sample survey interviews were supplemented with ethnographic data gathered through several months of participant observation in each of the communities included in the study. Unstructured, in-depth interviews were also conducted with key informants and recognized leaders in each community, as well as with government officials and other "outsiders" who had had extensive contact with the communities. Archival research included systematic searches for published government documents pertaining to the development of the communities, copies of petitions and correspondence in the possession of community leaders, and articles published in several Mexico City daily newspapers between 1954 and 1975. Finally, detailed life histories were gathered from several residents in each community to supplement the partial histories collected on the entire group of migrants interviewed in the sample survey.

The survey research findings reported in this study were constantly checked against qualitative data gathered through the less structured research methods I employed. Indeed, a meaningful interpretation of the survey data in many instances would have been virtually impossible without prolonged immersion in the day-to-day events and concerns of people living in the research communities and familiarity with the history of each community since its formation. As Field has pointed out (1973: 149), most survey research is actually a substitute for in-depth exposure to the population one is studying. In the present study, the sample survey constitutes only one of several complementary and mutually reinforcing methods of data-gathering.

Reconstructing local history bit-by-bit over a period of many months from the available documentary evidence and from the "oral histories" of community residents proved to be one of the most time-consuming yet uniquely satisfying aspects of my research experience. In many ways, the six communities I studied were little different from hundreds of other low-income neighborhoods in the Mexico City urban area. The conditions and events that brought them into being, and in several cases the sacrifices and struggles necessary to ensure their survival and development, were unknown to all but the residents themselves and a handful of government officials. The inhabitants of these communities were fully aware of their anonymity in Mexican society at large, yet anxious that their story be told. Many seemed both amazed and flattered that any outsider—particularly of upper social status—would seek them out as informants and friends.

As my rapport with community residents increased over the months of fieldwork, my role as a participant-observer expanded to include regular participation in family celebrations, providing transportation to medical facilities and government offices in the central city, typing of correspondence and petitions to be directed to public officials, and serving as "official" photographer at important community meetings and other events. My role as a recorder of conditions in the communities, and of the efforts being made by the residents to improve these conditions, seemed to be appreciated by most residents. Particularly in the three squatter settlements and the government "site and services" project included in the study, residents were concerned that their children have some record of the progress they had made in creating a livable community out of barren, seemingly uninhabitable land, with few resources and often in the face of strong resistance from powerful outsiders. To the extent that the chapters following serve as that record of determination and accomplishment, I will have fulfilled one of my principal goals in completing this study.

CHAPTER TWO

From Village to Colonia

MOST OF THE people whose attitudes and behavior are examined in this study began their lives in one of the thousands of small villages that still dot the Mexican countryside. And at some point after reaching the age of 15, each of them joined in the massive exodus from "village Mexico" that has fundamentally transformed the spatial distribution of the Mexican population since 1940. Their journeys led eventually to one of the six predominantly low-income urban communities (*colonias proletarias*) that were the research sites for this study. This chapter describes some of the most important aspects of this experience of migration and urban relocation, from place of origin to current place of residence within Mexico City.

THE FLIGHT FROM RURAL POVERTY

The mobility of the Mexican population has increased dramatically since 1940, to the point where in 1970 more than 15 percent of the people—or 7.4 million out of 48.4 million—had lived in at least one state other than the one in which they were censused. It has been estimated that between 1950 and 1970 approximately 4.5 million persons migrated from rural to urban localities (Unikel et al. 1973: 24). About one-third of Mexico's urban population growth from 1960 to 1970 resulted from such migration, and the proportion was close to one-half during the 1940–60 period. Although the relative contribution of internal migration to urban population growth has declined, the statistics are more reflective of a staggeringly high rate of natural population increase (averaging 3.4 percent per year during the 1960's) than of any significant decrease in out-migration from the countryside. In the 1950's and 1960's the bulk of the migrants were landless workers and small subsistence farmers, the poorest sectors of the rural population.

The proportion of Mexico's population living in localities of fewer than 2,500 inhabitants has declined from 60.9 percent in 1910 to 38.4 percent in 1970 (see Fig. 2.1). Small and medium-sized cities have generally been bypassed by those leaving the countryside, whose preferred destinations are large metropolitan areas, especially the national capital. More than 43 percent of the growth of the Mexico City urban area during the 1960's was due to migration—about 1.8 million migrants in that decade alone (Unikel 1972: 24). By 1970 the population of the capital's urban area—including the old urban core (Ciudad de México), the Federal District surrounding it, and contiguous *municipios* (counties) in the State of México—had reached 8.4 million, as compared with about 1.5 million in 1940. The figure is approaching 12 million in the mid-1970's, and is expected to reach 14.4 million by 1980. In 1975, the city's population was increasing by an estimated 2,600 inhabitants per day.[1] The proportion of Mexico's total population residing in the capital has risen continuously, from 7.9 percent in 1940 to 17 percent in 1970 and an estimated 25 percent in 1980.[2]

The reasons for both the large-scale transfer of population from rural to urban areas in Mexico and the increasing concentration of population in the capital are not difficult to identify. Rapid population growth, the mechanization of commercial agriculture, and an acute shortage of new cultivable land have put extreme pressure on rural employment opportunities (Martínez Ríos 1972). As a result, there was a 74-percent increase in the number of landless agricultural workers in Mexico between 1940 and 1960 (Stavenhagen 1970: 245), and wage levels for those who do succeed in finding work have been correspondingly depressed. The *bracero* program of temporary migration to the United States for agricultural work, which provided a highly important outlet for the rural labor surplus from 1951 through 1964, was terminated by mutual agreement of the United States and Mexican governments.[3] At

[1] Projections by Luis Unikel and his associates at El Colegio de México indicate an urban area population of 20.8 million by 1990, making Mexico City the third largest conurbation in the world, after Tokyo and New York. During the 1950–60 period the city grew at an average annual rate of 5.4 percent; in 1960–70 the rate rose to 5.7 percent; and from 1970 to 1975 it has been above 5.5 percent (Unikel et al. 1975). The potentially disastrous ecological and socioeconomic consequences of the city's expansion at such rates are analyzed in Benítez 1975.

[2] Statistics cited here are drawn from CEED 1970: Chaps. 4 and 5; Unikel 1972, 1973; R. Wilkie 1975; Bataillon & Rivière d'Arc 1973: 39–44. In 1970, one out of three residents of Mexico City was a migrant from another state.

[3] The importance of this program to the rural economy in Mexico is illustrated by Kemper's studies (1971b, 1974) of migration from the village of Tzintzuntzan. Over half of the economically active male residents in this village had participated at least once in the bracero program. For a more detailed analysis of the program and its impact on the Mexican economy, see H. Campbell 1972.

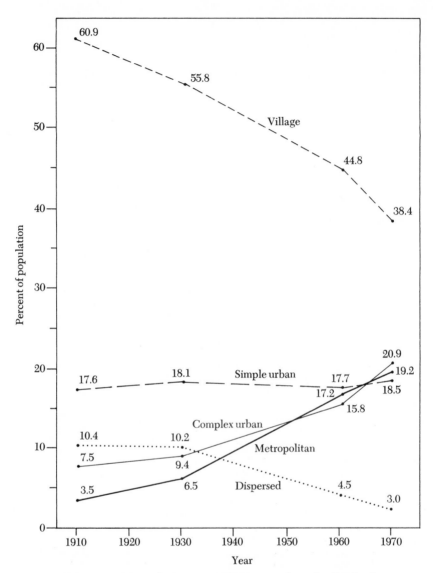

Figure 2.1. Percent of Mexican population at each rural-urban level, 1910–70. The population range of each level is as follows: dispersed settlement = population less than 100; village = 100–2,500; simple urban = 2,501–20,000; complex urban = 20,001–500,000; metropolitan = over 500,000. Source: R. Wilkie 1975.

the same time, employment opportunities (especially in the industrial sector), social services, and other amenities have become increasingly concentrated in the largest cities, and above all in the capital (see J. Wilkie 1970). Officially determined minimum wage levels in these cities are considerably higher than those set for rural areas, and the city dweller's advantage is not entirely offset by cost-of-living differences.

The struggling subsistence farmer or landless agricultural worker is increasingly aware of the great gap between urban and rural income levels and living conditions. He is likely to possess a transistor radio that receives stations located in the nearest city. The government's extensive road-building program has made it much easier for him to visit that city, and he is likely to have done so on numerous occasions. He is likely to know a number of persons—relatives, friends, and former neighbors or coworkers—who are permanent residents of a large city and who keep in touch with him through visits or correspondence. Within his own village, there may be many people who have lived or worked in the big city. All this, besides increasing the peasant's awareness of the relative advantages of city life, may well have made him envious of those who have moved to the city and succeeded in improving their incomes and living conditions; and it may have made him more confident of his own capacity to achieve the same result.

Much of the research on cityward migration in Mexico and other developing countries demonstrates that rural dwellers who choose to avail themselves of this opportunity for socioeconomic mobility tend to be younger, better educated, and more skilled occupationally than the average economically active resident in their community of origin (see Browning 1971; Balán, Browning & Jelin 1973a: 143–48). There is also some evidence that migrants tend to be positively "selective," as compared to other residents of their place of origin, in terms of such traits as innovativeness and achievement orientation (Kemper 1971b: 67–69). Although data were not gathered on the population characteristics of the communities of origin of the migrants to Mexico City included in the present study, it is clear that they were a selective group relative to the total population of Mexico. The vast majority of the migrants in my sample were young adults—nearly 80 percent of them under 30— when they left their place of origin. Most of them had not completed primary school, but only 20 percent had received no formal education at all before migrating. Before migration, 64 percent of them had been landless agricultural workers or small subsistence farmers. The selectivity of the most recently arrived migrants in the sample is not as great in terms of age and occupational skills as that of the men who came to Mexico City in the 1940's and 1950's, but they are not disadvantaged educationally relative to the "pioneers."[4]

The places of origin of most of these migrants could be characterized as small rural communities, mostly having fewer than 2,500 inhabitants and situated in the poorest, least developed municipios of the nation:[5]

Level of development	Percent of migrants
0	37.7%
1	32.1
2	15.3
3	8.6
4	6.2

In three-quarters of these communities of origin, the main source of employment was subsistence agriculture. The mean minimum wage level for all types of workers in the migrants' zones of origin was 24 pesos ($1.92) per day in 1970. In the same year, the mean minimum wage in the Federal District was 32 pesos per day. Even allowing for differences in living costs, the real income differential indicated by these wage levels is very large indeed, and there is no reason to believe that the gap would have been narrower in the year in which the migrants left their places of origin.[6]

The movement of migrants in the research communities from their

---

[4] The declining selectivity in migratory streams to large cities in Third World countries that have been urbanizing for several decades is a well-documented trend. See Browning 1971; Balán, Browning & Jelin 1973a: 147ff; Brigg 1973. This has led some observers to predict that the influx of individuals not so well equipped to cope with the problems of survival in an urban economy as those who preceded them will provide a basis for political radicalism among the less selective migrants. The relevant data from the present study do not support this expectation (see Chapter 3). Kemper (1974) also found declining selectivity on age, education, occupation, and other indicators among migrants to Mexico City from the village of Tzintzuntzan; but he notes that the less selective recent migrants have not experienced greater difficulties than did earlier migrants in coping with urban life, owing in large part to assistance received from Tzintzuntzeños already established in Mexico City. Similar assistance was available to most of the migrants in my sample.

[5] Level of development (0 is least developed, 4 most developed) is based on Stern's (1967) ranking of 111 socioeconomically homogeneous zones, as defined administratively by the Mexican government's Comisión Nacional de los Salarios Mínimos according to indicators of economic development drawn from the national census. The municipio in which each migrant's community of origin is located is a component of one of these zones. $N = 678$.

[6] Minimum wage levels for the migrants' places of origin were obtained from the government listing given in Comisión Nacional de los Salarios Mínimos 1970. A nationwide sample survey conducted in 1968 found that the average monthly income of families in the agricultural sector was 1,024 pesos (U.S. $82), compared with 2,483 pesos (U.S. $199) for nonagricultural families (Banco de México 1974: 8).

places of origin to Mexico City did not, for the most part, correspond with the pattern of "step migration" that has been observed in some Latin American countries (see Kemper 1971a). More than three-quarters of them had moved directly from their places of origin to the capital (that is, with no intervening residences of six months or longer).[7] Most of them had traveled relatively short distances—the average journey was between 150 and 200 miles—and more than 90 percent had considered no place other than the capital as a possible destination once the decision to migrate had been made. This finding, together with the migrants' lack of conformity to the stepwise model of migration, can be attributed to the unfavorable economic opportunity structure of small and medium-sized cities in Mexico, to the "high primacy" of Mexico City among the nation's urban areas, and, as we shall see, to the fact that most rural-urban migration in recent decades has occurred within networks of kinship ties that promote direct migration from small rural communities to the largest cities (see Balán, Browning & Jelin 1973a: Chap. 6; Crosson 1974).

Why did they migrate? In the vast majority of cases, economic factors were the most important determinants of the decision to migrate. The need to find work, or steady work, was cited as the primary reason by 48 percent of the respondents, and another 34 percent mentioned a general need to improve their economic situation. One out of four migrants acknowledged that his decision to migrate had been influenced by relatives already living in Mexico City, and 41 percent said that they had relatives already successfully established in the city at the time of their arrival. "Success" was defined by most respondents in terms of occupational mobility. Nearly half the total sample of migrants, and more than two-thirds of the most recently arrived ones, also acknowledged that their primary source of information regarding job opportunities and other attractions of life in the capital had been relatives already living there.

URBAN ASSIMILATION

The vast majority of migrants in the research communities came to Mexico City intending to remain there permanently. The remainder eventually decided to remain in the city because they had found lucra-

[7] Among the migrants in my sample, 58.9 percent had moved directly from a rural village to Mexico City; 18.0 percent directly from an urban locality (5,000 or more inhabitants) to Mexico City; 12.2 percent from a village to Mexico City with one or more intermediate destinations; and 10.9 percent from an urban locality to Mexico City with one or more intermediate destinations. The localities mentioned by each respondent were classified as "village" or "urban" according to official census data for the year closest to the respondent's departure. $N = 673$.

tive employment (by rural standards) or had experienced an improvement in their living conditions. Thus their behavior was consistent with the overall pattern of permanent rather than temporary rural-to-urban migration that differentiates the migratory process in Latin American countries from migration patterns in many parts of Africa and Asia. The decision of the low-income migrant, at the time of leaving his place of origin, to make a long-term commitment to urban life increases the likelihood that he will seek rapid and complete integration into community life in the urban area where he takes up residence (see Nelson 1975; Temple, in progress).

Most migration to large cities in Mexico has been mediated by kinship ties (Balán, Browning & Jelin 1973a: 159–64; Chance 1973; Kemper 1974; Ugalde et al. 1974). This pattern was characteristic of the migrants in my sample. Only 37 percent of them had moved to Mexico City as isolated individuals; the remainder came as members of nuclear or extended family units. Nearly two-thirds of the total sample had been preceded to Mexico City by other members of their immediate or extended families. Upon arrival, more than three-quarters of the migrants received some form of assistance from relatives already established in Mexico City, and more than half found permanent housing through the help of relatives. The migrants' initial destination within the city was also strongly influenced by kinship ties: more than half had relatives residing in the first colonia in which they lived for six months or longer.

Mexico City's occupational structure has been highly expansive during most of the period since 1940, and most migrants in the research communities were successful in finding employment and improving their incomes. Even though fewer than 1 percent of them had arranged for jobs in Mexico City before moving there, 46 percent had found work within a week after arriving in the city, and another 30 percent found jobs within a month. Only 4 percent remained unemployed for more than 6 months. Forty-three percent of the migrants reported having no difficulty finding their first job, and another 42 percent recalled that they had had "only a little" difficulty.

The data presented in Table 2.1 suggest that most migrants in the sample had achieved some degree of improvement in their economic situation since their arrival in Mexico City. Two-thirds of them had experienced a significant improvement in income level; and 35 percent had moved into higher-status occupations, as compared with their last occupation prior to leaving their place of origin. Nearly two-thirds of the migrants had also become landholders since moving to Mexico City, most for the first time in their lives. At the time they were interviewed

TABLE 2.1

Measures of Economic Improvement Among Migrants
Since Arrival in Mexico City

Measure	Percent
Family income level ($N = 656$)[a]	
Declined	3.9%
Remained stable	29.6
Increased one level	27.6
Increased two levels	12.6
Increased three levels or more	26.3
Occupational status ($N = 663$)[b]	
Declined	2.6
Remained stable	56.6
Increased one or more levels	34.9
Irregular	5.9
Acquired land since arrival ($N = 594$)	63.0
Acquired a major household appliance or motor vehicle since arrival ($N = 614$)	78.2

[a] Income level was defined as a ratio of the official minimum wage in the Federal District. Only those migrants who were economically active both on arrival in Mexico City and at the time of the interview were included in the analysis.

[b] For this analysis migrants were classified according to four occupational status levels defined in terms of the skill and social status characteristics generally associated with particular occupations in Mexico. The "lower manual" level includes such occupations as unskilled worker in production or services, street vendor, agricultural laborer, subsistence farmer, and low-ranking soldier. The "upper manual" level includes skilled workers and craftsmen, vehicle operators, small retail merchants, grocery clerks, and small commercial farmers. "Lower nonmanual" occupations include office worker, sales agent or clerk, supervisor or foreman, and owner or manager of a medium-sized or large commercial farm. Occupations in the "upper nonmanual" level include professional, technician or semiprofessional, manager or executive in production and service enterprises, and owner-employer in nonfarm business and industry. Migrants whose occupational mobility pattern is classified as "irregular" have experienced two or more changes in occupational status level, at least once in a downward direction and at least once in an upward direction. Cases for which sufficient information was not obtained have been excluded from the analysis.

in 1970, 53 percent of the migrants owned a television set; 54 percent had a gas stove; 12 percent had refrigerators; 43 percent had sewing machines; and 9 percent owned a car or truck. More than three-quarters had acquired these items since their arrival in Mexico City.

These measures of economic improvement compare very favorably with those encountered among larger migrant populations studied in Mexico City and in Monterrey (Balán, Browning & Jelin 1973a, 1973b; Muñoz & Oliveira 1973; Muñoz, Oliveira & Stern 1972, 1973). Fewer than 5 percent of the migrants in my study described themselves as unemployed at the time they were interviewed, but underemployment was a more serious problem, especially among construction workers and personal service workers.[8]

[8] The principal survey item regarding a respondent's current occupation encouraged him to specify the job he "usually held." Thus the low reported rate of outright unemployment does not include some respondents who were, in fact, unemployed

TABLE 2.2

Sources of Migrants' Satisfaction or Dissatisfaction
with Urban Life

Item and First Response Given	Percent Responding
In what ways would you say that living in this city is better than *living in [respondent's place of origin]?* ($N = 662$)	
More job opportunities, steadier work	65.2%
Higher wages	14.7
Better living conditions, housing	8.5
Educational opportunities	3.5
More opportunity to progress in life (no specific referent)	3.1
Recreational, cultural activities	2.0
Greater access to public services (including medical care)	1.1
Other	2.0
In what ways would you say that living in this city is worse than *living in [respondent's place of origin]?* ($N = 546$)	
Nothing—in no way is it worse	48.3
Environmental problems (pollution, overcrowding, noise, dirt, traffic congestion, climatic conditions)	22.6
High cost of living (prices of consumer goods, rent, taxes)	11.8
Employment difficulties (unemployment or underemployment, scarcity of good jobs, poor working conditions, etc.)	5.8
Crime, juvenile delinquency, vice, immorality of city life	5.5
Poor social relations (lack of "good" neighbors, friends; quarreling among family, friends, neighbors; feelings of isolation, impersonality of city life, etc.)	2.8
Housing difficulties (shortage of low-cost housing, lack of housing opportunities for large families, etc.)	2.6
Inadequate public services	0.6

NOTE: "Don't know" and unascertained responses have been excluded from the table.

Improvement in the migrants' economic situation is reflected in their positive evaluations of urban life in general as well as in their personal life situations. More than 97 percent of them reported that they were satisfied with having come to Mexico City (as opposed to having remained in their place of origin); and 80 percent said they would never consider returning to their place of origin to live, even if they had the opportunity to do so at some point in the future. One survey question asked, "Keeping in mind all aspects of life, where do you think that people are generally more satisfied and happy: in the country or in the city?" In response, 58 percent specified the city. The sources of this satisfaction with urban life are not difficult to identify. Table 2.2 shows

at the time of the interview and seeking employment—e.g., construction workers between jobs. Other recent studies of poor neighborhoods in Mexico City and Ciudad Juárez have encountered higher levels of open unemployment. See Lomnitz 1974; Ugalde et al. 1974.

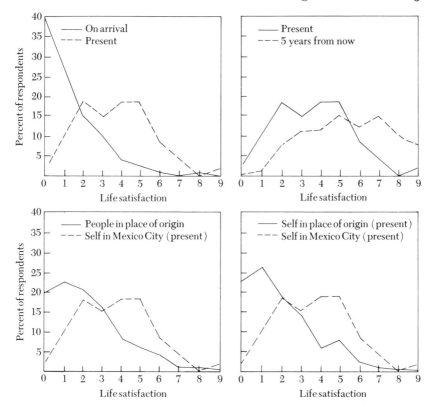

Figure 2.2. Personal life satisfaction among migrants. On the scale of satisfaction, 0 is the lowest rating and 9 the highest. The number of respondents represented in each graph varies from 641 to 667.

that greater employment opportunities and higher wages are overwhelmingly perceived as the most attractive aspects of residence in the city. Nearly half the migrants felt that there was no way in which life in Mexico City was worse than that in their place of origin. Those who could cite a specific source of dissatisfaction with the city stressed environmental problems (especially air pollution) or the high cost of living.

Migrants in the research communities were also asked a series of questions in the "self-anchoring striving scale" format (Cantril 1965) to elicit their perceptions of changes in their personal life situation since arrival in Mexico City. The introductory question in this sequence was as follows:

Everybody wants certain things in life. Think about what is really important for *you* . . . then think of the *best life* you can imagine, assuming that you could have everything just as you want it. Now think of the kind of life you would *not* want—the *worst possible life* you can imagine. Here is a picture of a ladder [with rungs numbered from 0 to 9]. Suppose we say that the top of the ladder represents the best possible life for you, and the bottom represents the worst possible life for you. Where on the ladder do you feel you personally stand at the *present* time?

Respondents were then asked where they thought they stood on the ladder when they first came to Mexico City, where they thought they would be five years from the time of the interview, where they would place the average person still living in their place of origin, and where they would personally be on the ladder if they had remained in their place of origin. The responses to this set of questions, presented graphically in Figure 2.2, show clearly that most migrants regard themselves as considerably better off since their arrival in Mexico City. They also tend to be optimistic about future improvements in their life situation; and they view their present situation as much superior to that of current residents in their place of origin, and to what would have been their own situation had they remained there.

URBAN HOUSING ALTERNATIVES FOR THE MIGRANT POOR

Rapid natural population increase has combined with large-scale in-migration to create a great demand for housing in the Mexico City urban area. At the same time, the supply of conventional low-cost housing in the city has been restricted by several factors. Land speculation is practiced by thousands of middle- and upper-class families and individuals, as well as by large-scale commercial agencies, and has driven up the cost of land available to individual, low-income home builders while reducing the incentives for low-cost housing construction by private enterprise. The city's existing stock of low-rent housing has been depleted as centrally located tenement slums (*vecindades*) deteriorate and are replaced by commercial structures and high-rise middle- and upper-income apartment buildings. Few housing opportunities remain in the surviving vecindades and *ciudades perdidas*,[9] whose populations tend to be highly stable, kept there both by the residents' low incomes and by the extremely low, controlled rents in many vecindades. Rent controls, initially applied in 1942 to vecindad housing with a rent below 300 pesos per month and maintained ever since, have also hastened the

---

[9] *Ciudades perdidas* are tiny, encapsulated shantytowns, usually occupying the interior of a central-city block and completely surrounded by commercial or industrial structures. Most residents—whose incomes are among the lowest in the city—rent their plots of land from private owners.

deterioration of the central-city tenements, whose owners have little incentive to invest in their upkeep.

Public policy has introduced other distortions that have restricted the housing options of the poor. From 1952 to 1970 there was a prohibition on the establishment of new residential subdivisions within the Federal District. Although many new upper- and middle-class subdivisions were in fact opened up during this period, the ban was selectively enforced by the head of the Department of the Federal District (D.D.F.) in a crude attempt to reduce the city's growth rate by preventing the sub-division of land for settlement by low-income families.[10] The lack of an effective or substantial tax on unimproved land has encouraged land speculation. Public housing programs have yielded a relatively small number of housing units, most of which are not accessible to the poorest sectors of the population for both political and financial reasons; indeed, the principal beneficiaries of public housing in the city have been government bureaucrats and other middle-class groups. Finally, the government has done little to expand the amount of credit available to would-be land purchasers or home builders among low-income *capitalinos.*

In sum, during most of the period since 1940, the government's intervention and nonintervention in urban land and housing markets have largely been detrimental to the interests of the poor, who have been left to find their own solutions to the housing problem—solutions embodied in the explosive growth of squatter settlements and other types of "non-planned" or "spontaneous" urban settlements.

The Expanding Periphery

Low-income migrants entering Mexico City during the period from 1930 to about 1950 usually settled in cheap, multifamily housing in the old urban core; then, when finances permitted, they moved toward the periphery, where land was available for squatting or purchase at relatively low cost, and single-family dwellings could be built. During the past two decades, however, as both the quantity and quality of low-cost housing in the central city declined sharply, the earlier arrivals have been joined by recently arrived migrants in seeking housing opportunities on the urban periphery. Also, earlier migrants who had moved to the peripheral colonias have been joined by friends and relatives, for

---

[10] The D.D.F. is the principal organ of local government for the Mexico City urban area, excluding contiguous urbanized municipios in the State of México. The head of the Department, a Presidential appointee and a member of the President's cabinet, is referred to as the Governor of the Federal District, or more popularly as the "mayor" (*regente*) of Mexico City.

whom proximity to established migrants is a major factor influencing the selection of a place of residence within the city. Finally, the opportunities afforded by residence in peripheral squatter settlements—rent-free housing, one's own plot of land, isolation from the noise and pollution of the central city, and the replication of some aspects of rural life (open space, tranquility, small-scale vegetable and livestock raising)—have made such settlements particularly attractive to recently arrived migrants.

For all these reasons, the central-city slums have ceased to be the primary receiving or "staging" areas for migrants from the countryside (Brown 1972; Lomnitz 1974; Ward 1975). Among the migrants in my sample, only about 20 percent had lived in a centrally located vecindad at any time since their arrival in the city, and only 14 percent (virtually all of them migrants who arrived prior to 1950) had selected such a slum as their first place of extended (six months or longer) residence in Mexico City. Limited exposure to central-city slums—by any standard, the worst low-income dwelling environments in the city—undoubtedly helps to explain the relatively high levels of personal life satisfaction and satisfaction with urban life among the migrants represented in my sample.[11]

The differing "place utilities" attached by both recently arrived and established migrants to housing alternatives in the central core and the periphery of the urban area have fundamentally altered the city's pattern of growth.[12] As illustrated in Figure 2.3 the Mexico City urban area

[11] In Mexico City and other major Latin American cities, residents of central-city tenement slums have often been found to exhibit significantly higher levels of social and political alienation, a higher incidence of alcoholism and drug addiction, more unstable family relationships, a great deal less socioeconomic mobility, and a weaker sense of community than residents of peripheral squatter settlements and other types of low-income neighborhoods (see Lewis 1961; Collier 1971: 139–40; Mangin 1970: xxix; Mercado Villar et al. 1970: 224–25, 262–63; Patch 1961; Andrews & Phillips 1970: 213). See Eckstein 1972a and Dietz 1974 for detailed descriptions of this type of dwelling environment in Mexico City and Lima. My own impressions, gathered during extended visits to two large and two small vecindades in central Mexico City, were consistent with many of the observations made in the studies cited above. Much smaller vecindades—usually occupying no more than a single 250-square-meter lot—are being constructed to provide rental housing in older squatter settlements and low-income subdivisions on the periphery of Mexico City.

[12] Wolpert (1965: 162) uses the term "place utility" to refer to the sum of the utilities, or positive and negative rewards, deriving from an individual's residence in a given locality. For detailed studies of Mexico City's pattern of growth since 1940, see Flores 1961: 200–213; Oldman et al. 1967; Unikel 1972. The growth of the urban periphery is given special attention in Deneke 1966 and Jackson 1973. For descriptions of land use and low-income settlement patterns in other Mexican cities, see Baker 1970; Balán, Browning & Jelin 1973a: Chap. 2; Montaño 1974; Portes & Walton 1975: Chap. 4.

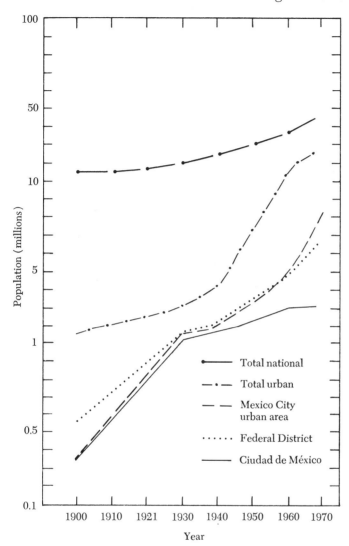

Figure 2.3. Population growth in Mexico and the Mexico City
urban area. Adapted from Unikel 1972: 9.

—embracing the central core (Ciudad de México), the Federal District
surrounding it, and adjacent parts of the State of México—grew more
rapidly in population during the 1960's than either the central core or
the Federal District taken by themselves. According to one estimate,
about 750,000 persons abandoned the central city during the 1960's,

whereas the peripheral colonias gained about 2.4 million inhabitants (Bataillon & Rivière d'Arc 1973: 42). By far the most explosive growth is occurring in four municipalities located in the State of México: Ecatepec, Tlalnepantla, Naucalpan, and Netzahualcóyotl. All these are now fully integrated into the Mexico City urban area, and attract both the poor fleeing from the decaying central city and newly arriving migrants from the countryside.[13]

Among the hundreds of *colonias proletarias* outside the central city, the prospective low-income settler may choose from two basic types, the squatter settlement and the low-income subdivision.[14] Squatter settlements (*colonias paracaidistas*) are formed through illegal occupation of public or privately owned land, which has been left uninhabited usually because of highly irregular topography or unstable subsoil conditions. For example, on the western edge of the urban area, there are numerous steep ravines formed by small rivers flowing toward the city; and the extreme irregularity of the topography makes street construction in nearby areas very difficult. The bottoms of the ravines often contain sandpits exploited by commercial mining firms. When the sand mines are exhausted (sometimes even before they are completely worked out) the land they occupy is invaded by squatters. Similarly, ancient lava flows in the area known as the Pedregal in the southern part of the urban area have left large tracts of land with highly irregular topogra-

[13] Two of these, Ecatepec and Netzahualcóyotl, more than quadrupled their populations between the 1960 and 1970 censuses, and the others either doubled or tripled their populations. Realizing that the battle to control urban settlement patterns has already been lost in the Federal District, government agencies have shifted their attention to the contiguous State of México municipalities. The shift is reflected in the establishment in that state of a comprehensive urban-planning agency (AURIS), and in a joint effort by the State of México and the federal government to create a new "growth pole," named Ciudad Cuautitlán-Izcalli, north of the existing Mexico City urban area in the State of México. The new settlement zone, with a projected population of 1.5 million, includes a large industrial complex to provide employment opportunities. Detailed planning for land use has been done, including steps to prevent the growth of squatter settlements—steps that will almost certainly fail, if experience with "new towns" in other Latin American countries is any guide (see Epstein 1973).

[14] There are no reliable estimates of the total number of *colonias proletarias* in the Mexico City urban area, since no comprehensive surveys of such neighborhoods have ever been completed either by the Mexican government or by private researchers. The official party (PRI) claimed in 1970 that about 620 such colonias existed in the Federal District, 120 of which were not officially recognized as residential zones. By mid-1975, the Department of the Federal District had "registered" 541 *colonias proletarias*, of which 151 were not legalized nor in process of legalization. Neither of these sets of figures includes the hundreds of *colonias proletarias* located in the State of México municipios bordering the Federal District.

phy, which is unsuitable for most conventional uses without a very large investment in urban infrastructure. These zones, too, have been occupied by squatters in large numbers. Other kinds of land bordering the urban area, such as the communally owned agricultural zones called *ejidos*, have also been invaded by squatters, especially those lands unfit for cultivation or abandoned for some other reason by the owners. Although invasions of this type of land have occasionally provoked violent clashes between *ejidatarios* and would-be squatters, many ejidos have actually encouraged squatting on some of their unused land, in hopes of receiving payments from the invasion organizers or indemnification from the government (see Antochiw 1974).

In some cases, squatter invasions take the form of a rapid, highly organized occupation; in others, a much more gradual and more or less spontaneous occupation occurs over a period of several months or years. Since the early 1950's, when *paracaidismo* (squatting, but literally "parachuting") became frequent within the Federal District, most land invasions have been resisted by government authorities, sometimes using riot police and even bulldozers. The resistance encountered has usually been proportional to the number of squatters involved in an invasion and/or the political influence of the owner of the invaded land. Invasions of land in the public domain have generally met with less resistance from the authorities.

In any event, government eviction attempts are rarely effective in the long run, since the invaded land is soon reoccupied, either by those who participated in the initial invasion or by another group of squatters.[15] As we shall observe in Chapter 8, government policy toward squatting in the Mexico City urban area has shifted since 1966 from unmitigated hostility and confrontation to acquiescence and even active assistance in the improvement of illegally formed settlements. The current approach involves expropriating the invaded land (if it is privately owned) and selling it to the invaders at low prices. The Department of the Federal District claims to have expropriated and released to squatters some 23.9 million square meters of land between 1966 and 1970 alone.[16]

---

[15] Motives for urban squatting are discussed in greater detail in Chapter 7. Of primary importance is the opportunity that the rent-free housing in a squatter settlement affords to accumulate savings or simply to increase one's disposable income. See also the excellent discussions of the advantages of "consumer-oriented" as opposed to "producer-oriented" housing in A. Leeds 1973 and Turner & Fichter 1972.

[16] Jackson 1973: 27. Jackson's source of data is a personal communication from the Director-General of Planning and Programs of the Department of the Federal District, dated November 4, 1970.

The typical squatter settlement begins as a jumble of hastily impro-
vised shacks made of *lámina de cartón,* a corrugated mixture of waste-
paper and petroleum byproducts. Once the survival of the settlement
seems reasonably certain, the construction of permanent housing begins.
Most of the labor and all of the building materials are provided by the
squatter himself, occasionally assisted by relatives and neighbors. The
completed constructions are typically one-story, single-family dwellings
with walls of *tabique* (a porous, inexpensive grade of brick), roofs of
lámina de cartón, and concrete floors. More elegant houses have concrete roofs and floors of *mosaico* (colored ceramic tile). Most are one-
or two-room dwellings, which are expanded over the years if space and
finances permit.

Squatter settlements usually lack most basic urban services for as long
as several years after their formation. Residents initially purchase water
for construction and other home uses from privately owned tank trucks
that circulate through the settlement. Later, a provisional water system
consisting of a small number of communal taps or hydrants may be
installed by the residents, at their own expense and with their own labor.
Sewage disposal is a much greater problem, and the expense involved
in dealing with it on even a provisional basis is usually so great that
the squatters await governmental action on a permanent sewage system.
Meanwhile, septic tanks are dug for individual dwellings, and the over-
flow simply runs off through surface ditches. Electricity is by far the
easiest service to obtain in a recently formed squatter settlement. Since
the federal power company is prohibited from selling current to residents of an "unregularized" settlement (i.e. one still awaiting government recognition), the residents illegally tap power poles and trans-
formers in nearby areas with regular electrical service. The resulting
supply systems may appear highly precarious, but they function amaz-
ingly well.

The second basic type of peripheral *colonia proletaria,* the low-income subdivision (*fraccionamiento*), may resemble some of the better-
planned squatter settlements in many ways, but its origins are very different. Fraccionamientos are created by private land companies, or even
individuals, who subdivide their property—generally into lots of 120–
250 square meters—and sell these off to individual purchasers. During
the 1950's and most of the 1960's, land in such subdivisions was within
the reach of families with very limited means, since the promoters offered very small individual lots and extended payment terms (usually
7–10 years). In recent years, however, land prices in many subdivisions
have been rising by as much as 20–40 percent per year, as the land re-

A squatter hooks his dwelling up to an illegally tapped power pole. Scores of similar connections form what the squatters call a *telaraña* ("cobweb"). Power company workers are routinely sent out to cut these networks, but the squatters usually reestablish them within a few hours.

maining for sale in them dwindles and as the subdivisions become more fully integrated into the urban area.

Initially, the land used for low-income subdivisions was among the least valuable property in the urban area. Most of it, especially the immense, almost dry Texcoco lakebed extending east of the international airport into the State of México, was not suitable either for agriculture (because of high soil salinity) or industrial use (having no convenient sources of water and electricity). It was bought up in the 1940's for a few centavos per square hectare by a handful of entrepreneurs—including some army generals—who were later to become millionaires from their minuscule investment.

Following the enactment of a 1958 law by the legislature of the State of México, individuals or companies subdividing a tract of land into lots to be sold on the public market were obligated to install certain basic services (piped water, sewage systems, and electricity), to pave the streets, to install curbs and sidewalks, and to set aside a certain amount of land within the subdivision for schools, markets, parks, and other public facilities. Those who had secured government authorization to subdivide before 1958 were not legally obligated to contribute anything to the improvement of their subdivisions, since the legislation was not retroactive.[17] In the great majority of these earlier cases, and even in some subdivisions opened for sale after 1958, the "urbanization" stemming from investment by the subdivider has consisted of little more than the creation of a more or less regular layout of unpaved streets. Not until a new governor was elected in the State of México in 1969 were any serious efforts made to enforce the 1958 regulative law and punish subdividers who refused to comply.

Housing in a fraccionamiento closely resembles the completed dwellings in a well-established squatter settlement. The houses are owner-built, one-story, single-family structures of tabique and concrete. Most construction is incremental, but precarious structures of *lámina de cartón* and other temporary materials are much less visible in a subdivision than in a squatter settlement. This can be attributed to the relatively higher income and security of land tenure normally enjoyed by subdi-

---

[17] In many cases it appears that would-be subdividers failed to obtain any sort of government authorization for their activities, and that some even lacked clear title to the land they were selling. The resulting *fraccionamientos clandestinos* have been completely lacking in basic services and improvements, and thousands of poor families who purchased land in them have found their tenure threatened when the subdivider's claim to the land was successfully challenged. The magnitude of land fraud committed in this way since 1950 has reached into the billions of pesos.

vision residents, who often finish construction of their dwellings in the subdivision while living in rented housing elsewhere in the city. However, although fraccionamientos have a more "planned" appearance than most squatter settlements, they tend to be devoid of trees and other vegetation and thus have a rather forbidding atmosphere. Also the density of settlement within them, though still high by conventional standards, is considerably lower than that in squatter settlements. This tends to reduce the frequency of social interaction among residents, and increases feelings of isolation and independence.

Selection of the Research Communities

The foregoing description of housing alternatives for the poor in Mexico City may leave an erroneous impression of homogeneity or uniformity among settlement zones of a given type. I would hasten to point out that there is actually considerable diversity within the types I have described. In fact, they often seem to vary on a bewildering variety of ecological, demographic, economic, sociological, and political dimensions, not to mention the variance introduced by purely idiosyncratic historical events and experiences. This heterogeneity greatly complicates the task of selecting communities that are in some way representative of basic settlement types.

My approach to this problem was first to identify the major settlement types that currently serve as the most important receiving areas or ultimate destinations (after one or more moves within the city) of low-income migrants entering the urban area. The second step was to choose one or more communities within each of the basic types.

Several kinds of data were collected to ascertain the location of the largest concentrations of low-income migrants within the Mexico City urban area. Official census data on income level and place of birth, disaggregated to the level of *delegaciones* and *municipios* (the basic politico-administrative divisions of, respectively, the Federal District and the State of México), were consulted. Articles describing low-income neighborhoods, published in Mexico City daily newspapers during the period from 1960 to early 1970, were reviewed. Government officials and social scientists familiar with low-income sections of the city were consulted. And informal interviews were conducted with numerous residents during my visits to more than 50 different *colonias proletarias* throughout the urban area. Finally, partial censuses (every other dwelling unit) were taken in two vecindades and one *ciudad perdida* in the centrally located colonias of Morelos, Guerrero, and Buenos Aires. More informal observations were also made in three other vecindades in other parts of the central city area. The results of this research strongly suggested that the most important settlement zones for low-income migrants were on the periphery of the city rather than in the old urban core.[18] Therefore, settlement types such as large vecindades and *ciudades perdidas*, which are now confined primarily to the central city, were eliminated from further consideration as possible research sites.

My attention then turned to the second major step in the site-selection process, that of choosing one or more colonias within each of the basic types on the urban periphery. I was constrained by the theoretical conceptions and empirical questions underlying my research to make this selection on a purposive rather than a purely random basis.[19] In the course of my preliminary interviewing and visits to possible research sites I had begun to form some judgments about the relative importance of certain community characteristics to political learning among residents of the *colonias proletarias*. Still other hunches stemmed from earlier studies of low-income settlements in other Latin American cities, especially those of Goldrich, Pratt, and Schuller (1970), Mangin (1967), and A. Leeds (1969). These judgments and expectations were eventually translated into a set of criteria for purposive sampling.

Apart from their geographical dispersion through the periphery of the urban area, the six communities finally included in the study were selected to maximize the range of variation among them on three dimensions of particular relevance to the research problem: (1) the age of the community; (2) how the community was originally occupied or established; (3) the overall developmental level of the community, defined in terms of access to basic urban services and improvements. The theoretical significance of these three variables will become apparent

[18] Corroborative evidence has been reported by Brown 1972 and Kemper 1971b, 1974. The data from my partial censuses of central-city vecindades showed that more than three-quarters of the residents had been born in Mexico City, and that most of the migrants still living in the vecindades had arrived in the city well before 1950. I subsequently discovered that many of the Mexico City natives had been born, as had many of their fathers, in the same vecindad in which they currently resided. This evidence is consistent with Eckstein's (1972a, 1973) observations regarding the high stability of residence that characterizes the populations of central-city tenement slums.

[19] Purposive or "theoretical" sampling of sites for comparative community studies —i.e. the selection of research sites according to a specified set of relevant independent variables—has been advocated most cogently by Bonilla 1964: 140–45; Walton 1973. See also A. Leeds 1968: 35. Bonilla and Leeds used this procedure in their research on *favelas* (squatter settlements) in Rio de Janeiro. Walton used the same approach in his comparative study of community power in four Mexican and Colombian cities (Portes and Walton 1975: Chaps. 4, 5).

to the reader as the study progresses; but it can be noted here that they largely determine the relative richness of the set of community-related political learning experiences to which a low-income migrant may be exposed.

The research communities selected are widely dispersed around the periphery of the urban area (see Figure 2.4). They include three squatter settlements at different levels of development (Colonia Nueva, Colonia Periférico, and Colonia Militar), one low-income subdivision (Colonia Texcoco), and two different types of government-initiated communities (Colonia Esfuerzo Propio and Unidad Popular).[20] The last two communities were included because of the potential future importance of government housing and site-and-services projects as low-income settlement types in Mexico City. At the time of my primary fieldwork (1970) the Department of the Federal District was actively experimenting with a number of such projects in different parts of the urban periphery, and it seemed appropriate to attempt a preliminary assessment of the impact of this type of dwelling environment on political attitudes and behavior.

Several of my research communities have characteristics or histories that might be regarded as atypical. Of course, there is considerable doubt about what constitutes "typicality" among such a diverse universe of cases. Given the plethora of important variables that seem to differentiate low-income settlements, the researcher can be concerned with the representativeness of his choices only to the extent that none of them exceeds, in his judgment, reasonable limits of variance on most of these dimensions. It is more important to attempt to include all the basic types of low-income dwelling environments on the urban periphery, and as wide a range of theoretically significant variables as can be accommodated within time and resource constraints. The time constraint is particularly relevant to a study such as this, which depends on in-depth knowledge of the research sites, obtainable only if the number of sites is sufficiently small to permit extended personal observation and interaction with community residents.

In short, my primary aim throughout has not been to understand how "the city" or "city life" affects political learning among a "representative sample" of the migrant poor in Mexico City—even if this were technically feasible. Rather, my goal has been to understand how particular *kinds* of urban dwelling environments with different sets of characteristics and historical experiences affect political attitudes and behavior

[20] Pseudonyms have been used throughout this study to identify both the research communities and their leaders.

among such people. In the remainder of this chapter I shall briefly sketch the most important of these characteristics and experiences.

THE RESEARCH COMMUNITIES

Colonia Nueva

Three of my research communities are squatter settlements formed by illegal occupation of publicly or privately owned land. The origins of the newest settlement, Colonia Nueva, can be traced to the actions of five taxi drivers and their families, who in the predawn hours of January 6, 1968, quietly occupied plots of land in an area formerly used as a garbage dump by residents of adjacent neighborhoods. Over the next 48 hours, the original invaders were joined by nearly a hundred more families, most of whom had been renting houses or rooms in immediately surrounding areas. The invasion, though largely spontaneous and unorganized, was consummated with great dispatch, to the considerable surprise and dismay of the landowners, who lived near by. At the insistence (and financial inducement) of these landowners, riot police were deployed on at least two occasions to evict the squatters, resulting in the arrest of 12 family heads and the destruction of numerous dwellings that had been hastily erected on the site. The shacks were soon rebuilt, however, and further resistance to the invasion proved futile.

In desperation, the landowners hired arsonists to set fires in various parts of the settlement, which caused the deaths of two adults and five children. The extensive, citywide newspaper and television publicity surrounding this event made it politically attractive, if not imperative, for the government to assume the role of defender of the settlement against its predatory enemies. Disaster-relief teams were promptly sent to distribute food and clothing to the affected families, whose dwellings were subsequently rebuilt with permanent materials contributed by the government.

Community leaders seeking legalization of the settlement soon found government officials more disposed to act favorably on their petitions; and in December 1969 the land was formally expropriated on the ground (probably contrived) that the landowners could not prove clear title to it. By 1972 Colonia Nueva's population had grown to about 1,800 (277 families). A large primary school had been built, regular electric service and piped water had been introduced, and most residents had replaced their original shacks with sturdy, one-room dwellings of tabique. In sum, the settlement had become a permanent feature of the urban landscape.

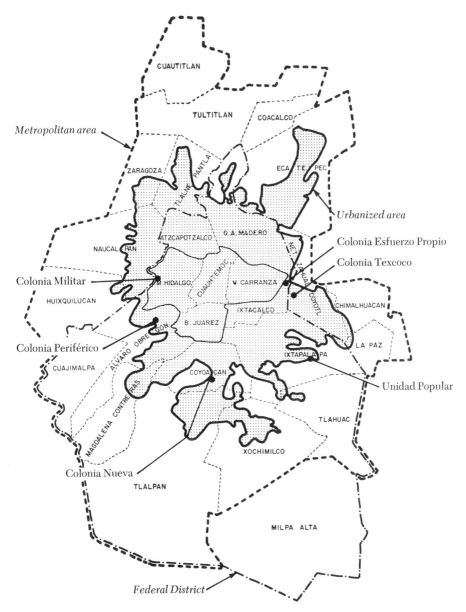

Figure 2.4. The location of the six research communities in the Mexico
City metropolitan area. Map adapted from Unikel 1972.

Part of Colonia Nueva. A dust storm swirls through the adjacent street at the left.
The stone wall at the right was built by the former landowner to impede squatting on
his property. Most of the dwellings are still makeshift structures of *lámina de
cartón*, but even so numerous television aerials have sprouted.

Another section of Colonia Nueva, showing the highly irregular volcanic terrain
occupied by the settlement. The natural vegetation around the houses
creates a semirural appearance.

Aerial view of Colonia Periférico (outlined in black), showing the totally
unplanned street pattern and the high density of settlement. Buses enter the colonia
via the only paved street (toward bottom of view).

Part of Colonia Periférico.

Colonia Militar. The cliff at right marks the edge of the sandpit that formerly occupied the site. The numerous solidly built houses, many of two stories, contrast with the temporary shacks that predominate in recently formed squatter settlements.

A residential street in Colonia Militar.

Aerial view of Colonia Texcoco (outlined in black). The many vacant lots are mostly held by land speculators. The open area in the center of the colonia is occupied by a new secondary and technical school.

A typical street in Colonia Texcoco, during the dry season. The open ditch carries a runoff of raw sewage.

Main street in Colonia Esfuerzo Propio, looking toward the headquarters of
the government's "Self-Help and Mutual Assistance Housing Program."

A typical unpaved side street in Colonia Esfuerzo Propio.

A family that chose not to join a mutual assistance group lays the foundation for a permanent house in Colonia Esfuerzo Propio. Their temporary dwelling of unmortared brick and *lámina de cartón* is in the background.

A mutual assistance group builds a house in Colonia Esfuerzo Propio, supervised by government engineers (in hard hats).

Aerial view of Unidad Popular.

A street in the paved section of Unidad Popular.

Colonia Periférico

The formation of the second squatter settlement, Colonia Periférico, followed a quite different pattern. The land invaded was the abandoned site of a large sand mine that had operated for more than 50 years. Title had been transferred to a private owner, who left the seemingly uninhabitable tract undeveloped. A few squatters appeared in 1954, followed in subsequent years by numerous families displaced by the construction of an expressway surrounding the city (popularly known as the Periférico) and other public works in nearby areas. The settlement grew through a process of gradual accretion over a period of 15 years. The first and most serious threat of eviction arose two years after the invasion commenced, when riot police surrounded the settlement and demanded that it be vacated. They were prevented from carrying out the eviction order by the intervention of an official in the office of the Presidency, whose help had been hastily secured by settlement leaders. Subsequently the landowner found it impossible to secure government action to evict the squatters.

The development of the settlement proceeded very slowly, and largely without government assistance. The residents themselves constructed a provisional school and a water system, and graded the main street of the settlement. Electricity, bus service, and a single public telephone were finally installed after frequent petitioning by the settlers. Even today, however, Colonia Periférico lacks a sewage system; and low-lying parts of it are often flooded during the rainy season, causing outbreaks of typhoid and other water-borne diseases. Protracted negotiations by various mutually antagonistic groups of settlers finally resulted in government expropriation of the land occupied by the settlement in August 1970 (after survey interviewing for the present study had been completed), by which time its population had swelled to more than 17,000. At present, the extremely high density of population and totally unplanned pattern of land use in the colonia make the installation of further services and improvements extremely difficult and costly. The fact that at least half the current inhabitants of the settlement would have to be relocated elsewhere in the city if these services and improvements were ever to be introduced was a major preoccupation of Colonia Periférico residents at the time of the fieldwork.

Colonia Militar

The third squatter settlement included in this study, Colonia Militar, originated in a highly organized, swiftly executed invasion of land that had formerly been the site of a commercial sand-mining operation. The invasion, in June 1954, involved about 700 families, led by low-ranking officers from a nearby military installation. The squatters set up a regular street layout and introduced other urban improvements—all at their own expense—in an effort to give the settlement an appearance of order and permanence and thereby reduce the possibility of eviction by the government. The fact that title to the land was held at that time by the federal government itself helps to explain the absence of serious eviction attempts during the early years following the invasion. Apart from an isolated incident in 1965, which resulted in the bulldozing of an adjacent strip of squatter housing erected prior to the invasion of Colonia Militar, the opposition of some officials and of residents in nearby upper-class neighborhoods to the settlement's survival was never translated into governmental action.

The settlers of Colonia Militar met with no success in their negotiations for "regularization" and development assistance from the government for more than a decade after the settlement's formation; but positive action on their petitions followed swiftly upon the appointment of a new Federal District governor in 1966. This was due in large part to the close relationship between the settlement's leaders and the incoming governor that had been developed over the preceding years. Colonia Militar was formally "regularized" in July 1966, and basic services and improvements—including a sewage system, piped water for individual dwellings, and paved streets—were installed within little more than a year.[21]

Colonia Texcoco

As noted earlier, a prohibition on new low-income subdivisions within the Federal District, in effect for most of 1950–70, resulted in a proliferation of subdivisions in surrounding municipalities in the State of México. Most explosive of all was the growth of the 56 subdivisions composing the municipio of Ciudad Netzahualcóyotl, east of the capital's international airport. The municipio's population grew from about 65,000 in 1960 to 650,000 by 1970 and 1.3 million by 1975, rendering it the fourth largest urban zone in the nation, exceeded only by central Mexico City, Guadalajara, and Monterrey (see Rosa 1975).

Among the first subdivisions to be opened up in this area was Colonia Texcoco, which I chose for inclusion in this study. Low down payments

---

[21] The history of Colonia Militar, particularly with regard to interactions between the settlers and government officials, is recounted in greater detail in my case study of the colonia's negotiations for "regularization," which appears in Chapter 7.

(50 pesos, or U.S. $4), extended payment terms (up to ten years), and promises of urban services and improvements to be financed by the subdivider, all extensively publicized through newspaper and radio advertising, attracted numerous poor families from the central city, as well as incoming migrants, to the new subdivision. As was typical of the land "developers" operating in this area, however, the subdivider of Colonia Texcoco defaulted on his promise of urban services. Because of this lapse, as well as an almost total neglect by municipal and state governments, Colonia Texcoco has remained without a functioning sewage system, paved streets, and other improvements. The public transportation serving this and other subdivisions in the municipio is ridiculously inadequate, since virtually all wage-earners must commute daily to their jobs in the Federal District. The colonia's water, supplied through a network of public hydrants installed by the residents in 1953, is usually contaminated and inadequate in quantity. Like other subdivisions in Ciudad Netzahualcóyotl, Colonia Texcoco lacks local fire protection, and fire engines arriving from the Federal District—invariably long after the affected buildings have burned to the ground—have sometimes been stoned by the residents. On several occasions, the notoriously corrupt municipio government fraudulently collected hundreds of pesos from each resident for a sewage system and other improvements that were never installed. Not until a new state government took control in 1969 were meaningful benefits provided to the colonia: regular electric service, a well to augment water supplies, and a large secondary and technical school.

As was true of most subdivisions in Ciudad Netzahualcóyotl, Colonia Texcoco's most severe developmental problems remained largely unsolved by 1970. Because of inadequate drainage and the lack of paved streets, it still suffered from intermittent flooding in the rainy season and fierce dust storms during the dry season. Nevertheless, it had become one of the most densely populated subdivisions in the municipality, and land prices had risen from 5 pesos per square meter in 1951 to 230 pesos per square meter in 1970, when the last of the 3,200 lots in the subdivision were sold. About 500 lots remained undeveloped, the majority of them held by nonresident land speculators. Since the colonia has no garbage collection service, these unimproved plots had been turned into garbage dumps by the residents, creating serious fire and health hazards. Disillusionment was widespread among the subdivision's 15,000 inhabitants, although some still hoped for assistance from the new state governor. Residents frequently remarked on the "backwardness" of their colonia, even by comparison with other parts of Ciudad Netzahualcóyotl, and blamed this condition on the unscrupulous subdivider and the previous state and municipal governments that had ignored their problems.

Colonia Esfuerzo Propio

Conditions in Colonia Texcoco contrasted dramatically with those in an adjacent area, which had been designated by the Department of the Federal District as the site of an experimental self-help (*esfuerzo propio*), site-and-services project. Initiated in January 1969, Colonia Esfuerzo Propio was intended to house 1,882 poor families who had been evicted from several central-city slums and peripheral squatter settlements that the government had chosen to remove, mostly to permit construction of the city's new subway system and other public works. The families, together with their dismantled shacks, were moved by truck to the project site and deposited on preassigned plots of land. Each lot was to be purchased from the government over a ten-year period, at a cost of 35 pesos (U.S. $2.80) per square meter, which included assessments for urban services and improvements. All residents were urged to participate in the "self-help, mutual-assistance" program of housing construction, in which they would have access to low-cost permanent building materials, technical assistance, and communal labor provided by other participants in the program.

The project site, formerly a barren, uninhabited area, was partially improved by the government before the arrival of the first residents, and development continued during the first year of the project's operation: the main streets were paved, sidewalks and streetlights were put in, and water, sewage, and electrical systems were installed. A large primary school was opened in 1971. At the time of my fieldwork in this colonia, however, most residents had not made sufficient progress on their permanent houses, according to the project specifications, to qualify for connection to the water and sewage systems, and most streets within the colonia remained unpaved. Dust storms and the insects swarming from an adjacent sewage canal presented major problems. Nevertheless, physical development of the site had been rapid; and the government's commitment to the success of the experimental project made residents confident that they would soon have full access to urban services and improvements.

At the time of the fieldwork, no payments on the land and improvements had been required of most residents by the officials administering the project. But the collection of these payments began in 1971, and as a result many of the colonia's poorest residents transferred their property rights to more affluent newcomers in return for large cash payments. By 1972, the bulk of the original inhabitants who had resisted the temptation to "sell out" could be expected to remain permanently. But the long-term financial burden—more than 11,200 pesos (U.S. $900) for both land and housing construction—would continue to weigh heavily on the survivors, most of whom had paid minimal rents and nothing at all for urban services in their former places of residence.

Unidad Popular

Site-and-services projects like Colonia Esfuerzo Propio had been initiated by the government chiefly as alternatives to the type of housing project exemplified by my final research community, Unidad Popular. Built in 1962–63 in an isolated area in the southern Federal District, the Unidad Popular project was justified by the government as an attempt to provide decent housing for several thousand *pepenadores* (scavengers or ragpickers) who made their living by collecting and selling scrap materials in a large municipal garbage dump adjoining the project site. Before the construction of the project, most of these people had lived in shacks erected precariously on heaps of trash inside the dump. Also among the first groups of settlers were numerous families who had been displaced by street-widening projects elsewhere in the city, as well as many government employees and policemen who had taken advantage of their official positions to acquire housing in the project. Unidad Popular had been provided with nearly all basic urban services and improvements, and construction of all its 3,300 small, depressingly uniform, concrete-block houses had been completed before the arrival of the initial residents.[22]

Like most of the government's low-income housing projects in the Federal District, Unidad Popular has largely failed in its stated purpose of providing housing for the neediest. House and land payments were set at 150 pesos (U.S. $12) per month, to be paid over a 15-year period. In addition, residents were required to pay regular bills for the electricity and piped water built into the project dwellings—services that many of them had been unaccustomed to paying for. As in Esfuerzo Propio, the expense proved beyond the means of many of the original settlers, who soon began selling out to more affluent families seeking housing in the project, or to the operator of the municipal garbage dump

---

[22] The fact that all the dwellings in Unidad Popular were built by the government distinguishes it from self-help projects like Colonia Esfuerzo Propio, in which all housing is owner-built. In a self-help project, residents are more likely to feel that they have had a personal share in the building and upgrading of their community.

and other wealthy nonresidents who sought rental properties.[23] Among the first to sell were most of the pepenadores, who went back to shacks inside the garbage dump.

At the time of the fieldwork, the most pressing problem confronting the newer residents of Unidad Popular was the need to negotiate an agreement with the government that would legalize their occupancy of houses in the project. Many residents had also begun demanding the removal of the adjacent garbage dump, which is still the main source of employment for the estimated 500 pepenadores remaining in the project. Other resident concerns included a barely potable water supply, unpaved streets in some sections, and inadequate telephone service.

For the migrants represented in this study, the paths leading to settlement in the six communities described here have been quite diverse (see Chapter 5). Although they may have been socialized into certain attitudinal and behavioral patterns in a rural environment or in other parts of Mexico City, residence in the research communities has exposed them to distinctive new mixes of political stimuli. In the following chapters I shall be concerned particularly with assessing the extent to which the attitudes and behavior currently exhibited by these migrants represent the outcomes of community-based processes of political learning.

[23] All such property transfers and rentals were illegal under the city regulations governing the project; but enforcement of the regulations was extremely lax, apparently because of the political connections of those seeking houses in the project.

CHAPTER THREE

Political Attitudes

NOWHERE IS THE imprint of the local urban community on migrants to the city more evident than in their attitudes toward the larger political system. The way in which a migrant perceives and evaluates the actors, institutions, and outputs of that system, as well as his personal relationship to it, is likely to be conditioned by the manner in which the system has affected his immediate residential environment. How a given set of political orientations comes to be shared by the residents of a low-income urban community will be the subject of considerable discussion in later chapters. But I wish first to examine some of the community-related sources of observed variation in the political attitudes of my respondents. I will begin with a general overview of the migrants' images of politics and the political system, and will then compare these with the images held by native-born city residents and by the migrants' own sons.

For the purposes of this analysis I distinguish between attitudes that reflect specific support for the political system and those that indicate diffuse support. Specific support, as in David Easton's (1965) use of the term, is here defined as support deriving from instrumental satisfactions or rewards obtained from the political system by individual citizens. It thus represents a *quid pro quo* in response to direct governmental action. Diffuse support implies a more generally positive, affective orientation toward the political system. It does not depend on the satisfaction of specific needs by the government, but instead derives from a reservoir of generalized trust or goodwill toward the political system that may even help citizens to "accept or tolerate [governmental] outputs to which they are opposed or the effects of which they see as damaging to their wants" (Easton 1965: 159). The absence of diffuse support may be reflected in a general sense of political negativism or cynicism about government and politics, or even in an advocacy of radical changes in the society and polity.

MIGRANT ATTITUDES TOWARD THE SYSTEM

Empirical studies of Mexican political culture since 1959 have consistently found that Mexican citizens entertain both a descriptive and a normative model of their political system.[1] The descriptive model emerges as a citizen evaluates the system's day-to-day outputs at local and national levels and the performance of specific political and governmental officials (except for the President, who remains largely exempt from critical evaluation). Citizens' evaluations of Mexican government outputs tend to be rather negative, especially as one moves from the national to the local level. Orientations toward politicians and public officials are even more critical, tending toward extreme cynicism about their motives and behavior, and about electoral politics in general (Fagen & Tuohy 1972: 108–13; K. Coleman 1972; Tuohy 1973: 275–76).

But these negative orientations represent only one side of what Joseph Kahl (1968: 114) has termed "the ambivalent Mexican"; for they are juxtaposed with the citizen's normative model of the political system, which includes highly positive orientations toward institutions such as the Presidency and the official political party (Partido Revolucionario Institucional, PRI), especially insofar as these institutions are associated with the stated goals and symbols of the Mexican Revolution (see Davis & Coleman 1974: 34). This is the idealized conception of the political system reflected in school textbooks, official party propaganda, government-controlled newspapers, radio and television broadcasts, and the rhetoric of Mexican political leaders from the President of the Republic down to the lowliest bureaucrat or community leader. According to this model, the political system operates in the best interests of the ordinary citizen, who can trust it to pursue the goals of the Revolution—and, more generally, to guide the country in the right direction. It is the internalization of this normative model by the bulk of the population

---

[1] The principal studies include Almond & Verba 1963: 414–28, 495–96; Kahl 1968: 114–16; Fagen & Tuohy 1972: Chap. 5; K. Coleman 1972; Davis 1974. For a particularly useful discussion of the tensions between a citizen's normative and descriptive models of the political system, see Cockcroft 1972: 259ff. The Almond and Verba data have been interpreted at length by R. Scott (1965, 1974, and forthcoming). See also Hansen 1971: 182–204 for a synthesis of findings from several of the survey studies just cited. Perhaps the most remarkable thing about these findings has been their consistency over time, from Almond and Verba's survey, completed in 1959, to Kahl's in 1963, Fagen and Tuohy's in 1966, Coleman's in 1969, my own in 1970, and Davis's in 1973.

that provides the underpinnings of what I have termed diffuse support for the political system (cf. Segovia 1975).

More often than not, particularly among the poor, a citizen's descriptive and normative models of the system are contradictory. The Mexican lower classes tend to have a descriptive model of their political system that is highly congruent with reality (see Fagen & Tuohy 1972: 111). But as Cockcroft (1972: 260) has pointed out, political ritual and directed political socialization through the schools, the mass media, and government-controlled voluntary organizations serve to blur the contradictions and increase the salience of the normative model of the system. As a result, dissatisfaction with government outputs and the performance of officials does not lead to a fundamental questioning of the legitimacy of the political system, but is more likely to give rise to a cynical criticism of corrupt and self-seeking politicians, bureaucrats, and labor and peasant organization leaders. Thus the average Mexican "believes in a government whose representatives he distrusts. . . . He does not blame the Revolutionary institutions for the chicanery of his fellow citizens, which he sees merely as a reflection of the Mexican temperament." (Kahl 1968: 116).

These general political orientations, so stable and so widely distributed through the Mexican population, are clearly reflected in the responses of migrants living in my research communities to numerous questions in the sample survey (see Table 3.1), as well as in comments made frequently during day-to-day conversations with me. The data illustrate once again the continuing success of the Mexican regime in identifying itself with the goals of the Revolution and progress toward the attainment of those goals. The majority of respondents believed that the federal government could be trusted to do the right thing (levels of trust in local government were lower, but not markedly so); that the government and the official party contributed to the welfare of the country, if not to that of the respondent individually; and that the government was the most likely source of concrete benefits for poor communities. Although a sizable minority of the migrants were mildly to extremely skeptical of the motivations of public officials, the level of political cynicism indicated by their responses was somewhat lower than national norms (see Almond & Verba, 1963: 414–28). The most cynical respondents often went to great lengths in their denunciation of politicians, describing the political process as a confidence game (*pura movida*) and a shameless money-making enterprise (*puro negocio*). Many more, however, though freely acknowledging the weaknesses and abuses of lower-echelon officials, were hesitant to attribute

TABLE 3.1

Migrants' Responses to Selected General Items About
Politics and the Political System

Questionnaire Item and Response	Percent Responses
149b. Believe that the ideals and purposes of the [Mexican] Revolution:	
have been achieved	11.2%
have not yet been achieved, but the government is still working to achieve them	81.3
have been forgotten	5.8
158b. Believe that the federal government can be trusted to do what is right:	
almost never	7.2
sometimes	32.4
most of the time, or almost always	60.5
159a. Is there any political party in this country that you think would do more good for the people of the country than any of the others?	
no, none	6.4
yes, PRI	89.7
yes, PAN (principal opposition party)	3.4
136a. Has the PRI helped to make [respondent's] life a better one or not?	
yes	50.7
no	49.3
131i. View government as the most likely source of help in solving community problems	97.3
164. Believe that the majority of public officials in the country are:	
trying mostly to help the people in general	60.0
trying mostly to advance their own personal interests or careers— working for their own benefit	37.2
some helping the people, others themselves	2.8
172. Believe that the present system of government and politics in Mexico is:	
good for the country	78.8
bad for the country	7.6
good in some ways, bad in others	13.6

NOTE: The number of respondents (cases) varies from item to item because of "don't know" or unascertained responses ("missing data"), which are excluded from this and subsequent tables of survey data. The minimum *N* for items included in the table is 567. Percentages for each item may not total 100.0 because of rounding. The numbers of items are those of the questionnaire sequence, reproduced in Appendix A, pp. 237–65.

selfish motives to specific higher-ranking functionaries, particularly those with whom they had had personal contact.[2]

In sum, the average migrant represented in this study believes in the legitimacy of existing authority structures and generally supports them. The most important determinants of this support emerge with greater

---

[2] The effects of such contact on migrants' political attitudes and behavior are discussed at greater length in Chapter 8.

clarity from the responses to two open-ended survey questions, which asked the respondent to explain his approval or disapproval of the present system of government and politics in Mexico (Table 3.2) and to give reasons for his electoral support for the PRI (Table 3.3). The many migrants who believed in the fundamental worth of the system felt that governmental and PRI concern for the needs of the poor was especially important, and they tended to attribute the social and economic development of the country as a whole in recent decades to political system performance. Some respondents cited a concrete example of system per-

TABLE 3.2

Migrants' Reasons for Believing That the Present System of Government and Politics in Mexico is Good or Bad for the Country

Response	Percent
System is good, because:	
Government helps the poor, is concerned about the needs and problems of ordinary citizens	31.0%
Country is progressing under the present system	24.8
Government builds schools, other public facilities; provides specific services, other kinds of benefits	12.0
System provides many freedoms for citizens	7.2
Other	8.5
System is bad, because:	
Government does not help the poor, is not concerned about the needs and problems of the poor	10.3
System is good; but government officials, police, politicians are corrupt, inefficient, mistreat citizens	5.1
Other	1.0

NOTE: If the respondent expressed an opinion in response to Item 172 (see Table 3.1), he was asked, "Why do you feel that way?" $N = 443$.

TABLE 3.3

Reasons for Supporting the Official Party (PRI) Among Migrants Who Voted for the PRI in 1964 and/or 1970

Response	Percent
PRI has done the most, can do more, for the poor or for the respondent and his family	29.9%
PRI always wins; other parties don't have a chance to win	23.6
PRI is the party of the government, of the Revolution	15.1
Almost everyone supports PRI, so it must be the best	11.8
PRI has done more for the country; helps the country progress	11.3
Officials and politicians who have helped this colonia are PRI; PRI helps the colonia solve its problems	5.2
Other	3.1

NOTE: The question was, "Could you tell me the main reason why you have supported the PRI?" $N = 413$. "Don't know" and unascertained responses have been excluded from the table.

formance as the primary reason for their support. A 23-year-old factory worker:

The government does good things like building roads and [improving] *colonias proletarias*. . . . They're concerned about things like that.

A 29-year-old taxi driver:

The PRI is the official party. . . . It does a lot to help the people. It gives classes in sewing and has laundries for poor people. It gives breakfasts for [school] children.

A 43-year-old unskilled worker:

I support the PRI because it has always concerned itself with the good of all the people of the country. To the peasants it gives credit so that they can work their land, and to the workers, better employment. It also organizes sports and cultural events.

As in this last remark, many respondents were either unwilling or unable to distinguish between "good works" performed by the government per se (e.g., providing agricultural credit) and those performed by the official party (organizing recreational activities).

Many migrants in the research communities, like those quoted above, were only generally aware of government or PRI activities that benefited the country as a whole or poor people as a social category. Others, however, had a more specific and personalized referent for political system performance, and explained their support for the system by mentioning specific assistance that they or their families had received personally.[3] A 34-year-old garage assistant:

I'm grateful to the PRI because doctors from the PRI cured my children. I know nothing about politics, but I vote for the PRI for that reason.

A 27-year-old factory worker:

I support the PRI because letters of recommendation from them helped me to get work.

A 22-year-old auto mechanic:

Because once the PRI gave away oil stoves, and I got one; that's why I'm going to support it.

A 40-year-old sales clerk (in the Unidad Popular project):

I appreciate the improvements and [public] works the government has built —like my house.

---

[3] For a more detailed description of the services provided to the poor in Mexico City by government and PRI agencies, see Chapter 8.

These comments suggest that the respondents' support for the political system is rooted in specific, personalized instances of governmental performance. These are not people who support the regime simply because of its "Revolutionary" origins or its continuing identification with national heroes and symbols.

Among a substantial proportion of migrants, particularly those in the research communities still suffering from insecure land tenure or a lack of public services, support for the government and the PRI may represent not only gratitude for whatever benefits they have received, but also a recognition that this support may help to extract additional rewards from the system or to preserve the gains already realized. The residents of insecure colonias consider themselves especially vulnerable to negative sanctions by government officials, as well as heavily dependent on favors from these officials.[4] Many of them assume, or are convinced by local leaders, that their community's chances for survival and for assistance from the government may be seriously diminished if they do not demonstrate support for the regime. Still others consider voting and other manifestations of support for the PRI to be essential to keeping their jobs. A 24-year-old plumber's apprentice:

I support the PRI because I also work for the government, in the Department of the Federal District, and I have to support it.

A 39-year-old unskilled factory worker:

Why the PRI? Because in my shop the union is with the PRI, and since I am a member I have to vote for it.

Although the "public" political behavior of such individuals may emphasize support for the system, in private they are not hesitant to criticize its performance in a wide variety of areas. The data reported in Table 3.4 reveal that in 12 out of 17 areas of government performance, less than half the migrants interviewed in the research communities felt that the government was doing "very well." The government got highest marks for its performance in providing electricity, public transportation, and public schools. Respondents were most critical of its deficiencies in providing police protection (and assuring fair treatment of the poor by police), providing economic aid for the needy, helping workers find employment, and redistributing wealth ("trying to even out the differences between rich and poor in Mexico"). However, dis-

---

[4] A similar explanation of support for the government party among urban squatters in Turkey has been advanced by Ozbuden (1973: Chap. 8).

TABLE 3.4
Migrants' Evaluation of Government Output Performance

Service or Benefit	Government Fulfills Its Responsibility		
	Poorly	Not so Well	Very Well
Potable water	9.8%	34.9%	55.3%
Electricity	7.0	30.3	62.7
Sewers	24.4	28.0	47.6
Paved streets	28.4	29.0	42.5
Public transportation	9.5	27.8	62.7
Police protection	20.8	39.2	40.0
Fire protection	26.8	20.9	52.4
Helping the poor find decent housing	25.9	30.1	44.0
Helping people secure land titles	18.1	35.0	46.9
Parks and recreation areas	30.4	23.6	46.0
Public markets	27.3	27.0	45.7
Public schools and teachers	8.0	25.7	65.9
Medical care for the poor	20.4	30.3	49.3
Economic help to those in need	32.3	29.6	37.1
Helping people find jobs	43.6	27.7	28.7
Assuring fair treatment of the poor by police	41.2	32.4	26.4
Trying to even out differences between rich and poor	36.5	38.7	24.8

NOTE: Question: "Now I am going to read a list of activities. As I read each type of activity, I would like you to give me your opinion of how well the government is doing in each of these areas. If you don't think the government *has* any responsibility for doing some of these things, please tell me. For example, providing potable water. Would you say that the government is doing very well, not so well, or poorly in fulfilling its responsibility for providing potable water?"

N's for each service range from 475 to 673, but most are well above 600. "Don't know" and unascertained cases, as well as those of respondents who perceived no governmental responsibility for providing a given service or benefit, have been excluded from the table.

Percentages sum across, with minor variation caused by rounding.

satisfaction with the government in these broad economic problem areas is unlikely to be translated into demand-making or protest behavior, since in these areas the migrants' *expectations* for government performance are relatively low.[5] As we shall see later in this chapter, evaluations of government performance in the community-related problem areas where migrants expect a great deal tend to vary considerably from one community to another, reflecting in large part the objective deficiencies in services and urban improvements provided by the government to specific communities.

To summarize, most of the migrants in the research communities appear to offer both diffuse and specific support for the Mexican political system. They have considerable respect for national political institutions and specific high-ranking officials, though criticizing the motives and

[5] The migrants' own priorities for governmental action are discussed at length in Chapter 7.

performance of underlings. They tend to view the regime as a benevolent provider of goods and services to the poor, though feeling that it could be doing a great deal more in many areas of responsibility than it is now doing.[6]

Both diffuse and specific support increase somewhat with longer residence in the city, apparently in response to improvements in a migrant's personal economic situation and to the gradual introduction of urban services and improvements into the community in which he lives.[7] Generalization in this vein is hazardous, however, because of sharp intercommunity differences in political attitudes. Another possible explanation for the apparent increase in support over time would be that the most discontented migrants soon forsake city life and return to their places of origin, leaving behind a system-supporting group with long urban experience. None of the evidence gathered in my study lends credence to this explanation, however. Almost all movement out of the research communities is to another part of Mexico City rather than back to the countryside. And the small amount of return migration to the countryside that does occur does not seem to be motivated primarily by dissatisfaction or by maladjustment to the urban environment. Rather, the returnees tend to be those who have retired from their jobs, those who have experienced family problems (usually involving relatives who remained in the migrant's place of origin after his own move to the city), or those who have been offered jobs or other economic opportunities in their places of origin.

Despite the generally supportive attitude toward the regime that exists in most of the research communities, small groups of migrants in each community are profoundly dissatisfied or alienated from the regime. These individuals are distinguished particularly by their uncommon political party affiliation. Migrants with the most negative attitudes toward the existing political system tend to support the National Action

[6] Both the quantity and the quality of the benefits provided by government figure in performance evaluations. My findings in Mexico City are thus at variance with those of Ugalde, who examined the medium-sized city of Ensenada in Baja California. He found (1970: 129–30) that "the lower economic groups . . . are not very concerned about the quality of [public services]."

[7] Andrews and Phillips (1970: 221) found that satisfaction with public services among squatters in Lima, Peru, also increased with longer urban residence. The simple correlation (r) between length of residence in the city and diffuse support for the political system among migrants in my sample is .134 ($p < .001$), and the r between length of urban residence and specific support for the system is .079 ($p < .026$). When objective socioeconomic mobility since arrival in Mexico City is held constant, the partial correlation between length of residence and diffuse support is .110 ($p < .003$), and the partial r for specific support is .054 ($p < .091$; not significant). Controlling for age has virtually no effect on either relationship.

Party (PAN), which provides the PRI's principal opposition at the polls. However, Panistas are much less common among residents of the *colonias proletarias* of Mexico City than among the general population of the city or the nation as a whole. Only 4.6 percent of the migrants in my sample identified themselves as PAN supporters, whereas 34.6 percent of the votes in the 1970 election in the Federal District were credited to the PAN presidential candidate. Even allowing for a certain amount of "social desirability" bias in the responses to my questions about political party preference, which would tend to reduce the number of self-professed Panistas in the sample, it is clear that PAN supporters are only a tiny minority of the population in the research communities and in similar neighborhoods throughout Mexico City.

Many low-income residents of the city seem to have accepted the government-propagated myth that the PAN is the exclusive party of the rich (especially big businessmen) and the clergy, and is therefore by definition a "counter-Revolutionary" movement. In fact, the PAN draws support from all social classes (see Ugalde 1970; Mabry 1973), and its substantive program is virtually indistinguishable in many areas from that of the PRI. But the PAN's principal *raison d'être* is simply opposition to the incumbent political elite. As described by Reyna (1971: 110), the PAN

has not had a well-defined political ideology, but from it stems a moral and critical position against the government and the PRI. It fights the monopoly of power and governmental corruption, and stresses the need for civic education among the population, which eventually may lead to a truly "democratic" government. It represents an institution through which some sort of protest can be manifested; an institution backed by growing numbers of people who know that PAN cannot win but who vote for it to express their political discontent with the established regime.[8]

This is clearly the most important motivation for PAN support among migrants in the research communities. Other minor opposition parties, such as the Popular Socialist Party (PPS) and the Authentic Party of the Mexican Revolution (PARM), are regarded, with considerable justification, as mere appendages of the PRI-government apparatus; but a vote for PAN is regarded, by both the voter and the government, as an expression of protest or of dissatisfaction with the present system. This is clear in the following responses to a survey question that asked PAN supporters to explain their party preference. An 18-year-old grocery clerk:

[8] For detailed analyses of the program and evolution of the PAN, see Mabry 1973; van Sauer 1974.

I will vote [in the 1970 election] for the PAN to show opposition to the PRI, and not because I think the PAN is necessarily any better.

A 32-year-old construction worker:

I support the PAN because I'm sick of the game of the PRI, which holds elections when everyone knows in advance who is going to win.

A 34-year-old accountant:

Because the PRI always wins, and it would be interesting to see if the PAN would keep its promises, or if it would be just like the PRI, which makes promises but never keeps them. The government is to blame for the problems of the country. . . . It devotes itself only to exploiting the peasants and the poor. . . . The *colonias proletarias* are without services, and the fault is the government's. . . . Also, the police are very arbitrary everywhere.

There was a nominal representative of the PAN in all but one of the six communities included in this study, but these people were much less active and visible than their PRI counterparts. They complained to me that most residents see nothing to be gained by supporting the PAN: the PRI always wins, and even if it lost, the incumbent regime would never allow a transfer of power to a Panista government at the national level. By supporting the PRI, the migrants reason, one stands a better chance of getting something out of the government.

MIGRANTS, NATIVES, AND THE "SECOND GENERATION"

In the 1950's and 1960's, one of the most pervasive themes of writings on the social and political consequences of urbanization in Latin America and other Third World regions was the argument that low-income migrants from the countryside were likely to become politically alienated or radicalized by the economic hardships and culture shock encountered in the big city. Migrants were viewed as the "available masses" from which opposition political parties and antisystem movements could recruit large followings. But virtually all of the empirical evidence reported thus far from a substantial number of research sites in all major Latin American countries has failed to support this view.[9] It should come as no surprise, therefore, that the migrants I studied in Mexico City were generally no less supportive of the established political order than the native city-dwellers around them. As shown in Table 3.5, migrants are slightly more positive in their orientations toward the political system than natives, but the differences on all but one measure (support

---

[9] The relevant theoretical and empirical studies are summarized and criticized, with special reference to Latin America, in Cornelius 1969, 1971; Kenski 1971: 32–132; Nelson 1969; Portes 1971c; and Schoultz 1972b.

TABLE 3.5

Measures of Diffuse and Specific Support for the Political System Among Migrants and Native-Born Residents of Mexico City

Index	Migrants (min. $N = 665$)	Natives (min. $N = 249$)	Signif- icant?[a]
Political party preference: PRI[b]	91.7%	86.6%	yes
(1) Affect for national political institutions	42.6	37.0	no
(130) Trust in government	53.8	52.9	no
(86) Political cynicism	53.8	57.4	no
(55) Overall diffuse support for political system	44.5	41.7	no
(76) Perception of governmental concern for the poor	36.1	38.9	no
(77) Perception of governmental respon- siveness to influence attempts	46.5	40.9	no
(91) Positive evaluation of public offi- cials' performance	49.7	50.0	no
(19) Satisfaction with government service outputs[c]	55.8	54.5	no
(70) Overall specific support for political system	53.1	50.0	no

NOTE: Percentages reported in Tables 3.5 through 3.8 represent the proportions of respondents having high scores on each summative index. (The number preceding each index name refers to its order of appearance in Appendix C, which may be consulted for specific item content.) Index scores were dichotomized into low and high categories, with the cutting point located as close as possible to the total sample median, computed on the basis of all respondents (both migrants and natives) in the weighted sample.

[a] Differences between groups are statistically significant, by Chi-square test, at the .05 level or beyond.

[b] Determined from responses to Questionnaire Items 159a, 159c, 159d, and 159e.

[c] Index of "dissatisfaction with government service outputs," with scores reversed.

for the official party) are not statistically significant. The strong prefer-ence of low-income migrants for the PRI, like their higher-than-average rate of voting, seems to be a carryover into the urban setting of a stable party identification developed in the rural communities from which most of them came.[10] It is doubtful, then, that in-migration from the country-side has contributed appreciably to the continuing erosion of electoral support for the PRI within the Federal District, or to the District's ris-ing electoral abstention rate (up nearly 6 percent between the 1964 and 1970 national elections). In fact, it is likely that both these trends would have been accelerated in the absence of large-scale in-migration.[11]

[10] Hypothesized relationships between rural political socialization and the mi-grants' attitudes and behavior in the city are discussed further in Chapter 4.

[11] Ames's (1970: 165–66) analysis of voting behavior between 1952 and 1967 in all Mexican states and in the Federal District also found "no evidence that rapidly urbanizing states are becoming less strong for the PRI. . . . Despite the increasing level of urbanization of Mexico, the PRI has become more rather than less dominant." Cf. Reyna 1971: 119–24.

Since the "radical migrant" thesis so widely diffused in the scholarship of the 1950's and 1960's has been effectively refuted, at least with respect to first-generation migrants to the city, efforts to assess the long-term political implications of cityward migration in Latin America and other Third World regions have focused increasingly on the question of differences in attitudes and behavior between migrants and their offspring. According to what has become known as the "second-generation hypothesis," the children of first-generation migrants will be less satisfied with their personal life situation and opportunities. They are also more likely than their parents to be dissatisfied with political system performance, and may even question the legitimacy of established political institutions. These attitudes are viewed as the outcome of more education, lifelong exposure to urban political stimuli (including partisan competition), and unfamiliarity with the deteriorating living standards, inadequate or nonexistent public services, and limited social mobility in rural areas.

The children of migrants are expected to have higher aspirations for personal socioeconomic mobility, higher expectations for government output performance, and a greater awareness of the inadequacies of the political system itself. All this makes them more likely to develop non-supportive orientations toward the system. In one of the most widely cited statements of the second-generation hypotheses, Samuel P. Huntington (1968: 282–83) compares the offspring of migrants in Third World cities with the discontented, riot-prone children of black migrants from the rural American South:

In Asia and Latin America, as well as North America, urban violence, political and criminal, is due to rise as the proportion of natives to immigrants in the city rises. At some point, the slums of Rio and Lima, of Lagos and Saigon, like those of Harlem and Watts, are likely to be swept by social violence, as the children of the city demand the rewards of the city.[12]

Empirical evidence bearing directly on this argument is still quite fragmentary; but previous studies in four different Latin American cities offer findings to the contrary. Members of the "second generation" were not found to be significantly more dissatisfied with public services, more frustrated with their personal life situation, or more ideologically radicalized than their parents. (Goldrich 1964: 332–33; Gurrieri 1965: 16–18, 24–27; H. Friedman 1969: 88; Andrews & Phillips 1970: 221.)

The evidence from Mexico City is somewhat inconclusive. As shown in Table 3.6, there are significant differences between migrant heads

[12] For other statements of the hypothesis, some with specific reference to the urban poor in Latin America, see Krickus 1968: 197–99; Ray 1969: 174–76; Mangin 1970: xxvii; and Epstein 1973: 182.

TABLE 3.6

*Diffuse and Specific Support for the Political System
Among Migrant Fathers and Eldest Sons*

Index	Migrant Fathers (min. N = 168)	Eldest Sons (min. N = 173)	Difference Significant at .05 Level?
Affect for national political institutions	41.1%	37.1%	no
Political party preference: PRI	91.8	83.5	yes
Trust in government	53.7	55.3	no
Political cynicism	60.2	53.3	no
Overall diffuse support for political system	49.2	54.9	no
Perception of governmental concern for the poor	43.4	40.2	no
Perception of governmental responsiveness to influence attempts	53.4	43.6	no
Positive evaluation of public officials' performance	50.6	55.7	no
Satisfaction with government service outputs	61.6	59.6	no
Expectations for government performance[a]	56.9	45.7	yes
Overall specific support for political system	58.0	52.8	no

[a] Index 22; see Appendix C for item content.

of family and eldest sons of migrants on only two measures of diffuse and specific support for the political system. Migrant fathers are more likely than their sons to be supporters of the PRI; and the fathers also have higher expectations for government performance.[13] There is, however, a tendency for sons who have spent all or most of their lives in Mexico City ("native sons") to be less supportive in their attitudes toward the system than those who were born and raised in the countryside and migrated to Mexico City with their parents ("migrant sons"). The data for this comparison (Table 3.7) show that native sons are less likely to be PRI supporters than migrant sons. The natives are also more distrustful of the government, and more negative in their evaluations of government service outputs and the performance of specific officials. These differences are statistically significant (though just barely), and they are consistent with the predictions of the second-generation thesis. However, the sample size is so small, and the differences on several other measures so slight, that no firm conclusions can be drawn. The native sons tend to be more highly educated than the migrants, and this

[13] Respondents being compared here are drawn from those families residing in the research communities in which both a migrant head of family and his eldest son (18 or older) were interviewed. Virtually all the sons who expressed a preference for some political party other than the PRI were supporters of the PAN.

TABLE 3.7

Diffuse and Specific Support for the Political System Among Migrant
Sons and Native-Born Sons of Migrant Family Heads

Index	Migrant Sons[a] (min. $N = 58$)	Native Sons[b] (min. $N = 115$)	Difference Significant at .05 Level?
Affect for national political institutions	40.4%	35.4%	no
Political party preference: PRI	88.3	81.1	yes
Trust in government	62.2	51.9	yes
Political cynicism	51.0	54.5	no
Overall diffuse support for political system	52.4	56.2	no
Perception of governmental concern for the poor	40.4	40.1	no
Perception of governmental responsiveness to influence attempts	42.1	44.4	no
Positive evaluation of public officials' performance	61.6	52.7	yes
Satisfaction with government service outputs	67.8	55.4	yes
Expectations for government performance	43.9	46.5	no
Overall specific support for political system	59.0	49.7	yes

[a] Sons who were born and raised in some locality outside the Mexico City metropolitan area.
[b] Sons who were born or raised in the Mexico City metropolitan area (spent most of their lives between ages 5 and 15 in Mexico City).

may be the primary determinant of their greater opposition to the regime. (In my sample as a whole, as in other surveys of urban populations in Mexico, educational attainment is positively correlated with negativism toward the political system.)

Thus the new generation of urban-born *colonia proletaria* dwellers may prove less willing than their migrant parents to acquiesce in the political status quo; but their critical stance may derive more from a greater awareness of the regime's flaws than from a lack of their parents' sense of relative material improvement. In any event, the second-generation hypothesis can be neither confirmed nor rejected on the basis of the present study.

POLITICAL ATTITUDES AND THE COMMUNITY CONTEXT

The immediate residential environment has a pronounced effect on migrants' political attitudes. When the sample of migrant family heads is disaggregated into territorially defined groups (Table 3.8), huge differences emerge on virtually every measure of support for the political system. Most of the attitudinal differences can be easily related to differences in the ways in which the six research communities were estab-

TABLE 3.8

*Diffuse and Specific Support for the Political System
Among Migrants, by Community*

Index	Colonia Nueva ($N = 125^a$)	Colonia Periférico ($N = 96$)	Colonia Texcoco ($N = 119$)	Colonia E. Propio ($N = 126$)	Unidad Popular ($N = 74$)	Colonia Militar ($N = 112$)
Affect for national political institutions	46.2%	26.0%	18.3%	74.8%	34.0%	49.0%
Political party preference: PRI	94.4	89.0	87.9	99.1	86.8	90.2
Trust in government	65.4	31.7	27.7	73.9	67.9	57.0
Political cynicism	40.7	69.1	60.3	31.8	71.7	59.8
Overall diffuse support for political system	40.6	29.1	23.2	61.8	52.8	59.7
Perception of governmental concern for the poor	37.4	47.5	6.2	44.8	49.1	38.1
Perception of governmental responsiveness to influence attempts	63.6	36.5	17.8	64.5	49.1	45.3
Positive evaluation of political and government officials' performance	71.8	38.1	1.8	81.0	43.4	56.1
Satisfaction with government service outputs	37.5	61.6	20.1	57.0	92.5	82.0
Expectations for government performance	53.3	45.5	30.3	79.4	45.3	58.6
Overall specific support for political system	59.3	45.2	6.2	77.1	71.7	64.0

NOTE: Intercommunity differences on all indexes with the exception of "political party preference: PRI" are statistically significant, by Chi-square test, at the .001 level or beyond. Differences in political party preference are significant at the .01 level.

^{a} All figures for N are minimum number of responses.

lished, to the kinds of local leaders who have emerged within them, to the kinds of interactions that have occurred between the communities and public officials, and to the absolute level of services and benefits provided by the government to each community. Each territorially defined group of migrants has its own distinctive attitudinal profile, which can be understood by reference to this set of variables.

The relationship between Colonia Nueva residents and the government was one of conflict and confrontation during the early months of 1968 immediately after the invasion that gave rise to that community; but it had become one of warm collaboration and mutual supportiveness by late 1969, after the colonia was "regularized" (the official euphemism for granting land occupancy rights to residents of an illegally formed settlement or subdivision). When interviewed in mid-1970, residents of Colonia Nueva were still euphoric over the success of their struggles for the survival of the community. However, they had become concerned about the government's slowness in surveying the land for a definitive assignment of plots to individual residents as well as its procrastination over introducing basic services and urban improvements into the community. The political learning experiences of migrants residing in this colonia are clearly reflected in their perception of the government as being highly responsive to citizens' requests, their generous evaluations of the way in which specific high-ranking officials perform their duties, their relatively low level of political cynicism, and their willingness to trust the government to do what is best for themselves and their community. The complete lack of urban services and improvements in Colonia Nueva at the time of the survey (with the exception of electricity, which was obtained through illegal hookups) is reflected in the migrants' expressed dissatisfaction with government service outputs (most of which are community-related).

Although Colonia Nueva residents were quite positive in their orientations toward the PRI and specific officials in the PRI-government apparatus, they were not as diffusely supportive of the political *system* as residents of three of the other research communities included in the study. My informal interviews with many residents of Colonia Nueva revealed that the basically affective relationship obtaining between the community and the government was highly personalized, to the point that one or two specific officials were almost universally regarded as the colonia's patrons and defenders. The informants seemed both aware and appreciative of the activities of these individuals on their behalf, and were not suspicious of intentions or motives; but they had not developed equally positive perceptions of the larger political system in which the patrons were enmeshed. Finally, the presence of strong, progovernment leaders in Colonia Nueva contributed greatly to developing a generally favorable view of government responsiveness among their followers.

Leadership differences are also important in explaining some of the divergence in political attitudes between migrants living in Colonia Nueva and those in Colonia Periférico. By the time of the survey interviews in 1970, the leadership structure of Colonia Periférico had become fragmented into at least three different, mutually competitive cliques, one of them led by the local *cacique*, who had formerly run the colonia as a tightly organized personal fiefdom.[14] For several years before 1970, the competing factions had worked at mobilizing support

[14] See Chapter 6 for a detailed discussion of the caciques, or local political bosses, who have operated in several of the research communities.

and discrediting their opposition in the eyes of the residents. The favored tactic was to designate a specific politician or government official as a patron of both the local leader and the community as a whole, and another politician or official as the community's principal enemy and the patron of a competing leader. The resulting polarization and confusion among Colonia Periférico residents had greatly lessened their support for the larger political system. Table 3.8 clearly shows the low level of trust in government and the high level of political cynicism among migrants in this community; these are coupled with unfavorable perceptions of government responsiveness to citizens' petitions and negative evaluations of the performance of specific officials. Whom can we trust? That is the question residents seemed to be asking, and their bickering leaders provided no useful guidance in the matter. Migrants in Colonia Periférico were moderately satisfied with government service outputs, and often mentioned the introduction of various provisional services and improvements during the colonia's 15-year history.

In Colonia Texcoco there is also a considerable congruence between the objective living conditions of migrants and their attitudes toward the political system. After 18 years of existence, this low-income subdivision still had very few services, and most residents expected little change for the better in the foreseeable future. Dust storms still howled through the community in the dry season, the rainy season invariably turned it into a quagmire, and children continued to sicken and die of intestinal diseases spread by open sewerage and polluted water. The fraudulent promotions of the colonia's subdivider ("your own lot with all services"), followed by the equally fraudulent collection of funds by successive municipal governments—ostensibly for a sewage-disposal system and other basic improvements that were never installed—have left the residents bitter and disillusioned. And it is not surprising that some of their hostility toward the subdivider and the municipal government has been transferred onto the larger political system. The prevailing attitude of Colonia Texcoco residents toward all governments —municipal, state, and federal—is perhaps best summed up in an observation by one of my informants in that community, a 44-year-old gardener: "Governments come and go. They work well for no more than a year or two, and afterward devote themselves only to filling their own pockets. That's the way they are, the public officials."

The cumulative neglect, unresponsiveness to petitions, and lack of government support for Colonia Texcoco residents during their long struggle to force the subdivider to install basic services have all left their mark on the general political orientations of community residents, as is evident from the data in Table 3.8. Migrants living in this community are far more negative in their political attitudes than those in any other community included in the study. By mid-1970, a newly inaugurated, progressive state governor was beginning to win back the confidence of some Texcoco residents; but the predominant mood remained one of disillusionment and cynicism.

As noted in Chapter 2, the situation of migrants residing in Colonia Esfuerzo Propio is dramatically different from that of their counterparts in the adjoining Colonia Texcoco. Most Esfuerzo Propio residents had been uprooted from some of the most run-down slums in Mexico City, and had been resettled by the government in a new community offering all the basic services and improvements that had been lacking in their previous surroundings. Moreover, the settlers had been offered ample technical and financial assistance in the construction of new single-family houses.

Most of those involved considered this a very good deal, and their appreciation was reflected in their highly positive attitudes toward the political system. In fact, the migrants interviewed in Esfuerzo Propio were more strongly supportive of the system in nearly every way than the residents of any other community in the study. The sole exception is their evaluation of government service outputs, which is less positive than the government's large investment in infrastructure development in this community would lead one to expect. At the time of the survey, however, most residents of the community had not yet benefited personally from this investment: for the most part, houses were still under construction and had not yet been connected to the community water and sewage systems; and the majority were located on streets that had not yet been paved, since paving was being extended slowly from the centrally located main street to the periphery of the colonia.

In general, though, Esfuerzo Propio residents were confident that they would eventually share in the improvement of their community, and they expected it to receive even more government benefits in the future. Many of them had watched the colonia develop from a barren, sparsely populated tract of dessicated lakebed, totally devoid of services and improvements, into a bustling, largely "urbanized" settlement in less than two years. Their optimism and sense of progress were reinforced by the frequent inspection tours of high-ranking officials through this "model" community as well as by the day-to-day presence of a government-employed development team.

Migrants in the two remaining research communities, Unidad Popular and Colonia Militar, were virtually as positive in most of their orientations toward the political system as residents of Esfuerzo Propio. The primary sources of their satisfaction appeared to be the many urban services and improvements to which most residents of these communities had access and the high security of land tenure they enjoyed. However, some differences in population characteristics also help to explain the attitudinal profiles of these two communities. Unidad Popular has the largest proportion of people with a high level of education (secondary or above) among the six research communities. This helps account for the high level of political cynicism among Unidad Popular residents, since political cynicism is moderately correlated with education ($r = .25$) among the total sample of migrants.

A substantial proportion of the residents of Colonia Militar are government employees—office clerks, school teachers, soldiers, policemen, and sanitation workers—who might be expected to have supportive attitudes toward the political system, or at least to express such views in a formal interview situation. This may account for some of the discrepancies between Colonia Militar and the other communities in the study. But a comparison of government-employed and privately employed residents in Colonia Militar revealed no striking differences between the two groups on at least half the measures of diffuse and specific system support. Moreover, I was constantly impressed with the willingness of the *militares* and other government employees I met in this community to speak their minds about politics and to criticize government performance in many areas. Far more important than occupational characteristics in explaining the generally system-supportive attitudes of Colonia Militar residents is the history of positive relationships between that colonia and various well-placed government officials (to be described in Chapter 7).

The findings presented in this chapter suggest that migrants' perceptions and evaluations of the government outputs directed toward their own local community color their perceptions and evaluations of the larger political system. In general, it is possible to understand a great deal more about the political attitudes of migrants if they are studied as members of specific residential communities. Far from being free-floating, "available masses" in the city—as they are frequently depicted in discussions of the urbanization process and its political consequences—such people are usually anchored quite firmly in a territorially based political subculture. This subculture helps them order their perceptions of the political universe and form evaluative judgments about it. The next two chapters will continue to explore the implications of this perspective on political learning among the migrant poor, with specific reference to learning that leads to political participation.

CHAPTER FOUR

Political Involvement

THE CONCERNS and activities of low-income Mexicans who migrate to the city are, understandably, centered on the particularistic needs and problems most important in day-to-day survival: securing stable employment, building or improving a house, increasing the family income, caring for the sick, and so forth. It is easy to suppose that migrants are almost totally preoccupied with meeting these basic needs, that they usually do not view political action as relevant to their problems, and that even those who perceive its relevance are too fearful of negative sanctions or too distrustful of politicians and officials to risk any activity aimed at influencing the decisions of such men.

Proceeding on these assumptions, casual observers of low-income migrants (and of the Latin American urban poor in general) have often depicted them as "marginal" to the political process. Marginality in this context usually means a lack of either cognitive or behavioral involvement in the formal political processes and institutions of the city and nation.[1] If confronted with an instance of political participation among the migrant poor, "marginality" theorists—like many students of the poor in U.S. cities—are likely to label it as aberrant behavior and ask how it could have happened at all (cf. Heffernan 1969; Orbell & Uno 1972; Mollenkopf 1973: 2). A very different perspective on political behavior among newly urbanized people is offered by another group of scholars, who emphasize the politicizing effects of city life. In this view previously apathetic and politically quiescent "urban peasants" are exposed to a large volume of stimuli that lead them—albeit with a time

[1] For detailed discussions of "political marginality" among low-income city dwellers in Latin America, see E. Cohen 1968; Mercado Villar et al. 1970; Nun 1969; Perlman 1971: 247–50; Quijano 1972; Vekemans & Giusti 1969–70. Useful critiques of the concept as applied to residents of squatter settlements are provided in Peattie 1974; Portes 1972; Vanderschueren 1973: 259–62.

lag—to develop high levels of political consciousness and participation. In this chapter I will present data to illustrate the ways in which both these paradigms are inadequate to explain the incidence and correlates of political involvement among the migrants in my six research communities.

I conceive political involvement as a phenomenon with both cognitive and behavioral components. The cognitions and behaviors examined in this chapter are quite diverse, and their selection has not been constrained by conventional definitions of political participation. Such definitions, which usually stress instrumental activity aimed at exerting influence upon government decision-makers, do not encompass the full range of politically relevant behavior I encountered in the research communities.[2] Overt "influence attempts" aimed at public officials do form an important dimension of political activity among the people included in this study. It is also clear, however, that such acts as voting in elections, working in an electoral campaign, joining a political party, or participating in community problem-solving activity are often *not* viewed by residents of the research communities as behavior that will have any discernible effect on the outputs of the citywide or national political systems. This applies particularly to some of the activities I have grouped under the term "community problem-solving."[3] But participation in these activities often has a great deal to do with "who gets

[2] For various definitions that stress the idea of participation as an instrumental act intended to influence governmental outputs, see McClosky 1968; Cataldo et al. 1968; Weiner 1971: 164; Verba, Nie & Kim 1971: 9. E. Leeds (1972: 7) found that the most appropriate definition of political participation among squatters in Rio de Janeiro is one that stresses instrumental motivation but includes both governmental and nongovernmental actors as targets for influence attempts: "Any action, interest expression, or attempt to maneuver public or private bodies which is aimed at extracting rewards from a given system." This broader conception is closer to my own view (and to that of Frey 1970b: 16ff) than are the conventional definitions of political participation.

[3] As defined in this study, "community problem-solving activity" includes: attending meetings or otherwise participating in the activities of community improvement organizations; contributing labor and materials to community development projects; making monetary contributions to community organizations or leaders engaged in negotiations with the government to secure needed improvements; and participating in the informal security forces or "vigilance committees" set up by some low-income communities to supplement the generally inadequate police protection provided by the city government. Of course, much of the behavior I have labeled "contacting public officials" also has community problem-solving as its principal object. However, contacting officials usually represents an attempt to extract rewards from the city or national political system and necessarily involves activity outside the local community. Community problem-solving, as I have defined it, does not necessarily lead to contact with supralocal political actors, and may have as its primary object the extraction of rewards from the authority structure of the community itself. (See Chapter 6 for a discussion of the ways in which local leaders may control the allocation of values within their communities.) In short, community problem-solving is

what" *within* the six communities, and we may therefore regard them as political in the broader sense of that term (see Verba & Nie 1972: 91). Finally, all the kinds of political activity examined in this chapter imply a concern with events, problems, power relationships, and allocation processes that transcend those occurring within the individual's own family.

URBANIZATION AND POLITICAL INVOLVEMENT

The impact of migration and urban residence on mass political awareness and participation, both in the Third World and in advanced industrial countries, has been the subject of much speculation and theorizing by social scientists.[4] In recent years a number of empirical studies have cast considerable doubt on the widely diffused notion that urbanization must always serve to increase mass involvement in politics. Before examining the relevant data from Mexico City, I shall summarize the most prominent theories that relate urbanization to political involvement, as well as the findings of other empirical studies that bear on the topic.

Some theorists view urbanization as a process that brings about important changes in social and political structure, changes which in turn stimulate greater political participation by individuals. Several writers have focused on the transfer of power from traditional, rural elites to modern, urban-based elites as the demographic balance of a country shifts from rural to urban. Others have emphasized the emergence of a new middle class, itself the product of increased economic complexity, role specialization, a growth of government bureaucracy, and other changes in the occupational structure that accompany urbanization. These analysts have documented the efforts of political leaders drawn from the "new" middle classes in several Latin American countries to achieve power by mobilizing the support of organized labor and other urban low-income groups on behalf of "populist" political parties (see Daland 1971: 238–39; Di Tella 1965; Horowitz 1967: 228–38, 247–48; J. Johnson 1958). Essentially, it is argued that the new middle classes,

---

highly parochial, internally oriented political activity; the contacting of officials is, by definition, externally oriented. The two forms of participation often require different attitudinal and material resources, and not all persons are likely to possess these resources in equal measure. In fact, my data (see Table 4.6) show that a substantial proportion of the migrants who frequently engage in community problem-solving never become substantially involved in other forms of political activity. On both conceptual and empirical grounds, then, it makes sense to distinguish between community problem-solving activity and the contacting of public officials. See also Dietz 1975 on the distinctiveness of community problem-solving as a mode of political behavior among squatters in Lima, Peru.

[4] In addition to the references to this literature cited below, see the studies summarized by Richardson (1973: 433–36) and White (1973).

seeking to wrest power from traditional upper-class elites, have greatly increased political involvement, particularly voting, among the urban lower classes.

Other theorists have stressed the importance of the cityward migration itself as a politicizing experience, irrespective of the many structural changes brought about by urbanization. Their basic assumption is that individuals whose life circumstances have been fundamentally altered by movement to new areas are particularly susceptible to politicizing influences and stimuli in their new environment: "Major clusters of old social, economic, and psychological commitments are eroded or broken, and people become available for new patterns of socialization and behavior" (Deutsch 1961: 494; cf. Germani 1973: 43–44). Moreover, the migrants acquire new kinds of needs and problems, for which governmental solutions may or must be pursued, and they become more conscious of the relevance of politics and government to their lives. People involved in movement from rural to urban areas can therefore be expected to vote more frequently and to make more demands upon government than they did before migration.[5]

Still another body of theory draws attention to those aspects of city life itself that contribute to greater political involvement. These aspects include: high population density (Daland 1971: 241); highly developed educational and communications systems (Lerner 1958: 60); modern occupational environments (Inkeles 1969: 1133–39); a great diversity of life-styles, consumption patterns, and organized group activity (A. Campbell 1962: 20; Kaufman 1971: 299); the formidable physical and psychological presence of the government (Bonilla 1964: 195–96; Cameron et al. 1972: 271; Milbrath 1965: 110–14); and the high salience of partisan political activity (Soares 1973: 26).

Urban life provides greater opportunities for interaction with people of differing life-styles and levels of affluence. The resulting "demonstration effect" creates new aspirations toward social and economic mobility, at the same time heightening awareness of one's "relative deprivation" that may be ameliorated through political action. The competition for political power is more visible in the cities than in rural areas where large landowners or local caciques hold sway, and urban dwellers are more accessible to the mobilizing and propagandizing ac-

[5] The extent to which this notion is embedded in the literature on political development can be gauged by consulting the 20 studies cited in Cornelius 1971: 120, n. 8. See also the references to more recent discussions of the relationship between urbanization and political demand-making in Chapter 7 of the present study. The most ambitious attempts at empirical testing of "social mobilization" theory in Latin American contexts appear in Domínguez 1971, 1974; Germani 1962; Prysby 1973.

tivities of the major political competitors. The urbanite's very proximity to the activities of government agencies makes him more aware of opportunities for influencing the decisions of public officials. Finally, greater educational opportunities and frequent exposure to mass media provide the city dweller with information that facilitates political involvement.

The basic principle underlying most theories that relate urban residence to higher political involvement has been stated succinctly by Milbrath (1965: 39): "The more stimuli about politics a person receives, the greater the likelihood that he will participate in politics and the greater the depth of his participation." And it is argued that people in cities are exposed to more political stimuli than those living in rural areas (cf. A. Campbell 1962: 20; Krickus 1968: chap. 4; Milbrath 1965: 113; Main 1966: chap. 2). It is not that the stimulation provided by urban life is totally absent in the rural environment; rather, cities provide a greater range and volume of political stimuli, as well as a greater number of opportunities for political involvement.

However plausible from the standpoint of basic behavioral-science theory, the conventional wisdom linking urban residence and greater political involvement has received only partial confirmation from empirical research. A number of early studies, using data primarily from the United States and other advanced industrial nations, documented significant rural-urban differences, with political participation highest in the largest cities and lowest in isolated rural areas (Milbrath 1965: 129–30). However, cityward migrants in the U.S. were found to have lower rates for both voting and membership in political organizations than other segments of the population (Campbell et al. 1964: 244; Bayes 1967). France, Germany, Britain, and Japan all emerged as "deviant cases" in which urban residence and voting participation had been negatively correlated throughout the postwar era (Milbrath 1965: 129; Benjamin 1972; Richardson 1973; White 1973).

It is noteworthy that most of the earlier studies indicating a positive relationship between urban residence and political involvement were based on aggregate statistics for nations or their subdivisions rather than on individual-level data gathered through sample surveys. The more recent studies that have employed survey data have yielded very different results. Several independent analyses of the survey data originally gathered for Almond and Verba's (1963) cross-national study of the United States, the United Kingdom, Germany, Italy, and Mexico have found no significant relationship (or a negative relationship) between urban residence and political participation when such variables as education, income, and organizational involvement are held constant (Nie, Powell & Prewitt, 1969: 361–68, 378; Di Palma 1970: 132; Burstein 1972). Nor did cityward migration itself have any significant independent effect on individual political participation (Main 1966: 63–64; Cornelius 1969: 847; Di Palma 1970: 132).

Negative findings also emerged from Inkeles's examination (1969) of survey data from Argentina, Chile, India, Israel, Nigeria, and East Pakistan. Inkeles and other researchers have found that residence in the largest cities actually decreases the probability that an individual will become involved in certain kinds of political activity (Inkeles 1969: 1138; Nie, Powell & Prewitt 1969: 368; Verba & Nie 1972: 240–41, 247). Single-city surveys conducted in several developing countries have also shown that length of residence in a city is a very poor indicator of some political activities (Perlman 1971: 413–18; Ross 1973a: 12). Even the more recent aggregate-data studies, which use more precise measures and control procedures than their predecessors, have found either no significant relationship or a strongly negative relationship between level of urbanization and voting participation.[6]

The findings reported in this chapter relate to a wide range of questions about the political involvement of migrants: How much involvement is there? What forms does it take, and to what extent are these interrelated? Are there any significant differences in political involvement before and after migration to the city? How do migrants differ in political involvement from native-born city dwellers? What changes in kind and degree of political involvement occur among migrants with longer urban residence? How do migrants differ from their offspring in terms of political involvement? Who are the politically active migrants, and what individual characteristics or experiences differentiate them from nonactivists?

POLITICAL MOBILIZATION AND PARTICIPATION
IN THE MEXICAN SYSTEM

Important to an understanding of why migrants—or any other segment of the Mexican population—engage in certain forms of political activity is the attitude of the Mexican government toward mass partici-

[6] See Adelman & Morris 1973: Table B1, p. 216, on 74 Third World countries; Rabinovitz 1969a: 117, on 20 Latin American countries; Ames 1970: 165, on Mexico; Reyna 1971: 115, on Mexico; Elkins 1971, on India; Sinding 1972: 784, on Chile; Cameron et al. 1972: 273, on France, India, Mexico, Switzerland, and the U.S.; Weiner & Field 1973, on India. Useful reviews of the literature, which highlight the weakness of urban residence or length of urban residence as a variable affecting individual political involvement, are provided in Fischer 1975; Schoultz 1972b; White 1973.

pation in the political process. In common with many single-party regimes in Third World countries, the leaders of the Mexican official party and government do not view political apathy among citizens favorably, and in fact regard it as potentially threatening to political stability.[7] Mexico's rulers rely on "a massive if diffuse grant of legitimacy to the Mexican regime by its citizens," provided mainly through ritualistic participation in elections that are never meaningful contests between the ruling party and its opposition (Fagen & Tuohy 1972: 38). The elections serve primarily to legitimize existing policies and to demonstrate mass support for the regime. If voter turnout is not high enough, or if the principal opposition party (PAN) makes a good showing, the legitimacy of the regime is diminished. Thus the official party and government are highly sensitive to any increase in support for the PAN; indeed, the loss of even a single precinct in Mexico City is cause for great dismay in PRI headquarters.

Nevertheless, most Mexicans are not moved to vote by any belief that their action will somehow affect what the regime does, much less who will rule. Among my sample of migrants, for example, 50 percent responded "true" to the suggestion that elections do not offer the voter a meaningful choice because the winners have already been selected by the PRI (Item 163); and another 10 percent believed this statement to be "partly true." In response to another question (Item 170), 47 percent of the migrants expressed the belief that the way people vote in elections has "only a little effect" on what the government does, and another 17 percent felt that election results have "no effect at all."

The fact that such beliefs are so widely held, together with the existence of a federal law obligating all eligible persons to vote, might lead one to conclude that most voting in Mexican elections is involuntary. But this is not the case. In practice, the voting law is never enforced; and it was evident from many of the survey responses, as well as from my informal discussions with voters on election day in 1970, that probably no more than 20 percent of those who voted felt compelled to do so. Most of this minority seemed to be voting because of pressure from their employers, labor union officials, or local community leaders who wanted a high turnout among their followers or employees. Others had to vote because they needed a validated credential indicating participation in the most recent national election: although the compulsory

[7] See R. Scott 1974. Other studies of one-party–dominant political systems that stress the need for mass participation in politics are Townsend 1967, on China; Fagen 1969, on Cuba; Field 1973 (esp. pp. 66ff), on India. The motives of such regimes in encouraging certain forms of mass participation are cogently explicated in Weiner 1971: 196–99; Tessler 1972: 177–78.

voting law per se is not enforced, a voter credential must often be presented when applying for employment or for certain kinds of licenses, permits, and social welfare services.

Despite intensive registration and get-out-the-vote campaigns by the government, over 35 percent of the registered voters in Mexico abstained in the 1970 national election, and many eligible voters did not even register. Nevertheless, the government's mobilization efforts have contributed significantly to the overall growth of the electorate (Reyna 1971; Segovia 1974). The proportion of those eligible voting in national elections has risen steadily from 25 percent in 1917 to 56 percent in 1970; and in recent years constitutional amendments have extended the franchise to women and to youths between the ages of 18 and 20 (see Cornelius 1973: 412).

Beyond the electoral arena, however, the Mexican regime has moved more cautiously in encouraging mass political involvement. Politicians and government officials invite personal contacts with the citizenry, "but on terms and occasions which they dictate and from which they hope to derive monetary or political benefits" (Fagen & Tuohy 1972: 134). Thus the urban and rural poor are periodically mobilized to participate in patriotic celebrations, official party meetings and rallies, the inauguration of public works, and peaceful demonstrations in support of the incumbent authorities. Approaching public officials to seek help in satisfying particularistic personal or local needs is both permitted and encouraged; but demanding major changes in public policy or government priorities is viewed as threatening and illegitimate activity.

In general, political mobilization in the Mexican context serves to channel the energies of the citizenry into carefully controlled, officially sanctioned activities. Controlled participation helps to build popular support for the regime, to legitimize its authority, and to minimize the possibility of "spontaneous" political activity that might have unpredictable consequences for the system's stability. When voting or working in electoral campaigns, most low-income citizens appear to respond to official exhortations to participate, viewing their activities on behalf of the official party as an opportunity to express their gratitude for assistance received from previous or incumbent administrations as well as their solidarity with the "goals of the Mexican Revolution" and its heirs within the PRI.[8] The average citizen's reasons for undertaking forms of

[8] Another study of a lower-class urban neighborhood in Mexico (Ugalde et al. 1974) observes that residents of such areas view the PRI as a conventional political party, with candidates and elections, but also as a "symbol of the Mexican Revolution and of modern Mexico. The PRI as a party does not solve many problems, but as a symbol it is to be supported with pride." George Foster (1967: 177) has also

political activity not directly related to the electoral process tend to be much more pragmatic: that is, he is usually bent on obtaining specific kinds of benefits from the government or the local community power structure.

Against this background, we may proceed to examine the patterns of political involvement among migrants in the research communities and the factors that influence the individual's propensity toward involvement.

HOW MUCH POLITICAL INVOLVEMENT?

Migrants living in the research communities exhibited higher levels of cognitive involvement in the political process than might be expected, given their predominantly low socioeconomic status and the relatively recent introduction of many to politics in an urban setting (see Table 4.1). It is likely, however, that the responses elicited by the questions about attention to political stimuli in campaigns and the mass media reflect higher than usual levels of attention, since the survey was conducted in a presidential election year.

The migrants' behavioral involvement in politics and public affairs varied widely according to type of involvement, and the electoral process engaged a far larger proportion of them than did any other form of political activity. Undoubtedly, the electoral participation figures in Table 4.1 reflect some overreporting, since the actual voting rates for the Federal District and the nation as a whole in 1964 and 1970 were much lower. In 1970, for example, 65.6 percent of the eligible voters in the Federal District voted in the national election, and the corresponding proportion for the nation as a whole was 56 percent. These statistics represent voting by both men and women, and they would be somewhat higher if based on males alone, as in my sample. Allowing for this factor, as well as for some artificial inflation in the self-reported voting rates, it is still reasonable to conclude that voting participation in the migrant sample was above national and citywide norms.[9] Participation in other forms of political activity was much less widespread.

---

noted that in Tzintzuntzan, a small rural community, elections "are, above all, a device to permit people to participate in a patriotic manifestation to declare their loyalty to Mexico and to their community and to express their pride in being Mexican."

[9] Ugalde and his associates (1974: 45) found that 87 percent of the residents in a low-income neighborhood in the Mexican border city of Ciudad Juárez had voted in the 1964 election, and some of those who had not were not old enough to vote. Voting participation in the Mexico City research communities also exceeds that encountered in low-income urban communities in other Third World countries. See, for example: Usandizaga & Havens 1966: 81, on Barranquilla, Colombia; Flinn & Camacho 1969: 54, on Bogotá, Colombia; Roberts 1970a: 367, on Guatemala City; Karpat 1973: 17, on Istanbul.

TABLE 4.1

Measures of Political Involvement Among Migrants in Mexico City and Among a National Sample of Lower-Class Male Urban Dwellers

Cognitive Involvement	Mexico City Migrants (av. N = 650)	National Urban Sample[a] (av. N = 290)
Interest in what the federal government is doing (Item 155a)		
much	28.1%	—
some	37.9	—
little	27.3	—
none	6.7	—
Interest in what the local government[b] is doing (Item 155d)		
much	38.7	—
some	36.6	—
little	20.1	—
none	4.6	—
"How much effect do activities of federal government have on your life from day to day?" (Item 158a)		
some or much	56.7	28.5%
none	43.4	71.5
Interest in campaigns (Item 157a)		
much	36.3	21.3
some or little	55.8	44.0
none	7.7	34.7
Follow reports of politics and public affairs at least once a week (Items 154a, 154b)		
in newspapers	49.9	—
on radio or television	69.1	—

Behavioral Involvement	Mexico City Migrants (av. N = 650)	National Urban Sample (av. N = 290)
Voted in most recent national election, if eligible[c] (Item 161b)	95.4%	73.8%
Intend to vote in 1970 national election (Item 161c)	96.7	—
Registered to vote in 1970 national election (Item 161d)	94.8	—
Attended political meeting or rally during past 6 months (Item 175e)	20.2	—
Worked in electoral campaign at least once (Item 175f)	8.0	—
Political party member (Item 159c)	32.1	11.6
Contacted a public official, on one or more occasions (Items 136c, 143c, 176a, 176m–176o)	25.8	8.3
Participated in community problem-solving activity in current place of residence on one or more occasions (Items 120b, 133a, 143c)	27.0	—
Discuss politics or public affairs with relatives, friends, etc. (Item 175a)		
at least once a week	4.1	7.8
from time to time	36.6	40.8
never	59.3	51.4

[a] Data for the national sample are drawn from a secondary analysis of survey data originally gathered for Almond and Verba's five-nation study (1963). A dash indicates that no comparable data are available from this source.

[b] Refers to the Department of the Federal District. Question was not asked of residents of Colonia Texcoco (located in the State of México).

[c] For Mexico City migrants, data refer to the 1964 election; for the national sample, data refer to the 1958 election.

Nevertheless, the migrants showed a relatively high level of involvement in comparison with a national sample of urban-dwelling, low-income, adult males; in fact, the migrants scored higher than the national sample on all but one of the seven measures of political involvement for which comparable data were available. Even allowing for the different time periods in which the data from these two sources were collected, the evidence suggests that migrants residing in the research communities had attained higher levels of political involvement than the nation's urban-dwelling population in general. However, the national sample used as the basis of comparison in Table 4.1 contains a relatively small number of cases from Mexico City. As we shall observe later in this chapter, migrants do not differ markedly from native-born residents of Mexico City on most dimensions of political involvement.

THE IMPACT OF THE URBAN ENVIRONMENT

Political Involvement Before and After Migration

Several questions in my survey were intended to provide information on changes in the migrants' level of political involvement before and after migration. Among migrants who were 20 or older at the time they arrived in Mexico City (55 percent of the total sample of migrant family heads), 37 percent reported that they had become more interested in politics and public affairs since they moved to the city. Slightly more than half of the same group reported that they belonged to more groups and organizations than they had before moving to the city (though nonpolitical organizations are included in the comparison). Finally, of those 20 or older at the time of migration who had worked in one or more electoral campaigns, 76 percent reported having done so only in Mexico City, whereas 22 percent had engaged in campaign activity only in their places of origin.

Of course, in the absence of detailed data gathered before migration, the respondents' self-reported changes in political involvement must be interpreted with great caution. Recall errors may be frequent in such reports. Nor can the reported changes be attributed solely to the migration experience itself, since they may well be related to other kinds of changes in an individual's life after migration to the city. The data do suggest, however, that a substantial proportion of the migrants became more politically involved in Mexico City than they would have if they had remained in their places of origin.

Migrant-Native Differences in Political Involvement

A comparison of the migrants in my sample with native-born residents of the research communities on various measures of political involve-

TABLE 4.2

*Political Involvement Among Migrants and Native-Born
Residents of Mexico City*

Index	Migrants (av. $N = 665$)	Natives (av. $N = 225$)	Difference Significant at .05 Level?
(81) Perception of relevance of government and politics to need satisfaction	51.9%	44.8%	no
(6) Awareness of governmental outputs affecting community of residence	40.2	35.1	no
(3) Attentiveness to electoral campaigns and political content of mass media	48.6	61.6	yes
(87) Political opinion-holding	22.4	34.2	yes
(37) Knowledge of government and politics	39.3	39.7	no
(133) Voting participation	70.2	60.7	yes
(8) Campaign involvement	28.4	28.3	no
(14) Contacting of public officials	27.2	20.6	yes
(71) Participation in community problem-solving activity	58.5	54.6	no
(16) Discussion of politics and public affairs	41.8	49.7	yes

NOTE: Percentages reported in Tables 4.2, 4.5, and 4.9 through 4.13 represent the proportions of respondents having "high" scores on various summative indexes. For example, 51.9 percent of the migrants exhibit a "high" perception of the relevance of government and politics to need satisfaction. Index scores were dichotomized into low and high categories, with the cutting point located as close as possible to the median for the total sample, computed on the basis of all respondents, both migrants and natives, in the weighted sample. The number in parentheses before each index name indicates its order of appearance in Appendix C, which may be consulted for specific item content.

The statistical significance of differences reported in this and subsequent tables in this chapter is determined by the Chi-square test.

ment reveals some interesting differences (see Table 4.2). The migrants are less attentive than the natives to campaign activities or to the political content of mass communications; they are also less likely to hold opinions about public issues. On other measures of cognitive involvement the differences between migrants and natives are not statistically significant. In terms of participant behavior, migrants are more likely than natives to vote and to contact public officials. They discuss politics and public affairs somewhat less frequently than the natives, however. The differences between migrants and natives in terms of campaign involvement and participation in community problem-solving are negligible.

The introduction of controls for age, socioeconomic status, and community of residence reduces most of the migrant/native differences to which I have referred, but the disparity in rates of voting participation remains significant. Why do migrants vote more often than native-born

TABLE 4.3

*Perceived Civic Duties Among Migrants and Native-Born
Residents of Mexico City*

Duty	Migrants (N = 650)	Natives (N = 258)
Vote in elections	44.1%	32.8%
Obey the laws	15.1	19.2
Pay taxes	1.2	1.4
Serve in armed forces	4.0	10.3
Send children to school	21.0	22.0
Keep informed about public affairs	1.0	1.0
Participate in community affairs	0.8	1.1
Work hard, do your job well	12.7	11.7
Other	0.2	0.6

NOTE: The question was: "What do you think a person ought to do in order to be a good Mexican?" The first activity mentioned in response is reported in the table; "don't know" and unascertained responses are excluded. Differences between migrants and natives are statistically significant at the .01 level.

residents of the city? One possibility is that more migrants than natives are involved in certain organizations commonly used by the government for electoral mobilization. But we find that there are no significant differences between the proportions of each sample group who belong to labor unions or the PRI; nor are more migrants than natives employed in government agencies.

A more plausible explanation for the difference in voting rates is suggested by the responses reported in Table 4.3, which indicate that migrants are more likely than natives to define their primary obligation to the nation in terms of political participation, and especially voting participation.[10] The migrant's sense of obligation to vote may also reflect his desire to support the authorities and symbols of the national political system, and his perception of voting as the most appropriate, officially sanctioned way of expressing this support (see Levenson 1971: 8). Such perceptions may well be a product of rural political socialization before migrating. Studies of electoral participation in Mexico since 1952 show that residents of predominantly rural states consistently vote in larger numbers than residents of predominantly urban states (Reyna 1971: 116, 134–35, 144; Ames 1970: 163). This pattern can be attributed in part to the mobilizational activities of local caciques, large landowners,

[10] Considerable research in both developing and advanced countries has demonstrated that a sense of civic obligation is strongly related to actual voting participation, especially among low-income people. See especially: Milbrath 1965: 60–64; 1968: 33; Nie, Powell & Prewitt 1969: 816; Di Palma 1970: 51–52; Levenson 1971: 11–15, 28.

comisarios ejidales (administrators of communally owned agricultural land), and other local notables who strive to turn out the largest possible vote for the ruling party in their communities.

The pattern of high voting participation in rural areas is also reinforced by greater "compliance observability" within rural communities. Nonvoting in such communities is both more visible and more likely to provoke negative sanctions than in large cities.[11] From this it might be expected that once a cityward migrant finds himself in a less constraining environment, with no *patrón* or political boss to "orient" him, his voting participation will decline (Sinding 1972: 789; Walton & Sween, 1971: 743). But the fact that the migrants in my sample continued to vote frequently, and even more often than native-born city-dwellers, long after their move to the city indicates the existence of a well-developed pattern of political behavior that may have been reinforced by the migrants' urban environment.

Political Involvement and Time in the City

The theoretical literature summarized earlier in this chapter implies that the longer a person resides in an urban area, the more likely it is that he will become involved in political activity. The first set of correlations (r_1) reported in Table 4.4 shows that among the migrant sample longer residence in Mexico City is positively related to all measures of cognitive and behavioral political involvement except the contacting of public officials and participation in community problem-solving. However, most of the correlations are of very low magnitude, with some falling short of statistical significance. Length of residence in the city is most strongly related to knowledge of politics and public affairs, voting participation, and campaign involvement. When we introduce controls for age and socioeconomic mobility (r_2), the relationship between length of urban residence and most measures of cognitive involvement in politics is strengthened, but the correlations remain relatively small. And controlling for these variables tends to reduce the strength of the relationship between longer urban residence and most types of participant behavior.

[11] Eva Hunt (1974: 15–16) has described a small rural community in the state of Oaxaca in which "village officials may fine or actually jail a man who refuses to register, pay dues [to the PRI], or vote. Actually, registration and voting are required by law, but dues for party membership are optional. But San Andreseños believe that they are also required to . . . pay dues to the PRI. They receive voter registration cards and party membership [cards] simultaneously. Both are seen as obligations like 'paying municipal tax.'" Corbett (1974: 160–61) describes another Oaxacan village in which public shaming of nonvoters is used by local leaders to ensure a high turnout.

TABLE 4.4
Correlations of Length of Residence in Mexico City with Measures of
Political Involvement Among Migrants

Measure (Summative Index)	Correlation	
	r_1	r_2
Perception of relevance of government and politics to need satisfaction	.115*	.109*
Perception of governmental outputs affecting community of residence	.032	.102*
Attentiveness to electoral campaigns and political content of mass media	.072*	.187*
Political opinion-holding	.058	.134*
Knowledge of government and politics	.171*	.188*
Voting participation	.293*	.197*
Campaign involvement	.155*	.148*
Contacting of public officials	.068*	−.002
Participation in community problem-solving activity	.003	−.061
Discussion of politics and public affairs	.016	.064

NOTE: Figures in the r_1 column are simple (zero-order) correlations; those appearing in the r_2 column are second-order partial correlations, controlling for age and socioeconomic mobility (Index 35). The number of cases used as a base for the analysis varies from 588 to 671. Correlations marked * are statistically significant at the .05 level or beyond.

The results of this analysis do not lend much support to the traditional conception of the large city as a politicizing environment. The migrant's general knowledge of government and politics, as well as his propensity to vote, do appear to increase significantly over time in the city. But we have found that this effect is not entirely independent of growing older and improving one's socioeconomic status. Outside the arena of electoral politics, it is clearly not the sheer amount of urban experience that determines the degree of participant behavior.

Intergenerational Differences in Political Involvement

As noted in Chapter 3, it has often been assumed that the city-born or city-raised offspring of migrants will be more dissatisfied than their parents with their personal situations, and are therefore more likely to make demands on the government. This higher political involvement is presumed to result from the younger generation's lifelong exposure to urban political stimuli, higher level of education, and lack of a rural standard of comparison in assessing one's life situation and opportunities for improvement.

Table 4.5 presents the data from Mexico City bearing on this hypothesis. The three groups of respondents compared here are drawn from those families in which both a migrant head of family and his eldest

TABLE 4.5
*Political Involvement of Migrant Fathers and
Eldest Sons of Migrant Fathers*

Index	Migrant Fathers[a] (av. $N = 179$)	Migrant Sons[b] (av. $N = 60$)	Native Sons[c] (av. $N = 116$)	Difference Significant at .05 Level?
Perception of relevance of government and politics to need satisfaction	49.5%	44.4%	47.0%	no
Awareness of governmental outputs affecting community of residence	35.6	29.9	33.8	no
Attentiveness to electoral campaigns and political content of mass media	52.1	49.6	61.2	no
Political opinion-holding	28.9	22.7	29.2	no
Knowledge of government and politics	45.2	28.8	57.2	yes
Voting participation[d]	95.4	78.3	84.0	yes
Contacting of public officials	29.2	12.2	0.0	yes
Participation in community problem-solving activity	66.1	43.8	48.9	yes
Discussion of politics and public affairs	46.8	31.4	55.7	yes

[a] Heads of family who were born and raised outside the Mexico City metropolitan area.
[b] Eldest sons of migrant family heads, sons born and raised outside Mexico City.
[c] Eldest sons of migrant family heads, sons born or raised in Mexico City.
[d] Refers only to voting in the 1970 presidential election, in which all members of all three subgroups were eligible to participate.

son were interviewed. The sons have been divided into two groups: those who were born and raised outside Mexico City, and those who were either born in Mexico City or brought there by their families in early childhood. Although native sons have a higher cognitive involvement in politics than migrant sons, which is consistent with the theory that lifelong urban exposure results in higher political consciousness, they do not differ significantly from the first-generation migrants on these measures. And when we compare the three groups in terms of behavioral involvement, the "second-generation" hypothesis seems even less likely: both migrant sons and native sons tend to participate in political activity less frequently than their parents. The intergenerational gap is greatest in community-related activities such as contacting public officials (usually with regard to some community need) and community problem-solving.

Statistically significant differences between the three subgroups persist when level of education is controlled. Sons were also found to be significantly less active in politics than their migrant fathers within all but one of the six research communities (the deviant case, Colonia Nueva, will be discussed shortly). The differences revealed by this analysis cannot be dismissed by arguing that the sons are politically inexperienced simply because of their youth. Because the research communities contained many extended families with representatives of two or three generations living under the same roof, the sons of migrants interviewed in my survey ranged in age from 18 to 45, and sons in their 30's and 40's were not uncommon.

The survey findings with regard to community-related political activity can be explained in large part by the different opportunities each generation has had for this kind of political involvement. In the older squatter settlements, few sons of migrants were involved (except perhaps as children) in the land invasions that created their communities; nor did they participate in the series of confrontations with the government or with private landowners that usually occurred while the communities were being established. Even in low-income communities that do not originate through squatting, the residents' most important opportunities for political participation often involve community-related problem-solving or petitioning—both activities that are most intense during the early years of a community's existence, when the need for basic services and improvements is most severe.

In half of the research communities, political activity aimed at meeting basic needs occurred before most of the sons of migrant settlers in my sample reached maturity. The sons, then, had little acquaintance with the experiences that had helped to politicize their fathers. My survey revealed that only 25 percent of the sons (whether migrant or native) had ever witnessed a land invasion or a confrontation between squatters and officials or landowners seeking to evict them; but 55 percent of the migrant fathers had had such an experience. Only 12 percent of the migrant sons, and not one of the native sons, had been involved in an attempt to contact a public official, whereas 29 percent of the migrant fathers had done so.

Further data to support this explanation of the intergenerational difference in community-related participation comes from Colonia Nueva, the most recently established squatter settlement in my study. The settlement had been established only two and a half years before the survey; and this period had been marked by emotion-charged struggles to retain control of the land, as well as intense petitioning to secure government assistance. Most of the community's residents had been caught up in some way in this effort to defend and consolidate their settlement.

All the sons of migrants I interviewed in Colonia Nueva had been at least 16 years old when the land invasion occurred, and both fathers and sons had frequent opportunities for political participation. The data gathered in this community—unlike those from all other neighborhoods in the study—show no significant differences in community-related political participation between migrant fathers and their sons.

CORRELATES OF POLITICAL PARTICIPATION

If mere length of residence in the city is not a powerful indicator of political participation among migrants, what *are* the most important variables? My approach to this problem involves splitting the sample of migrants into six subgroups: "complete nonparticipants," "voting specialists," "campaigners," "demand-makers," "community problem-solvers," and "complete activists." Each migrant has been placed in one of these subgroups, according to the particular kind of political participation in which he seems to have "specialized," usually the one he has engaged in most frequently.

For purposes of this analysis, the subgroups were defined as follows. Complete Nonparticipants are those migrants who rank below the median for the total sample on summative indexes of voting participation, campaign involvement, contacting public officials, and community problem-solving activity. Voting Specialists are those who score below the median on all indexes but that of voting. Excepting the respondents who are completely inactive in a political sense, a relatively high level of voting participation is characteristic of the migrant sample as a whole. Therefore, in identifying migrants who tend to specialize in a given form of political participation other than voting, I have defined such a subgroup as one whose members rank above the sample median in that form of political activity *in addition to* voting. Thus migrants classified as Campaigners are those who rank high on the indexes of voting and campaign involvement but low on the indexes of contacting officials and community problem-solving. Demand-Makers are those who have high scores on the indexes of voting and contacting of public officials but low scores on the indexes of campaign involvement and community problem-solving.[12] Community Problem-Solvers are those who score above the median on the indexes of voting and community problem-solving activity and below the median on the other two indexes of participation. The Complete Activists in the sample do not specialize in

---

[12] See Chapter 7 for a fuller discussion of the terms "demand" and "demand-making" as they apply to political activity among the residents of low-income urban communities in Latin America.

TABLE 4.6
*Defining Characteristics and Proportions of Types of
Political Participants Among Migrants*

| | Mode of Political Participation | | | | | |
Type	Voting	Campaign Involvement	Contacting Officials	Community Problem-Solving	N	Percent
Complete Nonparticipant	low	low	low	low	48	10.9%
Voting Specialist	high	low	low	low	136	30.8
Campaigner	high	high	low	low	36	8.0
Demand-Maker	high	low	high	low	52	11.8
Community Problem-Solver	high	low	low	high	148	33.3
Complete Activist	high	high	high	high	43	5.2

NOTE: "Low" indicates a score below the median score for the total sample of migrants on a given index of participation; "high," a score above the median score for the total sample.

any particular kind of political participation but score above the median on all four indexes.

Table 4.6 summarizes the defining characteristics of the six groups that I have differentiated. Respondents who could not be assigned to any one group—about 28 percent of the total sample—have been excluded from the analysis.[13] The exclusion of so many cases from the analysis is in some respects a liability; but I consider the disadvantage to be more than offset by the theoretical advantages of a typology that allows a clearly differentiated analysis of the correlates of political activism. The case for this approach has been made and documented most effectively by Verba and his colleagues (Verba, Nie & Kim 1971), whose study of political participation in Austria, India, Japan, Nigeria, and the United States revealed that the factors affecting the rate of participation—such as psychological predisposition, social status, or individual experiences and exposures—often differ from one mode of participation to another. Observing that the failure to distinguish between types of participation may be responsible for many of the ambiguities and contradictions in research findings about political participation and its correlates, these authors argue (1971: 8–9, 66):

Participation is multidimensional and must be treated as such if it is to be understood. Citizens differ not only in the overall amounts of participation they perform but also as to the types of acts in which they choose to engage. . . .

[13] This classification procedure approximates, in highly simplified form, the identification of types of political participators carried out by Verba and Nie (1972: chap. 5) using cluster analysis techniques. For an alternative approach, based on similar assumptions about the multidimensional nature of political participation, see Olsen 1972.

TABLE 4.7

Social-Status Characteristics of Types of Migrant Participants

Status Characteristic	Complete Nonparticipants	Voting Specialists	Campaigners	Demand-Makers	Problem-Solvers	Complete Activists	Difference Significant at .05 Level?
Education:							
None	23.0%	25.6%	35.4%	32.1%	41.6%	20.7%	yes
1–5 years of primary	63.3	57.8	54.0	57.7	50.1	72.0	
6 years of primary or more	13.7	16.6	10.7	10.2	8.2	7.3	
Occupational Status:							
Lower manual	43.0	58.6	45.5	78.0	61.1	45.1	yes
Upper manual or above	57.0	41.4	54.5	22.1	38.9	54.9	
Family Income:							
Below minimum wage for 1 worker	57.0	47.6	47.5	56.4	60.2	31.6	no
Minimum wage or above	43.0	52.4	52.5	43.6	39.8	68.4	
Intragenerational socioeconomic mobility[a]							
Low	63.7	59.9	59.4	61.8	48.1	64.5	no
High	36.3	40.1	40.6	38.2	51.9	35.5	

[a] Summative Index 35 (see Appendix C for item content).

Those who engage in each mode hold different attitudes and orientations about politics and participation. . . . There are different processes that lead to one type of participation rather than another.

I did perform a more conventional analysis of the correlates of political participation, using the overall summative index of participation (Index 62) developed for use elsewhere in this study; but in the end the typology just described seemed to reveal more about the correlates of participation in my migrant sample than did any scale or index in which the respondents were ordered from low to high on a single dimension of political activism.

I turn now to an examination of the socioeconomic and attitudinal characteristics of the six types of political participants.

Social-Status Characteristics

One of the most widely accepted generalizations in the literature on political participation holds that political activists come overwhelmingly from middle- and upper-class sectors of the population—that is, from citizens having higher-status occupations, more education, and larger incomes.[14] This is usually attributed to the greater time and greater financial resources available to such people, and also to certain cognitive and attitudinal correlates of high socioeconomic status (sense of personal and political efficacy, awareness of opportunities for influencing government decisions, etc.). The data presented in Table 4.7 indicate that a disproportionate number of the Complete Activists in the migrant sample do have above-average incomes; but this does not hold true for migrants who specialize in a particular mode of participation. Nor are educational attainment, occupational status, or socioeconomic mobility consistently related to political activism. Complete Activists are as likely as Complete Nonparticipants to have had no formal education, to be employed in lower-manual occupations, and to have experienced little improvement in their socioeconomic status since reaching adulthood.

The relative unimportance of social-status variables in affecting political participation is clearly illustrated by a correlational analysis performed upon the total sample of migrants (see Table 4.8). Most of the correlations are very weak, especially those summarizing the relationship between the status variables and the two activities that are

---

[14] The evidence on which this generalization is based is reported most extensively in Lane 1959: 220–34; Lipset 1960: 187–89, 206; Milbrath 1965: 114–28; Inkeles 1969; Di Palma 1970: 121–49; Verba & Nie 1972: 125–37; Huber & Form 1973: 120–31. See also, with reference to squatters in Rio de Janeiro, Perlman 1971: 426–28.

TABLE 4.8

*Correlations of Social-Status Variables with Political
Participation Among Migrants*

Type of Participation	Family Income	Occupational Status	Years of Education	Overall SES[a]
Voting	.15*	−.03	−.05	.08*
Campaign involvement	.13*	.12*	.10*	.16*
Contacting public officials	.09*	−.03	.01	.05
Participation in community problem-solving activity	.01	−.06	−.09*	−.08*
Overall political participation[b]	.12*	−.01	.01	.07*

NOTE: Table entries are Pearson correlation coefficients. Correlations marked * are statistically significant at the .05 level or beyond. The average number of cases is 670.
[a] Summative Index 69.
[b] Summative Index 62.

predominantly related to local community affairs, namely, contacting officials and participating in community problem-solving. In fact, some of the status variables are negatively related to participation. Overall socioeconomic status (SES) accounts for less than 1 percent of the variance in voting participation, contacting officials, and community problem-solving activity; and it explains less than 3 percent of the variance in campaign involvement.

The amount of variation in socioeconomic status within my predominantly lower-class sample is probably less than is encountered in most survey studies that have found SES to be a powerful explanatory variable; but the significance of the findings in Table 4.8 should not be discounted on this ground alone. Several of the communities included in the present study, particularly Unidad Popular and Colonia Militar, are quite heterogeneous in terms of SES, and a sprinkling of middle- or lower-middle-class residents can be found in most of the others as well. In fact, there is a substantial range of variation in scores on the finely calibrated SES index used in my analysis.[15] The low explanatory power of SES, then, is rather striking in view of the overwhelming importance usually attached to it in discussions of political participation. The finding is, however, consistent with a growing body of studies that have found measures of SES to be unrelated—or even negatively related—to political involvement among certain racial minority groups, urban populations in developing countries, and regionally defined groups in the United States (Flinn & Camacho 1969: 55; Goel 1969; G. Johnson 1971; Rabushka 1970; Salamon & Van Evera, 1973).

[15] The variance for this 23-point index is 8.05, and the range is 21.

General Attitudinal Orientations

Table 4.9 compares the six types of political participants in terms of several general orientations that are usually regarded as important correlates of political activism. The index of attitudinal modernity used in this analysis measures such traits as propensity to plan for the future, capacity to project oneself into the social or political roles of other people (empathy), felt need for achievement, sense of control over one's environment (the opposite of fatalism), and propensity to take risks in order to attain goals. Some scholars have suggested that these traits may provide important incentives or psychological resources for political involvement (Milbrath 1965: 78–79; Kahl 1968; Inkeles 1969; Inkeles & Horton 1974). My data are consistent with this view. Among migrants in the research communities, we find that Complete Nonparticipants are considerably less likely than any of the political activists to possess a high level of attitudinal modernity, whereas Complete Activists conspicuously outdistance all other groups in this respect.

High trust in people and a disposition to work with others in order to satisfy needs or solve problems have also been cited by some investigators as traits that incline people toward political participation (Milbrath 1965: 80; Goldrich 1970: 189–91). In my migrant sample, Demand-Makers, Problem-Solvers, and Complete Activists are all more likely to possess a high level of trust in people than other types of participants. Moreover, all types of politically active migrants except Voting Specialists exhibit a stronger preference for working collectively to satisfy needs than the Nonparticipants. These findings suggest that those whose political activity usually involves cooperation with other people —working in electoral campaigns, contacting officials, helping in com-

TABLE 4.9

General Attitudinal Orientations Among Types of Migrant Participants

Index	Complete Nonparticipants	Voting Specialists	Campaigners	Demand-Makers	Problem Solvers	Complete Activists
(51) Attitudinal modernity	22.2%	41.8%	48.0%	52.7%	38.0%	75.9%
(131) Trust in people	12.6	16.1	12.4	34.4	25.8	29.5
(18) Disposition to work collectively	19.8	16.5	32.6	33.1	23.5	42.3
(4) Authoritarianism	39.1	29.7	25.0	40.4	41.1	60.5
(12) Conflict orientation	46.4	47.7	19.2	73.7	55.2	72.3

NOTE: See Appendix C for item content of each index. Differences on all measures are significant at the .05 level or beyond.

munity problem-solving—are more likely to have a high degree of social trust and a generalized preference for collectively rather than individually pursued solutions to problems affecting them.

Research on the relationship of authoritarianism to political participation has produced contradictory findings; but the studies that do demonstrate a significant relationship find that highly authoritarian people are less likely to engage in political activity (Milbrath 1965: 84–86). Among migrants in the research communities, however, there appears to be a positive relationship between authoritarianism (defined here as a preference for strong, autocratic leadership and a low level of tolerance for minority opinions) and political participation. The relationship is strongest among the Complete Activists, who are much more likely than other types to exhibit authoritarian tendencies. One explanation for these findings may lie in the particular pattern of authoritarian leadership—*caciquismo*—that has existed in several of the communities. A cacique may devote considerable attention to political mobilization within the community under his control (see Chapter 6). Authoritarian-minded residents may be more receptive than others to his inducements, and may thus be drawn more readily into political activity.

A willingness to take sides in conflict situations has been identified as an important characteristic of certain types of political activists in the United States (Verba & Nie 1972: 84–94). The index of conflict orientation developed for the present study is based on several questions: whether the respondent had supported one of the contending groups in the 1968 disturbances in Mexico City; whether he was aware of any conflicts or cleavages among residents of his community; whether he felt such conflicts were harmful or beneficial to the community; and whether he would be willing to take a dissenting or "deviant" position (relative to majority opinion within the community) on matters of partisan politics and community development issues. Table 4.9 shows that the Demand-Makers and Complete Activists in the sample are much more likely than other kinds of participants to possess a strong conflict orientation. Since demand-making often places one in situations of potential or overt conflict with public officials, or even with one's neighbors, the Demand-Maker's tolerance for conflict equips him well for this form of political activity. Campaigners, on the other hand, are considerably below average on this dimension. Given the essentially noncompetitive nature of the electoral process in Mexico, most campaign workers (particularly in low-income areas of Mexico City) can usually avoid situations of intergroup or interpersonal conflict.

Perceptions of Self and the Social Order

The striking disparities in life-style and material affluence between upper- and lower-class residents of a large city have usually been expected to increase perceptions of "relative deprivation" among the disadvantaged groups in the urban population. And such perceptions, it is argued, may lead to increased participation by the poor in both conventional and unconventional (i.e., violent or disruptive) political activity (Weiner 1971: 168). This prediction is not borne out, at least with regard to nonviolent activity, by my survey results. As shown in Table 4.10, perceptions of being disadvantaged relative to other segments of society do not differentiate significantly between the several types of politically active migrants. However, Complete Nonparticipants show a much greater sensitivity to their disadvantaged position in the social order than do the participants. They are also more likely than most types of participants to perceive structurally rooted barriers to individual socioeconomic mobility in Mexico. Moreover, Nonparticipants are less likely than the activists to feel that the nation is progressing toward social and economic equality. The politically active migrant seems more willing to accept at face value the official view of Mexico as a country offering virtually unlimited opportunities for mobility; and he sees himself as having a meaningful stake in both the present and the future social order.

Perhaps the most plausible explanation for this pattern lies in the fact that the political activists in my sample are much more positive than

TABLE 4.10

Perceptions of Self and the Social Order Among Types of Migrant Participants

Index	Complete Nonparticipants	Voting Specialists	Campaigners	Demand-Makers	Problem-Solvers	Complete Activists
(121) Sense of relative deprivation	70.1%	58.5%	43.9%	53.6%	52.4%	55.5%
(82) Perception of social inequality	61.9	47.1	31.8	54.1	49.4	49.4
(118) Sense of openness in society	32.8	39.8	59.9	61.2	42.4	74.6
(116) Perception of national progress toward reducing social inequality	39.9	49.5	76.5	72.8	60.5	60.1

NOTE: See Appendix C for item content of each index. Differences on all measures are significant at the .05 level or beyond.

Nonparticipants in their attitudes toward the national political system. This makes them more receptive to government and PRI propaganda, which places considerable stress on Mexico's progress toward greater social equity. Moreover, their very activism, which often includes attendance at PRI or government-sponsored meetings and rallies, is likely to increase their exposure to the official view. Some people may bring with them a willingness to believe that the society's opportunity structure is open and that the nation's distribution of wealth is shifting toward greater equality; for others, such perceptions may result from political involvement.

Orientations Toward the Local Community

The way in which the migrant relates himself to his immediate residential environment is one of the most important factors influencing his propensity for political activity. Table 4.11 shows that Complete Nonparticipants are weakly integrated both socially and psychologically into their community of residence. Politically active migrants are considerably more likely to have attained a high level of integration. They tend to perceive themselves as permanent residents of the community in which they currently live, to have a personal sense of "belonging" to a territorially-based social system, to take a personal interest in community affairs, and to interact frequently with neighbors and relatives in the community. Those who actively participate in community-related political activity—i.e., Demand-Makers, Community Problem-Solvers, and Complete Activists—have also made a greater personal investment (both material and psychological) in their community. They are much more likely than the Nonparticipants or the other types of political activists to own their own homes, to have built their houses themselves, to have used permanent building materials, and to have obtained the land they occupy through participation in a land invasion. In short, they have a larger personal stake in political activity aimed at defending or improving the community as a whole.

Politically active migrants also differ markedly from Nonparticipants in their perceptions and evaluations of their community. They are more likely to perceive a high level of solidarity among residents of their community and are more sensitive to community norms. Political activists of all types express a higher level of satisfaction with their community as a residential environment, and they are also more likely than Nonparticipants to view their community as being upwardly mobile in a developmental sense.

This finding is consistent with those of other studies of low-income

TABLE 4.11
Orientations Toward Community of Residence Among Types
of Migrant Participants

Index	Complete Nonparticipants	Voting Specialists	Campaigners	Demand-Makers	Problem-Solvers	Complete Activists
(98) Psychological integration into community	8.5%	24.5%	30.1%	41.8%	44.1%	87.4%
(122) Social integration into community	28.0	37.0	40.3	44.7	35.9	69.3
(84) Personal investment in community	29.1	46.5	49.7	83.7	70.6	76.1
(73) Perception of community solidarity	58.7	86.7	71.7	96.0	90.9	87.4
(17) Disposition to conform to community norms	30.9	50.0	40.5	50.9	58.7	48.9
(109) Satisfaction with residential environment	32.3	46.6	49.7	59.9	51.7	52.0
(114) Sense of community progress	67.8	79.5	90.7	85.6	74.1	95.7
(5) Awareness of community leadership	8.5	22.5	44.8	55.2	61.4	77.5
(89) Positive evaluation of community leadership	21.9	45.8	48.4	59.9	64.9	68.8

NOTE: See Appendix C for item content of each index. Differences on all measures are significant at the .05 level or beyond.

urban communities in Latin America, which have demonstrated a significant relationship between residents' perceptions of rates of community development and the incidence of community-related political activity (Stokes 1962; Collier 1971: 123–24; Portes 1971a: 237–39; Mac-Ewen 1972). If after a number of years the settler feels that his community has failed to develop and that its long-term prospects for government assistance or secure land tenure are unfavorable, he has little incentive to become involved in activities aimed at securing community improvements. A fairly optimistic view of the community's developmental prospects, then, may be a necessary precondition for involvement in this kind of political activity; but it is also possible that political activism itself can lead to a greater sense of satisfaction with one's community and a greater sense of community progress. There is, no doubt, a reciprocal relationship between positive evaluations of the community and political activity that is successful in improving the quality of the residential environment.

Table 4.11 also shows that politically active migrants are very much aware of the identities and activities of political leaders within their community, and that they tend to evaluate the performance of these leaders in a positive way. Again, this is particularly true of the Complete Activists, Demand-Makers, and Community Problem-Solvers. These types appear to be responsive to the mobilizing efforts of community leaders, who often organize delegations of residents to petition public officials, solicit financial contributions for community improvements, recruit workers for campaign activities, and promote voter-registration drives (see Chapter 6).

In several of the research communities, most notably Colonia Nueva and Colonia Periférico, it was evident that confidence in the ability of local leaders to bargain effectively with politicians and bureaucrats was an extremely important factor in persuading residents to "stick their necks out" by directly approaching the authorities to secure aid for the community. But even residents who are less charitable in evaluating the performance of their leaders are usually aware of the sanctions that these leaders can often impose. (In a squatter settlement these sanctions are often rooted in the control that local leaders exert over the right to occupy land within the community.) The costs of political activity, whether in time, in money, or in discomfort at being exposed to conflict situations, may reduce an individual resident's responsiveness to his leader's appeals for participation; but in communities where local leaders are able to reward those who participate and penalize those who do not, any cost/benefit calculation regarding participation must include the costs of nonparticipation as well.

Political Awareness

A certain level of awareness of how the political system operates and how its outputs affect one's personal life is generally assumed to be a necessary precondition for most kinds of political activity. Table 4.12 presents data on several dimensions of political awareness among migrants in the research communities. On all dimensions the Complete Nonparticipants rank considerably below the various types of politically active migrants. There are also interesting differences between types of activists. Demand-Makers and Complete Activists, both types who have attempted to influence the distribution of government benefits to themselves as individuals or to the community in which they live, are more likely than other types to perceive the relevance of government and politics to the satisfaction of personal and community needs. Campaigners and Complete Activists distinguish themselves by their high level of attention to political stimuli in electoral campaigns and the mass media, as well as their greater knowledge of politics and public affairs. Voting Specialists and Community Problem-Solvers generally exhibit

TABLE 4.12
Political Awareness Among Types of Migrant Participants

Index	Complete Nonpar-ticipants	Voting Special-ists	Cam-paigners	Demand-Makers	Problem-Solvers	Complete Activists
(81) Perception of relevance of government and politics to need satisfaction	19.7%	55.9%	57.3%	64.9%	44.8%	77.5%
(6) Awareness of govern-mental outputs affecting community of residence	28.3	40.0	64.3	58.6	30.3	70.1
(87) Political opinion-holding	13.4	23.4	16.2	18.7	17.7	48.0
(3) Attentiveness to electoral campaigns and political content of mass media	25.5	44.4	64.0	55.7	33.9	79.3
(37) Knowledge of govern-ment and politics	9.1	20.9	59.1	32.3	29.1	89.2
(60) Overall political aware-ness	17.8	32.4	57.4	50.2	27.8	95.7

NOTE: See Appendix C for item content of each index. Differences on all measures are significant at the .05 level or beyond.

a lower level of political consciousness than other types of politically active migrants.[16] Of course, the kinds of political activity in which these two subgroups engage do not require the knowledge or the psycho-logical involvement in politics that may be needed for such activities as contacting officials. Voting Specialists and Problem-Solvers are not concerned with manipulating the supralocal political system to influence government outputs, and their participation does not depend on familiarity with political processes at the city or national level.

Political Attitudes

Numerous studies have shown that persons whose attitudes toward the political system are strongly positive or supportive are much more likely to engage in political activity than those whose political attitudes are less supportive.[17] The data for my migrant sample (Table 4.13) re-veal a strong relationship between participation and positive orienta-

[16] Verba, Nie & Kim (1971: 50) also found this to be true of Voting Specialists in most of the countries included in their cross-national study of political participa-tion. See also Field 1973: Chap. 5.

[17] Empirical evidence supporting this generalization has been reported in a large number of studies, based on data from both developed and Third World countries. See Milbrath 1965: 56–57, 78–80; Cataldo & Kellstedt 1968; Di Palma 1970: 3–4, 55–57; Fraser 1970; Hawkins 1971; Perlman 1971: 410–11; Olsen 1972: 27; Sallach et al. 1972: 889–90; Finifter 1972: 201; Field 1973: Chap. 6; Schwartz 1973.

TABLE 4.13
Political Attitudes Among Types of Migrant Participants

Index	Complete Nonpar- ticipants	Voting Special- ists	Cam- paigners	Demand- Makers	Problem- Solvers	Complete Activists
(1) Affect for national political institutions	24.2%	31.6%	46.1%	57.2%	40.1%	71.4%
Political party preference:[a]						
Official party (PRI)	73.3	95.7	93.5	100.0	91.7	100.0
Opposition party (PAN or PPS)	26.7	4.3	6.5	0.0	8.3	0.0
(130) Trust in government	34.7	60.5	47.7	63.1	48.6	59.8
(86) Political cynicism	61.7	54.6	45.7	40.6	64.3	47.2
(76) Perception of govern- mental concern for the poor	17.9	33.2	29.5	55.1	31.9	53.2
(77) Perception of govern- mental responsiveness to influence attempts	11.2	45.8	66.4	66.5	43.0	55.4
(119) Sense of political efficacy	22.2	33.8	45.0	58.8	32.4	89.7
(91) Positive evaluation of public officials' performance	33.9	43.8	43.8	67.0	45.7	80.6
(19) Satisfaction with govern- ment service outputs[b]	57.0	61.3	63.3	66.6	50.9	52.0
(22) Expectations for govern- ment performance	26.2	52.3	51.8	71.4	43.8	87.0
(64) Overall support for political system	22.2	55.2	58.1	85.5	39.7	74.9

NOTE: See Appendix C for item content of each index. Differences on all measures but "satis-faction with government service outputs" are significant at the .05 level or beyond.
  [a] Measured by questionnaire items 159a–159c, 161b, 161c (see Appendix A).
  [b] Index 19 (see Appendix C), "dissatisfaction with government service outputs," with scor-ing reversed.

tions toward the political system. Politically active migrants surpass the Nonparticipants by considerable margins in their esteem for national political and governmental institutions, their tendency to support the official party in elections, and their willingness to trust public officials. Moreover, they exhibit a greater sense of political efficacy, or confidence in their own ability to influence the actions of officials.[18]

The Demand-Makers and Complete Activists in the sample are even more positive in their attitudes toward the political system than other politically active migrants. These two types have in common the experi-ence of personal contact with officials. The impact of this contact on

[18] As I use the term, a sense of political efficacy does not necessarily imply that the "efficacious" person feels competent to influence government actions through efforts as an individual citizen acting alone. For a detailed discussion of this point, see Chapter 7.

political attitudes in the research communities will be explored more fully in Chapter 8, where positive orientations toward the political system are in fact treated as the outcome of certain kinds of personal contact with that system. But one might also argue, reversing the order of causation, that contacting officials, perhaps more than any other kind of political participation, seems to *require* a strongly positive set of orientations toward the system. Those who engage in it must first believe that officials want to know the needs and grievances of the average citizen and will respond in a nonpunitive fashion to direct influence attempts. They must also be confident that the government actually has the capacity to provide whatever assistance is being sought. Only by taking an optimistic view of the opportunities afforded by political action can poor people justify the relatively high degree of individual initiative, psychological stress, and commitments of time and money usually entailed in petitioning officials face-to-face.

Socialization Experiences and Organizational Involvement

Much of the political activity engaged in by residents of the *colonias proletarias* is collective in nature: Campaigners, Demand-Makers, and Community Problem-Solvers usually act as members of a task-oriented group. It might be expected that exposure to certain kinds of work environments, collective learning experiences, or voluntary organizations would increase the likelihood of an individual's becoming involved in collective political action. The data presented in Table 4.14 illustrate the importance of some types of socialization experiences and organizational ties in affecting political participation among the migrants in my sample. Recent research in developing countries has demonstrated the politicizing effects of employment in large-scale industry (Inkeles 1969; Inkeles & Horton 1974). Among my respondents, Voting Specialists and Campaigners were more likely to be employed in large factories than were the other types of participants. Most of these workers had been "encouraged" to participate in electoral politics by shop foremen or labor union officials affiliated with the PRI.

Participation in a land invasion seems to have been a highly important kind of socialization experience. Demand-Makers, Community Problem-Solvers, and Complete Activists in the research communities are drawn disproportionately from those who have participated in a land invasion, and they are also more likely to have witnessed at least one attempt by the government or a private landowner to evict squatters from invaded land (whether in their current community of residence or elsewhere in Mexico City). The invasion appears to be a more

TABLE 4.14
Socialization Experiences and Organizational Involvement
Among Types of Migrant Participants

Experience	Complete Nonpar- ticipants	Voting Special- ists	Cam- paigners	Demand- Makers	Problem- Solvers	Complete Activists
Employed in large factory	2.1%	12.1%	8.9%	2.5%	4.5%	4.7%
Participated in land invasion	0.0	7.0	10.5	36.2	35.1	38.5
Witnessed attempt to evict squatters	11.2	19.9	17.2	28.4	43.5	75.8
Overall exposure to collective stress situations (Index 24)						
Low	74.9	68.3	54.5	39.5	38.7	4.3
High	25.1	31.7	45.5	60.5	61.3	95.7
Membership in politically relevant organizations (Index 43)						
Low	93.8	71.5	54.9	40.9	68.7	14.3
High	6.2	28.5	45.1	59.1	31.3	85.7
Membership in politically nonrelevant organizations (Index 42)						
Low	61.3	46.1	56.1	50.6	56.0	22.5
High	38.7	53.9	43.9	49.4	44.0	77.5

NOTE: See Appendix C for item content of indexes. Differences on all measures except factory employment are significant at the .05 level or beyond.

powerful politicizing experience if it has met with strong resistance. This finding contradicts the argument advanced by Goldrich that eviction attempts and other negative sanctions imposed after a land invasion tend to depress political involvement among the invaders (Goldrich 1970: 182; Goldrich, Pratt & Schuller 1970: 193–95). A more comprehensive measure of exposure to collective stress situations—land invasions, negative sanctions by government or landowners, widespread flooding, major fires or other disasters affecting large numbers of community residents—reveals even more clearly the politicizing effect of such experiences. These situations increase the psychic investment of residents in the community, an investment they may seek to protect through political action.

Numerous studies have demonstrated that people who are members of voluntary organizations tend to participate in politics more than those who are not, irrespective of their social-status characteristics and attitudinal orientations toward politics.[19] My findings are quite consistent

[19] Cross-national studies reporting a strong relationship between organizational involvement and political participation include Nie, Powell & Prewitt 1969 and Bur-

with this generalization. Politically active migrants, especially Demand-Makers and Complete Activists, are much more likely to belong to organizations whose concerns are in some way related to political activity. Included in this category are political parties, labor unions, and community-improvement organizations. But even involvement in politically *non*relevant organizations appears to stimulate political participation. Politically active migrants are also more likely to belong to church groups, parent-teacher associations, and the like.

As we shall observe in the next chapter, organizational affiliation in general serves to locate an individual in networks of communication and interaction that are important in sensitizing him to community norms regarding participation. Moreover, membership in politically relevant organizations helps reduce the amount of individual initiative and other "costs" entailed in political activity. The availability of organizational resources for demand-making activity may also enhance one's sense of political efficacy (see Marshall 1971: 144–45; also Chapter 7 below). For all these reasons, politically active migrants tend to be those who are most involved in the organizational life of their community.

SUMMARY

This chapter has presented a general overview of political involvement among residents of the research communities. We find that the vast majority of migrants are at least minimally cognizant of the political and governmental activities that impinge on their lives. Most of them vote in elections with great regularity, and over half have engaged in some form of political activity beyond voting. Only a small proportion (less than 10 percent) can be considered completely "marginal" to the political process in terms of both cognitive and behavioral involvement. Differences between migrants and native-born residents on most dimensions of political involvement are not significant when other personal attributes are held constant. However, voting participation is appreciably higher among migrants than natives, regardless of age, socioeconomic status, or community of residence. I have attributed this difference to a stronger sense among the migrants of civic duty to participate in elections, which may be rooted in premigration political

stein 1972. Similar findings are reported in studies limited to the United States (Erbe 1964: 198; Marshall 1968: 210–11; Alford & Scoble 1968: 1197, 1203; Olsen 1972: 22), as well as in studies of low-income communities in several Latin American cities (Flinn & Camacho 1969: 55; McKenney 1969: 184; Goldrich 1970: 192, 197; Pratt 1971a: 532–39).

socialization. Political involvement among migrants tends to increase over time in the city; but much of the increase can be attributed to aging and (to a lesser extent) to improvements in socioeconomic status. Mere length of exposure to the urban environment explains little of the variation in political involvement among migrants.

The typical politically active migrant can be described as having an above-average family income (for my sample) but an average level of educational attainment and occupational status. Compared with politically inactive migrants, he possesses more modern attitudes, a greater willingness to trust people, a stronger disposition to work collectively to satisfy needs, a preference for authoritarian leadership, and a greater tolerance for conflict situations. He is less likely than the politically inactive migrant to have a sense of relative deprivation or to perceive socioeconomic improvement as being blocked for people like himself. He is more fully integrated into his community, both socially and psychologically; and his evaluations of the community and its leaders are generally positive. The politically active migrant is more knowledgeable about government and politics, and also more involved with them psychologically. His political attitudes are generally supportive of the existing political system. He views government officials as responsive to demands by the ordinary citizen, and has high expectations of receiving certain types of assistance from the government. He is more likely than the nonpolitical migrant to have been involved in collective politicizing activities such as land invasion. Finally, the politically active migrant is a "joiner" who often participates in the activities of voluntary organizations.

The data presented in this chapter have also revealed significant differences between the various types of politically active migrants. Voting Specialists, for example, are less likely than the other types to possess many of the attributes that are related to a general syndrome of political activism, such as a preference for collective problem-solving, a willingness to take sides in conflict situations, and a high level of political awareness. Demand-Makers and Complete Activists are more positive than the other types in attitudes toward the political system. Compared to other types of participants, Voting Specialists and Community Problem-Solvers have low levels of political consciousness. Demand-Makers, Problem-Solvers, and Complete Activists are the types most fully integrated into the community in which they reside. Many other differences may be observed between the various types of politically active migrants. Suffice it to say that the modes of political participation I have isolated in this chapter do vary significantly in terms of the characteristics and experiences of the migrants who engage in them.[20]

Any discussion of "correlates of political participation" raises an important point of interpretation. There is a tendency to treat variables that we find to be positively correlated with participation as "sources" or "preconditions" of political behavior. This implies a very definite causal ordering of the variables, according to which the "correlates" of participant behavior are assumed to be the independent variables *causing* the dependent variable—participation—to assume certain values. In many cases, however, the directionality of the relationship between participation and a given attribute or orientation cannot be established with any degree of certainty.

For example, migrants who have contacted a public official on one or more occasions are much more likely to feel that an individual can influence government decisions than those who have never contacted an official.[21] But how should this finding be interpreted? Since a sense of political efficacy (perceived ability to influence the government) is positively related to the act of contacting an official, we might conclude that this type of attitude is a "precondition" or "source" of this behavior. But it is entirely possible that feelings of political efficacy are a *result* of the participatory act, especially if the outcome of the act has been evaluated by the demand-maker as positive or successful in terms of some strategy of goal attainment. An individual whose contact with an official results in receipt of a land title or in a water system for his community is more likely to believe that he is capable of influencing government decisions; and he is more likely to repeat the influence attempt on some future occasion. Before making the initial contact, however, he may have lacked a sense of political efficacy. Attitudes such as political

[20] Similar findings are reported by Verba and his associates in their studies of political participation in the U.S. and four other countries. See Verba, Nie & Kim 1971: 44–53; Verba & Nie 1972: 82–101.

[21] Respondents were asked: "Some people say that one can only wait and accept government programs; others say that a person can have influence on the government and make the government help the people. How do you feel about this?" Of the 175 migrants who had contacted officials in the past, 57.2 percent felt that citizens could exert some influence; only 40.7 percent of the 500 who had never contacted officials held this view (the difference is statistically significant at the .003 level). Almond and Verba, in their cross-national survey (1963: 187), also found that an individual's estimate of his own ability to do something about government outputs is "closely related to actual attempts to influence the government. In all five nations . . . those who say they could influence the government, in comparison with those who say they could not, are at least three times as likely to have attempted such influence."

cynicism may also represent the residues of specific personal experiences in dealing with the political system.[22]

It could be argued that most of the attitudinal correlates of political activism among migrants identified in this chapter should not be regarded as necessary preconditions for participation. Many are just as likely to be the products of political learning experiences. I would argue further that the nature and frequency of these learning experiences are likely to vary considerably from one community to another. In the following chapter I will document the consequences of this phenomenon for individual political participation, arguing that in most cases the migrant's immediate residential environment, rather than the city as a whole, provides the stimuli and the reward (or reinforcement) structure most relevant to political involvement. In sum, it is not the sheer amount but rather the *kind* of urban experience that determines a migrant's political behavior.

[22] A similar interpretation of the relationship between political efficacy and participation has been advanced by Alford & Scoble 1968: 1206; Form & Huber 1971: 687; Mathiason & Powell 1972: 317–19; and Martinussen 1972. See also the following discussions of the impact of negative political learning experiences on political attitudes and behavior among the urban poor in the U.S.: Parenti 1970: 523–24; Savitch 1972: 54; and S. Greenberg 1974: 107ff.

CHAPTER FIVE

The Community Context of Political Involvement

SCHOLARS HAVE recently come to appreciate the role that residence in particular urban neighborhoods plays in the political socialization of the urban poor, including migrants from the countryside. However, there has been little systematic investigation of just *how* one's place of residence within a city comes to influence political attitudes and behavior. If the local urban community has a significant impact on political learning among the migrant poor, how does this "contextual effect" operate? What kinds of political learning experiences or patterns of social interaction help to generate and maintain attitudinal and behavioral norms in specific communities? What are the underlying social-psychological processes through which such norms are internalized by the residents? What individual characteristics determine whether (or to what extent) a particular migrant is influenced by his community of residence? Finally, why do some communities have a greater impact on political behavior than others? What characteristics of a community tend to increase its importance as an agent of political socialization among the migrant poor? These are the principal questions to be pursued in this chapter.

ORIENTATIONS TOWARD THE LOCAL COMMUNITY

The data presented in Table 5.1 show that migrants relate to their local communities in very different ways.[1] If they live in Colonia Nueva, the youngest of the three squatter settlements included in the study, they are much more likely to be knowledgeable about their community, to identify strongly with its interests, and to interact frequently with other community residents. As of mid-1970, residents of Colonia Nueva

[1] Statistically significant ($p < .05$) intercommunity differences on these dimensions persist when the age, socioeconomic status, and length of urban residence of individual respondents are held constant.

TABLE 5.1

Migrants' Orientations Toward Community of Residence

Index	Colonia Nueva ($N = 128$)	Colonia Periférico ($N = 98$)	Colonia Texcoco ($N = 121$)	Colonia E. Propio ($N = 128$)	Unidad Popular ($N = 73$)	Colonia Militar ($N = 112$)
(36) Knowledge of community	86.2%	59.4%	29.7%	46.0%	11.9%	30.3%
(98) Psychological integration into community	75.4	39.8	31.7	37.5	36.2	25.5
(122) Social integration into community	51.8	48.9	10.3	40.1	33.9	55.1
(17) Disposition to conform to community norms	76.1	64.2	47.8	56.7	42.4	36.6
(73) Perception of community solidarity	100.0	92.1	84.3	89.2	76.3	74.4
(80) Perception of positive social relations in community	89.8	56.0	58.6	70.0	62.7	66.7
(114) Sense of community progress	67.9	80.0	72.3	94.2	71.2	77.0
(109) Satisfaction with residential environment	50.8	68.1	13.7	50.8	44.1	64.3
(52) Overall community affect	72.2	54.1	19.3	50.8	32.2	44.6

NOTE: Percentages represent the proportions of migrant respondents having high scores on each index (e.g., in Colonia Nueva 86.2 percent of the respondents had a high level of community knowledge). Index scores were dichotomized into low and high categories, with the cutting point located as close as possible to the total sample median, computed on the basis of all respondents (both migrants and native-born city residents) in the weighted sample. See Appendix C for item content of each index. Intercommunity differences on all indexes reported are statistically significant, by Chi-square test computed on a 12-cell table (d.f. $= 5$), at the .001 level or beyond.

felt that the development of their community had not proceeded very far during the two-and-a-half years since its establishment, and they were disturbed by the continuing lack of urban services and improvements; but in general they regarded their neighborhood as a good place to live.

A migrant living in Colonia Texcoco, the unfortunate subdivision abandoned both by its "developer" and by the government, tends to have a very different set of orientations. He knows little about community affairs, has little personal identification with the community and little contact with other residents, and is generally negative in his evaluations of the community. He views Colonia Texcoco as a bad place to live and involves himself as little as possible in its affairs.

Residents of the Unidad Popular housing project and those of Colonia

Militar, the oldest of the three squatter settlements, also have relatively low levels of social and psychological integration into their communities, but view these communities somewhat more positively. Migrants living in Colonia Periférico and Colonia Esfuerzo Propio are closer to the highly integrated, affectively oriented residents of Colonia Nueva. Esfuerzo Propio residents seem particularly impressed with the developmental progress of their community in the year-and-a-half since it was opened for settlement—progress made possible by a massive infusion of capital, labor, and technical assistance from the city government.

Some of the findings reported in Chapter 4 (see especially Table 4.11) strongly suggest that the way a migrant perceives and evaluates his community will affect his propensity to participate politically. In the remaining sections of this chapter I shall attempt to document this relationship more fully and to identify some of the causal mechanisms that may be involved in it.

COMMUNITY CONTEXTUAL EFFECTS

The community context may either strengthen or weaken individual attitudes and behavioral predispositions toward politics. Relationships between the characteristics of individuals and those of the social collectivities to which they belong have been a major concern of sociological inquiry at least since the work of Durkheim on anomie and social integration.[2] Paul Lazarsfeld coined the term "contextual analysis" to designate a type of simultaneous, multilevel analysis that attempts to explain the behavior of an individual in terms of the social context or milieu to which he is exposed, when certain of his own personal attributes are held constant. A contextual approach to the analysis of sample survey data enables the investigator to overcome certain important limitations of conventional survey studies, which tend to focus on isolated individuals and largely ignore the larger sociopolitical setting in which individual attitudes and behavior occur.[3]

[2] Interest in the empirical investigation of such relationships was apparently revived by the research reported in Stouffer et al. 1949: 256ff. Other prominent sociological studies concerned with such problems include Barton 1970; J. Davis 1962; Lipset et al. 1956: 338ff. See also Dogan & Rokkan 1969; Eulau 1969; Sills et al. 1961.

[3] See Kendall & Lazarsfeld 1950: 195–96; 1955. Though they use a different terminology, analyses of "compositional effects" (J. Davis et al. 1961), "structural effects" (Blau 1960), and "clustering effects" (Katz & Eldersveld 1961) are based on the same principle. For reviews of the major variations of this research strategy see Frey 1970a: 288–94; and Lane 1959: 261–72. The technique is not without its difficulties of measurement and interpretation of results (see, for example, Barton & Hauser 1970 and the discussion by Frey cited above). The principal advantages of contextually grounded survey research and analysis are outlined in Barton 1968;

The theoretical assumptions underlying the contextual approach can be stated quite simply: "Individual behavior is influenced not only by individual characteristics but by the social context of the individual, both as it is perceived by the individual and as an objective situation influencing the possibilities of action." Moreover, "The behavior of an individual is influenced by the proportion of people in his environment who are engaged in that form of behavior" (Barton 1968: 8; 1970: 220–21). With reference to political behavior, it could be argued that a social unit whose members frequently engage in political activity provides a context that directly stimulates participation, and that it is perceived by individual members as sanctioning such behavior. Thus persons with the same set of individual attributes may participate politically in significantly varying degree, depending on the proportion of those within their immediate social environment who are politically active or who share some perception or attitudinal trait relevant to political activity.

Studies of contextual effects within local urban communities in the United States and England have documented significant relationships between community characteristics and individual attitudes toward education (Robson 1969: 216–34), social mobility orientations (Blalock 1967), anomia (Orbell 1970; Wilson 1971a, 1971b), racial attitudes (Orbell & Sherrill 1969), mental disorder and deviant behavior (Timms 1971: 14–31), propensity to help others in situations of collective stress (Barton 1970: 214ff), organizational participation (W. Bell & Force 1956; Warren & McClure 1973), and many other types of social behavior (W. Bell 1965; Greer 1956). Tingsten (1937: 126–27, 170–72, 180), using data from four Scandinavian countries, was perhaps the first student of political behavior to demonstrate empirically the effects of residential environment on individual voting behavior. Since the appearance of his work, numerous researchers, drawing primarily on data from the United States and England, have found that when individual characteristics are held constant, people will tend to vote for the party supported by the climate of opinion in the communities in which they live.[4]

J. Coleman 1961; Frey 1970a: 288–94; Horowitz 1970: 509–13; Verba 1969, 1971: 344–56. Contextual analysis, of course, requires a sample design in which sufficient numbers of respondents are interviewed in each social unit to enable the investigator to characterize the unit in terms of its social or political climate. For more detailed explications of the logic and theoretical assumptions of contextual analysis, see Barton 1970: 209–16ff; J. Coleman 1958–59; Lazarsfeld & Menzel 1961; and Scheuch 1969.

[4] See Almy 1973; Bayes 1967: Chap. 8; Berelson et al. 1954: 98ff; Cox 1970; Ennis 1962; Foladare 1968; Gosnell 1939: 91–125; Katz & Eldersveld 1961; Klorman 1971; Levin 1961; W. Miller 1956; Putnam 1966; Segal & Meyer 1969; Segal

In the contextual analysis reported below, the dependent variable will be *overall political participation*, including voting, campaign involvement, contacting public officials, and participation in community problem-solving activity. The partial correlation approach used for this analysis involves controlling the effects of individual sociodemographic attributes and attitudes toward political activity while measuring the relationship between selected characteristics of the community of residence and individual political participation. Each community is characterized in terms of the actual percentage of its residents who rank above the total sample median on summative indexes of overall political participation, civic-mindedness, disposition to conform to community norms, perception of external threat, and self-help orientation. These aggregations of individual responses to the survey questions are the independent variables of the analysis.[5]

The findings reported in Table 5.2 indicate a significant contextual effect. Both the overall frequency of political participation in a community and the frequency distribution of certain kinds of attitudes exert an independent influence on each resident's political participation. The relationships remain significant, and in some cases increase in strength, when the various personal attributes of the respondents are held constant. The addition of the five community contextual variables to a multiple regression equation results in an absolute increase of 12 percent in the explained variance in political participation beyond the effects of age, socioeconomic status, length of urban residence, and psychological involvement in politics.[6] Since these individual attributes account for only 20 percent of the variance in political participation, the explanatory contribution made by community characteristics is a meaningful one.

If the above analysis is repeated using a specific type of political participation rather than overall participation as the dependent variable, we find that those kinds of participation most closely related to the community of residence—contacting public officials and community prob-

---

& Wildstrom 1970; Tate 1974. The limitations of available data required some of these investigators to use data aggregated at the level of the county to specify the political complexion of the community environment.

[5] This approach to community contextual analysis is described more fully in Flinn 1970. As pointed out by Frey (1970a: 292–93) and by Tannenbaum and Bachman (1964), the partial correlation technique helps to avoid problems of interpretation deriving from failure to hold individual characteristics strictly constant. For examples of alternative approaches through analysis of covariance and path analysis, see Wilson 1971a, 1971b; R. Smith 1972. The older approach through multivariate tabular analysis is presented in Blau 1960 and J. Davis et al. 1961.

[6] The multiple $r = .562$; total variance explained = 32%.

TABLE 5.2
Correlations of Community Contextual Variables with Individual
Political Participation: All Migrants

Independent (Contextual) Variable	Dependent Variable	Control Variables	Correlation r_1	r_2
Level of overall political participation in community of residence (Index 62)	Individual political participation	Usual[a]	.317	.396
Degree of civic-mindedness in community of residence (Index 9)	Same	Usual + respondent's own degree of civic-mindedness	.301	.355
General disposition to conform to norms in community of residence (Index 17)	Same	Usual + respondent's own disposition to conform to community norms	.244	.295
Perception of external threat in community of residence (Index 75)	Same	Usual + respondent's perception of external threat	.279	.267
Strength of self-help orientation in community of residence (Index 113)	Same	Usual + respondent's own self-help orientation	.284	.262

NOTE: Correlations are based on an average N of 670, and all coefficients reported are significant at the .001 level or beyond. The r_1 correlations are simple (zero-order) correlations of the contextual variable with individual political participation. The r_2 correlations are fifth-order partial correlations of the contextual variable with individual political participation, controlling for the effects of various individual characteristics.

[a] The respondent's age, socioeconomic status (Index 69), length of urban residence, and psychological involvement in politics (Index 66) were held constant for each correlation.

lem-solving—are most strongly influenced by community contextual variables. Yet these variables also influence the individual's propensity to engage in forms of political activity not specifically related to community affairs, such as voting and campaign involvement.

Short of a laboratory study in which experimental groups are constructed according to randomization procedures, the causal interpretation of any kind of contextual effect is necessarily somewhat indeterminate. One potential source of this indeterminacy is what Ulf Himmelstrand has termed "homopolitical selectivity"—the conscious tendency of like individuals to seek each other as partners in formal or informal interaction (Himmelstrand 1960: 399–409; cf. Cox 1969: 164ff). If individuals are self-selected into groups according to their political characteristics, the relationship between individual and group characteristics may be spurious. At issue here is the question of whether the individual living in a community comes to reflect its attitudinal or behavioral norms or whether he has moved there because its norms already resemble his own. Herbert Gans, for example, has argued (1968: 14–16) that certain changes in the attitudes and behavior of newcomers to suburban neighborhoods in U.S. cities originated in the residents' motivations for moving into such communities and were not the result of socialization within the new environment.

One cannot entirely dismiss the self-selection hypothesis in relation to the migrants represented in this study, but its plausibility is reduced by a number of factors. Survey interviews, life histories, and accounts of the history of the research communities by key informants all suggest that the migrants studied had become neighbors primarily because of economic incentives or imperatives (low income, desire to save on housing expenses), occupational mobility (providing new resources to invest in land or housing construction), changes in job or family size, or displacement from a previous community of residence. Displacement by public works projects or slum clearance was particularly important in the movement of families to Colonia Periférico, Colonia Esfuerzo Propio, and Unidad Popular. The availability of cheap land was the major attraction in Colonia Texcoco. Participation in the land invasions that produced Colonia Nueva and Colonia Militar was influenced strongly by geographic proximity to the invasion sites: most of the initial invaders of Colonia Nueva had lived in rented housing in adjacent *colonias proletarias*, and the squatters of Colonia Militar were mostly persons employed at the nearby military base.

Several of the communities have experienced a substantial turnover in population since their establishment. This is especially true of Colonia Militar, where only 14 percent of the migrants interviewed in 1970 had been among the original invaders of the land in 1952—or would admit to having participated in the invasion. There is, however, no evidence to suggest that the motivations of latecomers to these communities were substantially different from those of the original settlers. Considerations of family income and savings on rent were overwhelmingly important; this applies even to the relatively prosperous middle-class families who have moved into Colonia Militar and Unidad Popular, sensing an opportunity for investment in potentially valuable real estate at a bargain price.

In the survey responses, the most frequently mentioned reasons for choosing one's current place of residence, as well as previous places of residence within the city, were economic advantage (low rents, rent-free housing), proximity to jobs or relatives, and opportunities to own one's own home or land. Cohort analysis of the responses by year of arrival in each community shows that motivations for moving into that particular community have remained essentially the same over time; the one exception was the importance of displacement from other areas among the initial settlers in Colonia Periférico, Colonia Esfuerzo Propio, and Unidad Popular.

Respondents were also asked to specify the most important things they would consider in choosing another place of residence, should they make such a move at some point in the future. In this case, the most frequently cited criteria were access to public services, proximity to jobs or to the central city, cost of land or housing, and opportunities for owning a home or land. These findings are consistent with those of other studies of residential mobility within Mexico City (Ward 1975), Monterrey (Vaughan & Feindt 1973), and Oaxaca (Butterworth 1973: 220), and within cities elsewhere in Latin America (Vernez 1973; B. Roberts 1973: 106–20; A. Leeds 1974; Uzzell 1974).

One must conclude that the recruitment processes drawing migrants to the communities under study here are largely independent of any particular orientations toward politics or political participation. Even if migrants were disposed to seek out neighborhoods where they would be surrounded by individuals sharing their own political preferences or propensities for political involvement, the selection process would be difficult and in most cases based on highly imperfect information. The political complexion of the research communities, in common with most low-income neighborhoods of the city, is by no means readily discernible to those unfamiliar with the communities; and this was even more true at the time when most current residents moved there. It seems reasonable, then, to conclude that the community contextual effects revealed by the foregoing analysis have not been rendered spurious by the respondents' self-selection into the communities. Migrants living in these communities *do* represent a self-selected population; but the selection processes have a great deal more to do with their perceptions of economic conditions and opportunities in their rural places of origin as compared with Mexico City, and with their awareness of the relative material costs and benefits of residence in different parts of the city, than with any foreknowledge of behavioral or attitudinal norms in their current community of residence.[7]

[7] Another way of determining whether it is actually the experience of living in a particular community that influences the attitudes or behavior of individual residents involves examining individuals who have lived in a community for varying lengths of time. If nonspurious contextual effects were operative, we would expect increased length of residence in a participation-oriented community to be associated with higher individual participation. This expectation is supported by the survey data from Colonia Nueva and Colonia Periférico, the two most highly participant

Models of Community Influence

A number of theories and models have been advanced to explain the way in which one's community of residence comes to influence one's behavior. One explanation, rooted in reference group theory and social learning theory, emphasizes direct, unmediated contextual effects resulting from a desire to conform to certain perceived community norms. According to this model, the community surrounds each resident with a certain normative structure or climate of opinion, as well as with pressures or sanctions that reinforce group norms; and people internalize the norms around them in response to sanctions or reinforcements by other members of the community (Orbell 1970: 636; cf. J. F. Scott 1971). Individual sensitivity to community influence thus depends on the extent to which a given resident perceives the existence of well-defined community norms and the existence of group pressure to conform to them. Individual receptiveness to community influence may also vary according to the visibility or "compliance observability" of a given type of behavior. For example, participation in community problem-solving activity and contacting public officials as one of a delegation of community residents are highly visible acts, and the individual resident of a community where such behavior is socially sanctioned may participate simply because his failure to do so would be easily detectable. Participation due to a positive desire to gain status through community service is also consistent with this "normative conformity" model.

An alternative explanation of the causal mechanisms at work stresses social structure and interaction: community influence is mediated by the network of social relationships in which the resident is enmeshed, including relationships with community leaders as well as with friends and relatives residing nearby (Barton 1970: 226–27). Thus the extent to which the community context will affect individual attitudes and behavior depends on one's exposure to social communication within the community and one's frequency of interaction—both formal and informal—with other residents. This "social interaction" model implies that people can be influenced by their community environment "even if they are not motivated to conform to community norms, indeed, even if they are unaware that such norms exist" (Putnam 1966: 641).[8]

---

communities in my study. Similarly, Portes (1971b: 831) found that leftist radicalism among Chilean slum dwellers rose with longer residence in communities where a left-radical political orientation predominated.

[8] See also Young & Willmott 1957: 135–36. For more detailed explications of these alternative models of community influence see Barton 1970: Chap. 5; A. Campbell 1958; Sherif & Sherif 1964. Empirical support for the social-interaction model

TABLE 5.3
Correlations of Community Contextual Variables with Individual
Political Participation Among Subgroups of Migrants, I

Subgroup Characteristic[a]	Correlation				
	r_1	r_2	r_3	r_4	r_5
Psychological integration into community					
Low ($N = 386$)	.300	.252	.163	.137	.179
High ($N = 276$)	.328	.292	.263	.258	.183
Perception of general concern in community for community problems					
Low ($N = 198$)	.174	.109*	−.022*	.020*	.075*
High ($N = 466$)	.420	.394	.346	.295	.300
Perception of one-party dominance in community of residence					
Yes ($N = 442$)	.410	.377	.326	.266	.294
No ($N = 220$)	.269	.248	.216	.250	.221
Perception of solidarity among residents of community					
Low ($N = 82$)	.311	.038*	−.092*	.019*	.165*
High ($N = 582$)	.403	.374	.321	.273	.275
Disposition to conform to community norms					
Low ($N = 299$)	.261	.214	–	.115	.166
High ($N = 365$)	.449	.417	–	.352	.301
Intend to move from community?					
Yes ($N = 77$)	−.116*	.023*	.098*	−.035*	.015*
No ($N = 589$)	.417	.360	.295	.273	.274

NOTE: The correlations reported in Tables 5.3 through 5.5 represent fifth-order partial correlations of the same community contextual variables employed in the analysis reported in Table 5.2 with individual political participation, controlling for the effects of the same control variables used in Table 5.2. The analysis differs only in the composition of the sample on which it is performed. Correlations r_1 relate the level of overall political participation in the respondent's community of residence to his own frequency of political participation. Correlations r_2 relate degree of civic-mindedness in community of residence to individual political participation. Correlations r_3 relate general disposition to conform to norms in community of residence to individual political participation. Correlations r_4 relate perception of external threat in community of residence to individual political participation. Correlations r_5 relate strength of self-help orientation in community of residence to individual political participation. Correlations marked * are not statistically significant at the .05 level or beyond.

[a] See Appendix C for item content of indexes used to measure subgroup characteristics.

By performing a contextual analysis like that reported in Table 5.2 upon different subgroups within the total sample of respondents one can gain greater insight into the underlying processes and mechanisms through which contextual effects operate in the research communities. When individual attributes are held constant, the magnitude of the par-

is provided in E. Campbell & Alexander 1965; Cox 1969: 165–69; Davies 1966: 162–65; Mollenkopf 1973: 4–5, 10; Putnam 1966; Robson 1969: 232–35. The model stressing conformity to perceived community norms receives empirical support in Barton 1970: Chap. 5; Flinn 1970; Sherif & Sherif 1964.

tial correlation coefficients computed for various subgroups can be interpreted as a measure of their relative sensitivity to the community political milieu (see Tannenbaum & Bachman 1964: 591; Sewell & Armer 1966: 168). Once again, partial correlations have been computed between individual political participation (the dependent variable) and certain aggregate characteristics of the individual's community of residence (levels of political participation, civic-mindedness, and so on).

Table 5.3 shows the relationships between individual and community characteristics among a number of subgroups, which are defined in terms of the way migrants perceive and orient themselves toward their community. We find that those who possess a higher sense of personal identification with the community ("psychological integration into community"), those who perceive themselves as permanent residents, and those who are more disposed to conform to community norms all exhibit greater sensitivity to the local political context. Those who perceive a high level of concern for community problems among their neighbors, those who regard most residents as supporters of a single political party, and those who perceive a high level of community cohesion are also influenced more strongly by the community context. These findings are consistent with the predictions of the normative-conformity model of community influence, which stresses psychological attachment to the community, awareness of community standards, and sensitivity to pressures for conformity.

The effect of social interaction within the community on sensitivity to the local political context is illustrated by the findings reported in Table 5.4. The political behavior of migrants having a higher level of social integration into their community is more strongly influenced by community characteristics. Specifically, those whose interaction with close friends and relatives is confined largely to their community of residence, those who participate in voluntary associations within the community, and those who frequently discuss local problems with other residents of the community are all more receptive to community influence.

Numerous studies have demonstrated that local leaders often serve as important channels for community influence (Eisenstadt 1965: 323–37; Frey & Roos 1967: 26ff; Jacob et al. 1972). Leaders in several of the communities included in this study have played a key role in the establishment of local behavioral and attitudinal norms (see Chapter 6). Thus we might hypothesize that those migrants in the research communities who perceive a well-defined leadership structure within their community and those who are positively oriented toward local leaders

TABLE 5.4
Correlations of Community Contextual Variables with Individual
Political Participation Among Subgroups of Migrants, II

Subgroup Characteristic	Correlation				
	r_1	r_2	r_3	r_4	r_5
Social integration into community					
Low ($N = 397$)	.304	.288	.228	.165	.228
High ($N = 264$)	.487	.409	.332	.388	.270
Discuss community problems with other residents?					
Infrequently ($N = 532$)	.363	.320	.235	.222	.243
Frequently ($N = 132$)	.475	.423	.404	.344	.275
Close friends in same community?					
No ($N = 360$)	.362	.359	.287	.213	.285
Yes ($N = 304$)	.415	.320	.298	.326	.201
Close relatives in same community?					
No ($N = 503$)	.364	.343	.270	.245	.253
Yes ($N = 162$)	.461	.360	.323	.312	.265
Participate in community-improvement organizations?					
No ($N = 411$)	.129	.153	.098	.089	.110
Yes ($N = 253$)	.466	.406	.386	.329	.284
Awareness of community leadership					
Low ($N = 319$)	.040*	−.015*	−.039*	−.130	−.021*
High ($N = 345$)	.348	.296	.269	.255	.229
Evaluation of community leadership					
Negative ($N = 282$)	.260	.184	.103	.018*	.127
Positive ($N = 382$)	.374	.342	.310	.295	.248

NOTE: For explanation of correlations and asterisks, see note to Table 5.3.

will be more exposed to community standards regarding political activity and more sensitive to those standards. And the data in Table 5.4 strongly suggest that local leaders do, in fact, transmit community norms.

The findings reported in Tables 5.3 and 5.4 indicate that the causal mechanisms specified by both the normative-conformity and social-interaction models of community influence are important in explaining why community characteristics are related to individual political behavior. To a large extent, local political influence is mediated by informal social interaction networks and formal organizational structure within the community. However, an awareness of community norms and motivated conformity to them also appear to be significant in determining individual behavior. Undoubtedly there are important interrelationships between these two mechanisms, with higher levels of social interaction strengthening perceptions of community standards and pressures for conformity to such standards. The two models thus provide complementary rather than alternative explanations for the transmission of community political influence.

It is instructive to compare my findings from Mexico City with those of studies of suburban neighborhoods in the United States. Suburban communities have apparently failed to exert much influence on the political attitudes and behavior of their residents. More specifically, the research completed thus far indicates that the suburban climate of opinion does not seem to play a significant role in determining individual voting preferences, attitudes toward local government, or opinions on certain public issues (see C. Bell 1969; Hensler 1973). These negative findings may be attributable in part to the low stability of residence in many suburban areas; but perhaps a more important explanation lies in the fact that suburbanites in the United States are likely to have a relatively wide range of social ties and interests outside their immediate residential zones. For such people one's place of residence is a "community of limited liability," distinguished by the partial or incomplete involvement of most residents in community life (Janowitz 1952; cf. Verba & Nie 1972: 231ff). The residential area is the locus for only a few of the basic social, economic, and political activities in which suburbanites engage. It is reasonable to expect that such people would be less susceptible to community contextual effects than the urban poor, whose social and organizational contacts are confined largely to their immediate residential environment (Cox 1969; Segal & Wildstrom 1970; M. Fried 1973: 86, 94–120).

INDIVIDUAL SUSCEPTIBILITY TO COMMUNITY EFFECTS

Much of the research on political communication and attitude change suggests that sensitivity to the political stimuli in one's social environment varies considerably according to certain individual sociodemographic and psychological characteristics (see Cox 1969: 160ff). To identify some of these individual variations among my respondents in Mexico City, I shall again examine the strength of relationships between individual political participation and aspects of community political context, measuring these relationships separately within subgroups of respondents.

In Table 5.5 the total sample of survey respondents (i.e. including both migrants and natives) is broken down into five subgroups defined in terms of length of residence in the Mexico City metropolitan area. We find that migrants in general—and those most recently arrived in the city in particular—exhibit a higher sensitivity to the community political context than native-born residents. These differences are understandable in light of what is known of the mechanisms of psychological adjustment among migrant populations (see Brody 1970; Morse 1971: I, 30–36; Nelson 1974: Chap. 3). It has long been recognized that mi-

TABLE 5.5

Correlations of Community Contextual Variables with Individual Political Participation Among Subgroups of Migrants and Native-Born Residents

Subgroup Characteristic	Correlation				
	r_1	r_2	r_3	r_4	r_5
Length of residence in Mexico City					
Less than 5 years ($N = 110$)	.593	.557	.572	.419	.503
5–9 years ($N = 155$)	.543	.538	.493	.391	.429
10 or more years, but not entire life ($N = 392$)	.280	.226	.106	.177	.142
Moved to city after age 15[a] ($N = 678$)	.396	.355	.295	.267	.262
Born in city ($N = 260$)	.348	.252	.190	.215	.160
Age of respondent					
Under 35 ($N = 266$)	.490	.462	.448	.377	.328
35 or older ($N = 398$)	.325	.281	.185	.189	.223
Respondent is:					
Migrant father ($N = 174$)	.395	.345	.291	.253	.252
Eldest son of migrant father ($N = 182$)	.382	.473	.304	.487	.357
Trust in other people					
Low ($N = 491$)	.392	.354	.265	.245	.260
High ($N = 174$)	.424	.324	.381	.310	.293
Disposition to work collectively					
Low ($N = 318$)	−.042*	−.004*	−.011*	.009*	.019
High ($N = 347$)	.359	.295	.250	.186	.246
Religiosity					
Low ($N = 398$)	.326	.308	.213	.207	.207
High ($N = 266$)	.477	.417	.415	.383	.374
Exposure to collective stress					
Low ($N = 317$)	.062*	.084*	.035*	−.003*	.093
High ($N = 348$)	.359	.295	.250	.265	.246
Employed in large-scale enterprise?					
No ($N = 383$)	.337	.306	.255	.204	.242
Yes ($N = 281$)	.473	.424	.371	.344	.308

NOTE: For explanation of correlations and asterisks, see note to Table 5.3.
[a] All migrant family heads in sample, regardless of length of urban residence.

gration from a rural to an urban environment places major burdens of adjustment on those who migrate, especially if the move is regarded as permanent. Although most rural migrants to Mexico City (and to other Latin American cities) seem to cope very well with emotional stress, some of them may develop a heightened sensitivity to community political norms because they are seeking to integrate themselves more fully into a new environment.

Eisenstadt's observations (1965: 317) on the felt need of international migrants to establish relations with people in their host communities seem relevant here: "The individual feels that he faces undefined, unknown behavior on the part of other people and is not certain of being able to establish stable relations with them. . . . This anxiety is closely related to the fear of not attaining, or of losing, one's place in the collectivity or wider society of which one is a member." As long as his uncertainty about his status within the community persists, the migrant can be expected to orient himself more strongly to the local community as a reference group, both because he lacks knowledge of proper behavior within the new environment and because he wants to win social acceptance among his neighbors. Moreover, the newcomer to the city is less likely to have personal links with the community power structure that controls the allocation of various government-provided benefits among residents. This may cause him to view the colonia *qua* political community as something he must learn about and become sensitive to if he is to get what he wants from local leaders.

Individual receptiveness to community influence is also likely to vary with different stages in the life cycle (Michelson 1970: 95–110; Orbell & Uno 1972: 485–86; Suttles 1972: 37). Since several of the communities included in this study are of relatively recent origin, older people in them may not differ appreciably from younger neighbors in length of exposure to the community political context. Yet socialization theory would lead us to expect that older residents are, by virtue of age alone, relatively less capable of "new" political learning than their younger counterparts. This appears to be true of migrants residing in the research communities. When the effects of socioeconomic status, length of urban residence, and individual political orientations are held constant, those under 35 years of age exhibit a considerably greater susceptibility to community influence, as does the subsample of eldest sons of first-generation migrants to the city (see Table 5.5). This difference is particularly interesting in light of certain conventional theorizing, which predicts that at the stage of life when a younger person is employed but still unmarried the local community may be weakest in its influence on his attitudes and behavior (Di Palma 1970: 126; Mann 1970: 575–76). A majority of the subsample of eldest sons are in fact young, single adults employed outside their community of residence; yet they appear to be sensitive to local political norms.

In several studies done in the United States, religious orientation has been found to be an important factor influencing individual susceptibility to community political influence (Foladare 1968; Putnam 1966: 648; Segal & Meyer 1969: 228). And in Table 5.5 we find that migrants exhibiting a higher degree of religiosity (as measured by Index 104, Appendix C) are also more sensitive to their local political context. It has been hypothesized that high religiosity helps to promote interpersonal trust, which may in turn predispose residents of low-income urban communities to certain forms of political involvement (Behrman 1971, 1972; Lutz 1970: 137). I suspect, however, that the differences observed in my sample can be attributed largely to the fact that frequent church attendance—almost always within the local community or in nearby churches frequented by one's neighbors—simply increases a migrant's contact with other residents of his community.

Finally, it could be hypothesized that certain basic attitudinal orientations and socialization experiences will increase an individual's susceptibility to community influence by predisposing him to cooperate politically with his neighbors. We would expect those who possess greater trust in others and have a collective orientation toward problem-solving to be more susceptible. Similarly, exposure to various kinds of collective stress situations—land invasions, eviction attempts by the authorities, or natural disasters—should increase one's receptivity to community influence. Occupational socialization may also contribute: it has been hypothesized that employment in large-scale enterprises (particularly factories and construction firms) predisposes individuals to cooperate politically with fellow workers and neighbors (B. Roberts 1970a: 368–69; Inkeles 1969; Inkeles & Smith 1974). The data reported in Table 5.5 provide support for all these hypotheses. Migrants characterized by a high level of interpersonal trust, a strong disposition to work collectively to satisfy needs, greater exposure to collective stress situations, or employment in large-scale enterprises do indeed show a greater sensitivity to the community political context.

COMMUNITY CHARACTERISTICS AND THE DEVELOPMENT OF PARTICIPANT NORMS

So far we have been concerned with specifying the major processes through which community norms for participant behavior are internalized by individual migrants, and with how this internalization may be affected by personal attributes or experiences. Certainly, an individual may become politically active in response to certain stimuli from his immediate residential environment. But this does not explain why local norms concerning participation vary across communities. Specifically, it does not explain why norms favoring political involvement develop in one community and not in another. If some communities are more effective than others in socializing their residents to political participation, they must have some set of characteristics particularly conducive to the development of participant norms. The most important of these characteristics, as revealed by my own research and that of other students of low-income urban communities, are as follows:

Size and Density of Population. As city planners and students of collective behavior in urban areas have long recognized, "The physical space that neighbors occupy is inversely proportional to the likelihood of interaction" among them (Schorr 1970: 720; cf. Festinger et al. 1950; Michelson 1970: 168–90). Studies of several low-income urban communities in Latin America have found that "smallness probably encourages a sense of community feeling and identification, communication, and communal interest within a settlement and reduces settlement problems to more manageable proportions" (Lutz 1970: 118; cf. B. Roberts 1970a: 365). Local leaders can more easily mobilize a small, densely populated community like Colonia Nueva for collective political action and self-help projects. Social control and pressures for conformity are also likely to be stronger in smaller communities, because of the more frequent opportunities these afford for social interaction and the scrutiny of one's neighbors' behavior (see Mann 1970: 580; J. Roberts & Gregor 1971; Rogler 1967: 521–27; Ross 1973b: 184). In small communities with a tradition of cooperative political activity, nonparticipation in such activity may be regarded as a form of deviant behavior. In general, smallness encourages and facilitates widespread participation in community problem-solving efforts.[9]

Socioeconomic Homogeneity. Community size is also important because it tends to be strongly correlated with internal socioeconomic differentiation. As Anthony Leeds (1969: 78) has observed in Rio de Janeiro and Lima, the larger the squatter settlement, "the more diversified the types of social groups, aggregates, and associations, and the more of them both absolutely and relatively." Studies of urban communities in the United States (Bleiker 1972; Foladare 1968: 525; Gans 1961a: 136–37; Milbrath 1965: 131; Tomeh 1969), Latin America (Calderón 1963: 162–63; Dietz 1973; MacEwen 1971; Vanderschueren 1973: 277), and the Soviet Union (Frolic 1970: 683) have demonstrated the importance of socioeconomic homogeneity in the development of community cohesion and a participatory political ethos. With homogeneity, there is more social interaction and communication within a community and the recognition of mutual interests is easier.

Unidad Popular in Mexico City is an example of the opposite situation.

[9] Research on political participation in the United States also suggests that an individual living in a small, isolated community is more likely to engage in community-related political activity than an individual of similar social characteristics living in a larger place (Verba & Nie 1972: Chap. 14). Corroborating evidence from cross-national survey studies is presented in Nie et al. 1969; and Inkeles 1969.

The extreme heterogeneity of its residents' social status has retarded a recognition of mutual interests, to the extent that affluent residents pre-occupy themselves with lobbying for the closing of the adjacent garbage dump, which is the main source of income for the poor scavengers the project was originally set up to house (cf. Quijano 1972: 99–100; Butterworth 1974). The presence of substantial numbers of middle-class residents in a predominantly lower-class community may also provoke conflict over such issues as leadership and strategies for political demand-making; yet having a few higher-status leaders may significantly increase a community's chances of receiving government assistance for development (see Fagen & Tuohy 1972: 36; Butterworth 1973; and the case study of Colonia Militar in Chapter 7).

Stability of Residence. A high rate of movement in and out of a community not only inhibits the formation of participatory norms but also breaks up the interaction and communication networks necessary to maintain these norms (McKenzie 1972: 43; B. Roberts 1970a: 349–50, 372–73; Savitch 1972: 25). Community cohesion and participatory norms are also weakened by the movement into the community of large numbers of people who have not shared key political learning experiences at earlier stages of a community's development, such as the original land invasion through which a squatter settlement is established (Maruska 1972: 24; Goldrich 1970). This turnover appears to be one of the most important reasons for the currently low incidence of cooperative activity in older squatter settlements, such as Colonia Militar.

Boundedness. The physical integration of a neighborhood into the metropolitan complex may have important implications for the development of community norms, since the community's degree of "boundedness," or spatial separation from other parts of the city, affects the residents' perceptions of the community as a distinct entity with which they may identify (T. Lee 1968; Verba & Nie 1972: 243–46). It is clear that residents of a highly compact community like Colonia Nueva (bounded on three sides by a high stone wall, a steep cliff, and a dense stand of trees) are much more likely to develop an awareness of their community's distinctiveness than residents of a community like Colonia Texcoco, whose street grid blends completely into those of adjacent colonias on all four sides, with boundaries marked only by two inconspicuous street signs. It is also true that leaders and improvement associations find it easier to represent residents of a community with unequivocally recognized territorial boundaries (Lutz 1970: 120; Peattie 1968: 54).

Origin. The conditions under which a community is established are often among the most important determinants of its subsequent development, and of the normative structure that may emerge within it. Formation of the community by land invasion—whether organized or spontaneously initiated—may be a crucial unifying and politicizing experience for residents (cf. Mangin 1970: xxxiii). This is especially true if the initial seizure of land is followed by repeated attempts at eviction by the government or private landowners, as in the case of Colonia Nueva.[10] The experiences of invasion and defense of one's settlement appear to figure importantly in the development of a collective orientation toward problem-solving among the squatters. This kind of generalized preference for collectively rather than individually pursued solutions to important problems is seldom encountered among peasants in rural Mexico (see Díaz 1966: 108–37; Lozier 1971; G. Foster 1967: 122–52; Núñez 1963; Torres Trueba 1969), despite a tradition of communal labor in some rural communities (D. Foster 1971). The illegal origins of squatter settlements and unauthorized commercial subdivisions also define their relationships with political and governmental agencies for many years to come, and create a major community problem—insecurity of land tenure—on which cooperative political action among the residents may focus. These conditions are less important for political mobilization in settlements whose growth has been gradual and largely unchallenged by landowners or the government (e.g. Colonia Periférico).

Relationships with Supralocal Authority Figures. As Suttles has noted (1972: 51), "Neighborhoods seem to acquire their identity through an ongoing commentary between themselves and outsiders." For the kinds of communities included in this study, the most important "outsiders" are usually government officials, politicians, and other authority figures who control resources needed for community development. These supralocal political actors may influence community orientations toward political activity in a variety of ways, but particularly through the eviction attempts and other negative sanctions they may impose on a community as a consequence of its illegal origins. Such negative sanctions tend to have an integrating effect upon the community. The old so-

---

[10] I must therefore take issue with the widely cited argument of Goldrich, Pratt & Schuller (1970: 198–201), to the effect that eviction attempts and other negative sanctions imposed by the government in the aftermath of a squatter invasion are likely to "depoliticize" residents of the affected settlement. Maruska (1972: 24), on the basis of fieldwork in the same "sanctioned" and supposedly "depoliticized" settlement studied by Goldrich et al., disputes their interpretations, and finds divisions and deceptions perpetrated by political parties to be a more plausible explanation of low politicization in the settlement. Another study based on Goldrich's own data (Lindenberg 1970) also concludes that the association between negative sanctions and depoliticization depends on a variety of factors, including the severity of the sanctions and the duration of their application.

cial-psychological maxim of "out-group hostility, in-group solidarity" (Becker 1963) appears to have considerable relevance here:

Without experiencing and resisting outside hostility, there is little likelihood of in-group solidarity; without in-group solidarity, there is no possibility of effective collective action; without the latter, there is no chance of accelerated progress.... A land invasion is an illegal and dangerous action; precisely because it is illegal and dangerous it is capable of giving rise to social processes powerful enough to form communities out of masses.... In general, the more protracted and difficult the initial invasion, the stronger and more durable the resulting cohesiveness among participants and the higher their capabilities for collective action. (Portes 1971a: 243)

The mere possibility that negative sanctions will be invoked by government authorities or other powerful outsiders may motivate conformity to community norms. Attitudinal studies in Western Europe have demonstrated that "increased threats to the values of the group would lead to increased tendencies to conform to common group policies, increased pressures on others to conform, and increased rejection of deviants from group policies" (Aubert, Fisher & Rokkan 1954: 27; cf. Rokkan 1955: 594). The data reported in Table 5.6 show that migrants in the research communities who perceive a high degree of external threat are significantly more disposed to conformist behavior in general and conformity with community norms in particular. Analysis by community reveals that this relationship is strongest among residents of Colonia Nueva, whose experiences with eviction attempts by police and private landowners had been highly traumatic.[11]

The responses of government officials to petitioning by community residents may also be crucial to strengthening participatory norms within the community. The positive or negative outcomes of petitioning experiences affect residents' perceptions of the likelihood of success in future contacts with public officials. To the extent that influence at-

---

[11] Evidence for the importance of external threat perceptions to the development of community cohesion and political mobilization in low-income neighborhoods has been reported by numerous investigators. With regard to urban communities in Latin America, see Butterworth 1973; Michl 1973: 160; Morse 1965: 55; Ornelas 1973; Portes 1971a; Rogler 1967: 514–16. Similar findings for a squatter settlement in Nairobi, Kenya, have been reported by Marc Ross (1973b: 194–95). Mollenkopf (1973: 1–4) also stresses the importance of external threat—"adverse, widely felt intrusions of the urban development process"—to neighborhood political mobilization in U.S. cities. See also the discussion of the "defensive mode" of politicization among low-income populations in Latin America in Goldrich 1965: 367–68 and the analysis of social behavior in "defended neighborhoods" within U.S. cities in Suttles 1972: 34ff. A theoretical model of community contextual effects that also stresses residents' reactions to some threatening external stimulus is proposed in A. Campbell 1958: 321–22.

TABLE 5.6

Impact of Perception of External Threat on Migrants' Disposition
Toward Conformist Behavior

| | Perception of External Threat | |
Conformity	Low	High
Overall disposition toward conformist behavior ($N = 671$)		
Low	66.5%	40.9%
High	33.5	59.1
Disposition to conform to community norms ($N = 675$)		
Low	53.8	25.5
High	46.2	74.5

NOTE: Differences between proportions are statistically significant (by Chi-square test) at the .001 level. See Appendix C for item content of indexes used to measure perception and disposition.

tempts have met with indifferent or inadequate responses from the authorities, it will be increasingly difficult to maintain a capacity for collective political action among community residents.[12] As students of urban community organization in the United States have frequently observed, a commitment to political involvement can be sustained over time among low-status groups only if their members have a reasonably high expectation of governmental responsiveness (Lipsky 1970; Lipsky & Levi 1972). Commenting on such problems as they affect community improvement organizations, Lutz (1970: 287, 292) observes that in Guayaquil, Ecuador, squatter organizations have brought their members into contact with a political system "unable or unwilling to respond satisfactorily to their petitions and demands. . . . Thus it is quite rational for squatters to learn through organizational experience that they have less competence in influencing government than they might otherwise have thought."

Among the communities included in the present study, negative learning experiences have depressed collective political activity most severely in Colonia Texcoco, whose dispirited residents were repeatedly deceived and ultimately abandoned by both the commercial "developer" who opened the community for settlement and most of the state and municipal governments in power during the community's two decades of existence.

Community Leadership. I have already referred to the key role that community leaders play in the generation and transmission of community norms. To the extent that norms defined by such leaders stress the

[12] This pattern is consistent with a basic tenet of social learning theory: "When a social group finds participation unrewarding, it will not enforce it as a social norm and will not offer its members training in social interaction that encourages participation" (S. M. Lipset, paraphrased in Di Palma 1970: 127).

need for high resident participation in community affairs (as in Colonia Nueva), leadership may contribute significantly to developing a local climate of opinion favoring political involvement. Residents may be less than receptive to such leadership, however, if the legitimacy of the community leaders is in question or if their performance in securing material benefits for the community has been poor (Behrman 1972: 279). Some low-income communities observed in Mexico City have had almost no strong, trusted leaders because they began through land invasions led by professional organizers. These men, who are often land speculators or the covert agents of politicians or bureaucrats, normally have no permanent interests in the settlements they help to form; and their early departure creates a vacuum that is often filled by co-opted or nonindigenous leaders imposed by the government.[13]

Government co-optation of the leaders of low-income groups is an effective and widely used tactic of political control in Mexico (see Anderson & Cockcroft 1966; Eckstein 1972a, 1973; Tuohy 1973b: 266ff). Many leaders in the *colonias proletarias* of Mexico City (including the caciques described in Chapter 6) manage to retain a measure of autonomy in their handling of community affairs, but many others do not. And as local leaders become increasingly dependent on external political actors and resources, their energies are diverted away from community problem-solving and toward political control and electoral mobilization on behalf of the regime. When supralocal interests and concerns become the dominant influence in "community" activities, resident participation usually declines, and local leaders cease to play a constructive role in the development of participatory norms.

Voluntary Organizations. The presence or absence of formal voluntary organizations in the community is another structural characteristic affecting local norms. Indirectly, such organizations can accelerate the political socialization process among community residents by facilitating the formation of informal social-interaction networks (cf. Litwak 1970: 587). And if a locally based organization concerns itself primarily with community needs and negotiations with the authorities to satisfy these needs, it may exert a direct influence on the internalization of political norms among its members.[14]

[13] This phenomenon was encountered by Eckstein (1972a, 1973) in a squatter settlement in Mexico City. Similar cases in other Latin American cities are reported in Collier 1971, 1973; Lutz 1967; and Ray 1969: 42–43.

[14] Participation in community-level improvement organizations in Latin American cities has been observed to have a rather selective impact on political attitudes and behavior. As in the present study, membership in such organizations has usually been found to be associated with higher participation in petitioning the government and other forms of political activity; but it has had little impact on level of political

Internal Political Cleavage and Competition. The fragmentation of a low-income community into competing political factions can seriously inhibit the development of participatory norms. In Mexico City, such factionalism usually stems from personal rivalries between community leaders who head local councils or improvement associations that are competing for the support of the residents. In other Latin American countries, where competition among the major political parties for the votes of the urban poor has often been intense, the divisive influence of partisan political activity is often a major source of factionalism in low-income neighborhoods.[15] In some of my research communities (e.g. Colonia Periférico) internal cleavages and competition have not posed insurmountable obstacles to successful collective action on behalf of the community; but most evidence suggests that it is an elusive goal under such conditions (cf. Butterworth 1973; B. Roberts 1973: Chap. 5). Moreover, the personal costs of becoming openly identified with one of the contending factions in a small community—social ostracism, economic sanctions, or even violent reprisal—may be so great that a climate of opinion favoring noninvolvement in community affairs develops.

Developmental Problems and Needs. In most low-income urban communities, the key stimulus to political involvement is a set of community-related development problems and needs that must be met if living conditions in the neighborhood are to be improved significantly. In Latin American cities, neighborhoods suffering from insecurity of land tenure place highest priority on securing officially recognized title to the land. Next in importance is the installation of basic services such as piped water, sewage systems, and electricity. And after these, demands may arise for the construction of schools, public markets, health-care centers, and other facilities.[16] While such improvements are still lacking, they provide a rationale for collective political action, aimed at influencing the allocative decisions of government agencies. But once the most acute problems are resolved, participation in community organizations and all other forms of cooperative political activity tends to decline sharply. Thus the lowest levels of participation are often encountered in the com-

---

information, sense of political efficacy, and other *non*behavioral dimensions or attitudinal correlates of political involvement. See Lutz 1970; McKenney 1969; Pratt 1971a, 1971b. See also Chapter 7.

[15] The forms and consequences of partisan political competition in low-income neighborhoods of Latin American cities are described in Collier 1973; Lutz 1970: 124, 294ff; Peattie 1968: 56ff; S. Powell 1969; Ray 1969: Chap. 7; B. Roberts 1973: Chap. 5; Rogler 1967: 520–21; Vanderschueren 1973. For a detailed analysis of the efforts of nominally nonpolitical agencies and institutions to penetrate and control squatter settlements in Lima, see Rodríguez et al. 1972.

[16] The agendas for community development that residents of the research communities establish for themselves are discussed in Chapter 7.

munities that have achieved the highest levels of tenure security and urban development.[17]

In the present study, this pattern is best exemplified by Colonia Militar, where the local improvement organization disintegrated within a year of the official recognition of land rights and the introduction of basic urban services. Other needs of this community remain unmet today—for example, local school facilities are badly deteriorated, and there is no public market building—but no attempts have been made to organize the residents to deal with these problems. Most residents make use of school and market facilities in nearby, higher-income colonias. This situation illustrates a necessary condition for the maintenance of participatory norms in the kinds of communities under discussion here: there must be a strong, continuing need for mutual assistance and cooperation, deriving from the existence of a set of high-priority, community-related problems that can be addressed *most effectively* through collective political action.[18]

On the other hand, the magnitude of a community's developmental problems must not be so great that the residents feel powerless to resolve them. They must view their community as being suitable for development and eligible to receive government assistance at some point in the not-too-distant future. Otherwise they are likely to regard it as little more than a temporary settlement, from which one should escape at the earliest opportunity; and they will be unwilling to invest their time and material resources in community development (see Portes 1971a: 244–46). Under such conditions, it is most unlikely that a norm structure supportive of cooperative political activity will develop.

SUMMARY

The evidence reported in this and earlier chapters suggests that there is considerable variation in the political learning experiences to which migrants to the city are exposed in different parts of the city. It does seem appropriate to characterize these local urban communities as agents of political socialization among the migrant poor. However, to

[17] This is a well-documented pattern in Latin America. See especially Butterworth 1973; Dietz 1974; Gauhan 1974: 38–39; Goldrich et al. 1970; Lutz 1970: 122; Portes 1972: 275–77.

[18] Of course, other factors may be involved in any marked decline in community participation over time. For example, local leaders may be rendered ineffective through government co-optation (see Eckstein 1972a, 1973). In other cases, withdrawal from overt political activity by the residents of a low-income community may reflect changes in the political opportunity structure at the city or even national level (e.g., in Brazil following the military coup of 1964, or in Chile after the coup of 1973), which make it futile or even dangerous to engage in such activity (see E. Leeds 1972; Portes & Walton 1975: Chap. 3).

demonstrate conclusively that the communities function in this manner, it would be necessary to link systematically the political characteristics of residential socialization settings with variations in socialization out-comes (political attitudes and behavior), as is done in the research on adult socialization in businesses, churches, bureaucracies, and other for-mal organizations (Brim 1966; G. Miller & Wager 1971; Wilken 1971). This will require a more sophisticated application of the type of con-textual analysis pursued above, to a wider range of social contexts than those included in the present study. The limited number of communities I studied in Mexico City does not allow an analysis in which one can control for potentially spurious relationships at the level of the com-munity. For example, it is not possible on the basis of my data to deter-mine whether it is a community's degree of civic-mindedness as such that affects individual political participation, or whether the causal agent is really some other attribute of the community that is correlated with its degree of civic-mindedness (cf. J. Coleman 1961: 610).

In a recent study of political participation in the United States, Aus-tria, India, Japan, and Nigeria, Sidney Verba and his colleagues propose a number of alternative models to explain the process of politicization. The findings presented in this chapter suggest that the most adequate conceptualization of the politicization process among low-income urban populations in Mexico and other Latin American countries would incor-porate elements from several of these models. Among these would be the "group consciousness" model (which specifies that individuals come to participate in politics "through development of a sense of group con-sciousness, usually based on a shared sense of some deprivation") and the "personal relevance of government" model (which predicts that people will participate "out of an awareness of the relevance to them of specific governmental programs . . . [that] impinge on their lives").[19]

The research reported in this chapter points to the importance of one additional factor—i.e. the *differential opportunity structure* of commu-nities of residence—in explaining the process of politicization among low-income urban groups. Here I refer to the range and frequency of opportunities for political involvement to which people have access by virtue of their residence in specific communities.[20] Residents of certain

[19] Verba, Nie & Kim 1971: 62. Verba and his associates find that the "group con-sciousness" model best approximates the process by which blacks in the United States come to participate in campaign and communal problem-solving activities; see Ver-ba, Ahmed & Bhatt 1971. This model is based on the same theoretical assumptions as Durkheim's "collective enthusiasm" theory of social participation; see Pizzorno 1970: 47–48.

[20] The importance of the local political opportunity structure to an explanation of political behavior has been emphasized by several students of urban politics in the United States. Greer and Orleans (1962), drawing on research conducted in the

types of low-income communities, particularly squatter settlements, are probably more exposed to community action, organization, and demand-making efforts than many urban dwellers who are economically better off (cf. Lutz 1970: 190). Certain characteristics of these communities —illegal origins, lack of services, "mobilizing" leadership, and so forth— provide incentives and opportunities for political participation. Age, socioeconomic status, sense of political efficacy, interest in politics, and other personal characteristics may of course influence the extent to which individuals are able and choose to avail themselves of these opportunities. But actual participation does not depend on individual attitudes or social status alone.[21]

Among a substantial proportion of the population in many low-income communities of Third World cities, it is evident that low levels of political knowledge, cultural norms discouraging political participation by the poor, and low socioeconomic status per se have not proven insurmountable obstacles to involvement in political activity (see M. Ross 1973b: 38–62). In fact, the accumulated evidence from field studies in such communities indicates that given sufficient opportunity for political learning, together with strong community leadership and organizational support, the urban poor may participate more frequently than those at considerably higher levels of the social hierarchy. Such findings demonstrate the need for a reevaluation of conventional explanations of political participation, as well as increased attention to the role of the local urban community in the process of political learning.

St. Louis metropolitan area, found that formal organizational participation, electoral behavior, degree of perceived political competence, and overall level of political involvement vary widely from one type of social area within the city to another. They explain these differences primarily in terms of variations in the structures of available opportunities for participation among urban subcommunities. Eisinger (1973: 11–12) has proposed a similar explanation for variations in frequency of protest behavior among urban populations in the United States.

[21] This perspective is consistent with a theory of neighborhood problem-solving behavior proposed by Orbell and Uno and tested with data from the United States. They suggest that an individual's political participation should be viewed as "a response to a need he experiences in his environment (or at least the neighborhood part of it), and as directed toward some agency, usually government, that has the power to do something about it" (Orbell & Uno 1972: 475–76). Complaints about the "individualistic" bias of much research and theorizing on political participation have been frequent but largely unheeded. See, for example: Alford & Scoble 1968: 1205–6; Houlihan 1970; Form & Huber 1971: 687; Verba 1971; Eckstein 1972b.

CHAPTER SIX

Community Leadership

THE THEORETICAL perspective I have employed in this study directs special attention to the structural and situational variables in migrant settlements that might be expected to affect individual political learning. Community leadership is one of these variables. As I use the term here, leadership is one of several types of linkages between community-level and individual-level phenomena that is of particular importance in explaining the impact of residential context on political attitudes and behavior.

Most observers of squatter settlements and other low-income neighborhoods in Latin American cities have been impressed by the importance of leadership differences in accounting for variations in the "developmental trajectories" of these communities. Leadership performance seems closely related to differences in the outcomes of demand-making, to the length of time needed to accomplish various developmental objectives, to the quality of the relationships maintained between a community and political or governmental agencies, and to the level of political organization within a settlement.[1] It is evident that effective leadership

[1] See, for example, Lutz 1970: 129; Perlman 1971: 399–403; B. Roberts 1973: 307–30. Despite the obvious importance of leadership in low-income urban communities in Latin America and other developing regions, there has been remarkably little systematic research on the topic. In addition to the studies just cited, see Havens & Flinn 1970: 93–107; Kaufman 1970; M. Ross 1973b: 169–79. Several studies have focused on voluntary associations (particularly local improvement associations) in low-income urban settlements in Latin America (Friedman 1968; Lutz 1970; Pratt 1968, 1971a, 1971b; McKenney 1969). Unfortunately these studies give no attention to leadership in such organizations, concentrating instead on the personal attributes of members and nonmembers, the attitudinal and behavioral consequences of participation in such organizations, and related topics. The same lack of specific attention to leadership has characterized broader studies of social and political life among the urban poor in Latin American countries (see, for example, Portes 1971a, 1971b, 1971c, 1972). The studies that do contain some specific information on the characteristics of leaders devote little or no attention to the *structural* aspects of leadership

can significantly increase the capacity of low-income communities to manipulate their economic, social, and political environment. Moreover, some of the findings reported in Chapter 5 suggest that leadership may be an important source of variance in individual attitudes and behavior among the residents of such communities.

The purpose of this chapter is to illustrate in greater detail some of the ways in which local leaders affect the *colonias proletarias* of Mexico City and their inhabitants. Most of the discussion will be devoted to a particular kind of leader, the urban *cacique*, who has been especially important in four of the research communities. I shall begin with a brief survey of leadership recruitment patterns in all six communities.

WHO BECOMES A LEADER?

The identification of leaders in the research communities was one of the first and most crucial steps in my fieldwork. First, it was necessary to determine whether the leaders in each community could be counted upon to cooperate with the fieldwork, or at least to raise no insurmountable obstacles to it. Moreover, the history of these communities is largely unrecorded, and local leaders are a key source for this type of background information. As I interviewed and observed the principal leaders over a period of many months, I gradually came to appreciate the importance of their role in community development and in political learning among residents of the communities. In an effort to gather more complete data on the residents' own perceptions and evaluations of their leaders, I included several questions bearing on leadership in my survey questionnaire. The responses to these questions were compiled continuously while the survey was in progress, and they were of great help in identifying the complete set of individuals who were regarded as leaders of the communities.[2] The group of 67 influential persons identified through this reputational approach, 64 of whom I interviewed on at least one occasion, included all the "principals" I had previously identified through informal interviews and participant observation; but there were also a substantial number of less visible individuals, especially those who had played conspicuous roles in earlier stages of their communities' development but who no longer occupied any well-defined leadership position.

—the nature of leader-follower relationships, relationships between leaders and supralocal political actors, and bases of a leader's influence within the community— that are most relevant to an assessment of the effects of leadership on the attitudes and behavior of community residents.

  [2] Only one of the persons identified by survey respondents as a community leader was himself included in the randomly selected survey sample.

Generalizing across the six communities, leaders tend to be long-term residents of their neighborhoods. In the three squatter settlements, most people regarded as influential at the time of the study either had taken part in the initial land invasions through which the settlements were formed or had moved in shortly thereafter. A majority had migrated to Mexico City from rural communities, although the proportion of migrants among community leaders was roughly the same as among the general population of each community. Their ages ranged from 18 (a college-preparatory student) to 76 (a retired military officer), but on the average did not differ significantly from the median age of male heads of families interviewed in each community. The leadership in all communities was predominantly male. However, the dominant leader of Colonia Periférico was female, and the two principal leaders of Colonia Nueva were a husband-wife team. (The husband was the cacique, but he preferred to have his attractive wife represent the community in meetings with outside authorities.) In general, community leaders were likely to have a better-than-average education, but in terms of influence the "exceptions" on this dimension were often important. For example, the dominant female leaders in both Colonia Nueva and Colonia Periférico were barely literate and had attended school for only two or three years.

The most obvious factors differentiating leaders from nonleaders were those of employment and occupational status (see Table 6.1). Professionals, technicians or semiprofessionals, and small merchants or salesclerks were greatly overrepresented among the leaders at the time of the study. The majority of these individuals are self-employed, and they have relatively high and stable incomes (apart from any income gained by virtue of their leadership status). They are, therefore, better equipped in terms of time and resources to play a leadership role. Retail merchants, most of whom own and operate stores in the communities where they live, have the added advantage of an occupation that brings them into frequent personal contact with large numbers of community residents. Leaders with higher-status (professional or semiprofessional) occupations were clustered in two of the communities, Colonia Esfuerzo Propio and Colonia Militar. Other settlements were dominated by people with such occupations as usher at a sports arena, general-store and tavern operator, and manager of a garbage dump. Economically inactive persons were more numerous among the leaders than among their followers, but most of these were housewives who served as assistants to the two most influential female leaders in Colonia Nueva and Colonia Periférico.

TABLE 6.1

Major Occupations of Community Leaders and Followers

Occupation	Leaders (N = 67)	Followers (N = 935)
Professional	11.3%	0.0%
Technician or semiprofessional[a]	20.1	1.0
Office worker	5.0	4.8
Small retail merchant or salesclerk	23.3	9.2
Skilled worker or craftsman	12.2	27.6
Unskilled worker	12.0	44.0
Street vendor	1.5	3.5
Other occupations	2.2	6.6
Economically inactive[b]	12.4	3.3

NOTE: Leaders include all individuals identified by respondents in the sample survey or by participant observation as "persons who have the most influence" in the six research communities. Followers include all heads of family (migrant and native) interviewed in the sample survey. Leaders and followers whose occupation was not ascertained are excluded.

[a] Includes schoolteachers, bookkeepers, reporters, and military officers.

[b] Includes housewives, students, and retirees, but not temporarily unemployed persons.

Since my interviews with most leaders concentrated on their activities during the period of their residence in the research communities, little information was gathered on their earlier activities and experiences. Hence it is not possible to assess the importance of those experiences in creating aptitudes or incentives for occupying leadership roles within the communities. However, the dominant leader—and cacique—of Colonia Nueva described himself as an activist in labor organizing in his hometown before migrating, and he had worked for a time as an apprentice printer—both experiences that gave him considerable facility with the written and spoken word.

The circumstances surrounding the creation of a low-income community, and the way it evolves over time, appear to be highly important determinants of recruitment into leadership roles. For example, the initial leaders of all three squatter settlements included in my study had gained prominence while organizing the initial land invasions or helping to defend their settlements against eviction attempts immediately thereafter. By 1970, most of the "founding fathers" of two of these settlements, Colonia Periférico and Colonia Militar, had been replaced as leaders by newer arrivals. Leadership turnover was particularly noticeable in Colonia Militar, where a military officer and his subordinates who had been instrumental in invading the land were succeeded by an opposition group of middle-class professionals, who moved into the colonia after the danger of government eviction had seemingly abated.

Leadership in the two government housing projects included in the study also reflects the manner in which the communities were established. The "conventional" housing project, Unidad Popular, having been built on a site adjoining the municipal garbage dump, immediately fell under the influence of the leader who operated the dump and oversaw the labor of the hundreds of *pepenadores* (scavengers) who worked within it. The site-and-services project, Colonia Esfuerzo Propio, had been set up and maintained as the virtual fiefdom of an architect employed by the Department of the Federal District. He and his assistants (all nonresident, government-employed professionals) constituted the effective leadership structure of the community, and they vigorously resisted the emergence of any indigenous leaders or organizations. Their success in this regard is illustrated vividly by the responses of Esfuerzo Propio residents to the survey question asking them to identify the leaders of their community: none of the respondents could name a single leader who was not a member of the architect's development team.

THE CACIQUE AS COMMUNITY LEADER

My study of the six research communities, both at the time of the fieldwork and at previous stages of their development, led me to the conclusion that wherever and whenever strong leaders existed, they were likely to exhibit those characteristics of leadership traditionally associated with the rural cacique in Mexico. This particular type of leadership was encountered at the time of the fieldwork in Colonia Nueva and Colonia Periférico, and I discovered that it had also existed at an earlier point in the settling of Colonia Militar. Leaders manifesting some attributes of the cacique were also prominent at the time of the fieldwork in Colonia Texcoco and Unidad Popular. My observation of several low-income neighborhoods bordering those included in the study, personal visits to many other colonias scattered throughout the Mexico City metropolitan area, and interviews with politicians and officials all indicate that caciquismo occurs with considerable frequency in the *colonias proletarias*, although it is by no means the only form of local leadership that can be observed.[3]

In Spanish-speaking countries the term cacique is often applied to any individual who is thought to exert overwhelming influence on local politics. Friedrich (1968: 247) has defined a cacique as a "strong and autocratic leader in local and/or regional politics whose characteristically informal, personalistic, and often arbitrary rule is buttressed by

---

[3] For descriptions of alternative leadership patterns in low-income neighborhoods of the capital and other Mexican cities, see Ugalde 1970: 143–46; Ugalde et al. 1974; Eckstein 1972a, 1973; D. Foster 1971; Butterworth 1973: 223–28; Ornelas 1973.

a core of relatives, 'fighters,' and dependents, and is marked by the diagnostic threat and practice of violence." He also notes that the existence of a *cacicazgo* (i.e. a concrete instance of caciquismo) has always implied "strong individual power over a territorial group held together by some socioeconomic or cultural system" and a certain degree of "detachment or freedom from the normative, formal, and duly instituted system of government."[4] Ugalde, who, like Friedrich, has studied caciquismo in a small Mexican rural community, offers a similar but less inclusive definition:

> We would define *cacique* as the leader who (1) has total or near total political, economic, and social control of a geographic area; (2) has in his power the potential use of physical violence to make his wishes become the law of his territory; and (3) is acknowledged and implicitly legitimized as the only leader of his realm by outside higher political leaders. (Ugalde 1973: 124)

Although my own fieldwork suggests that caciques operating in an urban setting may not share all of the traits listed in these definitions, their behavior seems to approximate the traditional model of caciquismo quite closely in most respects. The major departures from this model will be discussed below.

In Mexico, as in much of Latin America, caciquismo has been a historically ubiquitous phenomenon; and it is still an important (if largely covert) feature of the political landscape in rural areas.[5] During the past thirty years, as large numbers of *caudillos* and caciques in the countryside have either disappeared or lost their influence in state and national politics,[6] there has been an increasing tendency to refer to caciquismo as a phenomenon confined to the more backward areas, where it is closely tied to the isolation and the tradition of political control by a single family that have often characterized rural communities (González Casanova 1970: 33; Drake 1970: 407; Lambert 1967: 154). Padgett has observed (1966: 83): "The more remote the rural area and

---

[4] Friedrich's pioneering ethnographic work on Mexican caciquismo is reported most fully in his doctoral dissertation (Friedrich 1957) and in a more recent monograph (Friedrich 1970). See also Friedrich 1966.

[5] For a general survey of the phenomenon of caciquismo, both historical and contemporary, in Latin American countries, see Kern 1973. The most comprehensive, empirically-based study of rural caciquismo in Mexico is Bartra et al. 1975. See also Díaz Díaz 1972; Goldkind 1966.

[6] The term caudillo is usually applied to political strongmen who have made their influence felt on the regional or national level. As Wolf and Hansen (1967) have pointed out, there is much in the code of caudillo behavior—particularly its emphasis on personalized loyalties, frequent recourse to violence, and an arbitrary, autocratic style of governance—that is also characteristic of many local caciques, especially in rural areas.

the farther it is from ready accessibility to a large city, the easier it is for the cacique to establish and maintain himself in power." He implies that the decline in the number of old-style caciques in Mexico today can be attributed largely to the "growing urban character of the country."

More recent research, however, indicates that such statements about the decline of caciquismo are misleading. Large-scale field studies by researchers at the National University of Mexico recently found a great many caciques still operating in rural communities, including those located in areas with modern agricultural technology, good communications, and transportation links to urban centers (Paré 1972; Bartra et al. 1975; *El Día*, 23 May 1973: 2). My own observations in Mexico City, as well as those of researchers in other Latin American cities, suggest that there are also highly significant manifestations of caciquismo in urban contexts. Ray (1969: 59) found that many low-income neighborhoods in Venezuelan cities are dominated by caciques who are "the supreme, and almost absolute, authority in their barrios. They sanction, regulate, or prohibit all group activities and exercise a strong influence over any decisions that might affect their communities." Other instances of urban caciquismo have been observed in Venezuela (Bamberger 1968), Nicaragua (Toness 1967: 38), and Chile (Equipo de Estudios Poblacionales del CIDU, 1972b: 68); and there even appear to be analogues of the phenomenon in some small and medium-sized cities in Africa (see Barrows 1974: 290–93). Thus it would appear that urbanism per se does not inhibit the emergence of caciquismo as a pattern of leadership among low-income people. In fact, as I will argue below, the formation of squatter settlements and unauthorized commercial subdivisions on the periphery of most large cities in Latin America may provide important new opportunities for this type of leader.

In both urban and rural contexts in Mexico, a cacique is recognized both by the residents of the community in which he operates and by the supralocal authorities of the government and the PRI as being the most powerful person in the local political arena. Public officials invariably deal with him in all matters affecting the community, to the exclusion of other potential leaders. The cacique also possesses the de facto authority to make decisions that are binding on the community under his control, as well as informal police powers and powers of taxation (usually described as "taking up a collection" to finance a given project, service, or activity). Thus in some respects the traditional cacicazgo is a sort of government within a government, controlled by a single dominant individual who is not *formally* accountable either to those residing in the community under his control or to external authorities. As the cacique of Colonia Nueva bluntly put it, "Aquí no hay más ley que yo" ("Here there is no law but me").[7]

A cacique usually gains power through self-imposition, with the acquiescence (and occasionally the active support) of a majority of the community's residents. Since he holds no elective post and is not dependent on supralocal officials for appointment, he may remain in power until he voluntarily renounces his leadership role or is removed by force. As Friedrich has pointed out (1968: 258–59), the fact that a cacique's rule is temporally unrestricted is one of the most important distinguishing characteristics of his status in Mexican politics. Local caciques are virtually the only officially recognized political leaders whose tenure is not necessarily affected by the sexennial, constitutionally mandated changes of the national administration or the triennial replacement of municipal governments. In Colonia Periférico, for example, a single cacique had held power continuously from 1959 until the time of my study; and in Colonia Militar, the cacicazgo established during the invasion of the land in 1952 endured until 1964. In rural areas cacicazgos have been found whose origins antedate the Revolution of 1910 (see Reyes Heroles 1972).

The cacique is a truly indigenous leader: he emerges from the community over which he exerts his influence, and his following is confined to the residents of that locality. Moreover, his political activity is oriented primarily to local issues and concerns. Thus a cacique must be distinguished from local leaders who are simply "imposed" on a community by supralocal forces. Similarly, he must be contrasted with individuals who function only as local agents or representatives of the government, political parties, labor unions, or other organizations whose activity is oriented in some degree toward the local community but whose primary concerns are clearly supralocal.

The cacique's relationship to his followers tends to have a far more utilitarian character than that of other types of local leaders, whose influence derives largely from the esteem in which they are held.[8] Be-

---

[7] As we shall see, however, the urban cacique's actions are influenced to some extent by supralocal political actors, and he is informally accountable to them for the performance of certain political services.

[8] The cacique's relationship to his followers in certain respects approximates a patron-client relationship; yet the cacique does not operate exclusively with personally controlled local resources (as does the patron in a true clientage relationship), and the mutual rights, obligations, and types of interaction involved are usually different as well. For detailed explications of the patron-client relationship and how it may be distinguished from other types of leader-follower relationships, see Silverman 1965; Wolf 1965; J. Powell 1970; J. C. Scott 1972.

cause of this lack of affective underpinnings, the cacique's position can be quickly undermined by particularly flagrant financial indiscretions and abuses of authority, or by his failure to meet certain standards of performance over an extended period of time. Thus he must strive continually to legitimize his claim to leadership. At any given point, this process of legitimation may be incomplete and subject to reversal.[9]

The cacique may be heartily disliked and distrusted by many of his followers, who correctly suspect him of using his leadership position to advance his own financial interests. Like the old-style caudillos, whose code of behavior he frequently emulates, his primary aim is to increase his personal wealth.[10] He loses few opportunities to enrich himself and his principal aides; and despite the poverty of most of its inhabitants, the community he controls usually offers many such opportunities. In all three of the squatter settlements included in my study, caciques had been deeply involved in a variety of illicit moneymaking schemes— selling lots or "permits" to occupy land within the settlement before it was regularized, fraudulently collecting money for personal use, exploiting local mineral resources, and charging special fees for access to basic urban services such as electricity. To the economic returns from activities such as these, a cacique may add the income derived from property he owns within the community, often including small businesses and rental housing.

Although illicit land deals are by far the most important source of income for caciques in many communities, the frequent collection of "donations" (*cuotas* or *cooperaciones*) from the residents may be equally lucrative. The cacique usually justifies his requests for these payments in general terms referring to his ongoing negotiations with government officials to secure land titles, basic urban services, and other improvements for the community. The money is ostensibly used to cover travel costs for the cacique and his assistants, bribes or gifts for public officials, letter-writing fees, and similar expenses. The cuotas collected in Colonia Periférico and Colonia Militar were usually tied to specific community projects or needs, such as installing a provisional water system, repairing the community meeting hall, or grading the main street. It was evident, however, that the sums collected were far

---

[9] Friedrich (1968: 244) has argued convincingly that the legitimacy of a cacique should be viewed "as a matter of process and 'flux' rather than a static, fixed attribute of his leadership status."

[10] Undoubtedly, certain psychological satisfactions derive from exercising a leadership role in a squatter settlement; but it is clear that a cacique's primary motive for acquiring and retaining power is economic in nature.

in excess of the amounts actually spent by community leaders. The residents of Colonia Nueva were even persuaded to provide full financial support for the local cacique, his wife, and his six children in order to free the family for full-time attention to community affairs. Each family in the colonia contributed five to fifteen pesos each week for this purpose (yielding U.S. $100–200 per week). Individual cuotas were determined by the cacique on the basis of income, and he maintained a complete register of household heads and their estimated weekly income for this purpose. Special cuotas, in addition to the regular weekly donations, were also collected frequently—for example, an assessment of 100 pesos (U.S. $8) per family to purchase an automobile for the cacique's personal use (he subsequently demolished it in a traffic accident).

The barely concealed economic motivation of some caciques in assuming their position and maintaining themselves in power often leads to charges of fraudulent collection and mishandling of community funds. Some excerpts from my interviews are typical of these complaints. A small merchant in Colonia Texcoco:

Why would someone want to become a political leader? To make money fast, like Sr. González, who came here poor and now has two buildings and a lot of money.

A street vendor in Colonia Periférico:

Sra. Moreno asked each family for 1,040 pesos [U.S. $83.20] to pay for the *trámites* [bureaucratic procedures] needed to legalize our plots of land. This made me mad, because it was not true that all that money was needed. I sent a letter about these events in the colonia to the office of the Federation of Colonias Proletarias [a PRI-affiliated organization].

A factory worker in Colonia Nueva:

There are too many people living in the colonia now. This is because of Sra. Ortíz and her husband, who made it possible for them to settle here. In exchange for a certain amount of money, they give permission to move into the colonia. . . . One man refused to give her a cent, so they had his house torn down and later threw him out of the colonia. . . . They are getting rich from all that money, with which they are building their house here and also farming land in their hometown.

BASES OF THE CACIQUE'S INFLUENCE

What factors help to explain the influence of an urban cacique over the community he rules? What is it that induces others to follow his leadership, even when there is clear evidence of personal profiteering or other abuses on his part? To answer questions such as these we must examine the resources that a cacique brings to his leadership position, which serve to consolidate and legitimize his control over the community.

Personally Controlled Resources

Some resources take the form of personal skills or aptitudes that are viewed by a colonia's residents as equipping the cacique for a leadership role. For example, the cacique's skill at organizing and unifying a community is highly valued by its residents, who firmly believe that a high degree of unity and organization improves the community's position in negotiations with government officials for urban services, official recognition of land tenure, and other benefits. To the extent that the cacique can represent himself as effective in maintaining unity and organization within the area under his control, then, he will gain in influence and legitimacy. Moreover, his capacity to mobilize people, both for community-related purposes and for participation in political activity outside the community, tends to impress external political actors and to enhance his bargaining position in dealing with them.

A well-developed capacity for effective self-expression is another useful skill for a cacique. Since he is entrusted, among other things, with the task of seeking external assistance for the settlement, his ability to articulate the needs and aspirations of its residents is regarded as very important in dealing with public officials, as well as with media representatives who may be willing to publicize the settlement's needs and petitions for assistance. The oratorical skills of the caciques in both Colonia Nueva and Colonia Periférico were frequently displayed at community meetings, during which the caciques did virtually all the talking and often read from the petitions they had drafted for presentation to government officials.

Patronage resources also help the cacique to consolidate his grip on a community. He normally enlists the services of several close aides, who assist in mobilizing and organizing his followers, collecting money, and generally communicating and enforcing the cacique's will. In return, these assistants receive a share of the economic rewards flowing from the cacicazgo. The cacique usually adds to his *comitiva* (retinue of close subordinates) a number of people who are nominally representatives of the city government or the PRI in the settlement, whose appointments he has engineered through his contacts with higher authorities. The cacique may also appoint members of this group to positions in the community's improvement association (*junta de mejoras*) or governing council (*mesa directiva*). The members of the cacique's entourage are often bound to him not only through patronage rewards but through ties of fictive kinship (*compadrazgo*) as well, which strengthens their personal loyalty and responsiveness to his commands. They form a highly cohesive "political family," which supports, protects, and insulates the cacique against harassment by dissatisfied residents or predatory outsiders.

The cacique relies to some extent on coercive resources to compel financial cooperation and general obedience among his followers. He generally has exclusive control over the actions of city police within the community and makes effective use of them to intimidate dissidents and potential rivals. Like his rural counterpart, the urban cacique is characteristically accompanied by one or more armed supporters who are both personal bodyguards and "enforcers" within the community; they may also stand guard conspicuously outside his house. In Colonia Nueva and Colonia Periférico, overt coercion by the caciques occasionally took the form of breaking up meetings of suspected opposition groups, and on at least one occasion the cacique of Colonia Nueva incited a mob to demolish the house of a recalcitrant family.

Still, in Mexico City one does not observe the kind of consistent and highly visible application of physical force—including gunfighting and politically motivated homicide—that is apparently a normal part of community life in many rural cacicazgos (Friedrich 1965: 205–6, 1968: 265; Simpson 1967: 341–42). One possible explanation for this lesser reliance on physical force is that an urban cacique is under relatively close scrutiny by higher political and governmental authorities. A more convincing explanation, however, is suggested by the greater diversity of coercive tactics available to him, which may allow him to enforce "discipline" while avoiding the political costs generally associated with physical violence.

Most of the alternative forms of pressure are economic. For example, in a squatter settlement a cacique may possess nearly absolute control over the allocation of land within the settlement, at first through the illicit sale of credentials or permits to occupy land in the area, and later during the process of *lotificatión* (formal surveying and subdivision of the land occupied by the settlement) that follows government recognition or legalization of the settlement. This control over land distribution enables the cacique to build a strong following of families personally indebted to him for their landholding rights (cf. Ray 1969: 59). As a squatter settlement grows, and as virtually all land within it becomes occupied, the cacique may transfer parcels of land from the original occupants to more recent arrivals, particularly to relatives and close subordinates of the cacique himself. Some plots may be reallocated several times, and families refusing to submit willingly to displacement may be relocated on the least desirable land in the settlement—or simply expelled outright.

Among the migrants included in my study, residents of Colonia Nueva and Colonia Periférico, both squatter settlements with well-established cacicazgos, showed extreme sensitivity to the ability of their leaders to restrict access to land and to evict current occupants when their behavior failed to meet the caciques' expectations. The mere suggestion that one's plot of land might be reallocated to some other resident, or even to an outsider, was usually all that was needed to compel obedience.

Derivative Power

Still other kinds of resources explaining the influence of a cacique within his domain are external to the community and not subject to his personal control. The most important of these external resources are the cacique's relationships with political and governmental officials, professionals such as lawyers, doctors, architects, or engineers, and other nonresident, high-status individuals who have skills or resources that can help to satisfy community needs. Such contacts are highly valued by the residents of low-income neighborhoods (cf. Peattie 1968: 88–89; Maruska 1972: 67–68). They are viewed as enabling the cacique to deal effectively with external actors and to secure benefits beyond the reach of someone without regular access to higher levels of authority. And in fact, numerous studies of both rural and urban communities in Mexico show that personal ties between local leaders and higher authorities are the key to success in petitioning for government benefits.[11] Thus the cacique continually strives to impress his followers with the range and importance of the contacts he has established, depicting himself as enjoying the exclusive support of various high-ranking officials and stressing the importance of these contacts to the success of negotiations for community improvements.

In a broader sense, the cacique's relationships with external political actors are extremely important to understanding the influence he exerts

[11] This is a principal conclusion of the review of Mexican community studies by Purcell and Purcell (1973). See also Grindle 1975: Chap. 7; Ronfeldt 1972. My case study of the "regularization" of Colonia Militar in Chapter 7 also illustrates this point.

within the community; for the "derivative power" so gained can be used to consolidate his position and discourage challenges to his authority.[12] Hence he attempts to extend his contacts within the PRI-government apparatus as widely as possible, thereby increasing his own derived power. He must also demonstrate to his followers as often and as conspicuously as possible—preferably by congratulatory messages and even personal visits from officials—that he is in fact favored in high places.

Excessive dependence on external support may prove costly, however, if that support is withdrawn. To actually fall into disgrace with supralocal officials, and to have this become known among residents of his community, may seriously undermine a cacique's position. In fact, the most effective tactic of dissatisfied residents seeking to depose a given cacique is to work diligently at discrediting him in the eyes of outside authorities and, if successful, to inform as many residents as possible of the cacique's loss of official support. Once his usefulness to the community seems to be at an end, his former followers may be highly receptive to opposition efforts aimed at displacing him. This tactic was successful in securing the removal of a longtime cacique in Colonia Militar.

In Colonia Nueva, dissident residents began their effort to discredit the local cacique with the following petition, addressed to the President of the Republic, for whom the colonia had originally been named:[13]

> *Subject*: Protest against illegal acts of
> dispossession, caciquismo, anarchy,
> terror, and fraudulent sale of
> lots in Colonia Nueva

C. Presidente de los Estados Unidos Mexicanos
Los Pinos
México, D.F.
PRESENTE.

A large group residing in the colonia that proudly bears your name, we have gathered to send you our most energetic protest against acts of dispossession, caciquismo, anarchy, terror, and fraudulent sale of lots in our colonia, because, on being informed of the founding of our colonia you honorably and unconditionally granted us your highly valued support, with the firm intention, as has always been your way, that this land would be made available exclusively to

---

[12] The concept of "derivative power" employed here is elaborated in Adams 1967: 40, 250ff. The dependence of local leadership in low-income neighborhoods of Latin American cities upon derivative power has been noted by several investigators (Vaughan 1968; Toness 1967: 59, 68–70; Ray 1969: 56, 61–62; B. Roberts 1973: 306–30). It has also been characteristic of some caciques in rural Mexico (see Friedrich 1965: 199, 203; Friedrich 1968: 262–63; Ugalde 1973: 133–34).

[13] Translated by the author from a copy of the petition provided by informants in Colonia Nueva.

humble persons like ourselves, of few economic resources. But now it seems that the leveled and legalized lots have been given by the leaders not only to just a few residents of Colonia Nueva, but also to numerous outsiders, unknown to us, who have almost certainly given money to our leaders, Sr. Guillermo Ortíz and his wife Juana Ramírez de Ortíz, in exchange for these lots.

In the newspaper *El Día*, on September 20 of this year, there appeared a protest by another group of residents of Colonia Nueva, which denounced this situation. We consider it unjust that the denunciation involved the name of Sr. Ramón Valdéz,[14] whom we consider unassociated with these transactions; and we specifically identify as responsible the previously mentioned leaders, whom we accuse in addition of demanding unreasonable payments both to maintain themselves and for projects that are never carried out. It might also be mentioned that Sr. Ortíz asked the residents to buy him an automobile for his personal use—which was acquired for him by means of an additional cuota of one hundred pesos per family—without considering that the majority of us who live in this colonia have limited resources. But it was necessary to give this money or face the consequences, since the threat remained that he who gave no money might not receive the lot to which he was legally entitled.

We might mention, for your information, that the colonia has always cooperated in defraying the personal expenses of its leaders. We have paid for surgical operations and medical care for Sr. Ortíz, and for births and the medical expenses of his wife. Since Sr. Ortíz has no permanent employment, we almost always cooperate with them in giving two or three pesos daily for the maintenance of their home; in addition, they require of us each week a sum of five to ten pesos for the improvement of the colonia. The reason we have finally decided to send you our most energetic protest is that before they will turn the lots over to us, a payment of 150 pesos is required from each of us as a gift to Sra. Ramírez de Ortíz. Since many of us cannot pay this amount, we have been threatened with being left out when the lots are distributed.

We earnestly beg you to order an investigation of this matter, so that an early end can be brought to the exploitation we suffer and in this manner to protect your honorable name, which our colonia bears. We ask you not to mention this message to our leaders, so that the investigation can have positive results.

Finally, and as our duty to you, we should explain that we have abstained from signing this and identifying the persons who fully support our message, because on prior occasions there have been various protests like this one, but these have never succeeded because minor employees of official agencies have prevented such denunciations from reaching the hands of honest persons who, like yourself, would soon grant a just resolution of our problems. Instead, the petitioners, unmasked in the end, have been ridiculed by the colonia's leaders and branded as traitors.

We must make clear that certain messages earlier sent to you, to the Head of the Departamento Central [D.D.F.], and to other officials have nothing to do with our message. Those messages or petitions had but a single purpose: that the petitioners be given a lot on which to live. Ours is the same, but we ask in addition to this *that new leaders or representatives be given to us—*

---

[14] Pseudonym for an official of the Department of the Federal District.

honest persons strictly supervised by you, or by the offices whose duty it is, who can prevent in the future the conditions we now lament.

With full confidence in you, since we have called you our benefactor, we ask in the name of many humble Mexican homes your energetic intervention to end the unbearable situation of imposition, injustice, and abandonment in which we find ourselves, with the firm promise on our part that we will repay with our acts, for whatever they are worth, the attention which you doubtless will grant us.

A GROUP OF RESIDENTS OF COLONIA NUEVA

Copy to: C. Jefe del Departamento del Distrito Federal [Governor of the Federal District].

Neither this petition nor various follow-up visits by dissident residents to government offices led to direct government intervention to impose new leaders in Colonia Nueva. However, an engineer was sent by the Department of the Federal District to take charge of the distribution of lots among community residents. This deprived the local cacique of one of his principal means of control and personal profit.

Standards of Performance

Although initially a cacique is self-appointed to his leadership role, it is his later achievement in it that usually determines whether he is able to consolidate and legitimize his position. Demonstrated performance in securing benefits for the community is particularly important in this respect. In the eyes of most of his followers, the cacique's effectiveness as a leader is measured primarily by his success in maintaining a constant flow of material benefits both to the community as a whole and to individual residents. Such benefits as public services or legalization of a squatter settlement are collective goods obtained through the cacique's contacts with outside officialdom. Assistance provided to individual residents may include recommendations to prospective employers, help in procuring business permits or licenses, help in getting children enrolled in already overcrowded local schools, and so on.

As long as it appears that the individual and collective interests of community residents are being advanced under a cacique's leadership, his exploitative behavior will be tolerated by most of his followers. In Colonia Militar, for example, the cacique who organized the land invasion through which the settlement was established enriched himself for many years by illegally continuing to work the abandoned sandpit on the site; but it was only after a group of dissident residents proved that he had sabotaged the colonia's negotiations for official recognition of land tenure that he was deposed.[15]

[15] See Chapter 7 for a detailed discussion of this episode.

TABLE 6.2

*Migrants' Orientations Toward Community Leaders,
by Community*

Trait	Colonia Nueva (N = 125–30)	Colonia Periférico (N = 94–101)	Colonia Texcoco (N = 105–24)	Colonia E. Propio (N = 117–31)	Unidad Popular (N = 69–77)	Colonia Militar (N = 110–16)	ALL
Can identify at least one community leader[a]	98.5%	93.4%	59.8%	84.2%	49.1%	63.2%	76.2%
Have high awareness of community leadership[b]	98.5	87.2	25.4	45.0	18.9	31.1	52.6
Perceive "service to community" as primary basis of leader's influence[c]	41.1	60.1	12.0	27.2	15.1	8.9	27.5
Evaluate community leadership positively[d]	90.3	77.4	34.4	53.3	32.1	48.8	57.3

NOTE: Intercommunity differences on all orientations are statistically significant, by Chi-square test, at the .001 level.

[a] Question: "In your opinion, who are the three persons who have the most influence in [respondent's community of residence]?—that is, the persons who are most successful in getting their own way and getting things done."

[b] Index 5. See Appendix C for item content. Index scores were dichotomized into low and high categories with the cutting point located as close as possible to the total sample median, computed on the basis of all respondents (both migrants and natives) in the weighted sample.

[c] Question: "Why do these people [community leader(s), identified by respondent] have more influence in this colonia than others?"

[d] Index 89. Index scores were dichotomized into positive and negative categories with the cutting point located as close as possible to the total sample median.

The strongly instrumental nature of the ties binding the cacique to his followers requires him to be a highly visible actor in the community. His house must be a center of constant activity. He must be present at the scene of any major event or community development project. In a broader sense, he must seek to be identified personally with any and all public works, services, and other improvements introduced into the area under his control—whether or not he himself is actually responsible for securing these benefits. In many instances a cacique will claim full credit for an improvement for which he is in no way responsible, and which he may actually have opposed covertly in his dealings with political and governmental agencies.

The success of the caciques operating in Colonia Nueva and Colonia Periférico in cultivating the image of the "doer" in community affairs is amply demonstrated by the survey data reported in Table 6.2. Migrants residing in these colonias are far more likely than their counterparts in the other research communities to be aware of the existence and activities of local leaders, and virtually all of them who were able to identify one or more community influentials mentioned the incumbent cacique and his closest associates. When asked why these people had the most influence, a majority of respondents in Nueva and Periférico mentioned past or ongoing service to the community, and usually offered specific examples. In the other four communities, which lacked fully dominant caciques at the time of the study, the proportion of respondents viewing community service as the primary basis of leader influence fell off sharply.

Finally, when asked a series of questions requiring them to evaluate the accomplishments, responsiveness, and overall competence of local leaders, migrants in the communities recently dominated by caciques were much more positive in their evaluations than those in other communities. Although the survey data from Colonia Nueva were gathered before the erosion of the cacique's influence (following the petitioning just described), my informal interviews later on revealed no tendency to devalue his previous contributions to the community.

In dealing with certain problems, such as the legalization of land tenure within a community, the cacique may be confronted with a painful dilemma: the residents expect him to make a certain amount of progress toward resolving the problem over a given period of time; but the regularization of land tenure by governmental action may sharply diminish the cacique's own opportunities for extracting personal profit from control of land use within the community. In this and other problem areas, it is often in the personal interest of a cacique to act against the interests of his followers. Accordingly, he may choose to press for short-term ameliorative action by the government rather than seek permanent, comprehensive solutions to the settlement's developmental problems. He may even carry out elaborate deceptions regarding the actual progress of his negotiations for governmental action. In the long run, however, the cacique must clearly "produce"—or seem to do so. Otherwise, he will find it increasingly difficult to maintain the allegiance of his followers and block potential rivals.

Leadership Style

The overall style of leadership employed by a cacique is also important to an understanding of his control over the community. Style includes his manner of exerting influence among community residents, his approach to handling conflict and dissent, and his way of involving residents in community decision-making. Like the leadership of his rural counterpart, the urban cacique's style could be characterized as highly personalistic, pragmatic, informal, and autocratic (cf. Friedrich 1968: 246–48). However, his manner of dealing with community residents, either individually or collectively, need not be overly abrasive or domineering. He prefers to assert his influence in subtle ways, relying on the threat posed by the negative sanctions at his disposal to compel obedience and resorting to strong-arm tactics only against the most uncooperative and openly rebellious residents of the community (cf. Ray 1969: 61). Open conflict with recalcitrant individuals and opposition groups within the community is avoided if at all possible. To allow overt confrontations to develop would detract from the cacique's image as a unifier and peacemaker in the community, both in the eyes of his followers and in those of external authorities.

The same rule applies in presiding over meetings of a community-improvement association or other public assemblages. Open cleavages are not allowed to emerge in public; in fact, formal votes on community issues are hardly ever taken, "consensual" decision-making being the accepted practice. In a well-functioning urban cacicazgo the overt political factionalism and vicious interpersonal feuding characteristic of many Mexican communities are seldom in evidence.[16] Public meetings are handled (or more precisely, orchestrated) by the cacique in such a manner as to give the illusion of meaningful rank-and-file participation, with the cacique's role apparently confined to providing needed information or "orientation." In reality, of course, the cacique makes all important decisions affecting the community according to his own judgment, with no more than a ritualistic consultation of the residents. He demonstrates a certain degree of sensitivity to public opinion, but only to the extent necessary to forestall potential coups and avoid overt group conflicts within the community. The cacique's responsiveness to the preferences of his followers seems to vary directly with their ability to perceive alternatives to his leadership.

In sum, a cacique's influence within his domain is based on a number of demonstrated achievements, aptitudes, sanctions, and resident perceptions that enable him to compel obedience, if not affection, from his followers. He is regarded with a mixture of respect, cynicism, and fear. He is expected to use his power to line his own pockets whenever possible, but this will be overlooked as long as certain standards of performance are met. Most residents support the cacique for the reason expressed most vividly in the informal campaign slogan of a notoriously corrupt Brazilian politician: "He steals, but he gets things done."[17]

[16] For descriptions of such faction-ridden communities, see Friedrich 1965; Torres Trueba 1969; Butterworth 1973: 223–28; Ugalde 1973: 128–33; Ugalde et al. 1974.

[17] The slogan was that of Ademar de Barros, who served as mayor of the city of São Paulo and governor of São Paulo state, and was a perennial candidate for President during the 1950's and early 1960's. He garnered a substantial portion of his electoral support from *favelados* (squatters) and other elements of the urban poor.

LEADERSHIP ROLES

The kinds of roles performed by the cacique both within the local community and in its relationships with the external environment relate closely to his various bases of influence. The cacique gains in legitimacy to the extent that his followers perceive him as fulfilling widely shared expectations associated with the performance of such roles as formal organization leader, informal opinion leader, political mobilizer, and political broker or middleman.

In his role as formal organization leader, the cacique usually heads the community's improvement association (*junta de mejoras*) and customarily identifies himself to outsiders as president of this body. Depending on how seriously he regards the junta as a community institution and not just as an instrument of personal rule, he may have an important positive impact on that organization over time (cf. Ray 1969: 46, 54, 61). As head of the improvement association, the cacique has wide authority to define the community's objectives and organize them into an agenda for negotiation with external authorities. His performance of this role also helps to legitimize his control over the allocation of many of the benefits secured from external political and governmental sources.

As demonstrated in Chapter 5, the performance of community leaders as informal opinion leaders may have significant consequences for the development and internalization of community norms, value orientations, and traditions. Among the communities included in this study, opinion leadership by local leaders was most sustained and effective in the communities most completely controlled by caciques, Colonia Nueva and Colonia Periférico. The cacique of Colonia Nueva, Sr. Ortíz, was particularly adept at this role. One of his principal aims was to create a sense of community solidarity by fostering a collective perception of "external threat" to the community's chances for survival and development. Specifically, he sought to exploit the residents' insecurity of land tenure by exaggerating the threat posed by the legal and political maneuvers of the landowners whose property had been invaded to form the settlement, and he continued to do this long past the period during which such maneuvers could have been effective. These tactics enhanced Ortíz's reputation as a unifier and harmonizer of interests, while also strengthening his image as the community's foremost protector against powerful forces bent on its destruction.

Of equal importance in opinion leadership are the cacique's efforts to shape his followers' images of the supralocal political system. Through

overblown descriptions of his personal relationships with external political actors and overly generous accounts of his negotiations with them
to secure benefits for the community, he may create highly positive (and
often unrealistic) perceptions of the responsiveness of high-ranking officials to citizens' demands. The cacique also finds it politically expedient to cultivate a collective sense of dependence on the government
—and indirectly, on himself—for help in developing the community;
and to this end he may even try to undermine his followers' confidence
in the efficacy of self-help efforts. Self-help development activity was
uncommon in all of the research communities at the time of my study,
even though there were many needs that might have been met at least
provisionally in this way. A lack of initiative on the part of community
leaders was partly to blame.[18]

The cacique may also have a significant impact on the process of political learning among his followers in his role as political mobilizer.
Through frequent public meetings to discuss community affairs, visits
by delegations of community residents to the offices of politicians and
government functionaries, voter-registration drives, and other group efforts, the cacique involves his followers in politically relevant activities.
In doing so, he increases their awareness of the relevance of politics and
political participation to the satisfaction of individual and community
needs. Often, if participation in activities organized by the cacique is
necessary to prevent his imposing some negative sanction, extraordinarily high turnouts may be achieved.

The ability of some caciques to mobilize their followers for political
activities can be explained by their success in solving what has been
termed the "public goods dilemma" of community organizers:

> The benefits of collective neighborhood organization efforts are nondivisible
> public goods, and if there is no way to coerce all the members of the aggregate
> into paying their share of the costs of these goods—that is, in organizational
> participation—or unless there is some way to *exclude the noncontributor from
> the benefits of the collective goods*, there is very little incentive for the rational
> self-interested person to make a purely voluntary contribution to such efforts.
> (O'Brien 1974: 236–37)

In all three of the squatter settlements included in the present study,
caciques who controlled rights to land occupancy within the community
had made it known that "noncontributors" to collective political action
would be excluded from any benefits resulting from such action.

This kind of negative incentive structure had been developed most

---

[18] For further discussion of the factors that weaken self-help orientations and foster dependence on the government among the urban poor in Mexico, see Chapter 7.

Colonia Nueva residents on "comisión" assemble along President Díaz Ordaz's route to a school dedication. The motto on the colonia's banner reads: "The rich and powerful can defend themselves. The poor need someone to defend them: Gustavo Díaz Ordaz."

President Díaz Ordaz greets crowds near the school site, as residents of Colonia Nueva, arrayed on both sides of the street, try to attract his attention.

TABLE 6.3

"*Mobilized*" *Participation in Community Affairs by
Migrants in Colonia Nueva During One Year*

Participation	Percent ($N = 131-34$)
Times participated in *comisiones*	
0	26.7%
1–2	8.5
3–9	17.3
10–19	10.5
20–49	13.7
50 or more	9.2
Almost always, but can't recall number of occasions	14.0
Community meetings (*juntas*) attended	
0	17.2
1–2	3.3
3–9	12.2
10–19	4.9
20–49	27.1
50 or more	18.7
Almost always, but can't recall number of meetings	16.6
Times participated in security patrols (*guardias* or *veladas*)	
0	18.1
1–2	0.0
3–9	4.8
10–19	7.1
20–49	22.5
50 or more	34.9
Almost always, but can't recall number of occasions	2.5

NOTE: All data concern year from May 1969 to June 1970. For wording of questions, see Appendix A, Items 120c, 120f, and 120g.

fully in Colonia Nueva, where cacique Ortíz kept meticulous records of participation in the *comisiones*, community meetings, and security patrols he organized. "Comisión" was the term applied by Ortíz to a variety of group activities, such as attendance at public appearances of the President of the Republic and other high officials, ground-breaking and inauguration ceremonies for public works in many different parts of the city, and government- or PRI-sponsored meetings and rallies. Still other comisiones were visits by groups of community residents—led by Ortíz and his wife—to the offices of government functionaries with whom the cacique was negotiating for assistance to the community.

As shown in Table 6.3, migrants living in Colonia Nueva frequently participated in comisiones and other group activities organized by their cacique, even though most comisiones occurred on weekdays, when the male heads of family would normally be at work outside the community.[19] Although much of this participation no doubt resulted from pressures exerted by Ortíz and his assistants, my data from the sample survey and from participant observation suggest that the people involved also perceived their behavior as an instrumental act aimed at influencing government decisions. When asked why they had participated in comisiones, for example, more than 80 percent of the respondents replied that this kind of activity "helps the colonia." Asked to specify how it helped, four out of five respondents said that it increased official awareness of the needs and problems of the colonia or otherwise improved the colonia's chances of receiving government assistance.[20]

In the role of political broker or middleman, the cacique mediates in a number of ways between his followers and higher levels of authority.[21] He represents the community under his control before supralocal officials and has primary responsibility for articulating the demands and grievances of his followers to these officials. In doing so the cacique helps to bridge the gap between community residents—many of them recent rural emigrants who have little or no detailed knowledge of the city and national political systems—and the institutions of the larger society (cf. Friedrich 1968: 247). He serves as their protector against arbitrary governmental action, and passes on to them the information that flows from the PRI-government apparatus. He is primarily responsible for informing community residents of government programs or actions that will affect them individually or collectively. In sum, a cacique performing the role of political broker "stands guard over the crucial junctures or synapses of relationships which connect the local system to the larger whole" (Wolf 1965: 97).

[19] It was possible to collect such detailed data on resident participation through survey interviews because Ortíz had provided each adult resident of the colonia with printed forms for each type of activity, upon which the dates of all instances of participation were carefully stamped by the colonia secretary.

[20] The relevant questionnaire items are 120d and 120e.

[21] The concept of political brokerage has been developed principally by anthropologists concerned with relationships between the nation and the traditional rural community (see Wolf 1965; Silverman 1965; Betley 1971; and Rollwagen 1974). But it has also been employed in the context of linkages between traditional and modern sectors within the urban setting (Hanna & Hanna 1967, 1969, 1971; Ugalde 1970: 173–75; Bartolomé 1971; Snyder 1972). Numerous investigators have characterized local leaders in Latin American squatter settlements as political middlemen who broker the relations of politicians with their followers in the urban electoral arena. See especially Bourricaud 1970; Giusti 1971: 83; E. Leeds 1972: 24–29; Lopes 1970: 164–65; Ríos 1960; Toness 1967: 58–59; Vaughan 1968. For a general discussion of the importance of political brokerage activity by local-level leaders in Latin America, see Chalmers 1972: 110–11.

The cacique, as broker, seeks to monopolize all links between the community under his control and the political and bureaucratic structures in the external environment. He will take pains to portray himself as the only officially recognized intermediary, and thus the only person in a position to work productively with the government for the betterment of the community. And he will actively strive to minimize direct contact between his followers and outside officials, unless he himself is involved as broker or political mobilizer.

RELATIONS WITH OFFICIAL PATRONS

The cacique is usually linked as a client to one or more patrons in the PRI-government apparatus. These are most often upper-echelon functionaries in the various offices of the city government and the official party that deal with the problems of low-income sections of Mexico City.[22] Like all clientage arrangements, the relationships between a cacique and his external patrons are based on "reciprocal exchange of mutually valued goods and services" (J. Powell 1970: 412). Besides granting him a large measure of autonomy in the running of local affairs and the allocation of government benefits within his community, the cacique's patrons represent a source of derivative power that greatly affects his overall influence in the community. The cacique also relies on his patrons to expedite administrative actions favorable to the colonia, and thus to maintain an acceptable flow of material benefits to the community.

In return, the cacique is expected to mobilize large numbers of people within the area under his control to attend PRI meetings and rallies, public appearances of the President and other high-ranking officials, public works inaugurations, ceremonies held to commemorate the legalization of squatter settlements, and other civic events. Since the patron is usually vying with other ambitious *políticos* to demonstrate to higher authorities his capacity to turn out grass-roots support for the regime, the cacique's "available masses" take on special importance. The cacique is also expected to maintain "control" of his settlement—keeping order, preventing scandals and public demonstrations embarrassing to the government, and in general heading off any activities that might disturb the peace or undermine confidence in the regime. He also has

[22] These officials are in turn linked through informal clientage relationships to politicians and bureaucrats at higher levels of authority. This pattern has been referred to as an "extended patron-client relationship" or "clientele system" (J. Powell 1970; Nowak & Snyder 1970). The Mexican political system can be usefully conceived in terms of successive tiers of patron-client linkages, which operate at all levels of the system (see Fagen & Tuohy 1972: Chap. 2; Tuohy 1973; Grindle 1975).

obligations to "orient" his followers politically (i.e., to propagandize on behalf of the regime and strengthen local identification with it) and to organize their participation in elections, voter-registration campaigns, and other forms of officially prescribed political activity.

Finally, the cacique is expected to assist the regime in minimizing demands for expensive, generalized benefits that might "overload" the political system (for example, tax reform or extended social security coverage). He does this by encouraging his followers to view themselves as being "different" from residents of other *colonias proletarias* in the city and having their own unique problems and solutions. By promoting such parochial attitudes, he helps ensure that his followers' political demands will be focused on short-term, community-specific needs.

A flagrant violation of any of these basic terms of the informal contract between the cacique and his patron may be punished by a withdrawal of the patron's support and recognition, with all the negative consequences this may entail.[23] But this does not mean that the cacique is totally subservient to his patrons. He does not function simply as an appendage of the PRI-government apparatus, although he performs useful services for it and cooperates with his official patrons to the greatest extent possible. He retains considerable freedom of action in managing the internal affairs of his community, and it is clear that his position is not entirely dependent on derivative power from external authorities. The best evidence of this relative autonomy is provided by the caciques who succeed in remaining in power after the complete turnover of officials that occurs at the end of each presidential term.

ORIGINS AND DURABILITY OF URBAN CACIQUISMO

What factors help to explain the emergence and persistence of caciquismo as a pattern of local leadership in the urban setting? Ray (1969: 63) has argued that in the Venezuelan context, "What determines a barrio's choice of leadership is the economic, social, and political character, as it had developed in the postwar period, of the city in which the barrio is located." He goes on to assert that caciques are more likely

[23] One PRI leader interviewed by Schers (1972: 93) showed considerable sensitivity to the problems created by caciques who abuse their power. "[He] admitted that there are caciques in the *colonias* [*proletarias*], but [contended] that they have to behave: 'If the cacique has power he is recognized, but demands are made of him.' From the conversation it was clear that these demands do not include just loyalty to the Party but also a measure of honest behavior. Otherwise another leader will be helped to take over. To my question about how can they do it when the powerful cacique is present, the informant answered, 'We put him in jail for a while; when he comes out there is already another group in charge.'"

to emerge in cities relatively unaffected by the forces of modernization, whose occupational structures lack a strong, modern industrial sector. But the diversity of leadership patterns observed *within* many large cities in Latin America—including Mexico City—suggests that the most important variables in this regard are those relating to the character of the urban neighborhood rather than the city in which it is located.

In Mexico City, settlements that originate through illegal land invasion appear to provide a sociopolitical environment particularly conducive to the emergence of caciquismo. Caciques have also emerged frequently in the numerous illegal subdivisions (*fraccionamientos clandestinos*) on the periphery of the city. Both types of settlement suffer initially from extreme service deprivation and insecure land tenure, and often become the objects of negative sanctions or threats from the government or from private landowners. The emergence of caciquismo in such areas may be related both to the illegality of their origins and to the magnitude of the developmental problems they must confront. Since the government, until it grants official recognition to such a settlement, assumes no responsibility for its administration or improvement, there is greater latitude for individual strong men to assume control and deal with their followers in an autocratic manner.

If this is true, we might hypothesize that as a community's most acute needs are satisfied the cacique presiding over it will find it increasingly difficult to maintain his position.[24] Official recognition of tenure rights and the consequent subdivision of the land into individual parcels may be especially damaging to the cacique's influence in the community, for such acts simultaneously deprive him of important coercive resources (those deriving from his power to allocate homesites) and satisfy the single most deeply felt need of his followers. The cacicazgos in Colonia Nueva and Colonia Periférico were substantially weakened by government legalization of these squatter settlements.

The emergence of a cacique in a given community could also be related to the composition of its population in terms of rural and urban origins. Since a majority of the people in the squatter settlements included in this study are of rural origin, it might be argued that the leadership observed in these areas represents just another manifestation of residual ruralism—i.e. the "transference from the rural areas of institutions, values, and behavior patterns and their persistence or adapta-

---

[24] For perceptive discussions of the relationship between the satisfaction of basic needs and changes in local leader-follower relations, in both rural and urban contexts, see Silverman 1965: 183ff; González Casanova 1970: 35; J. C. Scott 1969: 1155–57; Wolf 1965: 98.

tion to the specific requirements of the urban setting" (Germani 1967: 179; cf. Cornelius 1971: 111–12). Thus it could be hypothesized that the migrant's support for a cacique represents a simple transference of leadership role expectations from his place of origin to the urban *colonia proletaria*.[25] Moreover, peasants as well as rural migrants to the city are often regarded as having a strong predisposition to submit readily to any kind of authority figure.

We might expect the stability of a cacicazgo to be threatened by changes in the distribution of these "supportive" role expectations and attitudinal orientations among the population of the community as the first generation of rural migrants internalizes new "urban" norms and the second generation—with little or no rural background—comes to maturity. But the survey data from Colonia Nueva and Colonia Periférico, the two communities still dominated by caciques at the time of the survey, lend little support to these hypotheses. They show that migrants do in fact exhibit a stronger predisposition toward authoritarianism and deference to authority than native-born city dwellers; but migrants are no more likely than the urban natives in these communities to evaluate local leadership positively. Nor are there any significant differences between migrants and their eldest city-born sons in terms of leader evaluation.

Perhaps the most fundamental threat to the durability of an urban cacicazgo—especially one situated in a squatter settlement—arises as the local community begins to develop a more complex set of social, economic, and political relationships to its external environment and becomes more fully integrated into the physical structure of the city. The influence of the cacique in his key role as broker between his followers and the institutions of the external environment may be substantially reduced through such evolutionary change.[26] As individual residents become more familiar with the contours of the larger urban society and political system, an increasing amount of direct, *nonmediated* contact will occur. The cacique may also be faced with increasing competition from nonresident brokers or middlemen who encroach upon his domain.

[25] Cooper (1959) has investigated the relationship between leadership role expectations and degree of orientation to urban-industrial life in the context of work situations in a rural village, a medium-sized town, and a large city in Mexico. He found that as one moves from the traditional rural community toward the modern urban-industrial environment of Mexico City, attitudes toward what constitutes "good" and "bad" leadership change markedly.

[26] Rogler (1974) has documented the negative consequences of urban assimilation for the influence of the local political boss in a Puerto Rican migrant community in the United States.

Eventually, he may be displaced as cacique by one of these competitors; more likely, the cacicazgo will simply dissolve, giving way to some form of externally imposed leadership, to a group of competing factions with no clearly dominant individual leader, or perhaps to no discernible leadership structure at all. Thus it might be most accurate to conceive of urban caciquismo as a transitory (though often long-lasting) phenomenon restricted to a particular phase in the evolution of a low-income community.

CACIQUISMO AND "POLITICAL REFORM"

The existence of widespread caciquismo in both rural and urban Mexico has become an increasingly controversial issue within the PRI and the government in recent years. It has been acknowledged and condemned repeatedly by high-ranking officials, including both the President of the Republic and the chairman of the official party.[27] The PRI chief pointedly warned that "it would be inconsistent to oppose rural caciquismo, a residue of the old prerevolutionary regime, while ignoring the threat of urban caciquismo" (*El Día*, 24 June 1972: 1). The topic also arose in the context of President Echeverría's efforts to introduce some limited democratizing reforms into the PRI's structure and procedures, in the hope of arresting or even reversing Mexico's recent trend toward greater electoral abstentionism (see Segovia 1974). The argument made by Echeverría, his party chairman, and other top officials is simply that the regime no longer needs caciques to turn out the vote for its candidates, and that continued reliance on them will contribute to rising abstentionism and political alienation among the masses. These concerns were clearly articulated by the PRI chairman in a 1972 speech to party workers (Reyes Heroles 1972):

There are comrades [PRI militants] who in good faith—at least I think it is—tell us that it is an error to fight caciquismo; that the caciques constitute part of the power of our Party . . . that we are breaking the backbone of the Party. I sincerely don't believe this. No ruler can base his support on cacicazgos. He is mistaken if he believes he can, for it is he who supports the caciques. It may be arguable that caciquismo has fulfilled a function [in the past], but it is completely unarguable that it should disappear in our time. In the brief experience we have had in this struggle, we have seen that the people, wherever

---

[27] The "struggle against caciquismo," in both rural and urban settings, has been a persistent theme in the rhetoric of President Luis Echeverría and PRI chairman Jesús Reyes Heroles since 1972. See especially their speeches reprinted in *El Día*, 3 Oct. 1972: 1; 22 May 1974: 3; 24 May 1974: 8; 6 Mar. 1975: 12; 1 June 1975: 4; and *Excélsior*, 10 Apr. 1975: 1A, 9A; 11 Apr. 1975: 22A; 13 Apr. 1975: 10A.

we fight caciques, have voted with enthusiasm and have stopped abstaining. They know that in voting they are deciding their own destiny and are conquering something [caciquismo] that holds back their community. In contrast to this situation, we see how abstentionism grows in localities where the Party, because of the internal play of forces or a deliberate resistance to change, has not been able to run candidates who would guarantee the elimination of the cacicazgo.... In these cases abstentionism grows. The people don't decide their own affairs, but resign themselves—only, perhaps, to explode later.

Not surprisingly, lower-ranking party politicians and government functionaries tend to have a much different view of the cacique's role in the political system. They are expected by their superiors to maintain social and political control within their jurisdictions, as well as to secure high turnouts for the PRI at rallies and at the polls. Caciques have found it easy to gain and hold power in small communities, both rural and urban, because they make it so much easier for an ambitious lower-echelon official to do his job (see Paré 1972). Such men tend to discount the argument that autocratic, exploitative caciques acting as ward heelers for the PRI are contributing to alienation and abstentionism among the poor.

Eliminating the caciques would require lower-level officials to invest more of their own time and energy in grass-roots political organizing, in social contexts with which they are largely unfamiliar. As presently structured, "The PRI ... can work with selected individuals who are strategically placed in the [social] structure, with the knowledge that they will deliver the support of their followers to the Party.... The Party thus does not always require a separate organizational structure; it can use personal contacts to work through other organizations and institutions" (Purcell & Purcell 1973). National leaders must also weigh the advantages of political control and mobilization through dependable, local caciques against the uncertainties and potential divisiveness of grass-roots organizing by outsiders; but they seem to have concluded that at least a strong rhetorical commitment to the eradication of caciquismo is essential to the drive for party reform.

From the standpoint of the rural and urban poor, too, the costs and benefits of caciquismo as a form of local leadership are mixed. In the urban context, the economic costs of caciquismo can be fearsomely high for individual residents of a low-income neighborhood. Yet the residents of such communities, especially the more recently formed squatter settlements, know that they confront a number of developmental problems that must be resolved if their community is to survive and become an adequate dwelling environment. The evidence from Mexico City suggests that strong leadership—whether provided by a cacique or by some other type of local leader—*can* significantly increase the capacity of a low-income community to manipulate the political system in order to secure assistance in community development. How this manipulation occurs, with what specific objectives, and with what consequences for the community are the principal topics to which we now turn.

CHAPTER SEVEN

Political Demand-Making

THE DELEGATION of petitioners from Colonia X has been waiting patiently for several hours—seven entire families, including restless children and family heads who have taken time off from their jobs, led by officers of the colonia's improvement association. The anteroom leading to the office of a Federal District functionary is crowded with dozens of similar delegations from other neighborhoods of the city. The people from Colonia X are urban squatters, and when finally granted admittance they present a laboriously typed petition requesting government recognition of their land tenure rights, signed by virtually all residents of their community. A spokesman for the group argues that land titles are essential to assuring a modest inheritance for their children. Moreover, he continues, security of tenure will stimulate investment in the construction of permanent houses and commercial enterprises within the community. The spokesman also observes pointedly that with property titles residents of the colonia may begin contributing to government tax revenues. To strengthen the image of their community as one deserving of government aid, other members of the delegation cite examples of the hardships they have endured in settling the land and the efforts they themselves have made to improve the community. They stress their belief in the government's commitment to humanitarian concerns, which should ensure that their request will be granted in the interests of social justice. The official promises that the colonia's situation will be thoroughly investigated. The session is concluded amid fervent expressions of the petitioners' support for the incumbent administration.

This scene, repeated many times daily in the city government's Office of Colonias, is the first step in a long, complex, and often frustrating effort to manipulate the political system and satisfy a deeply felt need. The rent-free housing provided by residence in squatter settlements is indispensable in fulfilling the material aspirations of millions of low-income *capitalinos*; but permanent residence in such settlements can only be assured by constant efforts to secure an official recognition of tenure rights.

Petitioning for such benefits as land titles and basic urban services is a very important, though undramatic, form of political participation that has received relatively little attention in the literature on cityward migrants or the urban poor in general. I refer to such activity as political demand-making, and define it as either individual or collective action aimed at extracting certain types of benefits from the political system by influencing the decisions of incumbent government officials. I therefore differentiate demand-making from political activity intended to influence government resource allocation by replacing or retaining the incumbent authorities (e.g. electoral participation) or by overthrowing or restructuring the political system itself (e.g. through violent revolution). Political demands, in this definition, have two characteristics: they stem from needs whose satisfaction is felt to depend on governmental action; and they are asserted by individuals or groups as specific claims upon the government. The term "demand" implies nothing about the way these claims are made. Particularly among low-income city dwellers in Latin America, demand articulation usually does not involve table-pounding, protest demonstrations, or other aggressive behavior.

Demand-making as a mode of political participation has several distinctive characteristics. Because an individual participant (or the leaders of the demand-making group he may belong to) determines the subject matter of his contacts with public officials, the outcome of his participation is certain to be both salient and important to him (see Verba & Nie 1972: 52); the linkage between participation and its results is more direct and visible than in any other mode of political activity. Moreover, the motivations for demand-making are almost entirely instrumental rather than expressive or system-supportive.[1] Although demand-making may sometimes have ritualistic, system-supportive overtones, it is nevertheless aimed primarily at manipulating the system and influencing value allocations. Demand-makers want explicit responses

[1] On the distinction between "instrumental" and "expressive" political participation, see Milbrath 1965: 12. Verba and Nie (1972: 2) also differentiate between instrumental participation and "ceremonial" or "support" participation, in which "citizens 'take part' by expressing support for the government, by marching in parades, by working hard in developmental projects, by participating in youth groups organized by the government, or by voting in ceremonial elections." See also the discussion of ritualistic and system-supportive participation in the Mexican political system in Fagen & Tuohy 1972: 38–39.

from the political system, and they perceive their behavior as "a tactic to enhance their chances of eliciting those responses" (Eisinger 1971: 984). For the urban poor in Mexico, participation within the demand-making mode is the most direct and often the most effective strategy for influencing government decisions.

URBANIZATION AND POLITICAL DEMAND-MAKING

Theorists of political and social change, as well as government policy-makers, have often posited a close relationship between increased rural-urban migration and changes in the types and frequency of demands made upon governments.[2] It has been argued that living in cities tends to expand the range of human needs that can be met through governmental action. At the same time, exposure to the urban environment is thought to increase political awareness among the migrant population. Finally, cityward migration places a larger proportion of citizens in close proximity to government officials, so that needs can be articulated at lower costs in time, effort, and money. The result, it is assumed, will be accelerated demand-making; and it is further assumed that demands for public services and other governmental benefits will increase much faster than the capability of the political system to respond to them. Applying this line of argument specifically to Latin America, Robert Scott has written (1973: 301–2):

As the character of the general population alters from predominantly rural and isolated to partly integrated and urban . . . shifts in the kinds, amounts, and intensity of demands on government occur. Both totally and proportionately more people leave subsistence agriculture and sharecropping to become part of the money economy in the city, or outside it as members of the rural proletariat and participants in commercial or market agriculture operations. To such persons, what happens in national politics is important, and the kinds of government programs they will condone change drastically. In the past . . . much of what government provided either was symbolic—a land-reform law that was not implemented, for instance—or not so much what the masses wanted as what government leaders felt they should have. Now, as the general populace becomes more knowledgeable, this sort of government activity does not satisfy them.

Such arguments appear to be based on rather mechanistic assumptions about the conversion of objectively defined needs into effective demands upon government. The demand for public services is viewed as largely a function of the number of potential clients, whose ranks are

[2] See especially Deutsch 1961: 498–99; 1974: 541; Huntington 1968: 5; Wriggins & Guyot 1973: 5–16. See also, with specific reference to Latin America, Duff & McCamant 1968: 1125–29, and the studies cited in Cornelius 1971: 100–101.

swelled not only by migration from the countryside but also by persistently high birth rates among the poor already living in cities. The evidence I will present in this chapter suggests that this kind of "one man, one demand" assumption may prove highly misleading in any attempt to estimate the potential impact of rapid population growth or migration on the functioning of political systems. Particularly with regard to low-income migrants from the countryside, the extent to which increased political awareness and objectively defined needs are actually translated into increased pressures on urban government is an empirical question, and one that has rarely been addressed in previous research.

Research bearing on this question must go beyond a measurement of the absolute level or frequency of political demand-making among newly urbanized sectors of the population. It must also seek to clarify the *process* by which objective needs are converted into political demands. How do the migrant poor perceive or define their most acute needs and problems? To what extent is the government perceived by them as the relevant problem-solving agency? What is the substantive nature of the demands presented? Are they concerned with individual needs or with the collective needs of urban neighborhoods and other social units? Toward what kinds of officials or agencies are the demands directed? What strategies are used in demand-making, and what factors determine its success or failure? In sum, how do those seeking to influence the distribution of government benefits accomplish their goals?

THE CONVERSION OF NEEDS INTO POLITICAL DEMANDS

It is possible to identify several distinct stages in the conversion of objectively defined needs into actual demands on government. Objective deprivations or problems must first be perceived by the individual as requiring some kind of solution or ameliorative action. Next, these felt needs must be viewed as needs particularly susceptible to satisfaction through governmental action. Finally, the potential demand-maker must be able to perceive a strategy or channel through which to articulate these "politicized" needs. These basic stages are summarized graphically in Figure 7.1.[3]

The assumption implicit in most discussions of the relationship of urbanization to demands on the political system is that the conversion

---

[3] For an alternative conceptualization of the process of demand creation at the level of the individual, see Medler 1966: Chap. 5. My model of the process differs from Medler's primarily in attributing a lesser importance to cognitive involvement in politics and sense of individual political efficacy as preconditions for demand-making. Cf. Graham & Pride 1971.

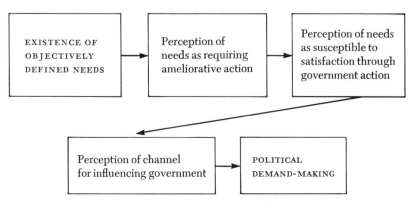

Figure 7.1. Basic stages in the process of demand creation.

of objective needs into political demands occurs almost automatically; but this notion remains largely unproved. In the following analysis I will attempt to demonstrate that there are often major lags in the process of demand creation among migrants to the city, and that many kinds of felt needs are in fact viewed by migrants as needs to be satisfied primarily through individual action rather than political demand-making.

Objective and Perceived Needs

The objective needs of migrants living in the communities included in this study are massively evident.[4] At the time of the survey interviewing, 70 percent of the households studied had no piped water, and an equal number lacked public sewerage. Most houses (75 percent) had no paved streets or sidewalks nearby. Nearly a third of the families lived in one-room houses, and 23 percent of the dwellings were temporary shacks of *lámina de cartón* or scrap materials. Only 4.4 percent of the homes lacked electricity, but 48 percent could obtain it only through illegal tapping of transmission lines in nearby colonias.

Physical conditions were only part of the problem. Only 4 percent of the migrant families had received formal title to the land they occupied.[5] Although only 4.7 percent of the migrant family heads were unemployed and seeking work at the time of the survey, there was substantial

---

[4] My figures are based on an average N of 671.

[5] This low figure is not just a reflection of the fact that two of the research communities were squatter settlements not yet fully legalized at the time of the survey. Even in communities where all landholders have officially recognized tenure rights, many residents cannot pay the fees that are needed to obtain a notarized property title (often more than 1,500 pesos, or $120 U.S.), even after all necessary payments for the land itself have been made.

underemployment, and those who held jobs were poorly paid (50 percent of the family incomes were below the legal minimum wage, then equivalent to about $60 U.S. per month). And the families to be supported on such incomes were large: 61 percent of the migrant family heads had six or more dependents living at home, and 90 percent of them had school-age children. Families remained large despite a high rate of child mortality: More than half the migrant families (50.6 percent) reported having had children who had died before reaching the age of six while residing in Mexico City. Subsequent interviews confirmed that most of these deaths had occurred during the families' residence in the colonias where they lived at the time of the study. Physicians in public-health facilities serving the communities informed me that the vast majority of deaths among children resulted from gastrointestinal diseases contracted from contaminated drinking water and from the raw sewage that flows through open ditches in the areas where children play.

In light of these very real economic and environmental problems, what do the migrants themselves perceive as their most urgent needs? The survey responses presented in Table 7.1 indicate that problems relating to socioeconomic mobility are uppermost in their minds. Increasing family income and having a steady job are the most important goals. Education—either for oneself or one's children—is another major concern, followed closely by the need to become a landowner or homeowner (or to obtain legal title to land presently being occupied). Surprisingly few respondents regard the improvement of living conditions (through ac-

TABLE 7.1
Migrants' Greatest Personal Concerns

Concern	Percent
Increasing family income	26.5%
Having steady work	22.4
Education (for oneself or for children)	15.2
Owning home or land, insecurity of land tenure	14.8
Improving living conditions (acquiring better house, improving present house, installing piped water, electricity, or sewage connection)	9.2
Health of oneself or family	7.7
Advancement in job, doing job well	2.3
Needs and problems of respondent's community (other than insecurity of land tenure)	0.8
Other	1.1

NOTE: The question was: "What about your worries? . . . What kinds of things do you worry about most?" This table reports the first concern mentioned by respondents. $N = 629$. "Don't know" and "have no worries" responses (7.3 percent of the sample) are excluded.

quiring better housing or access to basic urban services) as their most important concern.

One of the most striking findings of this and other studies of low-income people on the periphery of Latin American cities is the relatively low priority attached by such people to securing better housing. It is clear that they regard secure land tenure, basic services such as piped water, and infrastructure improvements like paved streets as more urgently needed than a spacious house built of permanent materials. Construction of permanent houses does proceed among residents of squatter settlements and low-income subdivisions, but only at a pace commensurate with a family's financial resources. Most families would be extremely reluctant to assume the long-term financial burden that payments on a government or commercially built house would impose, assuming that they were able to acquire one. Instead, they prefer to build and improve their own houses as time and money become available, even though the basic construction period may last 10–15 years (J. Turner 1971, 1974; Turner & Fichter 1972: Chap. 7; Dietz 1974).

The migrants in my study were also asked to identify the most serious problem or need facing their community of residence (see Table 7.2). Security of tenure was the overwhelming need in Colonia Nueva and Colonia Periférico, the two squatter settlements where the process of government recognition of individual land tenure rights had not been completed by the time of the survey. In the other four communities virtually no one perceived security of tenure as a key need. Instead, basic urban services and improvements—particularly piped water, sewage systems, and paved streets—were regarded as the greatest needs, followed by community facilities such as schools, public markets, and health-care centers. Environmental pollution, lack of parks and recreational facilities, and inadequate public transportation were perceived as problems only in the two most highly developed communities (Unidad Popular and Colonia Militar); and even in these communities, deficiencies in water supply and in community facilities such as schools and public markets were viewed as more serious. Only three respondents in all the research communities mentioned "poor housing" as the most important problem confronting people in their community. The overall frequency (across communities) with which water and sewage systems, paved streets, and security of tenure were mentioned as the most important community-related needs corresponds closely with the findings of other studies of perceived needs in similar contexts (Butterworth 1973: 231; Andrews & Phillips 1970: 217–18; Cornelius & Dietz 1973: 8; J. Turner 1970: 8–9).

TABLE 7.2

Most Important Community Problems Perceived by Migrants,
by Community

Problem	Colonia Nueva	Colonia Periférico	Colonia Texcoco	Colonia E. Propio	Unidad Popular	Colonia Militar	All
Water supply	23.4%	12.6%	32.5%	12.0%	35.6%	7.9%	20.1%
Sewerage	11.0	28.7	41.7	14.5	0.0	0.9	16.9
Security of tenure	46.7	45.8	0.8	0.0	0.0	2.6	16.5
Health care	2.0	0.0	10.4	20.5	13.6	13.2	10.0
Street pavement	2.3	8.9	7.5	19.6	3.4	2.6	7.7
Public markets	0.0	0.0	0.0	12.9	0.0	28.1	7.2
Schools	9.1	1.1	0.0	0.0	1.7	25.3	6.4
Environmental[a]	0.0	0.0	0.0	4.3	23.7	0.0	3.6
Electricity	1.0	0.0	5.0	3.4	0.0	0.0	1.8
Police protection	0.0	1.1	2.1	0.8	3.4	0.9	1.2
Garbage collection	0.0	1.9	0.0	0.0	0.0	3.5	0.9
Other	4.4	0.0	0.0	11.9	13.6	7.2	6.8
None	0.0	0.0	0.0	0.0	5.1	7.9	1.9

NOTE: $N = 663$. Intercommunity differences are statistically significant, by Chi-square test, at the .001 level. "Don't know" and "no response" cases are excluded. The question was: "In your opinion, what are the most urgent or serious problems and needs of this community? [Probe:] Of the problems or needs you have mentioned, which do you think is the most important?"
[a] Includes air pollution, insects, unstable subsoil conditions, overcrowding, etc.

The degree of importance attached to two particular needs—security of land tenure and public schools—warrants further discussion. The intensity with which migrants lacking legal title to their land feel a need to secure it is illustrated by the responses to three additional questions asked in the survey. When asked whether they had been personally concerned or worried about any particular community-related problem during the last year or so, more respondents mentioned insecurity of land tenure than any other single problem. In response to a related question, 30 percent of all the nonrenting migrants expressed the belief that their own claims to house and land were not yet secure, and the proportion holding this belief was far higher in Colonia Nueva and Colonia Periférico, the two communities whose official "regularization" was not yet complete at the time of the survey. Respondents were also asked whether they had ever worked or cooperated with other residents of their community to try to solve some common problem. A plurality (28 percent) of those who had done so reported that they had been concerned with the tenure problem.

The overriding importance attached to this problem by residents of an illegally formed community is not surprising, since the opportunity to acquire a homesite is one of the primary motivations for moving there in the first place. Apart from the important psychological satisfaction of owning land, ownership assures at least a modest property inheritance (*patrimonio familiar*) for one's children. But short-term economic advantages for the migrant and his family are equally important. Most migrants living in the research communities had built or were still building their own houses. In fact, housing construction was their principal form of capital investment. A rent-free, mortgage-free dwelling can provide economic security during periods of unemployment, major illnesses, and other family crises. If finances permit, a room may be added to the dwelling for rental purposes or to house a small store or other family-operated business. But protection of this source of security and supplemental income requires government recognition of land tenure rights. Moreover, land titles are often needed to obtain loans from banks and other institutions.

With regard to the need for more (or better) public schools, the reader may find it surprising that people who perceive education as a key personal concern (see Table 7.1) generally do not place schools at the top of their community's needs. Only in the most highly "urbanized" of the research communities, Colonia Militar, did public school deficiencies rank among the residents' principal community-related concerns. There, the problem involved rundown facilities and a poor teaching staff—not the complete absence of schools. In fact, all the communities included in this study had one or more public schools. Even in Colonia Nueva, which at the time of the survey lacked all basic utilities, the residents had built their own temporary school and engaged a teacher, whose salary was paid by the PRI. In general, despite extreme overcrowding in many primary and secondary schools, the performance of the PRI-government apparatus in building public schools and providing teachers for community-built schools is more impressive than in any other problem area affecting Mexico City's low-income neighborhoods.

Politicized Needs

What, then, is the "citizen agenda" for governmental action among the migrant population? That is, what kinds of needs do they perceive as satisfiable through government action? Residents of the research communities were asked to give their opinion of how well the government was doing in a wide variety of specific problem areas, and also asked to specify the areas for which they thought the government had no responsibility. Although some migrants were hesitant to claim that the government should provide economic help to those in need, provide employment, or redistribute wealth ("try to even out the differences between the rich and poor classes in Mexico"), they overwhelmingly viewed the government as responsible for providing most kinds of community-related services and improvements.

The degree to which community-related problems and needs have been politicized is further illustrated by the migrants' responses to several questions about the role of government in community development. In answer to the question, "Who or what is to blame for most of the problems of your community?" nearly two-thirds of the respondents mentioned "the government" in general or some specific government agency or official. Responding to another question, only 14 percent of the migrant sample felt that the most important problems of their communities could be solved by the residents themselves without external assistance. When asked who outside their community could help to solve its problems, more than 97 percent of the respondents mentioned some government agency or official. Only 1 percent mentioned private sources of aid (business firms, private land developers, the Church, etc.). In the communities included in this study, there had been no significant investments by outside businessmen, and the role of priests and Church-related organizations in community development had been negligible.

The perceived importance of government assistance in community development is also revealed by the migrants' responses to a fixed-alternative question that required them to identify the single most important factor for improving living conditions in their community (see Table 7.3). Most respondents in the research communities viewed government help as most important, followed by self-help efforts by the residents. Analysis by community shows that even among respondents living in squatter settlements, where the ethic of self-help is more deeply in-

TABLE 7.3
*Perceived Importance of Alternative Sources of Help
in Community Development*

Source of Help	Mexico City (N = 676)	Rural Mexico (N = 474)	Lima, Peru (N = 328)
Government	40.5%	57.6%	37.8%
Community residents	28.4	29.3	57.9
God	17.5	10.1	2.4
Good luck	13.5	2.1	1.8

NOTE: Mexico City data are for migrants in my six-community survey. Data for rural Mexicans are drawn from a study of four villages in the state of Michoacán (Arterton 1974). Data for squatters in Lima are from Dietz's (1974) survey of four squatter settlements (see also Cornelius & Dietz 1973). In all three studies, the survey question was: "Generally speaking, which is the most important for improving the conditions of life in this community: The hard work of the residents, God's help, the government's help, or good luck?" Differences between Mexico City migrants and squatters in Lima are statistically significant, by Chi-square test, at the .001 level.

grained, government assistance is regarded as paramount in the community development process.

Very significant differences emerge on the issue of self-help versus government assistance in community problem-solving when the responses of my sample are compared with those of residents of squatter settlements in Lima, Peru. More than 30 percent of the Lima squatters believed that the most important problems of their community could be solved by the residents alone; in Mexico City, only 14 percent of the respondents felt this way. Although cross-national differences in the distribution of responses within other categories ("God's help," "good luck") are also substantial, the noticeable disparity in the *relative* importance attached to self-help and government assistance is particularly relevant to our concern with the politicization of needs among the urban poor.

The most adequate explanation for the difference between Peru and Mexico may lie in the varying content of directed political socialization in the two countries. In both nations the government has strongly influenced mass perceptions of its responsibilities, though in very different ways. In Peru, most administrations since the late 1950's have sought to encourage and profit from the self-help efforts of low-income city dwellers, and this self-help orientation was reinforced by the efforts of U.S. Peace Corps volunteers during the 1960's. Moreover, until 1968, when a reformist military regime came to power, the strong governmental emphasis on self-help among the urban poor was accompanied by a relatively low level of official responsiveness to their demands. Partly in response to these conditions, large and effective self-help projects were launched in many of the squatter settlements ringing Peruvian cities.[6] In Mexico, the low propensity of the poor for self-help in both urban and rural areas (see middle column, Table 7.3) reflects the efforts of successive governments since 1940 to encourage a sense of mass dependence on the regime for community improvements and other types of social welfare benefits. As noted in Chapter 6, the local leaders of low-income urban communities, most of whom are tied to government bureaucrats or PRI functionaries through patron-client relationships, have also encouraged a sense of dependence on the government.

The comparative evidence thus suggests that the range of needs

[6] On self-help efforts in Peruvian *pueblos jóvenes* (squatter settlements), see especially S. Powell 1969: 211; Collier 1971, 1975; Maruska 1972; Rodríguez et al. 1972; Dietz 1973, 1974; Michl 1973. Squatters in other Latin American countries appear to place a relatively lower valuation on self-help efforts than the Peruvian *pobladores*. See Lutz 1970: 156–58 (Ecuador); Ray 1969: 85 (Venezuela). Cf. Karst et al. 1973: 50–51, 76–77.

viewed by the migrant poor as requiring governmental action is partly
a function of the presence or absence of overt governmental attempts
to create feelings of dependence among the lower classes. Where official incentives for self-help have been weak or lacking altogether, as
in Mexico, the range of politicized needs will be broader. However, the
conversion of diffuse claims on the government into specific demands
communicated to public officials will be impeded by an emphasis on
paternalism and dependence in the government's relationship with the
poor.

The responsiveness of the political system to petitioning by the poor
may also condition their attitudes toward reliance on government aid.
In countries where competitive party systems have induced incumbent
governments to be more responsive to petitions from low-income urban
communities, as in Chile since the early 1960's and Venezuela since 1958,
the urban poor have devoted most of their energies to petitioning rather
than self-help efforts (see Huntington & Nelson 1973: 5.33). In Mexico
the PRI has encountered little competition for the votes of low-income
city dwellers from opposition parties, but the regime's emphasis on
building support among the poor has nevertheless ensured a relatively
high level of responsiveness to petitioning by the *colonias proletarias*,
at least in Mexico City.

Perception of Channels for Demand-Making

Whether politicized needs will be translated into actual demands on
the government often depends on the ability of the potential demand-
maker to perceive an adequate channel for influencing government decisions. Though migrants to the city may take it upon themselves to
contact government officials and present requests for aid as individuals,
most data from Latin American cities (including my own) indicate that
the overwhelming majority of migrants' contacts with officials are made
by delegations of residents from particular communities. Since demand-
making groups are typically recruited from the members of existing
community-improvement associations and are led by officers of these
associations, the importance of such organizations and their leaders in
demand-making among the migrant population becomes obvious. If no
leadership or organizational resources are available to the migrant, he
will be much less likely to involve himself in any form of political demand-making.

Numerous studies of political participation in both developing and
developed nations have demonstrated that citizens who are involved in
any type of formal voluntary organization participate in politics more

frequently than those who are not so involved.[7] These studies have also shown that organizational involvement may lead to increased political participation even when the person involved lacks other attributes conducive to political activity (e.g. high socioeconomic status, sense of political efficacy, or high level of political information). Moreover, data from studies of low-income communities in Santiago, Chile, and Lima, Peru, indicate that members of community-improvement organizations in these cities are considerably more likely to engage in political demand-making than are their uninvolved neighbors (McKenney 1969: 184; Goldrich 1970: 192; Pratt 1971a: 536–37). Among the migrants in my Mexico City sample, those who had participated in local improvement organizations were *five times* more likely than the nonparticipants to have engaged in demand-making.

Community-improvement organizations provide important psychological support for the low-income migrant who wants something from the government. Participation in collective demand-making efforts requires much less individual initiative, and it provides the potential demand-maker with a clear strategy for influencing government decisions. Moreover, to the extent that community-based organizations are successful in securing benefits through collective demand-making efforts, they strengthen the migrant's perception of the political system as being subject to manipulation and thus increase his sense of political efficacy. He is then all the more likely to engage in future demand-making.

Participation in collective demand-making channeled through community organizations, however, may not increase a migrant's confidence in dealing with government officials as an individual. Community-improvement organizations in low-income urban neighborhoods seem to affect the attitudes of their members in much the same way that certain types of peasant unions do in rural areas:

The syndicate is something concretely visible and understandable to peasants. No ability to imagine oneself individually trying to influence national government is required for a sense of efficacy. A peasant need only learn that the syndicate exists as broker between himself and the government—and this lesson is learned by observing and especially by participating in the brokerage activities of the union. . . . Consequently, if the union is adept at brokerage . . . there is a greater likelihood that its members will be taught that they are, in fact, efficacious. (Mathiason & Powell 1972: 327)

This helps to explain why so few of the migrants in the research communities who have engaged in collective demand-making efforts have

[7] See Almond & Verba 1963: 262–65; Erbe 1964: 198; Nie et al. 1969: 813; Form & Huber 1971: 688; Verba & Nie 1972: 174–208; Burstein 1972: 1087; Ambrecht & Pachon 1973: 22; Ross 1973a: 19.

also attempted to contact government officials individually (see pp. 180–81). Individual demand-making with a particularistic objective apparently requires a different set of perceptions of the political system and one's own competence to influence its outputs—perceptions that are not necessarily fostered by collective demand-making experiences.

Political Demands

In most countries for which reasonably comparable data are available (see Table 7.4), demand-making appears to be a relatively uncommon form of political participation among the general population. Even in the United States, only about a third of the population report that they have contacted a government official at least once. Among my sample of migrants in Mexico City, about one out of four had contacted an

TABLE 7.4
*Frequency of Citizen-Initiated Contact
with Government Officials*

Country, Sample Composition and Data Source	Frequency of Contact[a]
MEXICO	
Lower-class, male, migrant heads of families in six low-income neighborhoods of Mexico City (my data in the present study)	25.8%
Lower-class adult residents in the city of Jalapa (Fagen & Tuohy 1972: 89)	20.0
Male household heads in four rural communities, state of Michoacán (Arterton 1974)	17.0
PERU	
Lower-class, male, migrant heads of families in four squatter settlements in Lima (Dietz 1974)	32.3
Lower-class male household heads in Lima (McKenney 1969: 181)	5.9
CHILE	
Lower-class male household heads in Santiago (McKenney 1969: 181)	11.1
BRAZIL	
Lower-class male residents of squatter settlements in Rio de Janeiro (Perlman 1971: 317)	42.0
UNITED STATES	
National sample of adult population (Verba & Nie 1972: 106)	33.0
Registered voters in New Haven, Conn. (Dahl 1961: 279)	27.0
Adult residents of Nashville, Tenn. (Graham & Pride 1971: 41)	27.5
Adult residents of five low-income urban neighborhoods in several cities (Curt Lamb, as cited in Perlman 1971: 316)	12.0
INDIA	
National sample of adult population (Field 1973: 355A)	20.0

[a] Percent who have contacted a government official on more than one occasion.

TABLE 7.5

Subject Matter of Migrants' Contacts with Government Officials

Subject	Percent	Subject	Percent
Security of land tenure	64.6%	Public transportation	1.0%
Water supply	11.4	Public sewage system	0.9
Postal service	4.1	Garbage collection	0.9
Paving of streets	2.8	Other community-related	
Electricity	2.2	problems	7.8
Schools, teachers	1.2	Personal or family-related	
		problems	3.1

NOTE: $N = 112$. "Don't know" and "no response" cases are excluded.

official on at least one occasion.[8] The incidence of demand-making activity varied considerably from one research community to another—from 45 percent in Colonia Nueva to 10 percent in Colonia Texcoco. These differences can be attributed partly to the nature of developmental problems that each community had confronted (e.g., demand-making was more frequent among migrants residing in squatter settlements like Colonia Nueva, as a result of the extended negotiations needed to secure government recognition of tenure rights); but differences in community leadership and organizational structure appear to be equally important determinants of demand-making propensities among the residents (see Chapter 6).

When migrants contact government officials, what is the substantive content of their demands? The relevant data for the Mexico City sample are presented in Table 7.5. Nearly two-thirds of the reported contacts with officials were concerned with the need for security of tenure. In the period immediately following a land invasion, demands relating to this need are essentially defensive in nature—i.e. simple requests that the settlers be permitted to remain on the land without fear of eviction by the government. Subsequently, tenure-related demands take the form of petitions for regularization of the community and the granting of legal land titles to its residents. Petitions relating to other kinds of community needs accounted for most of the remaining demand-making attempts reported by my respondents.

In their study of a national sample of the United States population, Verba and Nie (1972: 67) found that about one-third of all citizen-initiated contacts with government officials were concerned with the par-

[8] Because of the wording of the relevant survey questions (Items 136b, 136c, 137e, 176a), all of these reported contacts with officials involved a personal visit to the office of some functionary of the government or the PRI. Thus the data do not reflect contacts through letters or through petitions signed by the respondent but presented by others.

ticularistic problems of an individual demand-maker or his family; the remaining two-thirds had a broader social referent. By contrast, only about 3 percent of the contacts with government officials reported by migrants in Mexico City dealt with personal or family-related needs.[9] Thus the vast majority of demands upon government emanating from the migrant population are articulated in the name of an entire community and seek to gain nondivisible "public goods" that will benefit all residents of the community. Highly particularistic requests for jobs or other special dispensations benefiting only an individual or his immediate relatives were relatively uncommon among residents of the research communities.

The low frequency of particularistic demand-making reflects not only the urgency with which a migrant views such community-related problems as insecure land tenure or an inadequate water supply, but also his perceptions of what types of needs are most susceptible to satisfaction through governmental action. Perhaps the most important reason that individual needs for housing or employment are seldom expressed through demand-making is that a migrant usually views the satisfaction of such needs as an *individual* responsibility.[10] Alternatively, even when a problem is urgent (as when the migrant is out of work), seeking government assistance may not be viewed as an effective way to deal with it, either because of the complexities and delays involved in obtaining government help or perhaps because of the government's typically low responsiveness to individual petitions. By contrast, securing tenure rights and obtaining access to basic urban services are not viewed as being susceptible to "individual" solution. Even the most affluent residents of illegally formed communities in Mexico City have found it impossible to acquire title to their land through individual negotiations with gov-

[9] Among the reported contacts with PRI functionaries, about 13 percent had a particularistic (personal or family) referent; but contacts with PRI officials represented only 9 percent of the total number of demand-making attempts.

[10] Fagen and Tuohy (1972: 142–43) found a similar situation among residents of the city of Jalapa: "The major source of personal difficulties—the economic situation, and specifically the matter of jobs—is still widely perceived in the first instance as a private or individual domain. Individual mobility in the context of aggregate national growth is seen as the mechanism through which economic conditions will be ameliorated. A sense of personal blame and responsibility thus colors perspectives on these problems. . . . Despite substantial diffuse reliance on government, economics has not been connected with politics in ways that lead the average citizen to seek political redress for economic grievances." Equally particularized perceptions of the problem of unemployment have been observed among residents of squatter settlements in Lima, Peru (Rodríguez et al. 1972: 131). Such perceptions and expectations may help to explain the rarity of collective political action organized around the issue of unemployment among low-income residents of Latin American cities. Cf. Gutkind 1973 and M. Cohen 1974, both writing on African cities in which lower-class collective action has coalesced around unemployment and other broad economic issues.

ernment officials. Security of tenure can be achieved only through a government decision to recognize the tenure rights of all residents of a colonia; and such a decision is almost always the result of collective demand-making attempts by the residents involved.

STRATEGIES OF DEMAND-MAKING

What strategies of demand-making are likely to be employed by low-income migrants? To help identify my respondents' preferences, I presented them with a hypothetical situation (Item 176j): "Suppose a group of people in this city strongly feels that the government is treating them unfairly. I'm going to read a list of some of the things these people might do to try to get the government to change the situation. Which do you think would be the most effective way?" The responses (Table 7.6) showed a very marked preference for working through conventional bureaucratic channels (specifically, by sending a representative or a delegation to talk with a government official). My investigation of past and current demand-making efforts by residents of the research communities had already revealed that they often sought to circumvent regular bureaucratic processes by cultivating personal ties with key officials, so this tactic was also specified as an alternative in the survey question. About one in four of the respondents endorsed it (as "working through personal connections with government officials"). Much smaller proportions of respondents favored working through the PRI, organizing a protest demonstration, or trying to mobilize other citizens through public meetings or rallies.

Parties as Demand Articulators

Working with party politicians in order to influence the government bureaucracy is a common strategy among the poor in some Latin Amer-

TABLE 7.6
Migrants' Preferred Strategies for Demand-Making

Strategy	Percent
Sending a representative or delegation to a government office	47.9%
Working through personal connections with government officials	25.2
Working through the PRI	11.5
Organizing a protest demonstration	9.5
Organizing public meetings or rallies to get other people interested in the problem	5.8

NOTE: $N = 545$. "Don't know" and "no response" cases are excluded.

ican cities, primarily those in which there are competitive multiparty systems.[11] In Mexico, however, neither the PRI nor any opposition party is viewed by the urban poor as an important vehicle for demand-making, especially when the matter at issue is a community problem. It is not difficult to understand why working with opposition parties is considered a waste of time. These parties are known to have no resources of their own to distribute to low-income neighborhoods. Moreover, their electoral weakness vis-à-vis the PRI insures that they will have no chance of gaining control of the government agencies that do allocate resources. The reasons why the PRI itself is not viewed as an effective vehicle for interest articulation are more complex.

Despite the absence of any real threat to the PRI's hegemony, the Mexican regime continues to place a high premium on maintaining and even increasing the official party's already overwhelming margin of support at the polls. Nevertheless, residents of low-income communities often find it difficult or impossible to take advantage of this emphasis on voter mobilization. Most *colonias proletarias* in Mexican cities are relatively small, at least by comparison with low-income communities in other Latin American cities, and hence cannot deliver a substantial bloc of votes to the PRI. Moreover, the boundaries of electoral districts are rarely coterminous with the boundaries of specific colonias; as a result, electoral statistics do not reflect the loyalty or disloyalty of a given colonia. In short, *colonias proletarias* typically have little or no bargaining power in terms of granting or withholding electoral support from the regime.

In some provincial Mexican cities, the PRI has been observed to act as "a decentralized clearinghouse through which [lower-class] demands can be articulated and, at times, attended to" (Fagen & Tuohy 1972: 31. Cf. Ugalde 1970: 139–49; Ugalde et al. 1974). There is, however, considerable variation in the performance of this function from city to city, and even within single cities. For example, in the Ciudad Netzahualcóyotl section of the Mexico City metropolitan area, community-improvement organizations are tied administratively to the local PRI structure, and they direct their petitions to the party office. Where such direct ties do not exist, demand-making is not usually filtered through the PRI. In general, working exclusively through PRI functionaries is viewed by the urban poor as a highly indirect strategy. They believe that better

[11] See Peattie 1968: 67–70 (Ciudad Guayana, Venezuela); Ray 1969: 98–127 (various Venezuelan cities); E. Leeds 1972: 24–29 and Epstein 1973: 113, 130–31 (both on Brazilian cities prior to the military coup of 1964); S. Powell 1969: 194–95 and Uzzell 1972: 240 (both on Lima, Peru, before the military coup of 1968); Pratt 1971b: 509–10 (Santiago, Chile).

results can be achieved through direct contacts with government offi-cials, and turn to PRI functionaries only when their negotiations with government officials have failed. Such tactics reveal a highly realistic perception of the locus of decisional authority in the Mexican political system: government bureaucrats rather than party politicians are the men who control the allocation of the resources most needed for meet-ing community needs.[12]

The PRI, mainly through its "popular sector," provides a limited amount of patronage for individual residents of low-income neighbor-hoods. It may, for example, provide medical care, assist in obtaining a license or permit for commercial activity, or help one to find a low-level job in the public sector. But as I have already noted, demand-making with an individualized referent is very infrequent among the people in-cluded in this study, regardless of the type of official (PRI or govern-ment) toward which it is directed.

The Politics of Protest

The low preference of migrants in the research communities for pro-test demonstrations as a strategy for demand-making is particularly sig-nificant, given the extensive literature that views cityward migrants as having a high potential for protest behavior (see Nelson 1969, Cornelius 1969 and 1971, and White 1973 for reviews of the literature). In re-sponse to another survey question (Item 145), almost half of the mi-grants in my sample expressed the belief that it would be wrong for a man to join in a protest march or demonstration "to get public officials to correct an unjust situation." By a margin of 59 percent to 15 percent (with 26 percent expressing no opinion), they also condemned the pro-test activities of the students who had demonstrated against government violations of university autonomy (among other things) in Mexico City during the summer and fall of 1968 (Item 129e). Not surprisingly, the migrants' personal involvement in overt protest activities had been quite low. Only 3 percent had ever gone with a group of people to protest or complain to a public official about some problem, and only about 2 per-cent of the migrants had ever participated in a protest meeting or dem-onstration (Items 176o, 176p). The handful of actual demonstrators had themselves been students involved in the antigovernment movement of 1968. In my interviews with community leaders, several expressed the

[12] Drawing primarily on research conducted in the provincial city of Jalapa, Tuohy (1969: 8–9) concluded: "Only persons and organizations which lack adequate po-litical resources articulate demands to and through the Party. And since it is not a major decision-maker, those articulators can only hope for the party's services as a broker or intermediary connected with the government." See also Schers 1972: 68.

view that if some need of their community were particularly acute, and if the government had ignored community petitions, they would try to organize a demonstration outside the office of some high-ranking government functionary; but no leader was able to recall an instance in which he had actually taken this kind of action.

Even in the context of conventional petitioning activity, communications to officials by residents of the research communities were never worded as antigovernment protests, complaints, or expressions of anger at being unjustly deprived of some particular service or government benefit. Petitions like the one reproduced in Chapter 6 may protest against the misdeeds of local leaders or condemn unspecified "minor officials" who fail to do the bidding of their superiors, but the superiors themselves are never criticized. In general, both the written petitions and the language used in presenting them to government officials—an act I was able to observe on several occasions—are filled with expressions of deference toward authority and hope that the benefits being sought will be granted as a "special favor" to residents of the community.[13]

The migrant's deferential, nonthreatening approach to negotiating with public officials, as well as his avoidance of protest tactics in general, can be viewed as a reflection of his commitment to abide by the political rules of the game in the Mexican system. Violent or clearly illegal forms of political action are never considered as a means of bringing pressure to bear on the authorities because they would be a fundamental violation of these rules. Participation in a land invasion is usually the only instance in which a migrant may be willing to deliberately contravene social and political norms. And since land invasions in Mexico City are often carried out with the covert support of politicians or officials, it is unlikely that they are even construed by many of the participants as a form of antisystem political action.[14]

The migrant's low tolerance for the risks and uncertainties of unconventional political action also reflects his perception of what kinds of demand-making strategies are most effective in gaining tangible ben-

[13] The reluctance of residents of low-income neighborhoods to formally protest or complain about deficiencies in public services is strikingly reflected in a recent compilation of data on citizens' complaints received by the city government and Mexico City newspapers and television stations (*El Día*, 8 July 1973: 13). During the period from January through June, 1973, more than 61 percent of the complaints received were concerned with trash collection—a problem viewed with very little urgency in most low-income neighborhoods. More than three-quarters of all complaints came from people residing in predominantly upper- or middle-income areas.

[14] Government officials and politicians have also figured prominently in land invasions occurring in Santiago (Chile), Lima, and several Venezuelan cities. See Vanderschueren 1973: 267–68; Collier 1971, 1974; Ray 1969: 33–37, 42–43.

efits for himself and his community. He sees little or nothing to be gained by offending the authorities through protest activities, and perhaps a great deal to lose. Examples of both the futility and the potential costs of protest demonstrations abound in recent Mexican history. In the countryside, open protest by peasants has been systematically and often ruthlessly suppressed. And the 1968 student demonstrations in Mexico City were violently put down by police and military forces; at least 300 persons were killed, and the students accused of organizing the protests were sentenced to 15 to 20 years in prison. Most of those jailed were released in 1971, but the government had made its point. More lives were lost in June 1971, when a group of high-level government and PRI officials sponsored an attack by a terrorist street gang on student demonstrators in the capital. And since 1968 perhaps a dozen more student protesters have been killed by riot police in Puebla, Culiacán, and other provincial cities.[15] These events have greatly increased the people's awareness of the formidable coercive apparatus that can be activated by the government in response to overt protest. As in some U.S. cities where protest has elicited a violent response from the authorities, poor people are more likely than ever to rely upon less aggressive strategies of political demand-making.[16]

From the standpoint of the community leaders who actually organize demand-making efforts, protest strategies are risky and unproductive because they may damage the leaders' own clientage relationships with public officials. Overt protest actions in effect threaten the reputation of an official as a "capable manager," and hence his prospects for future advancement (cf. Fagen & Tuohy 1972: 71). When confronted with such a threat, he is far more likely to respond with retaliatory measures than with positive action aimed at meeting the protesters' demands. And the leaders of the offending community will henceforth be regarded as troublemakers who should be refused further patronage.

The need for caution is compounded by the vagueness of the distinction made by many public officials [in Mexico] between legitimate articulation [of demands] and personal or political attack. . . . There is a tendency, still present but diminishing with the increasing competence of government leaders, to regard all criticism as destructive. (Tuohy 1973b: 277)

---

[15] In a recent analysis of historical trends in the use of violence as a repressive tool by Mexican authorities, Evelyn P. Stevens (1974: Chap. 9) notes that such practices are still fairly common at the local level in rural areas, and even at the level of state governments in some parts of the country. The use of small-scale violence against peasants in rural areas is discussed further in Cockcroft 1972: 254; cf. Fagen & Tuohy 1972: 27.

[16] See Eisinger 1973: 27. Fear of physical and economic coercion has also depressed political participation among minority groups in the U.S. South. See the empirical analysis reported in Salamon & Van Evera 1973.

In short, overt protest actions are unlikely to be rewarded by the Mexican system, and this political truth is widely known among the poor.

Finally, the attractiveness of protest tactics to the urban poor is diminished by the demonstrated efficacy of conventional demand-making strategies in securing at least some community improvements. In Mexico City, the authorities have worked diligently to cultivate a popular image of accessibility and responsiveness to lower-class needs—though their responses often take the form of symbolic reassurances (e.g. making inspection tours or committing the problem at hand to technical study) rather than allocations of material benefits. Petitioners from low-income neighborhoods are seldom refused access to lower or middle-echelon government officials; and almost all of those who have visited a government or PRI office report that they were treated courteously and fairly by the officials they approached (see Chapter 8). Furthermore, over two-thirds of the migrants in my sample who had participated in demand-making believed that their contacts with officials had been successful, in the sense of having contributed to the solution of some community problem. Table 7.7 summarizes the outcomes of demand-making attempts by the residents of the research communities since settlement of the communities began, as reported in my interviews with community leaders. These leaders tended to depict *any* benefit received by their community as a result of demand-making (organized by themselves) rather than governmental initiative. However, subsequent interviews with the relevant government decision-makers confirmed that most of the benefits reported by community leaders would not have been provided in the absence of persistent petitioning by the communities.[17]

Even the residents of communities whose petitions for recognition of tenure rights or urban improvements have not yet elicited positive responses from the government are aware of nearby communities that have been so favored. These examples foster a perception of the political opportunity structure as being relatively open, and thus discourage protest tactics. Residents of *colonias proletarias* are thus likely to feel that by working together they can influence at least some of the government

[17] One might suspect that the research communities have benefited from an atypically high level of governmental responsiveness. However, most of the benefits they received were the result of persistent petitioning, often extending over five to ten years. And many serious needs of the communities have gone unmet. Even today, functioning sewage systems, schools, public markets, and health-care facilities are inadequate or nonexistent in three of the six communities. In some cases these unmet needs reflect an absence or suspension of demand-making efforts by residents of the community; in others, a lack of skill or commitment among community leaders has led to unproductive negotiations with the authorities. Still other unmet needs reflect a sheer lack of responsiveness by particular government officials.

TABLE 7.7
Outcomes of Demand-Making Efforts, by Community

COLONIA NUEVA	COLONIA PERIFÉRICO	COLONIA TEXCOCO
Destruction of stone wall erected by former landowner to restrict access to land	Introduction of regular bus service	Installation of provisional electric service
Rebuilding of houses destroyed by fire	Installation of temporary water system	Construction of secondary school
Government expropriation of land occupied by community (first step toward regularization)	Construction of primary school	Installation of temporary water system
Construction of primary school	Installation of regular electric service and streetlights	Construction of child-care center
Installation of regular electric service and streetlights	Paving of main street	**COLONIA MILITAR**
Piped water for individual dwellings	Installation of one public telephone	Government recognition of tenure rights
COLONIA E. PROPIO	Government expropriation of land	Installation of regular electric service and streetlights
None; water, sewerage, electricity and other services and improvements all installed at government initiative	**UNIDAD POPULAR**	Installation of sewage system
	Installation of water purification plant	Installation of piped water for individual homes
	Postponement of property tax payments	Construction of primary school
	Construction of two primary schools, one secondary school	Paving of streets
	Installation of several public phones	Installation of public and private telephones
	Some streets paved	

decisions affecting the development of their community; and most believe that they can do so through conventional bureaucratic channels. If a community's petitions are consistently denied by the government, and if deeply felt needs seem likely to remain unsatisfied in the foreseeable future, an individual resident is far more likely to respond to the situation by moving to another community with better prospects than by engaging in some form of protest activity.[18]

Conventional Demand-Making Strategies

The most commonly used strategy among the poor in Mexico City is that of forming a committee or delegation of community residents to visit the office of an official and present a formal request for assistance.

[18] Of course, numerous factors beyond governmental neglect may contribute to a decision to abandon a community suffering from insecurity of tenure or service deprivation. Useful conceptualizations of the decision-making process leading to intra-

What kinds of officials are the primary targets of such petitioning? In nearly half of the demand-making attempts reported by my sample of migrants, some high-ranking official within the Department of the Federal District (D.D.F.) had been contacted. Another 31 percent of the attempts had been directed toward the head of the Office of Colonias, an appendage of the D.D.F. that had special responsibility for the land tenure problems of low-income neighborhoods. Only 9 percent of the reported contacts with officials involved a PRI functionary, and only 6 percent involved a *delegado* (a lower-echelon D.D.F. official who is nominally responsible for all residential zones within a given political subdivision of the Federal District).

This choice of targets for demands shows an accurate understanding of the highly centralized nature of government decision-making in Mexico. In attempting to influence its outcomes, "both efficiency and security argue that it is wise to seek support and decisions as close to the center as possible lest time be wasted with those who don't count and whose decisions may subsequently be overturned."[19] Thus residents of a community seeking a water system may send copies of their petition to a delegado, to the head of the city's water department, and to other middle-echelon officials; but they will seek to negotiate directly with the Governor of the Federal District or one of his closest deputies. Direct approaches are also made occasionally to the President during his inspection tours in various parts of the city, as well as to the First Lady and top-level presidential aides; and copies of all major community petitions are routinely sent to the office of the President. Of course, access to officials with personal political power and decisional autonomy is more difficult to obtain; yet the potential rewards flowing from contacts with them are likely to be far more substantial and immediate than any benefits provided by subordinates.

In presenting a request for government assistance, community leaders take pains to emphasize the willingness of the residents to pay for any services extended to them ("We don't want you to 'give' us anything . . ."). Since residents of low-income communities in Mexico City are usually required to repay most or all of the cost of installing basic urban services and improvements (normally through individual assessments, to be paid over five to ten years), evidence of successful fund-

---

city residential mobility among the poor in Lima and Rio de Janeiro are provided in Uzzell 1974 and A. Leeds 1974. Much of these writers' analysis seems applicable to the migrant poor in Mexico City. See also Ward 1975.

[19] Fagen & Tuohy 1972: 23. For more detailed discussions of the mechanisms and consequences of political centralism in Mexico, see Tuohy 1973b; Furlong 1972; Purcell & Purcell 1973b.

A local government official discusses Colonia Texcoco's most recent petition for a sewage system and announces an inspection tour by the state governor.

raising campaigns to finance past improvements may be presented to demonstrate the community's credit-worthiness. Offers of free labor to help in the installation of improvements are also made routinely. Occasionally, gifts or outright cash bribes are presented to an official. For example, in Colonia Nueva an otherwise unemployed resident was regularly "commissioned" by community leaders to paint landscapes for presentation to government officials with whom they were negotiating.

If these and other inducements fail to produce the desired results, the demand-makers may attempt to exert indirect pressure on the government by publicizing their needs. One major newspaper in Mexico City maintains a section for "complaints and petitions" by residents of predominantly low-income neighborhoods; and delegations of residents from such communities often visit the paper's offices to present copies of their petitions or to request news coverage of the situation in their community. The resulting stories may be embarrassing to unresponsive bureaucrats. Another indirect tactic, less frequently used, involves asking PRI functionaries or congressmen to intercede with the government officials responsible for acting on community petitions.

Negotiations for the official recognition of tenure rights and the installation of basic urban services are usually quite complex and require frequent action by the demand-makers over a long period of time. A government decision to "regularize" an illegally formed community must be followed by several other administrative acts before individual tenure can be considered secure: expropriation of the land, if it was privately owned before it was invaded or illegally subdivided; completion of technical studies to determine the feasibility of installing certain types of services and improvements; a census of current residents in the community; surveying and subdivision of the land into parcels assigned to individual residents; and a determination of land prices, service assessments, and terms of payment. At any of these stages, serious difficulties and delays may develop; hence the necessity for numerous follow-up visits to officials, both to check on the processing of the community's petitions and to cultivate personal ties.

During this follow-up period, the demand-makers take every possible opportunity to renew their claims. Officials making inspection tours, PRI social workers, or politicians on electoral campaign visits may be confronted by a delegation that reminds them of pending petitions. A disaster of some sort—particularly on a scale sufficient to warrant coverage by the mass media—provides additional opportunities to dramatize the community's plight and put pressure on the authorities. For example, a fire set by the original owner of the land occupied by Colonia Nueva squatters, which caused seven deaths, greatly facilitated that community's negotiations for official recognition of tenure rights.

The competition for government attention among many communities whose needs are equally acute is often fierce, but persistence and skill in negotiating with officials can often make a great difference, particularly when the allocation of government benefits is not governed by systematized developmental or planning criteria. In Mexico City there have been no clear administrative guidelines for determining which low-income neighborhoods will receive which services and improvements, and when (see Bataillon & Rivière d'Arc 1973: 99–104; R. Fried 1972: 680; cf. Fagen & Tuohy 1972: 28–29). In fact, the idea of comprehensive physical planning, even as an eventual goal, was discarded shortly after World War II and never revived. Nor has there ever been a single government office with responsibility for overall planning and resource allocation in low-income areas of the capital. Instead, many separate agencies, as well as individual politicians and bureaucrats, act—or claim to act—on behalf of the *colonias proletarias*.[20]

_____

[20] As Schers (1972: 71–72) has noted, PRI functionaries are aware that neighborhood leaders "know very well how to make use of this situation [to] 'get things

These conditions are clearly reflected in the highly erratic responses of officials to petitions from low-income neighborhoods. Official behavior toward such communities has fluctuated sharply between overt hostility and benevolent permissiveness as top-level personnel changes have occurred in the city and State of México governments. Stubborn refusals to urbanize a squatter settlement on technical grounds (e.g., that topography or subsoil conditions would make the introduction of basic services prohibitively expensive) have sometimes given way virtually overnight to a decision to provide all necessary services.

Although they afford certain opportunities to lower-class petitioners, the absence of formally established criteria for evaluating needs and the multiplicity of access points within the government bureaucracy may create other kinds of obstacles, especially for communities whose leaders have failed to develop connections with high-ranking officials. The particularism of bureaucratic behavior "makes it hard for the [petitioner] to get a firm commitment on the part of any agency. He may even find it hard to find out what agency policy is, because agency policy may not exist; it may be that various bureaucrats each have their own mutually conflicting policies. . . . In such a system, it is quite true that an agreement with one official one day does not commit the agency" (Peattie 1968: 89).

A CASE STUDY: THE "REGULARIZATION" OF COLONIA MILITAR

The dynamics of the demand-making process, as well as some of the major factors affecting the outcomes of demand-making attempts, are well illustrated by the experience of Colonia Militar in securing official recognition of land tenure rights. The land occupied by this community had formerly been the site of a commercial sandpit. After the mineral deposits were exhausted, the land was sold to the National Defense Ministry, which intended to develop it as an extension of a nearby military base. But this plan was never carried out, and control of the land reverted to the Ministry of National Patrimony, an agency responsible for federal land use.

The availability of undeveloped land for settlement attracted the attention of one Major Rodríguez, a young officer stationed at the adjacent military base, and early in 1952 he began organizing a group of fellow officers and enlisted men to invade the land. This group was soon ex-

done.' " Other observers have also documented the advantages offered to petitioners from low-income neighborhoods in Lima and Guatemala City by ambiguities in the jurisdictions of various government officials and agencies. See Dietz 1973; Uzzell 1973; B. Roberts 1974: 230.

panded to take in civilian relatives and other interested parties, including a number of schoolteachers, policemen, and white-collar workers. However, the bulk of the invasion group consisted of low-income families, most of whom had migrated to Mexico City from rural areas and at that time occupied rented housing in other parts of the city. The prospective squatters met frequently over a two-year period to plot a strategy for occupying the land "discovered" by Major Rodríguez; and each of them purchased from him a legally meaningless "permit" to occupy a lot in the settlement-to-be.

From the outset of the invasion, in June 1954, the leaders of Colonia Militar sought to imbue it with an image of permanence and orderliness. "We didn't want to create problems for the government," recalled one of the original settlers, "or give them an excuse to run us off the land." Through the device of the land-occupancy permits, access to the settlement was carefully restricted during the organization of the invasion group and after the invasion. The leaders sought to exclude "undesirables," whom they defined as either persons with criminal records or persons lacking the income to build a permanent house within a relatively short period of time. This selective recruitment was also helpful in providing technical skills to assist in community development. Among those who received permits were an engineer who later supervised the layout of streets and individual lots and a doctor who advised the settlers on methods of waste disposal and other public sanitation measures.

Much attention was devoted to self-help development during the five years following the invasion. Heavy machinery was brought in by the military officers to level off the land and grade streets. Since shacks made of *lámina de cartón* or other temporary materials were discouraged by community leaders, construction of brick or cement-block dwellings began almost immediately. Septic tanks were installed. Residents provided both labor and money for the construction of a primary school, a church, and a small public park. They also contributed 300 pesos per family to finance the installation of a regular electrical system. Streets and vacant lots were kept free of rubbish. Taverns, houses of prostitution, and other "centers of vice" were barred. Although many of these projects and regulations improved living conditions for the settlers, they were also intended to provide government officials with evidence of the community's potential for subsequent development.

No immediate eviction attempts followed the formation of Colonia Militar, probably because the invasion site was undeveloped federal land rather than privately held property. Significant threats to the survival of the community remained, however. It was virtually surrounded by upper-class residential areas, whose inhabitants began to pressure the government to prevent the emergence of a permanent squatter settlement almost literally on their doorsteps. The community's improvement organization, headed by Major Rodríguez, commenced negotiations for the recognition of tenure rights in 1955. Delegations of community residents were dispatched to visit officials in the Ministry of National Patrimony, as well as the Governor of the Federal District, Ernesto P. Uruchurtu. Uruchurtu's hostility toward squatter settlements was widely known and he soon came to be regarded by the residents of Colonia Militar as their principal enemy. Uruchurtu argued that legalization of the community would have to be negotiated with the Ministry of National Patrimony; but he bluntly informed the petitioners that even if these negotiations were successful, he would refuse to extend basic services to the community.

The opposition of Uruchurtu and of officials in the Ministry of National Patrimony was cited by Major Rodríguez and his allies as an insurmountable obstacle to gaining tenure rights. After nearly five years, during which no discernible progress was made, a group of dissatisfied residents began to investigate the situation. It was then discovered that Rodríguez himself had suspended negotiations with the government, covering his tracks with a fraudulent documentation of petitioning activities and with faked reports on the "progress" of the negotiations, which had regularly been delivered at public meetings of the improvement organization.

Rodríguez in fact had every reason to preserve the community's illegal status. While this situation prevailed, he was free to continue selling occupancy permits, which had risen in price from 7 pesos (about 56¢ U.S.) at the time of the invasion to more than 10,000 pesos ($800) by 1960. At a climactic meeting demanded by the dissident residents, Rodríguez was denounced and accused of fraud in representing the community by a government representative who had been summoned to the meeting. He was subsequently convicted of the illegal exploitation of federal property and confined to a military prison for several months. These events led to the creation of a new community organization whose members immediately renewed the negotiations for regularization and government assistance.

In this second round of negotiations, a different set of officials was approached. Since Governor Uruchurtu remained intransigent, allies had to be sought within the Ministry of National Patrimony and other government agencies. The key to developing the necessary connections with these officials was provided by a young schoolteacher residing in the community, Juan Suárez, a youth organizer for the PRI in the Federal District. Sr. Suárez numbered among his personal friends the man who was soon to become federal deputy (Congressman) for the district in which Colonia Militar was located. This friendship was exploited to develop contacts with officials in the Ministry of National Patrimony and with Alfonso Corona del Rosal, the former military man who was then serving as national chairman of the PRI. The interest of Suárez's friend in the problems of Colonia Militar had been ensured in the first place by an offer of the colonia's vocal support for his nomination as a Congressional candidate. "It was politics," lamented one community leader, "but it was necessary."

The new deputy's intervention in these negotiations proved decisive. On several occasions he acted as an intermediary between community residents and government bureaucrats, either directing them to the appropriate officials or accompanying them to government offices to present petitions. Meanwhile, Sr. Suárez himself had become National Youth Director for the PRI, and as such was in an even better position to curry favor with the head of the Party, Corona del Rosal. The advancement of Corona himself was also highly beneficial to the community's fortunes. He soon became head of the Ministry of National Patrimony, which had become the principal target of the community's demand-making attempts. Each week during this period, delegations of community residents visited the Ministry or other government offices to urge action upon their petitions. At the urging of the deputy who had befriended the community, Gustavo Díaz Ordaz visited Colonia Militar during his campaign for the Presidency in 1964. He was presented with petitions for regularization and improvement of the community, and his speech to the assembled residents included a promise of assistance once he assumed office.

A final stroke of good fortune for the community was provided by Díaz Ordaz's dismissal of Governor Uruchurtu in 1966, partly in response to the public furor created by Uruchurtu's bulldozing of a squatter settlement elsewhere in the city. The new governor was Colonia Militar's most important patron, Corona del Rosal. Corona visited the community shortly after taking office, and a presidential decree regularizing the community was issued several weeks later. After regularization was secured, residents continued to negotiate with officials of the Department of the Federal District for the installation of basic services and improvements; but this task was rendered much easier by Corona's apparent willingness to introduce whatever services were needed. Except for a small section extending beyond the Federal District boundary into the

State of México, the complete urbanization of Colonia Militar—including the installation of a sewage system, piped water for individual dwellings, sidewalks, and paved streets—followed within a 15-month period in 1966–67.

The success of Colonia Militar's demand-making efforts can be attributed to a number of factors: selective recruitment of settlers, effective (if belated) leadership, substantial self-help efforts, and excellent connections with high-ranking politicians and government officials. Partly as a result of these advantages, the community was able to forestall government action to remove it. Moreover, its most urgent problems were resolved within a relatively short period of time after serious negotiations were undertaken. It should not be assumed that all the factors mentioned must be present to ensure the success of demand-making attempts by a low-income community; but the experience of communities like Colonia Periférico and Colonia Texcoco, which have pursued the same goals as Colonia Militar with far less success, suggests that where most or all of these factors are lacking, government assistance will not be forthcoming.

In particular, the case of Colonia Militar illustrates the importance of close, highly personalized relationships with key decision-makers. Although the leaders of most low-income communities in the city seek to establish such relationships, they are seldom as successful as the demand-makers of Colonia Militar. And the relationships they established were rendered more productive than usual by the element of chance: Colonia Militar's patrons were advanced to positions of authority directly relevant to the satisfaction of its needs.

ANTICIPATING DEMANDS AND SYSTEM "OVERLOAD"

We have observed that most demands articulated by migrants in the research communities deal with concrete problems very close to the individual's own everyday concerns. But what happens after the most immediate, parochial, and acutely felt needs of migrants for such things as land titles and urban services are satisfied? Should we expect a "spillover" of demand-making into other issue areas of broader social and economic import, such as inflation, unemployment, or inequalities in the country's distribution of wealth?

One prominent student of the urban poor in Asian countries has hypothesized that as economic and social conditions in low-income neighborhoods improve there will be a shift in the role of community-improvement associations "from selfishly particularistic pressure groups to more general welfare-oriented lobbies" (Laquian 1972: 199–200). He notes, however, that this may require "a generation of educated, upwardly mobile slum children" whose concerns extend beyond the developmental problems of their neighborhoods.

The demand-making activity observed among migrants to Mexico City and other major Latin American metropolitan areas lends little support to such expectations. After several decades of large-scale migration to these cities, demand-making by communities populated mostly by low-income migrants or their offspring remains confined to parochial, small-scale needs.[21] Moreover, demand-making tends to fall off sharply within these communities once security of land tenure has been assured and basic urban services have been introduced. In many cases community-improvement organizations are created solely to negotiate for land titles or some other specific benefit. When this purpose is fulfilled, they lose their *raison d'être* and quickly disintegrate (this was, for example, the fate of the successful community-improvement organization in Colonia Militar). Cases of community organizations that start with a narrowly defined function and subsequently evolve into general-purpose lobbying groups are extremely rare.

In assessing the potential impact of cityward migration on demand-making aimed at local and national governments, one must also take into account the limited *scope* of the demand-making activity in which migrants are likely to engage. In Mexico City and other major Latin American cities, attempts to aggregate demands across the various communities in which migrants take up residence are almost nonexistent, as are attempts by such communities to influence the overall content or scale of government policies and programs. For example, communities in Mexico City often negotiate for government recognition of land tenure rights in their own cases but almost never seek to alter general government policies regarding land use or the legalization of squatter settlements. Thus most demand-making by low-income migrants to the city attempts to influence the government decision-making process only on the *output* (policy-implementation) side.[22]

These observations are quite consistent with those of students of the urban poor in the United States, who often stress the difficulties of or-

---

[21] As reported in Chapter 4, the adult sons of migrants to the city have been *less* likely than their parents to engage in political demand-making.

[22] Similarly, John Walton has observed that neighborhood action groups in Cali, Colombia, "have a dismal record in redressing any of the larger problems that prompt their organization" (Portes & Walton 1975: Chap. 4). Lisa R. Peattie reports that in Quito, Ecuador, even a large-scale "land-for-the-poor" movement with adherents drawn from numerous low-income neighborhoods has failed to make any generalized demands on the government (personal communication, 4 May 1973).

ganizing the poor around larger policy issues.[23] Yet there are a few Latin American cases of low-income urban groups that present important exceptions to this general pattern, to the extent that they have addressed themselves from time to time to concerns transcending their immediate, parochial needs for security of tenure and basic services. In urban neighborhoods in Cuba under Castro, residents were organized into Committees for the Defense of the Revolution; and a substantial number of squatter settlements (*campamentos*) in Chilean cities were organized in the early 1970's by members of the extreme-left MIR (Movement of the Revolutionary Left), the MAPU (a party originating from a 1969 split in the Christian Democratic Party), and some elements of the Socialist and Communist parties. Whereas the Cuban committees have often served primarily as instruments of political control or mass mobilization in support of the Castro regime, the squatter organizations in Chile were ostensibly aimed at stimulating demand-making based on perceptions of class interests and class solidarity. They were viewed by their organizers as "instruments of political education" that would stimulate demands for government benefits going far beyond land titles and community services.[24]

During the administration of President Salvador Allende, delegations of residents from the campamentos in Santiago and other Chilean cities carried out numerous *tomas* (temporary seizures or occupations) of government buildings (including ministries), streets, and other public facilities to force officials to receive and act on demands for assistance.[25] Many—perhaps a majority—of these instances of direct action were motivated by the needs of the settlements for water and sewerage, schools, medical facilities, and other local improvements; but other tomas were

[23] See, for example, Hillman & Seever 1970: 284–85; Kramer 1969: 235–37. My research does suggest, however, that the poor in Mexico City possess a greater capability for organizing themselves for demand-making with regard to *community-related* needs and problems than has often been observed among the urban poor in the United States. On the failure of neighborhood-improvement associations established in U.S. cities during the 1960's, see Gove & Costner 1969; O'Brien 1974, 1975.

[24] Detailed descriptions of the Chilean campamentos are provided in E. Petras 1973: 53–89; Vanderschueren 1973: 281–82; Duque & Pastrana 1972; Equipo de Estudios Poblacionales del CIDU 1972a, 1972b; and Castells et al. 1973. The following discussion of demand-making by campamento residents is based primarily on these sources and on supplemental information provided by Richard R. Fagen (personal communications, April–May 1973). For a detailed analysis of demand-making by squatter settlement residents in Santiago during the Frei administration (1965–70), which stresses the nearly total preoccupation of the demand-makers with parochial tenure problems, see Cleaves 1974: Chap. 8. The political organization of low-income neighborhoods in Havana under Castro is described in Butterworth 1974.

[25] In Chile the word "toma" is also used to refer to illegal seizures of land for permanent occupation by urban squatters. These tomas do not represent political demand-making as defined in this chapter, although they may lead to such behavior.

staged to protest high prices, shortages of food and other commodities, and unemployment. Some campamentos in Santiago also organized committees to seek jobs for unemployed residents through conventional approaches to politicians and government bureaucrats. In sum, the organizers of these efforts drew the attention of squatters to a variety of large-scale problems that were manifested concretely at the community level, and encouraged them to view these problems as national in scope, origin, and import.

Perhaps even more important, the Allende regime took a generally permissive stance toward demand-making by the poor, regardless of the subject matter of the demands or the tactics employed in articulating them. Occasionally local authorities retaliated against a toma with tear gas and arrests; but in general this type of demand-making activity was tolerated, and the resulting negotiations between squatters and government officials often produced prompt and acceptable solutions to the problems at issue, or at least to their local manifestations.

The case of Chile under Allende suggests that if migrants and other elements of the urban poor in Latin American cities are to undertake any kind of demand-making beyond that related to immediate, community-specific problems, they will do so only as a result of intensive, sustained mobilization by leaders of political groups external to the low-income communities themselves. Moreover, this mobilization must occur in the context of a national political environment that tolerates aggressive demand-making by low-income groups in many issue areas. Demands concerning nonparochial needs are likely to be made by the urban poor only when they feel that the risk of violent repression by the authorities is minimal and that the likelihood of getting some redress of grievances is quite high. The amount of time and energy involved in petitioning public officials is too great to be squandered on matters that are not regarded by the government as legitimate objects of demand-making by the poor. In the absence of both external mobilization efforts and perceptions of governmental receptivity to nonparochial, "class-based" or cross-community demand-making, the potential for this activity among the migrant poor will remain very low.[26]

The evidence presented above indicates that low-income migrants to

[26] The obstacles to demand-making by low-income migrants based on perceived class interests are legion, but perhaps the most important derive from the extreme occupational heterogeneity of the migrant population and its concentration within the tertiary sector of the urban economy. For discussions of these and other factors inhibiting class-based demand-making by the poor in contemporary Latin American cities, see Goldrich 1965: 368–71; Touraine & Pécaut 1967–68; González Casanova 1968: 76–80; J. Petras 1970: 13–23; Hamburg 1972: 18–19; Huntington & Nelson 1973: 5.21–5.29; A. Leeds 1974.

Mexico City should not be viewed as a "nondemanding" sector of the population, even though the demand-making in which they engage is considerably less frequent than has often been assumed. However, their demands on the political system remain highly parochial and limited in scope. They are the kinds of demands that can be satisfied most easily by incumbent authorities without fundamental changes in government priorities or patterns of resource allocation. A political system in which most demand-making by the poor is confined to seeking satisfaction of community-specific needs is one that tends toward preservation of the basic sociopolitical order:

Pressures which might otherwise take collective form, and be directed to earlier states of policy formation or to the composition of the government itself, are diverted into discrete, separable, and small-scale demands which can be met in full or in part or rejected one by one. . . . Even where the incidence of neighborhood organization is high . . . the sporadic nature of small-scale independent collective action means that only a fraction of all associations are likely to press for assistance at one time.[27]

Rural-urban migration has undoubtedly increased the number of demands made on governments in Mexico and other Latin American countries. But apocalyptic visions of mushrooming popular demands that might overwhelm local or national political systems and generate pressure for major shifts in resource allocation are clearly premature, if not altogether unfounded. Most of the demands on government stemming from the large-scale redistribution of population from rural to urban areas are, regrettably, those that are least likely to threaten the highly inequitable distribution of power and privilege in Mexican society.

[27] Huntington & Nelson 1973: 5.51. Bryan Roberts (1974: 230), on the basis of fieldwork in Guatemala City and Lima, concludes that even though residents of low-income neighborhoods in these cities are often able to take advantage of ambiguities in the urban power structure to obtain needed services, these manipulative strategies "have little lasting impact on the existing structure of power or on the distribution of resources. . . . The major impact of these local-level political activities . . . is that of creating a state of political uncertainty for those who control political and economic resources." See also B. Roberts 1973: 307–37.

CHAPTER EIGHT

Political System Performance

POLITICAL AND governmental activities impinge on the lives of urban citizens in countless ways, many of which are largely imperceptible to those affected. But the migrant poor in Mexico City and elsewhere are often in a better position to perceive the consequences of governmental acts than more affluent city dwellers. The illegal origins of many of the neighborhoods they inhabit, together with the acute service deprivation from which these areas usually suffer when established, lead to frequent contact with governmental agencies whose assistance is needed. Inadequate incomes render the migrants more dependent on government for medical care, education for their children, and other goods and services. Moreover, the government devotes special attention to this sector of the urban population in order to mobilize electoral support or other participation in regime-supportive political activities. This chapter will explore the general hypothesis that the migrants' attitudes toward the political system and their willingness to become politically involved are significantly influenced by system performance.[1]

I shall define political system performance in Mexico City as including outputs of goods and services for individual citizens, administrative actions or sanctions affecting whole neighborhoods, responses to indi-

---

[1] The impact of government outputs on political attitudes and behavior has received little attention in studies of the urban poor in Latin America. As I have argued elsewhere, American political scientists, "in their haste to plunder the sociological and psychological literature in search of concepts and theories to apply in their research . . . have neglected a host of matters involving the operation of the political system itself which bear importantly upon the behavior of urban populations" (Cornelius 1971: 115). With few exceptions (Eldersveld et al. 1968: 97–106; C. J. Lee 1971; Kaufman 1966: 44–100; Kaufman et al. 1973), this criticism can be applied to studies of urban political behavior in most developing countries. Even in the United States, research on the impact of citizen-government contact and governmental outputs on political attitudes and behavior among city-dwellers has been quite limited (Eisinger 1970, 1972; Glassberg 1972; Schuman & Gruenberg 1972).

vidual or communal demands directed at specific officials, and efforts at electoral mobilization by the PRI. No attempt will be made to distinguish between the performance of the government and that of the PRI. There is in fact a considerable overlap in the functions of some governmental agencies and some sectors of the official party with regard to the urban poor; moreover, distinctions between governmental and PRI outputs are often not perceived as important by the low-income population. Neither will I distinguish between the performance of specific levels or agencies of government. All but one of my research communities are located within the jurisdiction of the Department of the Federal District, which is functionally part of the federal government and is headed by an appointed governor who serves in the President's cabinet. For the remaining community, Colonia Texcoco, the relevant agencies are the government of the municipio in which it is located and the government of the State of México. As noted in Chapter 7, most contact with government among residents of the research communities has involved the Department of the Federal District.

After a general survey of the nature and extent of political system outputs relating to the poor in Mexico City, I shall examine the pattern of contacts between the PRI-government apparatus and the research communities. Measures of system performance will then be related to the political attitudes and behavior of community residents. How much and what kind of contact is there between public officials and community residents? What individual and community-related services are received by the residents? Does what the individual gets from the political system affect his perceptions and evaluations of it? Does contact with political and governmental agencies motivate the individual to become more politically involved? And does it lead him to expect more from the system? What kinds of system outputs or contacts with officials are most important in producing these attitudinal and behavioral consequences? These are the principal questions to be addressed in this chapter.

DIMENSIONS OF POLITICAL SYSTEM PERFORMANCE

The Mexican regime tends to concentrate its expenditures, particularly those for social services, in states or cities where it encounters the strongest electoral opposition (see Ames 1970: 167; Hogan 1972: 495); and Mexico City has traditionally been the principal stronghold of the nation's opposition parties. For this and other reasons relating to Mexico's highly centralized patterns of political and economic activity, the capital has enjoyed a grossly disproportionate share of federally funded urban services, education, and other social welfare benefits (Wilkie 1974: 217).[2]

In recent decades the government's stance toward low-income neighborhoods in Mexico City has shifted from one of neglect and occasional repression under the autocratic Federal District Governor Ernesto P. Uruchurtu (1952–66) to one of relative benevolence under Governor Alfonso Corona del Rosal (1966–70) and his successors (see R. Fried 1972: 669). Under Uruchurtu the government sought to discourage further migration to the capital by prohibiting the subdivision of land for low-income housing, acting immediately to evict squatters from invaded land, and denying tenure rights and basic urban services to most existing colonias formed through squatter invasions. Since 1966, restrictions on land for low-income families have been relaxed. Though continuing to resist the formation of new squatter settlements (often half-heartedly), the governors of the Federal District and the State of México have increased official assistance to these and other types of illegally settled colonias within the metropolitan area.[3]

The shift in policy has been particularly evident in the area of land tenure rights. Justifying its actions as an attempt to end land speculation, fraudulent land sales, and other abuses committed by subdividers of land for low-income settlement, the government has increasingly acted to "regularize" low-income zones by expropriating the land and selling it to its occupants at a price well below market value, usually with 5–10 years to pay. In 1971 alone, the government formally "intervened" in this way in 186 *colonias proletarias* within the Federal District. In recent years, several hundred land titles have been distributed each month to residents of newly regularized colonias, and during a 40-month period from 1967 to 1970 more than 20,000 titles were dis-

---

[2] For discussions of the origins and consequences of political centralism in Mexico, see Fagen & Tuohy 1972: Chap. 2; R. Fried 1972: 652ff; Furlong 1972; Tuohy 1973; Purcell & Purcell 1973.

[3] The number of government evictions of squatters has been greatly reduced in recent years. The regime's new (but unstated) policy is reflected in the answer of a high-ranking PRI leader to a question about the Party's response to land invasions in the Federal District: "First, one can call the owner of the land and agree on a reasonable payment by the settlers. Second, if the value of the land is very high, the owner may be asked to give 'compensation' to the settlers so they can make down payments on lots in another area. Finally, INDECO [a federal housing agency] may prepare a survey and offer other solutions to the problem. Actually, this third course generally means a preservation of the status quo. In very few cases are the people driven out." (Schers 1972: 69–70)

tributed. This policy clearly has extraordinary potential for building support among the urban poor, whose major preoccupation is often gaining security of land tenure.

Once official recognition of tenure rights has been granted, the government's stated policy is to assist in a colonia's "urbanization" by introducing regular electric service, streetlighting, water and sewage systems, paved streets, sidewalks, and so on. Residents must eventually repay the cost of these improvements through individual assessments based on lot size, location, and other factors; and they are often asked to donate the manual labor needed to install basic services in their community.

Thus far, the actual commitments of government resources for upgrading *colonias proletarias* in the Mexico City metropolitan area have fallen far short of the needs. In 1968, 83 of 350 colonias included in a government survey were completely lacking in piped water, sewerage, "legal" electricity, street paving, and schools (Instituto Nacional de la Vivienda 1968: 10). In 1970 a technical advisory group affiliated with the PRI estimated that the metropolitan area contained more than 500 recently settled colonias, mostly low-income, that had no basic urban services (*El Día*, 25 Oct. 1970: 9). Later in the same year the Governor of the Federal District admitted that no fewer than half the metropolitan area's population—or about 4.5 million people, at that time—had no access to these services (*El Día*, 24 Dec. 1970: 9; cf. PRI 1970: 137–311, 461–96). The government claims to have introduced piped water and sewage systems in 300 colonias during the 1971–75 period, but perhaps twice that number have remained "unurbanized."

By contrast, urban services are rarely lacking in upper-income neighborhoods, and are sometimes provided to such areas regardless of need (for example, streets may be resurfaced frequently, even if they have not deteriorated). It is this high level of government performance in middle- and upper-class colonias that gives the Federal District such a high ranking on national indexes of urban service and infrastructure development. Within the metropolitan area, in fact, the distribution of many public services is only slightly less unequal than the distribution of personal income. Still, the government has begun to make good its pledges to assist the *colonias proletarias* more actively; and residents of these areas have come to expect greater governmental responsiveness to their petitions for community improvements.

The regime also provides a variety of social welfare services. Most medical care available to the poor in Mexico City is provided by free government clinics or by doctors paid by the PRI. The Party also supplies teachers for makeshift schools in low-income settlements, and sponsors classes in domestic arts, hygiene, nutrition, family planning, first aid, and adult literacy. A federal agency, the Instituto de Protección a la Infancia (INPI), distributes free breakfasts to schoolchildren, operates kindergartens, and provides other kinds of child care. The government-owned Companía Nacional de Subsistencias Populares (CONASUPUO) operates stores in most parts of the city offering food, cooking oil, clothing and shoes, student supplies, medicines, and other essential goods at prices well below those charged by private retailers (see Alisky 1973; Grindle 1975). Since 1969, these stores have been supplemented by temporary, mobile markets (*mercados sobre ruedas*) that give peasants and rural artisans an opportunity to sell their products directly to low-income *capitalinos*, thus eliminating middlemen and price markups. In 1973–74, when retail prices for several of the basic staples in the diet of poor families rose by more than 200 percent, the government began financing the establishment of consumer cooperatives in predominantly low-income sections of the metropolitan area. Seven large social-service centers have also been established in poor areas of the city, offering services ranging from recreational programs to low-cost funerals.

Among the most visible and widely used of the regime's welfare services are those provided during the *"jornadas de mejoramiento ambiental"* conducted each Sunday in various *colonias proletarias* throughout the city. To carry out these highly organized, one-day "health operations," large teams of public-health workers and other skilled personnel provided by various government agencies and PRI organs appear in the colonias, usually invited by local leaders or by lower-echelon officials in whose districts the neighborhoods are situated.[4] In each colonia a speaker's platform and several tents, all prominently bearing the PRI emblem, quickly spring up. Residents are given free medical and dental attention, vaccinations for children, rabies inoculations for dogs, and legal advice. There are talks on drug abuse, alcoholism, personal hygiene, child care, and nutrition. Houses are fumigated to eliminate pests; garbage is collected from streets and vacant lots; and CONASUPO trucks distribute free food, medicine, and ornamental plants. Children get free breakfasts, haircuts, and entertainment by musical and theatrical groups.[5] The government has claimed that such jornadas benefited

[4] Schers (1972: 67) was told by a PRI functionary that a particular colonia had been designated as the site of a jornada because the opposition National Action Party (PAN) had become active in the area. My own impression, based on observation and interviewing done in 1970, is that the site selection is not dictated primarily by electoral concerns. Jornadas seem to represent just another kind of reward periodically dispensed to local political leaders from their patrons higher up.

[5] For a detailed account of a jornada, which closely resembled those I observed

A PRI-sponsored domestic arts class in Colonia Nueva displays its handicrafts in the community meeting hall.

A jornada in Colonia Texcoco. Residents line up at the PRI tents to receive free medical and dental care, haircuts, and gifts of ornamental plants, while being entertained by the musical group at left.

"directly or indirectly" at least 1.5 million residents of the city between May 1967 and July 1968, and another million between December 1970 and August 1972 (*El Día*, 1 July 1968: 12; 25 Aug. 1972: 11).

Still other opportunities for demonstrating the regime's concern for the welfare of the poor are provided by the floods, fires, and other disasters that frequently afflict low-income areas of the city. Both the government of the Federal District and the "Popular Sector" of the PRI have organized efficient disaster-relief teams, much in the style of the big-city political machines of the United States in their heyday.[6] Victims are swiftly provided with food, clothing, and temporary shelter. Like the sporadically conducted jornadas, this kind of crisis-oriented, ambulance-chasing assistance is highly visible and has a deep and lasting impact on the recipients. At the same time, the costs of providing such aid are relatively small, and no commitment to any form of continuing assistance is involved. These qualities make disaster relief highly attractive to the government as a means of building support among the most disadvantaged sectors of the city's population.[7]

---

in several *colonias proletarias* in 1970, see Schers 1972: 82–90. Schers notes (p. 89) that the master of ceremonies "suggested sending a telegram to the President of Mexico expressing the support of the people in this neighborhood, and asking him to 'act with a firm hand' in dealing with the problems of the country. This was 10 days after the bloody events of Corpus Christi day in Mexico City [when a student demonstration was broken up by a paramilitary group organized by high-ranking PRI and government officials opposed to the incumbent President] and five days after the gigantic demonstration [in support of the President] in front of the Presidential Palace. The people agreed enthusiastically. It was hard to say how many really knew what the real issue was."

[6] The similarities between the PRI-government apparatus in Mexican cities and big-city machines in the United States have been noted by numerous observers (see especially Purcell & Purcell 1975a; Ugalde et al. 1974; Eckstein 1973; Needler 1971: 86). Although it is more useful to consider the entire Mexican political system rather than any particular local subsystem as a machine on the classic U.S. model, some important aspects of "machine politics" as practiced specifically in urban Mexico have analogues in U.S. experience. I refer especially to the institutionalized trading of votes and other manifestations of system support for highly particularistic goods, services, and jobs; to a personalistic, opportunistic, and nonideological political style; and to a social base consisting largely of poor people of rural origin. Many consequences of machine politics are also similar in the two cases. In both countries, the "machine" has had the effect of increasing the political fragmentation of the lower class, inhibiting the formation of class-based political organizations and movements, and discouraging far-reaching demands (i.e. demands for goods and services benefiting more than isolated individuals or neighborhoods) on local officials (see Rosenbaum 1973). There are, however, some key differences between the U.S. and Mexican machines in terms of organizational structure and sociopolitical context (see Purcell & Purcell, 1975a).

[7] One can easily envision a PRI functionary mouthing the words of Tammany Hall politician George Washington Plunkitt: "It's philanthropy, but it's politics, too— mighty good politics. Who can tell how many votes one of these fires brings me? The

The regime's preference for low-cost, high-impact assistance to the urban poor is also reflected in the high priority attached to its program of expropriating or otherwise regularizing illegally settled *colonias proletarias* and providing land titles to their inhabitants. The initial expenditures involved in the regularization process may be considerable; but they are soon regained through resident assessments, and the government's long-term income from property taxes paid by the new landholders is substantial.

Regularizing already established squatter settlements and unauthorized subdivisions as a solution to the problem of housing the urban poor has taken precedence in recent years over the construction of conventional low-income housing projects. Although no fewer than 12 different federal and state government agencies operating in the Mexico City metropolitan area continue to build conventional public housing units, they have failed to provide housing for all but an insignificant proportion of the city's poor. In fact, most government-built housing has been occupied by more affluent working-class and white-collar elements, even in housing projects supposedly destined for occupancy by the neediest families (e.g. Unidad Popular). Although corrupt or inefficient administration of the projects since they were completed is partly to blame, the basic problem has been that only the more privileged working-class families with stable incomes can afford such housing. Moreover, the huge capital investment involved in building public housing limits construction to a few thousand dwelling units per year, at a time when the demand for low-cost housing is increasing rapidly because of a 3.5 percent annual rate of natural population increase as well as in-migration from the countryside. In the face of rising demand and resource constraints, the government's rhetorical commitment to providing housing for the poor is being translated increasingly into a policy of providing "secure" land on which low-income families can construct their own dwellings.

PERSONAL CONTACT WITH PUBLIC OFFICIALS

To assess the impact of some of the government policies and programs just discussed on residents of the research communities, survey respondents were asked about their personal experiences with political and governmental agencies, and about the benefits they had received from these agencies. The responses reveal that migrants living in the research

poor are the most grateful people in the world, and, let me tell you, they have more friends in their neighborhoods than the rich have in theirs" (as quoted in Riordan 1963: 28).

communities have come into contact with government and PRI representatives in a variety of ways; but the most important of these, in terms of influencing political attitudes and behavior, are contacts initiated by the migrants themselves, usually for the purpose of demand-making.

As reported in Chapter 7, about one out of four migrants interviewed had contacted a public official at least once, either alone or as one of a group. Almost 90 percent of those who had done so reported that they had received "good" or "very good" treatment from the officials visited, and more than two-thirds believed that the contacts had been beneficial in some way, either to themselves individually or to their community. Most of the remaining respondents did not know whether their contacts with officials had resulted in any specific benefits.

Expectations of favorable treatment from government and PRI officials appear to be held even by those who have never had any contact with these officials. Among this group—representing three-quarters of the total sample of migrants—more than 67 percent believed that they would be treated "well" or "very well" if they had occasion to visit some PRI office to discuss a personal problem or need, and nearly 73 percent expected good treatment from a government office. When asked why they thought many people had never contacted a PRI or government official (Item 176c), a majority of respondents cited ignorance or naiveté—not being aware of opportunities for contact or not knowing which official to contact. Only 27 percent explained citizens' inaction as a result of political cynicism—a belief that contacting officials would do no good or an expectation that citizens would be badly treated by officials. A slightly smaller proportion expressed the belief that those who had not contacted an official had probably had no problem or need about which to complain or petition.

It is questionable whether responses to such an abstract question in a survey interview should be taken at face value. But the responses to many other survey items, as well as many months of informal discussion with residents of the research communities, suggest that residents who lacked faith in the government or PRI would not have hesitated to give a cynical answer to a question about citizens' avoiding contact with officials. The Mexican political culture as a whole is quite supportive of such cynical attitudes (see Almond & Verba 1963: 106–14), and I had expected most responses to the question to reflect them. Thus the low proportion of respondents who mentioned expectations of poor treatment, inability to gain access, or lack of responsiveness is of particular interest.

Direct personal contact initiated by officials themselves appears to be quite limited: only 5 percent of the migrants in my sample reported that they had ever been contacted personally by an official of the government or the PRI. About 7 percent reported that they had been approached individually by a PRI campaign worker, but virtually all these party workers were residents of the communities where the respondents lived.

Substantial numbers of people, however, have been brought into contact with the regime through visits to their communities by government or PRI functionaries. In most cases the visits have involved lower-echelon officials; but Colonia Militar was visited in mid-1964 by the presidential candidate of the official party, as were Colonia Nueva and Colonia Periférico during the electoral campaign of 1970. Well over half the migrants in my sample had witnessed at least one official visit to their current community of residence. Most of these visits were perceived as vote-getting attempts; but 22 percent were viewed as inspection tours by officials seeking to investigate community needs and problems, and 19 percent were reportedly made for the purpose of announcing some government policy or action involving the community. Nearly two out of three respondents were unable to identify any specific consequences of these official visits, but 15 percent viewed the installation of a public service or some other improvement in the community as the direct outcome of such a visit.

Most of the negative contacts with officials reported by migrants in the research communities stemmed from the government's opposition to the land invasions through which three of the six communities had been formed. About 17 percent of the migrants had observed at least one attempt by the government to forcibly remove squatters in their current community of residence; and 5 percent had witnessed a similar incident elsewhere in the city. More than three-quarters of those who had been exposed to any government eviction attempts believed them to have been unjust. But in general this form of negative contact has been sporadic among residents of all six communities; and its impact on attitudes toward the political system has been largely offset by more frequent, positively evaluated contacts with PRI and government officials.

Other data strongly indicate that the most important negative experiences of migrants with "the authorities" result from police behavior. As in urban ghettos in the United States, the conduct of police officers is a prime source of irritation in the *colonias proletarias* of Mexico City. My survey respondents were asked whether they or any members of their families had ever had "some experience with the authorities—that is, with some government office or with the police—that caused you

The ceremony marking the "regularization" of Colonia Nueva in 1970. City officials stand behind the dais while a community representative addresses the assembled residents.

Carlos Hank González, Governor of the State of México, arrives in Colonia Texcoco to inaugurate a new secondary and technical school.

Residents of Colonia Nueva prepare to welcome PRI presidential candidate
Luis Echeverría during the 1970 electoral campaign.

PRI presidential candidate Luis Echeverría addresses the residents of Colonia Periférico
in January 1970. The many placards labeled "CNOP" represent the PRI's major
"Popular Sector" organization. The speaker's platform, hastily erected by the PRI for
the occasion, was torn down immediately after the candidate's departure by
residents seeking building materials.

pain." Nearly 13 percent of the migrants reported such an experience, and virtually all of these involved contacts with the police. In over half of these cases the respondents simply felt that they had been arrested without justification or provocation; other complaints involved police brutality, attempts to extract a bribe while the respondent was being detained for some offense, or failure to act on a complaint that the respondent had attempted to lodge against another individual.

Even migrants who had had no personal encounters with the police felt that people like themselves were systematically preyed upon by local patrolmen, generally with the aim of extracting bribes and payoffs. They tended to view all police as incorrigibly corrupt and arbitrary in their behavior toward poor people, and often charged that those "serving" their areas had been recruited from the ranks of known criminals (who have the financial means to bribe recruiting officers). Such beliefs were shared by most residents of the research communities, but they were strongest in Colonia Texcoco, which is located in a municipio where police corruption and brutality reportedly exist on a scale surpassing even that in the Federal District. It came as no surprise, then, to find that more than 78 percent of the migrants interviewed anticipated only bad treatment in any encounter with the law (Item 176g). When asked to specify what they meant by "bad treatment," most said that they would probably be beaten or otherwise harmed physically if detained by the police.

Given the ubiquity of police abuses in poor neighborhoods of the capital and the deep feelings of resentment that these arouse, one might expect that police misconduct could seriously affect the migrants' perceptions of government officials or authority figures in general—a common finding in studies of the urban poor in the United States (see, for example, Rossi et al. 1974: Chap. 12). But neither the survey data nor my informal interviews, including several conducted with people I knew had been interrogated in local police stations, provided any clear evidence that residents of the research communities held "the government" responsible for abuses of authority by the police. This reluctance to blame the regime seemed to extend to all situations except squatter evictions, which are usually undertaken by riot police who are clearly acting under orders from government officials.

BENEFITS RECEIVED FROM GOVERNMENT

A measure of what migrants in the six research communities have actually received from their government in terms of personal and community-related services is provided by the data in Table 8.1. The substantial commitment of the regime to providing health care for the

TABLE 8.1
Receipt of Public Services by Migrants

Service	Percent (min. $N = 665$)
Personal services received on one or more occasions	
Medical care at government hospital or clinic	79.0%
Medical care in community of residence, from personnel sent by government or PRI	66.8
Benefits (other than medical attention) from Social Security Administration	16.6
Government help in finding employment or housing	28.1
Free legal services from government or PRI	7.0
Food or other goods from CONASUPO store or "market on wheels" (received or purchased)	65.1
Services at government social center	4.0
Assistance from government social worker	7.5
Basic urban services and improvements	
Regular electric service	47.4
Connection with sewage system	30.0
Running water inside house	29.7
Paved street adjoining house	24.8

urban poor is reflected in the high proportion of respondents who report having received such attention in some form. Nearly two-thirds of the migrants had benefited from the government's marketing of low-cost foodstuffs and other commodities through CONASUPO stores or mobile markets. My inquiries about government help in finding employment or housing were asked as a single question; however, virtually all of the 28 percent* who responded affirmatively to this question were residents of the two government housing projects, Colonia Esfuerzo Propio and Unidad Popular, and had received only houses or homesites, not jobs. Much smaller proportions had received other benefits—legal aid, assistance from a government social worker, or disability compensation from the Social Security Administration (but only 44 percent held jobs covered by Social Security).

The government's performance in providing basic urban services and other "collective" benefits has been generally less satisfactory. Less than a third of the migrants interviewed had sewage connections or running water in their homes at the time of the survey, and even fewer homes were located on paved streets. The substantially higher figure for regular electrical service reflects the inordinately high priority given by the government to electrification projects in the *colonias proletarias* of the city. Electrification can be completed with relative speed, it is highly visible, and it costs much less than a water or sewage system. It is also, in most cases, much less needed: the residents of *colonias proletarias* are adept at providing their own power by illegal tapping, and 46 percent of the migrant families in my sample were doing so at the time of the survey.

Government benefits in the form of basic urban services and improvements were distributed very unequally among the communities represented in this study. The proportion of residents with access to *all* the urban services and improvements mentioned in Table 8.1 varied from none in Colonia Nueva and only 37 percent in Colonia Texcoco to 88 percent in Unidad Popular and 95 percent in Colonia Militar. These extreme disparities arose from the varying conditions under which specific communities were formed, as well as from accidents of local leadership and other community-specific factors discussed in previous chapters. All these have influenced the quality of the communities' relationships with political and governmental officials over time.

THE IMPACT OF POLITICAL SYSTEM PERFORMANCE
ON POLITICAL ATTITUDES AND BEHAVIOR

Political Involvement

At the outset of my research I hypothesized that personal contact with government and receipt of public services would stimulate a greater awareness of political and governmental activities, and would also strengthen individual predispositions to use the political process in satisfying needs.[8] These general hypotheses were supported by the data gathered in the research communities; but the impact of political system performance on political involvement among the migrants varied

---

[8] The analysis reported in this section makes use of several indexes summarizing responses to the relevant survey questions. Index 88, "positive contact with officials," includes both contacts initiated by the respondent and contacts initiated by officials themselves, the outcomes of which were evaluated by the respondent as being favorable to himself or his community. Most positive contacts reported occurred during negotiations for regularization or government assistance in community development. Index 46, "negative contact with officials," measures exposure to eviction attempts by the government in addition to personal contacts with PRI or government officials whose outcome was evaluated as negative. Index 54, "overall contact with officials," combines all types of personal contacts with the government and the official party, irrespective of outcome. Finally, two indexes were constructed to measure the extent to which respondents had benefited personally from various kinds of governmental outputs. Index 101, "receipt of personal services," includes medical care, help in finding housing or employment, legal services, receipt of low-cost commodities through CONASUPO or other government outlets, and other types of social welfare benefits. Index 102, "receipt of urban services," measures the respondent's access to regular electric service, piped water, sewage systems, paved streets, and sidewalks. The survey items used in constructing each index are listed in Appendix C.

TABLE 8.2

Impact of System Performance on Political Involvement Among Migrants

Dependent Variables	Independent Variables				
	Contact with Officials			Services Received	
	Overall	Positive	Negative	Personal	Urban
Awareness of government outputs affecting community	.190	.194	.000*	.314	.117
Perception of general relevance of government and politics to satisfaction of needs	.204	.165	.025*	.262	.031*
Attentiveness to electoral campaigns and political content of mass media	.257	.169	.006*	.206	−.039*
Interest in politics and public affairs	.165	.140	−.120	.168	−.087
Knowledge of government and politics	.490	.414	.149	.334	−.107
Discussion of politics	.275	.239	−.006*	.187	−.017*
Voting participation	.181	.183	.027*	.219	.023*
Campaign involvement	.593	.407	.115	.303	−.123
Participation in community problem-solving	.420	.408	.266	.261	−.257

NOTE: Minimum $N = 670$. All table entries are third-order partial correlations (controlling for age, socioeconomic status, and length of residence in Mexico City), and all but those marked * are statistically significant at the .05 level or beyond. Summative indexes are used as the measures of all variables in Tables 8.2 through 8.6; see Appendix C for item content.

significantly according to the type of personal contact experienced and the kind of benefits received (see Table 8.2). When one controls for the effects of age, socioeconomic status, and length of residence in the city, there is a positive relationship between overall contact with government and most measures of political awareness and participation, particularly involvement in electoral campaigns ($r = .593$) and community problem-solving ($r = .420$). It should be kept in mind that even the correlations under .20 often reflect large percentage differences. For example, among migrants in my sample having low overall contact with government, only 46 percent have a high perception of the relevance of government and politics to the satisfaction of needs. Among those who have had frequent contact with government, 64 percent perceive political and governmental activity as highly relevant to need satisfaction.[9]

[9] These percentages derive from a cross-tabulation of respondents' scores (dichotomized into "low" and "high") on Index 54, "overall contact with officials," with scores on Index 81, "perception of relevance of government and politics to need satisfaction." The differences reported are statistically significant, by Chi-square test, at the .001 level.

The analysis also indicates, however, that only contacts whose outcomes are evaluated positively by the respondents have a significant impact on political involvement. Negative contact is only weakly related to most of my measures of political awareness and participation. Research on the urban poor in Lima and Santiago (Chile) indicates that negative contact with government must be particularly severe in its personal consequences and must be experienced repeatedly over an extended period of time if the political interest and involvement of such populations are to drop significantly (Lindenberg 1970: 178, 187). These circumstances did not apply to any of the research communities. Even in the most severely "sanctioned" community, Colonia Nueva, the period of government eviction attempts was relatively brief, and it was followed by several instances of government assistance in defending the settlement against harassment by private landowners.

My finding of a positive relationship between personally initiated contacts with public officials and participation in voting and campaign work is consistent with the findings of studies done among city-dwellers in the United States. It is obviously difficult to determine the direction of causation implied by such a relationship. As one investigator has noted, it seems probable that "impressions gained in contact [with government officials] carry over into other areas of political behavior. The reverse is also true: political activity [unrelated to contacting officials] provides incentives and opportunities to initiate contact" (Eisinger 1972: 63). Personal contact with officials undoubtedly increases one's general knowledge of points of access within the bureaucracy and procedures for articulating demands.

The relationship between receipt of public services and individual political involvement appears to depend on the nature of the services received. Among my sample of migrants, the extent of *personal* services received is positively related to all measures of political awareness and participation. Since most voting and campaign activity in the research communities are on behalf of the PRI, migrants may engage in such regime-supportive activity at least partially as a quid pro quo for personal services received from the PRI or the government. However, the receipt of *community* services and improvements does not promote involvement in these and other forms of political activity; in fact, it is negatively related to most measures of involvement. This finding reflects the fact that most respondents having high access to basic urban services and improvements live in communities (Unidad Popular, Colonia Militar) where the incentives for political involvement are weakest.

Political Efficacy and Powerlessness

It is commonly assumed that feelings of political efficacy or power-lessness among low-income people may be strongly influenced by personal contact with the government. Specifically, we might expect such contact to increase the individual's self-confidence in dealing with officials and his sense of personal competence to influence their decisions. The analysis reported in Table 8.3 confirms these expectations with regard to migrants in the research communities. Again controlling for the effects of age, socioeconomic status, and time in the city, we find overall contact with officials to be positively related to a feeling of political efficacy, and negatively related to a sense of powerlessness. Once again, only contact whose results are positively evaluated by the respondents contributes significantly to these relationships. Receipt of personal services shows the same relationships with perceived efficacy and powerlessness, but access to basic urban services is essentially unrelated to these perceptions.

As we shall see, those who have benefited substantially from personalized services are also more inclined to be generally supportive of the political system; and their greater sense of political efficacy may derive mainly from an uncritical acceptance of the government's claims of being highly responsive to demands by the citizenry. By contrast, those who currently enjoy most basic urban services may not view themselves as politically efficacious, either because they were not personally involved in the collective demand-making that obtained these benefits (perhaps having moved into the community at a later stage in its development) or because their community received these services at the initiative of the government rather than the residents (as in the case of Unidad Popular).

Both the survey data and the unstructured interviews suggest that a low-income migrant who has personal contact with government in the

TABLE 8.3

Impact of System Performance on Feelings of Political Efficacy and Powerlessness Among Migrants

	Independent Variables				
	Contact with Officials			Services Received	
Dependent Variables	Overall	Positive	Negative	Personal	Urban
Sense of political efficacy	.284	.233	.023*	.219	−.072
Sense of political powerlessness	−.197	−.153	.016*	−.200	.040*

NOTE: $N = 670$. Controls, correlations, and significance as in Table 8.2.

context of demand-making attempts often emerges with an enhanced sense of political efficacy, especially if the outcomes of the attempts are evaluated positively (cf. Mathiason 1972: 75). Those who have experienced the satisfaction that comes when some action in which they have voluntarily participated brings them closer to their goals have greater faith both in the feasibility of obtaining government assistance and in the means employed to obtain it.

Attitudes Toward the Political System

We shall now assess the impact of political system performance on migrant attitudes toward the system, retaining the distinction made in Chapter 3 between the different attitudes that reflect diffuse or specific support for the system. Table 8.4 treats system performance as a determinant of diffuse support. Overall contact with government is positively related to affect for national political institutions, trust in government, and perception of governmental concern for the poor but negatively related to feelings of political cynicism. Only contact that is negatively evaluated by the respondents appears to increase nonsupportive attitudes toward the political system (cf. Lindenberg 1970: 115–24).

These findings contrast sharply with those of Fagen and Tuohy (1972: 114), who found that in the city of Jalapa "a citizen [who] actually comes into contact with the political process in other than routine fashion . . . is more likely to be extremely negative about politics." This relationship held true within all family income levels. The apparent conflict between the Jalapa study and my findings in Mexico City may be attributable to the more highly developed capabilities for responding to the needs of the poor that government in the capital possesses. In Mexico City lower-class petitioners have many more points of access to the government and PRI bureaucracies. Moreover, the comparatively greater resources that officials in the capital are able to expend in low-income neighborhoods increase the likelihood of a favorable response to petitions. Contact with government under these circumstances could easily generate diffuse support for the political system.

A particularly interesting pattern of relationships emerges when political system performance is correlated with specific support for the system. As shown in Table 8.5, personal contact with government (especially positively evaluated contact) is positively related to a favorable evaluation of the performance of specific (and mostly high-ranking) public officials, as well as to a general perception of the government as responsive to demands by ordinary citizens. Negative contacts with the regime do not seem to adversely affect the migrants' evaluations of

TABLE 8.4

*Impact of System Performance on Diffuse Support for the
Political System Among Migrants*

	Independent Variables				
	Contact with Officials			Services Received	
Dependent Variables	Overall	Positive	Negative	Personal	Urban
Affect for national political institutions	.257	.248	−.025*	.355	−.032*
Trust in government	.214	.206	−.104	.227	.047*
Perception of governmental concern for the poor	.198	.133	.040*	.217	.053*
Political cynicism	−.190	−.168	.146	−.219	.107
Perception of need for radical socio-political change	−.014*	−.053*	.072	−.138	−.005*
Overall diffuse support for political system	.236	.183	.024*	.276	.098

NOTE: Minimum N = 675. Controls, correlations, and significance as in Table 8.2.

TABLE 8.5

*Impact of System Performance on Specific Support for the
Political System Among Migrants*

	Independent Variables				
	Contact with Officials			Services Received	
Dependent Variables	Overall	Positive	Negative	Personal	Urban
Positive evaluation of public officials' performance	.268	.302	.099	.254	.030*
Dissatisfaction with government service outputs	.014	.016*	−.057*	−.086	−.337
Perception of governmental responsiveness to influence attempts	.294	.351	.003*	.269	−.025*
Overall specific support for political system	.238	.260	.045*	.280	.150

NOTE: Minimum N = 663. Controls, correlations, and significance as in Table 8.2.

the performance of high-ranking officials, perhaps because they usually attribute negative experiences with the authorities to the failings of low-ranking politicians or bureaucrats, whose corrupt or arbitrary behavior subverts the will of those higher up (cf. Kahl 1968: 114–16).

The hypothesis that those who receive objectively better public services are likely to evaluate political system performance more positively is confirmed by the data reported in Table 8.5. The receipt of personal services is positively related to favorable evaluations of the performance of public officials and the government's responsiveness to influence attempts. And the receipt of basic urban services is inversely related to dissatisfaction with government outputs. It is possible, however, that some people may express dissatisfaction with public services for reasons unrelated to the objective quantity or quality of the services themselves. For example, dissatisfaction with service outputs may be simply one facet of a general syndrome of political alienation or negativism (cf. Schuman & Gruenberg 1972: 372–87). To explore this possibility, the analysis reported in Table 8.5 was repeated, this time controlling for feelings of general political alienation and perceptions of social injustice in the country. The negative relationship between dissatisfaction with government service outputs and receipt of basic urban services remained virtually undiminished—suggesting that evaluations of political system performance in this area are in fact influenced by objective levels of service deprivation.

In this chapter I have so far not considered differences between migrants and city-born residents in the research communities, inasmuch as the relationships I have reported did not vary significantly between the two groups. There are, however, some important differences in the impact of political system performance on migrant and native attitudes toward the system. Table 8.6 shows that, in general, personal contact with government and receipt of public services are more important predictors of diffuse and specific support for the system among migrants than among native-born residents of Mexico City. This pattern persists if the analysis is performed within single communities—i.e., in each of the research communities, system performance has a greater impact on the political attitudes of migrants.

An explanation for these findings may lie in the relatively low expectations for government assistance that migrants often have when they first arrive in the city. Most migrants in the research communities were born and raised in small towns or villages where public services were minimal and personal contact with government and PRI officials was limited and, as they described it, mostly unrewarding (cf. G. Foster 1967: 109, 170; Arterton 1974; Corbett 1974). Low initial expectations are also consistent with a more general "migrant ethic" in which urban opportunities for material advancement and improvement of living conditions are perceived as potential gains to be realized through individual (or community) action rather than as basic rights accruing to all residents of the city (Portes 1971c: 716). Given this set of perceptions and expectations, the migrant who experiences positive contact with public officials and benefits from a variety of governmental services after his arrival in the city is likely to evaluate the political system more favorably than his native-born neighbor. The native city-

TABLE 8.6

Impact of System Performance on Political System Support Among Migrants and Native-Born Residents

	Independent Variables									
	Contact with Officials						Services Received			
	Overall		Positive		Negative		Personal		Urban	
Dependent Variables	Migrants	Natives	Migrants	Natives	Migrants	Natives	Migrants	Natives	Migrants	Natives
Overall diffuse support for political system	.236	.102	.183	.175	.024*	.155	.276	.151	.098	.027*
Overall specific support for political system	.238	.129	.260	.202	.045*	.046*	.280	.228	.150	.186

NOTE: Minimum *N* for migrants = 670; *N* for natives = 377. Table entries are second-order partial correlations, controlling for age and socioeconomic status. Correlations not marked * are statistically significant at the .05 level or beyond.

dweller may take such things for granted; and if he lacks access to certain public services, he may even feel that the government has deprived him of legitimate benefits.

SYMBOLIC OUTPUTS AND SUPPORT FOR THE SYSTEM

It is probable that the political attitudes and behavior of the poor in Mexico City, including residents of the research communities, have been conditioned by political system performance in a number of ways not directly examined in the preceding analysis. As noted in Chapter 7, the granting of land tenure rights to squatters is probably, for those people, the most important measure of governmental performance. The provision of educational opportunities is another critically important area, and one in which the government has made great strides within the Mexico City metropolitan area. (More than 90 percent of the migrants in my sample with school-age children had at least one child who attended a public school regularly, and in 55 percent of the families with school-age children all eligible children attended.) The symbolic outputs of the regime—channeled through the press, radio and television, the schools, labor unions, and local leaders tied to the government by clientage relationships—have also shaped the attitudes and behavior of the urban poor in important ways. Symbolic reassurance of the regime's concern for the poor is also conveyed by elaborately staged public events and ceremonies (*actas*), during which land titles are distributed and new schools and other small-scale public works are "presented to" the people by high-ranking officials, even including the President of the Republic. Residents of *colonias proletarias* in many different parts of the city are usually transported to the site of an acta in buses chartered by the government or the PRI.

The significance of these symbolic outputs, relative to the material benefits provided by the regime, should not be underestimated. A comparison of Mexican government expenditures and economic policies with those of other Latin American governments is illuminating:

Excepting the impact of land distribution, in no other major Latin American country has less been done directly by the government for the bottom quarter of society. Trends in prices, wages, and occupational opportunities in Mexico have probably left most of the families within this stratum with a standard of living at or below that which they enjoyed in 1940. (Hansen 1971: 87)

Although this observation is far less applicable in the capital than elsewhere in Mexico, it nevertheless redirects our attention to the striking juxtaposition of objectively inadequate government performance in many problem areas and highly supportive mass attitudes toward the regime, as revealed by virtually every attitudinal survey completed in Mexico City during the past decade, including my own (cf. Kahl 1968: Chap. 6; K. Coleman 1972: 45–56; C. Davis & Coleman 1974).

Murray Edelman has advanced the hypothesis that government actions chiefly satisfy or arouse people "not by granting or withholding their stable substantive demands, but rather by changing the demands and the expectations" (Edelman 1971: 7; cf. Edelman 1965: Chap. 2). Many social scientists now similarly stress the importance of expectations of future welfare or deprivation in predicting mass attitudes and behavior. For example, recent studies in frustration/aggression theory hold that "much greater weight must be given to *anticipations of the goal* than merely to the duration or magnitude of deprivation per se" in accounting for most motivated behavior (Leonard Berkowitz, quoted in Edelman 1971: 8; cf. Klassen 1972).

The Mexican regime's symbolic outputs, which stress its commitment to the pursuit of social justice and other goals of the "continuing Revolution," have strongly influenced mass expectations of future welfare. And these expectations have been tied not only to continued economic progress for the nation as a whole but to the prospect of direct governmental assistance to the poor. Among my sample of migrants, personal contact with the government appears to reinforce such expectations, since overall contact with officials is positively related to higher expectations of future governmental assistance in solving important personal and community-related problems.[10] This creates a nasty dilemma for the regime: Citizen contact with public officials, at least in areas where the government has been relatively responsive to demands by low-income groups, can increase support for the system; but it will also raise expectations for government performance. Barring a radical shift in government priorities and expenditure patterns at the national level, many of these expectations will not be met.

It has been observed that the Mexican regime "encourages structured and controlled political contacts [by citizens] to a greater degree than perhaps any other in Latin America with the exception of Cuba" (Fagen & Tuohy 1972: 88–89). Such contacts undoubtedly decrease the citizen's sense of remoteness from the regime and may even convince him of its concern for his well-being. But in a situation of limited resources for meeting the needs of the urban poor, whose numbers are

---

[10] The partial correlation between respondents' scores on my index of "overall contact with officials" (54) and scores on the index of "expectations for government performance" (22), controlling for age, socioeconomic status, and length of residence in Mexico City, is .26, significant at the .001 level.

swelled constantly both by migration from the countryside and by natural population growth, the long-term effect of encouraging contact with public officials may be to undermine confidence in the regime's capacity for effective response to mass needs. Machine-style politics and limited perceptions of the scope of governmental responsibility on the part of the poor may continue to insulate the Mexican political system from demands for a major increase in resources allocated to the poor. Among those who have already benefited from government outputs in some way, however limited, symbolic rewards may eventually replace actual receipt of goods and services as the basis for according legitimacy to the system (cf. Kaufman et al. 1973). But among a large proportion of the urban poor, the initial development of supportive orientations toward the political system will continue to depend substantially on the delivery of concrete benefits from that system.[11]

[11] This conclusion is also supported by the findings of some students of political socialization in the United States. See especially Merelman 1966.

CHAPTER NINE

Conclusion

THE COMMUNITY AS AN ARENA OF POLITICAL LEARNING

One of the recurring themes of this study has been the importance of the immediate community context to the process of political learning among the migrant poor. In fact, the research project was in large part suggested by my dissatisfaction with highly generalized treatments of the people flowing into Third World cities as undifferentiated "masses" who would respond in uniform fashion to a given set of conditions or stimuli, to which all rural migrants to large cities were presumably exposed. The empirical reality, as I have demonstrated, is far more complex; even within a single city, there is considerable variation in the socializing influences to which a migrant is exposed. These differences in neighborhood socialization patterns are an important source of variance in individual political attitudes and behavior.

The evidence presented here even suggests that certain characteristics of a migrant's local community are often of greater importance in determining his political attitudes and behavior in the urban setting than his individual socioeconomic attributes or psychological state. The intense political involvement, affect for the political system, and sense of community that characterize a young, upwardly mobile squatter settlement such as Colonia Nueva bear little resemblance to the passivity, political negativism, and weak sense of community in a stagnating subdivision like Colonia Texcoco. Given this diversity in local socialization contexts, it is not surprising that the outcomes of the political learning process among migrants to the city show little uniformity.

The intercommunity differences that have been detected in Mexico City and other large Latin American cities help to explain why the mere fact of residence in an urban area, or length of residence in such an area, is such a poor predictor of political attitudes and behavior. As Oscar Lewis has argued (1965: 497), the city as a whole may not be the proper unit of comparison or analysis for most studies of social and political life, because variables operating at the level of the city are not the crucial determinants of individual attitudes and behavior. In any event, generalizations about urban life and its impact on political orientations must be tested against evidence from studies of neighborhoods, social networks, and other relatively small groupings of city-dwellers. Only in this way can we begin to understand why urbanization has failed to produce uniform political responses among mass publics.

We have observed that under certain conditions the local urban community may function as an agent of rapid, intense political socialization. This finding has important implications for those attempting to deliberately mold political attitudes and behavior. Specifically, it suggests that such attempts need not involve stimulating individuals to develop a generalized interest in politics or psychological commitment to political involvement. It may be enough to create (or to capitalize on) situations that will induce people to behave in the intended manner and to then establish an appropriate, localized incentive or reinforcement structure for this behavior. This is the strategy that has been followed, with minor variations, by governments and political parties in Chile, Cuba, and mainland China, all of whom have sought to utilize the local urban community as a vehicle for directed political socialization and mobilization.[1]

The extent to which attitudes and behaviors are situationally determined raises important questions about their stability. As Becker points out (1964: 45),

> The perspectives a person acquires as a result of situational adjustments are no more stable than the situation itself or his participation in it. Situations occur in institutions. . . . When the institutions themselves change, the situations they provide for their participants shift and necessitate development of new patterns of belief and action. . . . Similarly, if an individual moves in and out of given situations, is a transient rather than a long-term participant, his perspectives will shift with his movement.

Of course, political attitudes and behavioral predispositions are not infinitely mutable, and there is undoubtedly some carry-over of orientations learned in a given situation to future situations. It is clear, however, that structural and situational variables relating to a migrant's

---

[1] The competition among major political parties in Chile for permanent control of organizations in low-income urban neighborhoods is recounted in Friedmann 1972: 27–28; Vanderschueren 1973. (See also p. 198, n. 24.) On the use of neighborhood-based committees for political control and socialization in Cuba under Castro, see Fagen 1969; Butterworth 1974. The use of neighborhood organizations to alter socialization patterns in the wake of the Cultural Revolution in China is described in Salaff 1971.

community of residence are highly important determinants of his incentives and opportunities for political involvement.

We have noted that political participation among migrants is very sensitive to changes in community needs, degree of "external threat" to the community's survival, and other situational factors. The resolution of key problems of community development, for example, tends to depress participation. Rewards to participants in community problem-solving may change drastically as the control of local leaders over their communities begins to wane. However, these and other changes in the community context of political learning may not lead to "depoliticization" or the "unlearning" of political orientations. What is learned by a resident in one situation is not necessarily forgotten; it may simply become irrelevant in the context of new community needs or behavioral norms. For example, residents may once have developed a capacity for cooperative political action that is now latent but can be reactivated when new needs arise or supralocal constraints on political activity are altered. It is evident that long-term studies of specific communities will be needed to determine the relative "staying power" and generalizability of community-induced political learning.

POLITICS AND URBAN POVERTY IN MEXICO

Another central concern of this study has been the way in which migrants and others among the urban poor interact with political and governmental agencies. We have observed that among residents of the research communities, contact with politicians and government officials usually takes place in the context of community-related activity. It has been argued that territorially based demand-making is not likely to overload the city or national political system, since the demands concern parochial, short-term needs and are rarely aggregated across communities. Instead, a host of particularistic requests for government assistance move upward through tiers of patron-client relationships. These petitions can be satisfied by piecemeal administrative action, at relatively little cost to the regime, as compared to the cost of responding to broadly based demands on behalf of whole categories of people or territorial units. Migrants' conceptions of the scope of governmental responsibility in many problem areas are quite limited, and they are not inclined to seek governmental solutions for problems far removed from their immediate life space. Moreover, compared to native city-dwellers migrants tend to be more deferential toward authority figures in general, more supportive of the PRI, and less likely to support groups or movements threatening to the established regime. They do not perceive violence as a legitimate or effective response to material deprivation; in fact, many of them harbor a deep-seated fear of the personal consequences of radical social or political change. All this greatly reduces the willingness and capacity of the migrant poor to challenge the political system as it presently operates.

In fact, it might be argued that the regime's interest, at least in the short run, lies in promoting cityward migration, both as a conservatizing influence on the urban population and as a safety valve for rural discontent. Government officials also realize that most of the migration in recent decades represents a response to extreme poverty and unemployment in the countryside, and they tend to view widespread underemployment in the cities as preferable to high open unemployment in rural areas. Eventually, as the nation's population becomes increasingly concentrated in the larger cities, opposition to the existing political system—electoral and otherwise—will almost certainly increase. But this will have little to do with the presence of large numbers of recent migrants in the cities. Of far greater potential importance as a source of opposition to the regime are the more highly educated, city-born offspring of migrants and native-born city dwellers in general, who may even find themselves at a disadvantage vis-à-vis recent migrants in competition for certain kinds of jobs (cf. Weiner 1973a, 1973b).

Although migrants are not readily available for recruitment into antisystem political movements, many of them *are* available for system-supportive activity. The most important sources of tension within the Mexican political system in recent years have been conflicts between elite groups, especially between the commercial-industrial elite and the dominant faction of the PRI-government apparatus. The incumbent regime uses its control over low-income sectors of the population as a political resource in bargaining with the wealthy capitalist sector (Tuohy 1973: 265–66; Purcell & Purcell 1975a). For this reason, if for no other, the regime finds it expedient to continue building support among the urban poor, who are more strategically located and more easily mobilized than their rural counterparts. Such policies as the regularization of squatter settlements through expropriation of the invaded land are designed to prepare for the day when an incumbent government might have to fall back on mass support to withstand a major economic crisis or a challenge from some dissident elite. The same general objective is served by such practices as systematically co-opting local leaders in low-income communities and buying off unionized workers with wage increases.

The regime's support-building efforts, especially among the more disadvantaged, unorganized workers in commerce and services, may be complicated in future years by changing economic conditions. During most of the 1940–70 period, Mexico's gross national product grew by more than 6 percent per annum—one of the highest rates in Latin America or elsewhere in the Third World. Since 1970 the country's rate of overall economic expansion has slowed, and soaring population growth and inflation have combined to wipe out much of the economic gain achieved in these years. By 1974 the annual rate of increase in consumer prices, which had remained below 4 percent throughout the 1960's, had risen to 23.3 percent nationally and even higher in Mexico City (see *Latin America*, 30 May 1975: 163; López Rosado 1975.). It remains to be seen whether the hope for socioeconomic mobility generated by the boom years of the 1950's and 1960's will now fade, and whether lower-class tolerance for material deprivation will decrease sharply, as some have suggested (Hirschman 1973).

The willingness of the poor to support or at least acquiesce to existing political arrangements has been based at least in part on their perceptions of an "open" opportunity structure in Mexican society. Only 29 percent of the migrants interviewed in the research communities in 1970 believed that it was very difficult or impossible for one to move from a lower social class to a higher one (Item 86b). As reported in Chapter 2, many migrants have experienced some upward mobility themselves, and even those who have not are aware of relatives and friends who have significantly improved their economic situation. Not surprisingly, the migrants' expectations for their children are quite high. In response to another survey question, more than 94 percent of them thought that their children's lives would be better or much better than their own (Item 71a), with three-quarters of these citing "more education" as the explanation for this. Over half the migrants wanted their children to obtain a university education, and 60 percent believed that it would be economically feasible for them to give their children such an education (Item 77). The children's access to high-status occupations was assumed to be high. When asked, "What kind of work would you like your oldest son to do?," 56 percent mentioned professional or semi-professional occupations, and an additional 22 percent wished their children to become skilled service workers. Fifty-nine percent of the migrants thought it likely that their sons would have the kind of occupation that the parents preferred for them.[2] An equal proportion thought that their children would eventually belong to the middle class.

[2] When asked whether a working man's son who is "intelligent and hardworking" might become the owner of a small business, 62 percent replied that such a person would have much opportunity to do so (Item 73). Thirty-eight percent believed

Whether any of these expectations will be met will almost certainly depend on the continued expansion of the urban occupational structure, and on the growth of labor-intensive industry in particular. The migrants themselves are well aware of this: when asked about the causes of poverty in Mexico (Item 69a) most of my respondents mentioned the scarcity of jobs; and when asked to identify the most important problem facing the country, more of them cited unemployment or the need to create new sources of employment than any other problem. Unfortunately, recent trends in this problem area are not encouraging. In 1974 an estimated 5.7 percent of Mexico City's economically active population were unemployed (6.3 percent in the Ciudad Netzahualcóyotl section), and 35.3 percent were underemployed (*Excélsior*, 21 June 1975: 10A; Manuel Gollás, quoted in Moiron 1975: 7).[3] The rate of job creation in the city, especially in the industrial sector, has declined significantly in recent years, at a time when the age structure of the population and rates of in-migration and natural population growth all dictate that many more jobs are needed if even higher unemployment and underemployment rates are to be avoided (Contreras 1972; Muñoz et al. 1972; López Rosado 1975; Robles Quintero 1975).

Previously, the poor have credited the government with more than its actual share of responsibility for the country's rapid and sustained economic expansion; they may now hold it responsible for any major constriction of employment opportunities. Evidence from a number of Latin American, African, and Middle Eastern countries indicates that the potential for antigovernment protest behavior among the urban poor is greatest under conditions of high unemployment.[4] The most disruptive individuals tend to be young workers who have been steadily employed and then lose their jobs. As Horowitz (1967: 219) has noted, the historical evidence seems to support the generalization that only when cities do in fact ameliorate material deprivation by expanding employment opportunities does urbanization significantly reduce the potential for political unrest.

Viewed in this context, government policies that would sacrifice high rates of overall economic growth in order to reduce Mexico's depen-

---

that such a person had a good opportunity to become a high-ranking public official; 46 percent felt he had a similar chance to be a physician; and 63 percent thought he could easily become a white-collar worker (*empleado*).

[3] The national unemployment rate in 1974 has been estimated at 15–17 percent, primarily reflecting the acute shortage of jobs in rural areas (*Excélsior*, 2 Feb. 1974: 1A; 12 May 1975: 1A; 20 June 1975: 4A).

[4] See M. Cohen 1974; Hobsbawm 1967: 65; Gutkind 1973; Kazemi 1973; Moreno 1970: 92–96, Portes 1971c.

dence on foreign investment and to achieve a more equitable distribution of wealth within the country—policies advocated by increasing numbers of officials and academic economists[5]—may actually generate more frustration and political alienation among the poor than a perpetuation of the "high growth" policies that have contributed to extreme income concentration. In 1968 the poorest 20 percent of Mexican families received only 3.6 percent of the total personal income, while the richest 20 percent received 67.6 percent of the total income (Banco de México 1974: 17).[6] Within Mexico City itself personal income was more unequally distributed during the 1960's than in most major Latin American cities (only Monterrey, Mexico, and Asunción, Paraguay, ranked higher on a standard measure of income inequality; see Figueroa & Weisskoff 1974: 136).

Nevertheless, data from all available studies, including my own, indicate that the urban poor are more concerned about unemployment and job creation than about the national or citywide distribution of income. They are well aware that they are materially disadvantaged relative to other sectors of the population, but they do not expect this gap to be narrowed significantly in the near future—or even, perhaps, in their own lifetimes. Nearly three-quarters of my migrant respondents felt that the government was doing "poorly" or "not so well" in evening out differences between the rich and the poor in Mexico (Item 141a), yet less than 10 percent of them regarded unequal distribution of wealth as the country's most important problem.

The obstacles to upward mobility for the great majority of the urban poor are already formidable; but they may become insurmountable if the rate of overall economic growth falls sharply and inflation erodes real income. Thus the hopes of most poor city-dwellers for their own economic improvement and for the occupational mobility of their chil-

[5] Taking their cue from President Luis Echeverría, government officials since 1971 have regularly stressed in their public statements the problem of income inequality and the "incapacity" of the Mexican model of economic development pursued in recent decades to ameliorate it. The economic rationale for the alternative strategy of development they have advocated is set forth lucidly in a volume by one of President Echeverría's most influential economic advisors (Solís 1972); the political considerations that may have prompted the policy shift are outlined in Reyna 1974: 50ff. For a recent justification of the same policy prescriptions by a North American development economist, see Keesing 1974. Some of the redistributive policies implemented by the Echeverría administration since 1971 are described in F. Turner 1973: 168–69.

[6] For detailed analyses of trends in national income distribution in Mexico, and the contributions of government policies and programs to these trends, see Banco de México 1974; Barkin 1971, 1975; Cockcroft 1974: 276ff; ECLA 1972: 65ff; Hansen 1971: 71–95; Navarrete 1970; Solís 1972: 63–70; Tello 1971.

dren are pegged primarily to a continuation of the so-called "Mexican miracle" of economic expansion, regardless of the consequences for national income distribution, the physical environment, or other matters of concern to government technocrats and academicians. They do not expect to profit much from government programs to redistribute income or reduce dependence on capital-intensive foreign enterprise, even though success in dealing with both of these problems would in fact help to reduce unemployment and would stimulate job creation in the long run.

Great caution must be exercised, however, in predicting the behavioral response of the migrant poor to deteriorating economic conditions. Even if migrants grow more frustrated in the future as a result of declining job opportunities and rising inflation, their discontent may be difficult to exploit. The success of any overt protest movement aimed at redressing migrants' grievances against the sociopolitical order would probably depend in large part on the availability of independent, indigenous leaders capable of mobilizing this sector of the urban population. As we have observed, the poor in Mexico City have their own leaders; but these are rarely autonomous of government authority, and they are not inclined to mobilize their followers in behalf of "unauthorized" demands that go beyond the problems of the local community.

The responses of residents of the communities included in this study to questions regarding the legitimacy and efficacy of protest activity and political violence suggest that they would be quite resistant to efforts to recruit them for overtly "antisystem" activities, regardless of the leaders involved. They would resist not simply out of deference to authority or fear of government retribution, but out of a deeply held conviction that it is more productive to try to manipulate the system to satisfy needs than to confront it or overturn it. It is this pragmatic view of the options afforded by the existing political situation that makes the supposedly "available" migrant in many Latin American cities much less susceptible to appeals for political upheaval than has been generally assumed by both the militant left and incumbent elites.

It must be emphasized that this reluctance to take to the barricades or join class-based political movements dedicated to overturning the existing sociopolitical order, even in the face of glaring material inequalities, does not result from irrationality, "false consciousness," or lack of awareness among the poor that they are being manipulated by the political system. On the contrary, their unwillingness to confront the system reflects a rational adaptation to the rules of the political game, a low propensity for risk-taking, and an awareness of which kinds of political action are rewarded by the authorities and which kinds are likely to be ignored or violently repressed. In Mexico City, as elsewhere in Latin America, the struggle of the migrant poor for recognition and material benefits will go on, but most probably within an overall framework of opportunities and constraints carefully fashioned and maintained by ruling elites.

Appendixes

Sample Survey Questionnaire

English version

For space reasons the pages of the questionnaire have been reproduced two to a page, turned 90 degrees. The first page appears below.

SAMPLE SURVEY QUESTIONNAIRE

Good morning (afternoon). We are doing a study for a large university in order to find out more about the people of (Mexico City/ Ciudad Netzahualcóyotl) -- about their opinions and needs. We are interested in the problems of this place, as seen by the people who live here; and above all, in your point of view concerning these matters. Could we please ask you some questions, that are also being asked in other parts of the city. We assure you that your answers will be strictly confidential; no one else will know how you have answered. The information obtained from each family will be used only in combination with that obtained from the other families being interviewed in the city.

According to the instructions for this study, I must ask some questions of the head of the family, Mr. _____. Are you that person?

1a. Do you have a wife living with you?

1b. (IF YES:) Are you married by civil ceremony, by the Church, or by civil ceremony and by the Church?

1c. (IF RESPONDENT HAS NO WIFE:) Are you single, widowed, divorced, separated, or abandoned?

2. (IF MARRIED:) How long have you been married?

3a. How many children do you have? (IF CHILDREN ASK 3b, 3c, 3d)

3b. How many of them live here with you?

3c. How old are they--those that live with you?

3d. Did you have any children who died before reaching the age of six? (IF YES:) How many? How old were they when they died?

4. (ALL RESPONDENTS:) How many people altogether are living in this house, including yourself? Who are they--not their names, but how they are related to you: how many sons and daughters, brothers and sisters, mothers-and fathers-in-law, and so on?

5. How long have you lived in Mexico City? (We understand, as "Mexico City" [SHOW MAP] not only the Federal District, but also the municipalities of Chimalhuacán, Ecatepec, Naucalpan, Netzahualcóyotl, and Tlalnepantla of the State of México; so if you have lived in one of these municipalities, please remember that they form part of Mexico City.)

(IF RESPONDENT HAS LIVED IN THE METROPOLITAN AREA OF MEXICO CITY ALL HIS LIFE, SKIP TO QUESTION 36a.)

NOTE: Some instructions to the interviewer have been omitted from this reproduction of the questionnaire. The complete version, in Spanish, is available from the author upon request.

12a. How old were you when you moved to Mexico City?

12b. In what year did you come to this city?

12c. Did you come alone, or with other members of your family, or with other persons?

12d. (IF RESPONDENT DID NOT COME ALONE:) Who were these other persons?--Not their names, but how they were related to you, or how you came to know them.

12e. (IF RESPONDENT CAME TO MEXICO CITY ALONE:) Were you the first member of your family to come to live in Mexico City?

13a. Upon your arrival, were there other relatives, compadres, or friends of yours living in Mexico City at that time? (IF YES, ASK 13b, 13c, 13d)

13b. Who were they? Not their names but how they were related to you, or how you came to know them.

13c. Had any of these relatives (friends) been successful in Mexico City? (IF YES:) In what way?

13d. Did any of these persons ever encourage you to come to the city, perhaps in their letters, or by sending you money or a ticket for the trip, or in some other way? (IF YES:) How?

14. (IF RESPONDENT WAS NOT FIRST MEMBER OF HIS FAMILY TO COME TO LIVE IN MEXICO CITY:) The first member of your family to come to Mexico City--what reason did he have for leaving the place where he lived and moving to Mexico City? (If he had several reasons, please give them all, beginning with the most important and ending with the least important reason.)

15a. (ALL MIGRANTS:) In your case, was moving to Mexico City the result of a personal decision, or a decision which depended on other persons?--Such as your parents, aunts, or uncles, etc.

15b. What reason did (you have/the persons who made the decision have) for leaving the place where you lived and moving to Mexico City? (If there were several reasons please give them all, beginning with the most important and ending with the least important.)

15c. (IF RESPONSE TO QUESTION 15b INCLUDED MENTION OF EMPLOYMENT OR EDUCATIONAL OPPORTUNITIES, HOUSING, ACCESS TO SERVICES, LAND OWNERSHIP OPPORTUNITIES, MEDICAL ATTENTION, OR OTHER ATTRACTIONS OF THE CITY:) How did you (they) learn about these things? Who told you (them) about these things?

6a. Now I would like to ask you some questions related to the fact that you have lived in some other place before coming to live in Mexico City. If you have come to live in Mexico City more than once, the questions refer to the last time you came here to live. Where were you born?

6b. Where is it located?--In what state or territory?

7a. When you were fifteen years old, where did you live? Where is it located?--In what state or territory?

7b. Were you living in: (IF RURAL LOCALITY:) a rancho? a pueblo? an ejido? (IF URBAN LOCALITY:) a colonia proletaria? a vecindad or patio? some other type of colonia?

7c. What was the most important source of jobs in (PLACE MENTIONED IN RESPONSE TO QUESTION 7a)? (IF NO FACTORIES OR INDUSTRY MENTIONED IN RESPONSE TO QUESTION 7c:) Did this place have some factory or industry--for example, mines, or factories where certain products were made? (IF YES:) What kinds? Did you work in this (factory, mine, industry, etc.) for some period of time? (IF YES:) How long?

8a. (IF RESPONDENT IS MARRIED:) When your wife was 15 years old, where did she live?

8b. Where is it located?--In what state or territory?

8c. Was she living in: (IF RURAL LOCALITY:) a rancho? a pueblo? an ejido? (IF URBAN LOCALITY:) a colonia proletaria? a vecindad or patio? some other type of colonia?

9a. How old were you when you left (PLACE NAMED IN RESPONSE TO QUESTION 7a)? (IF RESPONDENT LIVED IN MEXICO CITY AT THE AGE OF 15, ASK QUESTION OF HIS PLACE OF BIRTH)

9b. In what year did you leave there?

9c. About how long before you left (PLACE MENTIONED IN RESPONSE TO QUESTION 7a) were you seriously thinking about leaving? (IF RESPONDENT LIVED IN MEXICO CITY AT THE AGE OF 15, INSERT NAME OF PLACE OF BIRTH)

10. Do you know any other people living in this colonia--(INSERT RESPONDENT'S CURRENT PLACE OF RESIDENCE)--who came from (PLACE NAMED IN RESPONSE TO QUESTION 7a)? (IF RESPONDENT LIVED IN MEXICO CITY AT THE AGE OF 15, INSERT NAME OF PLACE OF BIRTH). That is people outside of your own family. (IF YES:) How many?

11a. After leaving (PLACE NAMED IN RESPONSE TO QUESTION 7a, OR OF BIRTH), did you live in any other places before coming to live in Mexico City? (IF YES:) What are the names of these places? Where is this place (are these places) located?--In what state or territory?

11b. How long did you live in this place (each of these places)?

15d. (IF RESPONSE TO QUESTION 15b MADE NO MENTION OF PROBLEMS EXPERIENCED BY THE RESPONDENT IN HIS PLACE OF ORIGIN:) Before making the decision to leave the place where you lived before coming to Mexico City, did you have any problems in (PLACE MENTIONED IN RESPONSE TO QUESTION 7a, OR IF RESPONDENT LIVED IN MEXICO CITY AT AGE 15, INSERT NAME OF PLACE OF BIRTH)? For example, problems with relatives, friends, neighbors, or with the authorities? (Remember, we assure you that your answers to all questions that we ask will be strictly confidential; the information obtained from each person will be used only in combination with that obtained from the other persons who are interviewed in the city.) (IF YES:) Could you tell me something about these problems?

16a. (ALL MIGRANTS:) How well did you know Mexico City before coming here to live? Would you say that you knew it well, fairly well, not very well, or not at all?

16b. (IF "VERY WELL" OR "FAIRLY WELL":) How did you come to know the city? Had you spent some time here before coming to live in the city? (IF YES:) How much time? For what purposes?

17a. (IF RESPONDENT MIGRATED AS A RESULT OF PERSONAL DECISION:) Before you came to this city, when you were thinking about where to move, did you ever consider going to live in some place other than Mexico City? (IF YES:) What place was this? (IF RESPONDENT CONSIDERED ALTERNATIVE DESTINATION, ASK 17b and 17c.)

17b. What made you think of (NAME OF PLACE MENTIONED IN RESPONSE TO QUESTION 17a)?

17c. Why did you decide to come to Mexico City rather than (PLACE OR PLACES MENTIONED IN RESPONSE TO QUESTION 17a)?

18a. When you first arrived in Mexico City, did you expect to stay permanently or only for a while?

18b. (IF RESPONDENT DID NOT EXPECT TO STAY PERMANENTLY:) For how long did you intend to stay?

18c. (IF RESPONDENT DID NOT EXPECT TO STAY PERMANENTLY:) Why did you decide to remain in the city?

19a. Was it more or less difficult to live in Mexico City than you had expected?

19b. (IF "MORE DIFFICULT" OR "LESS DIFFICULT":) In what ways?

20a. (IF RESPONDENT MIGRATED AS RESULT OF PERSONAL DECISION TO MIGRATE; IF DECISION TO MIGRATE WAS NOT AN INDEPENDENT ONE, ASK ABOUT HEAD OF RESPONDENT'S FAMILY AT THAT TIME:) Upon coming to Mexico City did (you/the head of the family) have some job assured or promised, or had (you/he) heard something about some definite job possibility, or did (you/he) only hope to find something?

20b. Did (you/he) receive help from someone in finding a job? (IF YES:) Who helped (you/him)? (IF NO:) Then, how did (you/he) get a job? Through the newspaper ads, searching from door to door, or how else?

20c. (ALL RESPONDENTS:) Would you say that (you/he) had much, little, or no difficulty in finding that first job in the city?

20d. After setting out to find a job, how long did it take (you/him) to find one?

21a. Did someone help (you/him) in finding a place to live? (IF YES:) Who helped you?

21b. Did (you/he) receive any other kinds of help in establishing yourself in the city? (IF YES:) What kinds of help? Who provided this help?

22a. In what part of Mexico City did you live just after arriving?

22b. In this colonia apart from those living with you, was there some relative, compadre, or friend of yours living there? (IF YES:) Who was that? Not their name, but how they were related to you, or how you came to know them.

22c. (IF PERSONS MENTIONED:) Did you live with this person (these persons) upon arriving in the city?

23. In what kind of house did you live when you first began living in (COLONIA MENTIONED IN RESPONSE TO QUESTION 22a)?

24. At that time, did you and your family receive your income usually by the week, by the quincena (every two weeks), or by the month? (SHOW APPROPRIATE CARD) Using this card, I would like you to show me which of these groups, from "A" to "I", comes closest to the total amount of the income of the members of your family when you began living in (COLONIA NAMED IN RESPONSE TO QUESTION 22a), including the income from all sources, such as wages, rent, or any other source.

25. When you moved to (COLONIA NAMED IN RESPONSE TO QUESTION 22a), did you bring a sum of money with you--for example, money you had saved or had borrowed from your relatives or friends?

26. (IF YES:) About how much money had you brought with you?

27a. (IF RESPONDENT'S CURRENT PLACE OF RESIDENCE IS DIFFERENT FROM PLACE MENTIONED IN RESPONSE TO QUESTION 22a, ASK 27a TO 28c.)

27b. How long did you live in (COLONIA NAMED IN RESPONSE TO QUESTION 22a)?

27b. Why did you move from this place?

27c. At the time you moved from (COLONIA MENTIONED IN RESPONSE TO QUESTION 22a), what kind of work were you doing?

28a. Where did you move to after leaving (COLONIA MENTIONED IN RESPONSE TO QUESTION 22a)?

28b. Why did you move to this colonia rather than some other place?

(IF RESPONDENT'S CURRENT PLACE OF RESIDENCE IS DIFFERENT FROM PLACE MENTIONED IN RESPONSE TO QUESTION 28a, ASK 28c, 28d, 28e, AND 29a.)

28c. In what kind of house did you live in (COLONIA MENTIONED IN RESPONSE TO QUESTION 28a)?

28d. How long did you live in (COLONIA MENTIONED IN RESPONSE TO QUESTION 28a)?

28e. Why did you move from this place?

29a. Is there any other place in the city where you have lived? (IF YES:) Which place? (IF YES, ASK 29b TO 30a)

29b. Why did you move to this colonia rather than some other place?

29c. In what kind of house did you live in (COLONIA MENTIONED IN RESPONSE TO QUESTION 29a)?

29e. Why did you move from this place?

30a. Are there any other places in the city where you have lived? (IF YES:) Which places?

(QUESTIONS 30b, 30c, and 30e REFER TO THE FIRST ADDITIONAL PLACE MENTIONED IN 30a).

30b. Why did you move to this colonia rather than some other place?

30c. In what kind of house did you live in (COLONIA MENTIONED IN RESPONSE TO QUESTION 30a)?

30d. How long did you live in (COLONIA MENTIONED IN RESPONSE TO QUESTION 30a)?

30e. Why did you move from this place?

31. (ALL MIGRANTS:) Do you consider yourself more capitalino than (INSERT NAME OF STATE OF BIRTH PLACE OF RESPONDENT, e.g., OAXAQUEÑO, MICHOACANO, ETC.), or do you feel you haven't changed much at all? (IF NO CHANGE:) Why do you feel this way?

32. Now that you know Mexico City, are you satisfied with having come here, or would you prefer to have remained in your place of origin? (REFERS TO THE PLACE MENTIONED IN RESPONSE TO QUESTION 7a, OR IF RESPONDENT LIVED IN MEXICO CITY AT AGE 15, TO HIS PLACE OF BIRTH.)

33a. Would you say that the house you have now is much better, somewhat better, more or less the same, worse, or much worse than your house in (PLACE NAMED IN RESPONSE TO QUESTION 7a, OR IF RESPONDENT LIVED IN MEXICO CITY AT AGE 15, HIS PLACE OF BIRTH)?

33b. Think about the house in which you lived just after arriving in Mexico City. Is your present house much better, somewhat better, about the same, worse, or much worse than that in which you lived when you first came to the city?

(IF SATISFIED WITH HAVING COME TO MEXICO CITY, ASK 34a AND 34b).

34a. If you had the opportunity to do it, do you think you might want to return some day to (PLACE MENTIONED IN RESPONSE TO QUESTION 7a, OR IF RESPONDENT LIVED IN MEXICO CITY AT AGE 15, HIS PLACE OF BIRTH) to live?

34b. (IF YES:) What would cause you to return?

(IF NOT SATISFIED WITH HAVING COME TO MEXICO CITY, ASK 34c, 34d, and 34e.)

34c. How likely is it that you will return to (PLACE MENTIONED IN RESPONSE TO QUESTION 7a, OR IF RESPONDENT LIVED IN MEXICO CITY AT AGE 15, HIS PLACE OF BIRTH) to live?

34d. (IF "VERY LIKELY" OR "SOMEWHAT LIKELY":) How soon do you think you will be returning to (PLACE NAMED IN RESPONSE TO QUESTION 7a, OR IF RESPONDENT LIVED IN MEXICO CITY AT AGE 15, HIS PLACE OF BIRTH)? What would cause you to return? (IF NECESSARY:) What reasons would cause you to return to (PLACE NAMED IN RESPONSE TO QUESTION 7a, OR IF RESPONDENT LIVED IN MEXICO CITY AT AGE 15, HIS PLACE OF BIRTH)?

34e. What might prevent you from returning to (PLACE NAMED IN RESPONSE TO QUESTION 7a, OR IF RESPONDENT LIVED IN MEXICO CITY AT AGE 15, HIS PLACE OF BIRTH)?

35a. (ALL MIGRANTS:) In what ways would you say that living in this city is better than living in (PLACE NAMED IN RESPONSE TO QUESTION 7a, OR IF RESPONDENT LIVED IN MEXICO CITY AT AGE 15, HIS PLACE OF BIRTH)?

35b. (ALL MIGRANTS:) In what ways would you say that living in this city is worse than living in (PLACE NAMED IN RESPONSE TO QUESTION 7a, OR IF RESPONDENT LIVED IN MEXICO CITY AT AGE 15, HIS PLACE OF BIRTH)?

35c. Do you have any relatives still living in (PLACE MENTIONED IN RESPONSE TO QUESTION 7a)? (IF YES:) Who are they?—Not their names, but how they are related to you.

35a. Since you came to live in Mexico City, how often have you visited (this person/these relatives)? Would you say that you have visited (him/her/them) very often, occasionally, (from time to time), not very often, almost never, or never?

35e. (IF RESPONDENT HAS VISITED RELATIVES IN PLACE OF ORIGIN:) How many days did you spend visiting this person (these persons) in (PLACE MENTIONED IN RESPONSE TO QUESTION 7a, OR IF RESPONDENT LIVED IN MEXICO CITY AT AGE 15, HIS PLACE OF BIRTH), during the past 12 months?

35f. Since your arrival in Mexico City, how often have you been visited by (this person/these relatives)?--Here in Mexico City.

36a. (IF NATIVE OF MEXICO CITY:) What is it that you like most about living in this city?

36b. (IF NATIVE OF MEXICO CITY:) What is it you like least about living in this city?

37a. (ALL RESPONDENTS:) Do you know of any relatives, friends, neighbors, or co-workers who came to this city and lived here for a while, but decided to return to their place of origin? (IF YES:) Who were these people?--Not their names, but how they are related to you, or how you came to know them.

37b. Do you know what caused (this person/these persons) to leave the city? (IF NEEDED:) Did they have some kind of unpleasant experience, or did they have trouble finding a job or a place to live, or what other kinds of problems did they have?

38a. Through your encouragement and help have any relatives or friends of yours come to live in Mexico City? (IF YES:) Who are they?--Not their names, but how they are related to you, or how you came to know them.

38b. Where did they come from?

39. (ALL RESPONDENTS:) Keeping in mind all aspects of life, where do you think that people are generally more satisfied and happy--in the country or in the city?

40. (ALL MIGRANTS:) Would you say it is easier, more difficult, or just about the same to make friends here in Mexico City than it is in (PLACE MENTIONED IN RESPONSE TO QUESTION 7a, OR IF RESPONDENT LIVED IN MEXICO CITY AT AGE 15, HIS PLACE OF BIRTH)?

41a. (ALL MIGRANTS:) Do you think it is more difficult for a provinciano to get ahead in this city than for some one born and raised here, or don't you think it makes any difference?

41b. (IF "MORE DIFFICULT" OR "EASIER":) In what ways do you think it is (more difficult/easier)?

42a. (ALL RESPONDENTS:) If it were up to you to decide, would you be in favor of allowing all the people who are able to come and live in this city, or would you be in favor of stopping so many people from coming here?

42b. Why do you feel that way?

43a. Could you tell me something about your main occupation? What do you do for a living? (IF NECESSARY:) Could you describe the work you do? (IF UNEMPLOYED: ASK QUESTION ABOUT JOB LAST HELD OR USUALLY HELD)

(IF PRESENTLY EMPLOYED ASK 43b TO 43g.)

43b. How many hours a day do you work at this job?

43c. How many days a week do you work at this job?

43d. How many weeks each month do you work at this job?

43e. How many months out of the year do you work at this job?

43f. In addition to your main job, do you have any other jobs? (IF YES:) What kind of job? (IF NECESSARY:) Could you describe the kind of work you do in this job?

43g. In all, how many hours a day do you spend working, counting your main job and any other jobs you may have?

(IF CURRENTLY UNEMPLOYED, ASK 44a, 44b, AND 44c)

44a. For how long have you had no work?

44b. Throughout your life since you began to work full-time, what is the longest length of time you have been without work?

44c. Why are you not working at the present time?

45. (ALL RESPONDENTS:) How long have you worked in your present main occupation, adding together all the time you have worked in this occupation, even if it has been for various short periods?

(IF EMPLOYED IN A FACTORY, OFFICE, STORE, RESTAURANT, SHOP, OR FARM, ASK 46a TO 46d.)

46a. Could you tell me something about the place where you work--that is, the (factory, office, store, restaurant, shop, farm) where you work? For example, about how many people work at this place?

46b. What does this (factory/office/store/restaurant/shop/farm) for which you work do? (IF NEEDED:) What does it sell, produce, or offer as a service?

46c. Where is it located?

46d. How long have you worked there?

(IF EMPLOYED, ASK 47a, 47b, AND 47c.)

47a. Speaking about your main job, on which you spend the most time during the year, how satisfied are you with your present work? Would you say you are very satisfied, somewhat satisfied, only a little satisfied, or not at all satisfied?

47b. Which of these phrases comes closest to your opinion about your present job?: (READ LIST)
"It's a bad job"
"It's a job, like any other"
"It's a good job"
"It's a fine job"

47c. In some jobs there are many opportunities to get ahead and improve your situation, while in others there are no such opportunities. In your present job, how good are your chances for getting ahead and improving your family's economic situation? Would you say that your chances are very good, good, average, not very good, or poor?

48. (ALL RESPONDENTS:) What job do you think you will be working at five years from now?

49. Which would you consider to be better? (READ ALTERNATIVES)
—A job that is steady and secure, but without many opportunities to get ahead (or)
—A job that is unsteady and insecure, but with many opportunities to get ahead?

50. Suppose that you had a chance to get a much better job than you have now. How important would each of these things be in stopping you from taking the job?
Would they actually stop you from taking it, or would they not stop you from taking it? (READ LIST)
—Having to postpone having a child
—Having to learn new skills to do the job
—Having to give up free time
—Having to keep quiet about your political opinions
—Having to leave your friends
—Having to leave your relatives (apart from those who live here with you)
—Having to leave your family (those who live here with you) for a while
—Having to travel a lot from place to place in the new job

51. (IF NATIVE OF MEXICO CITY:) Since you began to work full time, have you done any other kind of work besides the work you are presently doing? (IF YES:) What of work, and for how long? (IF NOT SPECIFIC ENOUGH:) Exactly what did you do in this job?

52a. (IF MIGRANT WHO WORKED BEFORE MIGRATING:) What was the last job you had before moving to Mexico City? Were you owner of
(IF RESPONDENT HAD JOB RELATED TO AGRICULTURE:) a small farm, owner or manager of a medium-size or large farm, an ejidatario, a tenant farmer or sharecropper, a landless farm worker, or what other kind of situation were you in?

52b. (IF RESPONDENT HAD NOT WORKED IN AGRICULTURE:) In that job, did you work for an employer or boss, or were you an owner or business partner?

52c. (ALL MIGRANTS:) What was the first job you had after arriving here in Mexico City?

52d. Other than your present job, have you done any other kinds of work since you came to Mexico City? (IF YES:) What kind of work, and for how long?

53. (ALL RESPONDENTS:) Do you remember the hopes you had about your work when you first started to work? Have you gotten farther than you expected, or not as far?

54. (IF MIGRANT:) If you had a job in (PLACE MENTIONED IN RESPONSE TO 7a, OR IF RESPONDENT LIVED IN MEXICO CITY AT AGE 15, HIS PLACE OF BIRTH), how do you consider your present job compared with that job? Would you say that your present job is much better, somewhat better, about equal to, worse, or much worse than the job you held in (PLACE NAMED IN RESPONSE TO 7a)?

55. (ALL RESPONDENTS:) In your opinion, what is the best occupation that a person of your experience and ability can hope for?

56a. Can you tell me anything about the new Federal Labor Law? For example, what kinds of things is it supposed to gain for the workers?

56b. (IF HAS HEARD OF LAW OR CAN IDENTIFY IT:) Do you think that this law will have any effect on your own job, in particular? (IF YES:) In what ways?

57. (ALL RESPONDENTS:) Thinking back to your childhood—What was the main occupation of your father during the first 15 years or so of your life? (IF RESPONDENT DOESN'T KNOW OR DOESN'T REMEMBER, ASK OF HIS MOTHER).

58. Where was your father born? Where is it located?—In what state or territory?

59. Where was your mother born? Where is it located?—In what state or territory?

60. Here are some questions about different aspects of life and work. Each question has two parts, or statements. For each question, we want to know which part you believe is more true. In some cases you may believe that both parts are true. In other cases you may think neither part is true. But for every question, we want you to choose the part which you believe is more true. (READ LIST)

60a. The only important thing is to work hard--that is the only way to progress in life.
Getting ahead in life is mostly a matter of having better luck than others.

60b. People with wild and strange opinions should not be allowed to speak in public in this country.
Anyone with something to say should be allowed to speak out, regardless of what ideas or point of view he may have.

60c. You sometimes can't help wondering whether life is worthwhile anymore.
Life is often hard and unfair, but one must always make the best of what he has.

60d. In the long run, we ourselves are responsible for having bad government.
Someone like me doesn't have any say about what the government does.

60e. Nowadays a person has to live pretty much for today and let tomorrow take care of itself.
It is necessary to prepare ourselves for the future and make plans for it.

60f. The best job to have is one where you are part of a group all working together.
It is better to work alone and achieve your own goals than to work with other people and have to depend on them.

60g. Listening to all the different points of view on something is very confusing; it's better to hear just one point of view from somebody who is informed.
Before making a decision, it's good to consider the opinions of as many different people as possible.

60h. One of the major causes of war is that people do not take enough interest in what is happening in the world.
However, I might try, I feel more and more helpless in the face of what is happening in the world today.

60i. A person should strive to be successful even if it means he will lose friends and others will be jealous of him.
In the long run, it is more important to be liked and respected by one's friends and neighbors than to become successful in life.

60j. Any leader should be very strict with the people under him in order to gain their respect.
Being respected as a leader comes only from treating one's followers well.

60k. I usually feel that I'm very much a part of the things going on around here.
These days I get a feeling that I'm just not a part of things.

60l. It is essential for effective work that our bosses tell us just what is to be done and exactly how to do it.
We can usually get the job done just as well without any instructions from our bosses.

60m. Sometimes politics and government seem so complicated that a person like me can't really understand what's going on.
If a person just pays attention to what is going on in politics and government, he should be able to understand what is happening.

60n. No matter how hard some people try, it's difficult for them to get ahead in life.
Most people who don't get ahead just don't have enough will power.

60o. It is best to make plans for the things you want in life.
It is best to leave things to fate.

60p. It's hardly fair to bring a child into the world, the way things look for the future.
No matter how bad things may look at times, we should always have hope for what the future may bring.

60q. It's useless to kill yourself working, if you have little time left for anything else.
The job should come first, even if it means sacrificing time from recreation or from one's family.

60r. What young people need most of all is strict discipline by their parents.
Young people today should have more freedom and independence from their families.

60s. You can always count on someone to help you out if things get bad enough.
When you get right down to it, no one is going to care much about what happens to you.

60t. The secret of happiness is not to expect a lot and be content with what comes your way.
One should make any sacrifices in order to succeed in life.

60u. What we need most is a strong leader to tell us what to do.
We are better off trying to figure out what we should do by ourselves than listening to some leader who claims to know what's best for us.

60v. A person can pretty well make whatever he wants out of his life.
No matter how much a person tries, it is hard to change the way things are going to turn out.

60w. It's good to pay attention to election campaigns, because it is important that the best candidate wins.
It doesn't matter much whether the people elect one candidate or another, because nothing is going to change, anyway.

60x. Everything is so uncertain these days that it almost seems as though anything could happen. In spite of everything, it's really not hard for a person to know where he stands from one day to the next.

61. Now here is a different sort of question. Some people say that a man should work for his goals in life participating with others as a member of organized groups, while others think it is best to work for one's goals by acting alone, without belonging to organized groups. How do you feel about it? Is it better to work for one's goals by working with others as a member of a group, or is it better to work alone?

62. Now I'm going to read a list of things that a young man may need to learn in life. Would you please tell me which one of these you think is most important? (READ LIST OF ALTERNATIVES)

   --Knowing how to do his job well
   --Being a good father and head of the family
   --Being a good Mexican
   --Making a good income
   --Being a good friend
   --Practicing his religion faithfully
   --Helping his fellow man

   And what would be the second most important? (REPEAT LIST OF ALTERNATIVES)

63. It has been said that if a man works hard, saves his money, and is ambitious, he will get ahead in life. How often do you think this really happens? (SON'S QUESTIONNAIRE VERSION: Some people say that a man born into a poor family will not get ahead in life, even if he is ambitious and hard-working. Do you think that such a man will surely fail to get ahead, that he will probably fail to get ahead, that he could well succeed in life, or that he will almost certainly succeed?)

64. Everybody wants certain things in life. Think about what is really important for you...then think of the best life you can imagine, assuming that you could have everything just as you want it. Now think of the kind of life you would not want--the worst possible life you can imagine. Here is a picture of a ladder (SHOW LADDER). Suppose we say that the top of the ladder represents the best possible life for you, and the bottom represents the worst possible life for you.

10
9
8
7
6
5
4
3
2
1
0

64a. Where on the ladder do you feel you personally stand at the present time?

64b. Where on the ladder do you think you stood five years ago?

64c. And where do you think you will be on the ladder five years from now?

64d. (IF MIGRANT:) At about what step were you when you first came to live in Mexico City?

64e. Nowadays, where on the ladder would you place the average person in (PLACE NAMED IN RESPONSE TO QUESTION 7a, OR IF RESPONDENT LIVED IN MEXICO CITY AT AGE 15, HIS PLACE OF BIRTH)? That is, someone who was born and raised in that place and who lives there now.

64f. And about where would you be now if you had stayed in (PLACE MENTIONED IN RESPONSE TO QUESTION 7a, OR IF RESPONDENT LIVED IN MEXICO CITY AT AGE 15, HIS PLACE OF BIRTH)?

65. (ALL RESPONDENTS:) Some people say that getting ahead in life depends on fate or destiny. Others say that it depends on the person's own efforts. Do you think the position a man reaches in life depends more on fate and luck or more on his own efforts?

66. Do you think that most people would try to take advantage of you if they got the chance, or would they try to be fair?

67. Do you think you have more, the same, or fewer opportunities than the majority of people in Mexico to live a good life--that is, to live happily and in comfort?

68a. Taking into account what you see around you, would you say there is a great deal of injustice or not so much injustice in this country?

68b. Why do you feel that way?--Could you give me an example of what you mean?

69a. What do you think causes poverty?

69b. Do you think there will always be as much poverty in Mexico as there is now?

70. I am going to read a list of statements. Would you tell me with which of the following three statements you agree most? (READ LIST OF ALTERNATIVES)

   --The government should not intervene in the economic life of the country, but should leave economic questions in the hands of private citizens.
   --The government should not own businesses but should control some aspects of their operation.
   --The government should own all businesses and industries and should control the entire economic life of the country.

   (IF RESPONDENT HAS CHILDREN, ASK 71a TO 72d.)

71a. In general, do you think that the lives of your children will be better or worse than yours? How much better or worse?

71b. (IF "MUCH BETTER" OR "SOMEWHAT BETTER":) Why do you think that your children will have a better life than yours?

71c. (IF "SOMEWHAT WORSE" OR "MUCH WORSE":) Why do you think that your children will have a worse life than yours?

72a. Consider the chances that are open to your children to improve their lives. How do these chances compare with those of other young people in this city? Would you say that they are much better, a little better, about the same, a little worse, or much worse?

72b. Do you think there are some young people whose chances to improve their lives are better than those of your children? (IF YES:) Who are they?

72c. Are there some young people whose chances are not as good as those of your children? (IF YES:) Who are they?

72d. (IF DIFFERENCES MENTIONED:) What do you feel are the reasons for these differences between the opportunities of your children and those of others?

73. (ALL RESPONDENTS:) If the son of a working man is intelligent and hard-working, how much opportunity does he have of becoming the owner of a small business, if he really tries? Or the owner of a large business? A high-ranking public official? A high-ranking military officer? An important politician? An office worker? A doctor?

74. What do you think is the most important thing one needs in order to get ahead in life?

(IF RESPONDENT HAS SCHOOL-AGE CHILDREN, ASK 75a TO 77.)

75a. Do your children presently attend school? (IF YES:) How many of them attend regularly?

75b. What school(s) do they attend, and where are they located?

75c. (IF SCHOOL AGE CHILDREN DO NOT ATTEND SCHOOL:) Why don't they attend school? (IF MORE THAN ONE REASON GIVEN:) Which of these things which you have mentioned is the most important--the main reason why your children don't attend school?

IF RESPONDENT HAS CHILDREN OF SCHOOL-AGE OR YOUNGER THAN SCHOOL-AGE, ASK 76a AND 76b.)

76a. How much education do you want your children to get?

76b. (IF "NONE":) Would you like your children to learn some trade? (IF YES:) What trade?

77. You can never tell exactly how things will work out. Here are some statements. Please tell me, as far as you can see, which statement comes closest to the one that you would agree with: (READ LIST OF ALTERNATIVES)
--For a person in my economic situation, it is practically impossible to keep children in school past primary school.
--For a person in my economic situation, it is practically impossible to keep children in school past secondary school.
--For a person in my economic situation, it is practically impossible to put children through a university carrera (degree program).
--If a person in my economic situation is willing to make the necessary sacrifices, it should be possible to give his children as much education as they want.

(IF RESPONDENT HAS CHILDREN OLDER THAN SCHOOL-AGE, ASK QUESTIONS 78a TO 79.)

78a. How much education did your children get? What was the last year of school completed by each child?

78b. (IF MIGRANT WITH OLDER THAN SCHOOL-AGE CHILDREN:) Did your children begin school in (PLACE MENTIONED IN RESPONSE TO QUESTION 7a, OR IF RESPONDENT LIVED IN MEXICO CITY AT AGE 15, HIS PLACE OF BIRTH), in Mexico City, or some other place?

78c. (IF RESPONDENT'S CHILDREN BEGAN SCHOOL IN HIS PLACE OF ORIGIN:) Did they complete their studies there, or did they continue in this city?

79. About how much schooling would you have liked your children to have?

(IF RESPONDENT HAS SON UNDER 30 YEARS OF AGE, ASK 80a AND 80b.)

80a. What kind of work would you like your oldest son to do?

80b. What are the chances that he will have that kind of occupation. Would you say that it is very likely, somewhat likely, not very likely, or not at all likely?

81. (IF RESPONDENT HAS SON 30 YEARS OLD OR OLDER:) When your oldest son was younger, did you have any ideas about what you wanted him to be? What kind of work did you want him to do?

82a. (ALL RESPONDENTS:) If a son of yours were actually choosing a job at this moment, which would you prefer (assuming there was nothing special he wanted to do)? (READ ALTERNATIVES)
--An auto mechanic's job paying 2000 pesos a month
--A school teacher's job paying 1500 pesos a month

82b. Suppose he had the choice of a government clerk's job paying 3000 pesos a month, or an electrician's job paying 3500 pesos a month. Which would you prefer him to choose?

83a. Would you have more respect for a man if he were: (READ ALTERNATIVES)
—The mayor of a large city
—The rector of a university
—The head of a large industry

83b. Why would you feel that way?

84a. Some people think that they can plan their lives and strive for distant goals—for example, what they will be doing ten years from now. Others say, "whatever will be will be," and take things as they come. How do you feel about this? (IF NECESSARY:) Do you think it is better to try to make plans and strive for distant goals, or do you think it is better not to try to make plans and to just take things as they come?

84b. Have you ever made any long range plans for yourself, your family, or for some other group of people? (IF YES:) How did this work out?

85. Now I would like to ask you some questions about different groups of people and their social position in this country. Here is a picture of a ladder. Imagine that this ladder represents the social position of all the people in the country. This means that in the top part of the ladder are those persons who have the highest social positions. In the middle part of the ladder are those persons who have a middle social position; and in the lower part of the ladder are those persons who have a lower social position.

85a. Now, I would like you to point to the position on the ladder of the people who have the same social position as you.

85b. (IF RESPONDENT HAS SCHOOL-AGE CHILDREN:) And about where on the ladder do you think your children will be when they are grown?

86a. Sometimes one hears the term "social class," as in "middle class," "upper class," "working class," "lower class," and so forth. What term would you say is most applicable to you and your family?

86b. How difficult do you think it is to move from a lower social class to a higher one? Would you say it is very difficult or almost impossible, somewhat difficult, not very difficult, or not difficult at all?

86c. (IF SCHOOL-AGE CHILDREN:) To what social class do you think your children will belong?

87. (ALL RESPONDENTS:) Now I would like to talk for a while about the colonia in which you live. Here is a piece of paper. Could you draw me a rough map of this colonia, showing where it begins and where it ends? I don't need anything detailed, just a rough sketch showing the boundaries of the colonia. (IF RESPONDENT FINDS IT DIFFICULT OR IMPOSSIBLE TO DRAW MAP:) Could you tell me where you think the colonia begins and where it ends?

88a. How long have you lived here in this colonia?

88b. Then you came to this colonia in what year?

89a. At the present time, do you feel yourself to be a part of the colonia and are settled in it? (IF NECESSARY:) Do you feel that you "belong" and are really established in this colonia?

89b. (IF YES:) When did you begin to feel this way?

89c. (IF NO:) I see. Why do you say that? Could you give me an example of what you mean?

89d. (IF NO:) Is there any other place in this city or perhaps in some other place where you feel most at home? (IF NECESSARY:) That is, some place which you feel is really "home" for you. (IF YES:) What place is this?

89e. (IF OTHER PLACE MENTIONED:) Why do you feel that way about (COLONIA OR BARRIO MENTIONED IN RESPONSE TO QUESTION 89d)?

90. (ALL RESPONDENTS:) Do you think you have a great deal in common with other people living in this colonia, quite a bit in common, little in common, or nothing in common with them?

91. Has there been any important change in your life since you moved to this colonia? (IF YES:) In what sense? What are the most important things that have changed?

(IF RESPONDENT IS RESIDENT OF "ESFUERZO PROPIO," ASK 92a AND 92b)

92a. Taking everything into account, are you satisfied or dissatisfied with your move to this colonia? Would you say you are very satisfied, somewhat satisfied, a little dissatisfied, or very much dissatisfied?

92b. (IF "DISSATISFIED":) Why do you feel that way? Could you give me an example of what you mean?

93a. (ALL RESPONDENTS:) The house in which you live...is it owned by you, rented, or borrowed?

93b. (IF OWNED:) Is the house completely paid for, or are you still making payments on it? Did you ever own your own home before coming to (COLONIA IN WHICH RESPONDENT CURRENTLY LIVES)? (IF YES:) Where was this house?

93c. (IF RENTING:) How many pesos per month do you have to pay for rent?

94. (ALL RESPONDENTS EXCEPT THOSE LIVING IN UNIDAD POPULAR:) Did you build this house yourself? (IF YES:) How long did it take you to build it?

95. (ALL RESPONDENTS:) Has your house ever been flooded? (IF YES:) How many times? When was the last time this happened?

96a. And the land...how did you obtain it?

(IF LAND WAS OBTAINED THROUGH A GROUP INVASION, ASK 96b TO 96j.)

96b. Did you participate in the original occupation of the land which forms this colonia?

96c. (IF YES:) How did you learn of the plans for occupying the land?

96d. Altogether, how many families participated in the occupation of land in this colonia? Was your family with you at that time?

96e. What was the most important reason why you decided to participate?

96f. Did you play a special role in the occupation of this land? For example, were you in charge of any special kind of activity or particular job? (IF YES:) What was it? (IF NECESSARY:) Could you give me a description of what you did in that special job?

96g. Could you tell me something about your feelings while you were participating in the occupation of this land? Could you give me an example of what you mean?

96h. At the time that you were occupying the land, did you think that you would have no serious difficulty in occupying and holding it, or did you believe it would be necessary to struggle to hold onto it?

96i. Had you ever participated in such a land occupation by many families before the occupation of land in this colonia? (IF YES:) Where was that?

96j. (IF YES:) How long ago was this? How did it turn out? What did the landowner or the authorities do about it?

(IF RESPONDENT PARTICIPATED IN MORE THAN ONE INVASION, ASK ABOUT MOST RECENT ONE.)

(IF RESPONDENT PURCHASED LAND FROM PRIVATE LANDOWNER, SUBDIVIDER, OR GOVERNMENT, ASK 97a TO 97g.)

97a. Have you finished paying for the land?

97b. (IF YES:) How much did you pay for it, altogether?

97c. How many square meters of land do you have?

97d. Have you received your title to the land?

97e. (IF STILL PAYING FOR LAND:) How much have you paid thus far, altogether?

97f. How much do you still owe?

97g. How much do you have to pay monthly?

97h. How many square meters of land do you have?

(IF RESPONDENT PURCHASED THE LAND FROM A PRIVATE SUBDIVIDER [FRACCIONADOR] ASK 98a TO 98d.)

98a. In your contract for this land, are the obligations of the subdivider for urbanizing the land clearly specified? That is, responsibilities for water, sewage disposal, electricity, sidewalks, street pavement, and so on.

98b. (IF YES:) Has the subdivider complied with any of these obligations? (IF YES:) Which ones?

98c. Do you think the government has done anything to make the subdivider meet his obligations?

98d. (IF NO:) Why do you think the government hasn't done anything?

(IF RESPONDENT RENTS LAND, ASK 99a AND 99b)

99a. How much do you pay each month in rent?

99b. How many square meters of land do you rent?

(IF RESPONDENT DID NOT PURCHASE LAND FROM A PRIVATE LANDOWNER, SUBDIVIDER, OR FROM THE GOVERNMENT, DOES NOT RENT THE LAND, AND DID NOT OBTAIN IT THROUGH A GROUP INVASION, ASK 99c TO 99f.)

99c. Did you have to pay someone for the land?

99d. (IF YES:) Who did you have to pay?

99e. (IF YES:) How much did you have to pay, altogether?

99f. How many square meters of land do you have?

(IF RESPONDENT IS RESIDENT OF "ESFUERZO PROPIO," ASK 100a TO 100h)

100a. Do you participate in the program of Self Help and Mutual Assistance in this colonia? (IF YES:) Do you participate as an individual or as a member of one of the Mutual Assistance groups?

100b. Some people in this colonia have become participants in the Self Help and Mutual Assistance Program, while others have not participated. (IF RESPONDENT IS A PARTICIPANT:) Why did you decide to become a participant in the program? (IF NOT A PARTICIPANT:) Why did you not become a participant in the program?

100c. What do you regard as the most important advantages and disadvantages of participating in this program?

100d. (IF A PARTICIPANT:) Do you think the officials or administrators of the program are really trying to help you?

100e. (IF A PARTICIPANT:) Do you feel that the program officials really understand your problems?

100f. (IF A PARTICIPANT:) Do the program officials seriously consider your own point of view? For example, with regard to the manner in which your house is to be built, or the manner in which building materials are to be paid for, or some matter related to your participation in the program.

100g. Do you think that the Self Help and Mutual Assistance program is connected in some way with political or governmental affairs? (IF YES:) In what way do you think it is connected?

101a. (ALL RESPONDENTS:) Did you own any land before coming to live in this colonia?

101b. (IF YES:) Where was this? (IF NECESSARY:) Where is that located—in what state or territory?

102a. Do you know if there have been any attempts by the government or the police to evict or force off the land or to tear down the houses of any residents in this colonia?

102b. (IF YES:) When did this happen?

102c. Were you living in this colonia when this happened?

102d. How did this come about?

102e. About how many families were affected by this?

102f. What actions were taken? That is, how did the authorities carry out these eviction attempts?

102g. What were your feelings when this happened? For example, did you feel that the actions taken by the authorities were just or unjust?

102h. Were you or your family affected in some way by these actions? (IF YES:) In what way?

102i. Can you recall any other incidents of this nature? (IF YES:) How many? Did these things also happen here in this colonia, or somewhere else?

103a. Do you know if there have been any actions of this kind taken by private landowners or subdividers in this colonia?—That is, sudden evictions, destruction of houses, and other kinds of abuses.

103b. (IF YES:) When did this happen?

103c. Were you living in the colonia when this happened?

103d. How did this happen?

103e. About how many families were affected by this?

103f. What actions were taken? That is, how did the (land owner/subdivider) carry out these eviction attempts?

103g. What were your feelings when this happened? For example did you feel that the actions taken by the (landowner/subdivider) were just or unjust?

103h. Were you or your family affected in some way by these actions? (IF YES:) In what way?

103i. Can you recall any other incidents of this nature, that happened in this colonia? (IF YES:) How many?

104a. (ALL RESPONDENTS:) Do you recall any incidents of this kind which took place in places where you may have lived before coming to (COLONIA IN WHICH RESPONDENT CURRENTLY LIVES)?

104b. (IF YES:) Where was this?

104c. When did this happen?

104d. Who was involved in this—the government, the police, a land-owner, a subdivider?

105a. (ALL RESPONDENTS:) What about your present situation...do you feel that your claim to your house and land is secure?

105b. (IF INSECURE:) Who is likely to challenge or threaten your possession?

105c. What would you do if they tried to evict or relocate you?

106a. (ALL RESPONDENTS:) Do you have any specific plans for improving your house or land? (IF YES:) Could you tell me about them, briefly?

106b. (IF PLANS FOR IMPROVEMENT:) How likely is it that you'll be able to carry out your plans? Would you say it is very likely, somewhat likely, not too likely, or not at all likely?

107a. (ALL RESPONDENTS:) In general, how would you rate this colonia as a place to live?

107b. What is it in particular that you like about living in (COLONIA IN WHICH RESPONDENT CURRENTLY LIVES)?

107c. What is it in particular that you don't like about living here?

108. Do you think this colonia is progressing? Would you say it is progressing rapidly, progressing slowly, that it is not progressing, or is it getting worse?

109. In general, how much movement of families in and out of the colonia would you say there is? Would you say that there is a great deal of such movement, some movement, not very much or hardly any?

110. Do you think that in relation to the rest of Mexico City this colonia is very isolated, not very isolated, or not isolated at all?

111a. As far as you know now, do you intend to stay here permanently, or do you intend to move within the foreseeable future?

111b. (IF INTENDS TO MOVE OR IS UNDECIDED:) What is the most important reason why you haven't moved from here already?

111c. (INTENDS TO MOVE OR IS UNDECIDED:) To what kind of place would you like to move? In what ways would it be different from (COLONIA IN WHICH RESPONDENT CURRENTLY LIVES)?

111d. (IF INTENDS TO STAY IN CURRENT PLACE:) If you were thinking of moving to another place, what would be the most important things that you would consider in choosing that place?

112a. (ALL RESPONDENTS:) When you think about this colonia, in what ways do you think it has changed since you arrived here? Could you tell me the two or three most important changes that have taken place? (IF ONLY ONE CHANGE MENTIONED:) Are there any others?

112b. (ABOUT THE FIRST CHANGE MENTIONED:) On the whole, has this first change you mentioned been good or bad?

112c. (ABOUT FIRST CHANGE:) Who do you think was most responsible for this change?

112d. (ABOUT SECOND CHANGE MENTIONED:) On the whole, has this second change you mentioned been good or bad?

112e. (ABOUT SECOND CHANGE:) Who do you think was most responsible for this change?

112f. (ABOUT THIRD CHANGE MENTIONED:) On the whole, has this third change you mentioned been good or bad?

112g. (ABOUT THIRD CHANGE:) Who do you think was most responsible for this change?

113a. (ALL RESPONDENTS:) Can you recall any event, incident, or experience that may have occurred in this colonia since you have lived here...something that you considered very important or something about which you felt very strongly? (IF NEEDED:) Something that made you feel really angry or really happy?

113b. (IF YES:) What was that about? How did it come about? What happened? How did it turn out?

113c. Why did this make you feel angry (happy)?

113d. (IF POSITIVE EXPERIENCE MENTIONED:) Who do you think was responsible for this? (IF NEEDED:) Who do you think deserves the credit for this? What person or group or office?

113e. (IF NEGATIVE EXPERIENCE:) Was anyone to blame for this? What person or group or office?

113f. Did you do anything about this at the time? (IF YES:) What was that? (IF NO:) Do you think anything could have been done about it? (IF YES:) What kind of thing?

114a. (ALL RESPONDENTS:) Think about the changes that may take place in this colonia in the next five years or so. What do you think the colonia will be like five years from now? In what ways do you think it will be different from its present condition?

114b. (IF NO CHANGES FORESEEN:) Why do you think there will be no changes? (ALL RESPONDENTS:) Here is a set of photographs. Which one of these looks most like what you think this colonia will look like five years or so from now?

115a. Suppose you heard a rumor that the government was going to build a new health center for the people living in this colonia and others nearby. To what person or group or office would you go to get more information about such a matter?

115b. (IF RESPONDENT CAN IDENTIFY A POTENTIAL SOURCE OF INFORMATION:) (IF SOURCE IS A PERSON:) Does this person live here in (COLONIA IN WHICH RESPONDENT LIVES)? (IF SOURCE IS GROUP, OFFICE, ETC.:) Is this (group/office) located here in (COLONIA IN WHICH RESPONDENT LIVES)?

116a. (ALL RESPONDENTS:) Now I would like to ask a few questions about the people who live in this colonia. Do you have many friends in this colonia?--For example, would you say that your neighbors are your friends? All your neighbors, some of them, or none of them?

116b. (IF "ALL" OR "SOME":) Why do you feel that way? (IF NECESSARY:) For example, what kinds of things do you do together with your neighbors?

116c. (IF "NONE":) Why do you feel that none of your neighbors are your friends? Could you give me an example of what you mean?

117. (ALL RESPONDENTS:) About how many people in this colonia do you know well enough to talk to?

118a. Now think about your three closest neighbors--those whom you know best. How often do you get together with them?

118b. Now think about your three closest friends. In what area or areas do they live?

118c. How often do you get together with them?

118d. Think of your three closest relatives, other than those who live with you in this house. In what areas do they live?

118e. How often do you get together with them?

118f. In the past two years, how often have you received the following kinds of help from these relatives? (READ LIST)
--Advice on a decision you had to make
--Help on special occasions, such as childbirth or sickness
--Help in caring for children
--Financial assistance, such as money or a loan
--Help in finding a job or a place to live
--Handwork such as sewing, help in building or repairing your house, etc.
--Any other kinds of help

118g. In the past two years have you given these relatives any kind of help you can recall? (IF YES:) What kinds of help? How often?

118h. In general, would you say that you now feel closer to your relatives (that is, those who do not live here in this house) than when you were living in (PLACE MENTIONED IN RESPONSE TO QUESTION 7a, OR IF RESPONDENT LIVED IN MEXICO CITY AT AGE 15, HIS PLACE OF BIRTH), or not so close?

119a. (ALL RESPONDENTS:) Are you or any other persons living in this colonia related to any other persons living in this colonia through compadrazgo? (IF YES:) To how many persons?

119b. (IF MIGRANT:) How important is compadrazgo in your life here in the city? Would you say it is very important, somewhat important, not very important, or not important at all?

119c. (IF MIGRANT:) In comparison with your life in (PLACE MENTIONED IN RESPONSE TO QUESTION 7a, OR IF RESPONDENT LIVED IN MEXICO CITY AT AGE 15, HIS PLACE OF BIRTH), would you say that compadrazgo is more important for you here in Mexico City, less important, or is it about the same?

119d. (IF "MORE IMPORTANT" OR "LESS IMPORTANT":) Why do you feel that way? In what way is it (more/less) important for you here? (IF NECESSARY:) For example, would you say that, in general, you receive (more/less) help from the compadres you have here in the city than you received from your compadres when you lived in (PLACE MENTIONED IN RESPONSE TO QUESTION 7a, OR IF RESPONDENT LIVED IN MEXICO CITY AT AGE 15, HIS PLACE OF BIRTH)?

120a. (ALL RESPONDENTS:) Do you think that the people who live in this colonia are very united, more or less united, only a little united, or not united at all?

120b. What kinds of work have you done together with other residents of this colonia? For example, when the residents have done something for the colonia, such as building a meeting hall or installing some public service (water, light, drainage, etc.), or when assistance has been provided to families affected by floods or fires--have you taken part in any of these activities? (IF YES:) What kinds? How many times have you done this?

(IF RESPONDENT IS RESIDENT OF COLONIA NUEVA, ASK QUESTIONS 120c TO 120g.)

120c. Do you ever go on comisiones with other residents of this colonia? (IF YES:) During the past year--that is from June of 1969 to May of this year--in how many comisiones did you participate?

120d. (IF YES:) Which one of the following statements best describes how you feel when you go on comisiones? (READ LIST OF ALTERNATIVES)
"I feel bothered; it's a waste of time."
"I go because they make me go."
"I go only because it is my duty."
"I feel satisfied because it is helping the colonia."

120e. (IF "SATISFIED BECAUSE IT IS HELPING THE COLONIA":) In what ways does this help the colonia?

120f. Do you ever attend meetings (juntas) of the colonia? (IF YES:) During the past year--that is, from June of 1969 to May of this year--how many juntas did you attend?

120g. Do you ever participate in the vigilancia for the colonia? (IF YES:) During the past year--that is, from June of 1969 to May of this year--in how many guardias or veladas (night watches or patrols) did you participate?

121a. (ALL RESPONDENTS:) In many places there are groups that are opposed to each other. Thinking about (COLONIA IN WHICH RESPONDENT LIVES), what are the major groups that oppose each other here?--That is, the groups that have differences of opinion or who have controversies.

121b. (IF OPPOSITION GROUPS MENTIONED:) Do you think these differences are good for the colonia or not so good?

122a. (ALL RESPONDENTS:) In your opinion, who are the three persons who have the most influence in (COLONIA IN WHICH RESPONDENT LIVES)?--That is, the persons who are most successful in getting their own way and getting things done. What kind of work do they do?

122b. Why do these people have more influence in this colonia than others? (IF NECESSARY:) Why do people come to them in search of help, advice, or orientation?

123. Suppose two men are talking about some problem of this colonia, and of the best way of solving it. The first man says: "It is better for each person to form his own opinion of what should be done and to defend his point of view before his neighbors. If there are large differences of opinion among the residents of the colonia, then the matter should be decided by taking a vote." The second man says: "As soon as you begin deciding questions like that by taking a vote, you'll see that some people are with you and some are against you, and in that way divisions and quarrels develop. It's best to get everybody to agree first, then you don't have to vote." With which of these two men are you most in agreement? (IF "NEITHER":) Why do you feel that way?

124. Do you think that most people around here tend to be hard on a person who does not agree with his neighbors on something like politics? Or do you think it does not matter with most people?

125a. Some people feel that when they are troubled by a problem of the colonia, they can do something about it, such as speak out for or against a solution to the problem or in some other way attempt to get their opinions considered. Other people feel that this kind of activity can only lead to problems for them. We would like to know your feelings about such matters. Suppose some problem of the colonia comes up, and you are troubled by it, and you decide to do something about it. Would any of the following things be likely to happen? (READ LIST)

--Your friends and neighbors would disapprove of your efforts
--Your family and your other relatives would disapprove
--You would get a reputation as a trouble-maker
--You would get fired from your job or get a warning from your boss
--You would get a warning from the leaders of the colonia
--The authorities would threaten you or try to evict you
--(ASKED EVERYWHERE EXCEPT UNIDAD POPULAR AND ESFUERZO PROPIO) The (subdivider/landowner) would threaten you or try to evict you

125b. (IF "YES" OR "DON'T KNOW":) If (this thing/any of these things) that you mentioned actually happened to you because you were trying to do something about a problem of the colonia, what would you do then? Would you continue trying to do something about the problem, or would you stop trying?

126a. (ALL RESPONDENTS:) When you meet someone for the first time in this colonia, should you: (READ LIST)
--Trust him until he proves to be unworthy of that trust
--Be cautious about trusting him until you know him better
--Not trust him because he may take advantage of you?

126b. Do you think what you say applies only to people in this colonia, or does it apply to people in general?

126c. (IF "DOES NOT APPLY TO PEOPLE IN GENERAL":) In what way is there a difference between people around here and others elsewhere? Can you remember any incidents or experiences that illustrate this difference?

126d. (IF MIGRANT AND RESPONSE TO QUESTION 126a DOES NOT APPLY TO PEOPLE IN GENERAL:) In what way is there a difference between people around here and those living in (PLACE MENTIONED IN RESPONSE TO QUESTION 7a, OR IF RESPONDENT LIVED IN MEXICO CITY AT AGE 15, HIS PLACE OF BIRTH)? Do you recall any incidents or experiences that illustrate this difference?

127a. (ALL RESPONDENTS:) Some people are inclined to help others. Other people are more inclined to look out only for themselves. Thinking again about the people in this colonia, which of the following statements do you think applies most to them? (READ ALTERNATIVES)
--Most people around here are helpful to others
--Most people around here only look out for themselves

127b. (IF RESPONDENT CHOOSES AN ALTERNATIVE:) Why do you say that? Can you remember any incidents or experiences that illustrate this?

127c. Do you think that what you say applies only to people in this colonia, or does it apply to people in general?

127d. (IF "DOES NOT APPLY TO PEOPLE IN GENERAL":) In what way is there a difference between people around here and others elsewhere? Can you recall any incidents or experiences that illustrate this difference?

127e. (IF MIGRANT AND "DOES NOT APPLY TO PEOPLE IN GENERAL":) In what way is there a difference between people around here and those living in (PLACE MENTIONED IN RESPONSE TO QUESTION 7a, OR IF RESPONDENT LIVED IN MEXICO CITY AT AGE 15, HIS PLACE OF BIRTH), with respect to this tendency to (help others/look out only for one's self)? Can you remember any incidents or experiences that illustrate this difference?

128a. (ALL RESPONDENTS:) Do your neighbors sometimes quarrel or argue with you? (IF YES:) How often does this happen?

128b. (IF MIGRANT:) Do you think that there is more or less quarreling among neighbors here than in (PLACE MENTIONED IN RESPONSE TO QUESTION 7a, OR IF RESPONDENT LIVED IN MEXICO CITY AT AGE 15, HIS PLACE OF BIRTH)?

129a. (ALL RESPONDENTS:) There are some people who say that violence should never be used to settle personal quarrels or disputes—that is, those involving relatives, friends, neighbors, co-workers, and so forth. Others say that in some cases it may be necessary to use violent means to settle a dispute. How do you feel about this? Should violence never be used to settle personal questions, or may it be justified in some situations?

129b. (IF "VIOLENCE MAY SOMETIMES BE USED":) In what kind of situation? Could you give me an example of some situation in which violence may be justified?

129c. (ALL RESPONDENTS:) How about political questions or disputes? Do you think that violence should never be used to settle this type of dispute, or may it be justified in some situations?

129d. (IF "VIOLENCE MAY SOMETIMES BE USED":) In what kind of situation? Could you give me an example of some situation in which violent means may be justified?

129e. (ALL RESPONDENTS:) During the student demonstrations in Mexico City in August and September of 1968—that is, at the time of the Olympic Games—were you on the side of the government or of the students?

129f. (IF RESPONDENT CAN RECALL DEMONSTRATIONS:) What were your feelings about what happened—especially about the government's actions toward the students? (IF NECESSARY:) For example, did you feel that the actions taken by the government were justified or not?

129g. Why do you say that?

129h. (ALL RESPONDENTS:) Can you imagine any kind of situation in which you might take part in demonstrations like the ones in Mexico City in 1968? (IF YES:) What kind of situation? Could you give me an example of what you mean?

130a. (ALL RESPONDENTS:) Here is another kind of question. Suppose something were to happen to your family—say, for example, a case of serious illness or accident, the sudden loss of your job or of your house, etc. Is there some person, group, or office which you could rely upon for help in such a situation? (IF YES:) Who are they? (Does this person live/is this office, group, etc. located) inside or outside of (COLONIA IN WHICH RESPONDENT LIVES)?

130b. Can you give me any examples of special help you have received from this person (group, office) in the past five years or so?

130c. Compared with your situation of five years ago, would you say that it is easier now to find someone to count on in case of special need, about the same, or harder now to find someone?

130d. (IF MIGRANT:) Compared with your situation before coming to Mexico City, would you say that it is easier now to find someone to count on in case of special need, about the same, or harder now to find someone?

131a. (ALL RESPONDENTS:) The main concern of our work is to find out what the needs and major concerns of the people are. We want to know as fully as possible what concerns and problems they have. Think now about the most important needs and problems of (COLONIA IN WHICH RESPONDENT LIVES). In your opinion, what are the most urgent or serious problems and needs of this colonia? (IF MORE THAN ONE PROBLEM MENTIONED:) Which of these needs or problems is the most important one for you?

131b. Who or what is to blame for most of the problems you have mentioned?

131c. Are many of the other people in this colonia concerned about problems of this sort, or are most of them unconcerned?

131d. When you think of problems of the sort you have mentioned... can they be solved by those living within the colonia, or would help be needed from outside the colonia?

131e. Within this colonia, who may be able to help in solving these kinds of problems or in meeting these kinds of needs? (IF NEEDED:) What persons or groups?

131f. (IF "NO ONE":) Some people believe that residents' associations are needed to solve the problems of the colonias proletarias of this city, while others do not think them necessary. How do you feel about it?

131g. (IF POTENTIAL INTERNAL SOURCE OF ASSISTANCE IDENTIFIED:) How certain are you that you would receive help from (FIRST PERSON, GROUP, OFFICE MENTIONED IN RESPONSE TO QUESTION 113e)? Are you very certain, not so sure they would help, or do you think they are not likely to help?

131h. (IF TWO POTENTIAL INTERNAL SOURCES OF ASSISTANCE IDENTIFIED:) And what about (SECOND PERSON, GROUP, OFFICE MENTIONED IN RESPONSE TO QUESTION 131e)? Are you very certain that they would help, not so sure, or do you think they are not likely to help?

131i. (ALL RESPONDENTS:) And who is it from outside of this colonia who may be able to help in solving the kinds of problems you have mentioned? (IF NEEDED:) What persons, groups, or offices?

131j. (IF POTENTIAL SOURCE OF OUTSIDE HELP IDENTIFIED:) How certain are you that you would receive help from (FIRST PERSON, GROUP, OFFICE MENTIONED IN RESPONSE TO QUESTION 131i)? Are you very certain they would help, not so sure, or do you think they are not likely to help?

131k. (IF TWO POTENTIAL SOURCES OF OUTSIDE HELP IDENTIFIED:) And what about (SECOND PERSON, GROUP, OFFICE MENTIONED IN RESPONSE TO QUESTION 131i)? Are you very certain that they would help, not so sure, or do you think they are not likely to help?

132. (ALL RESPONDENTS:) Generally speaking, which is most important for improving the conditions of life in this colonia: The hard work of the residents, God's help, the government's help, or good luck? And which is the second most important? (REPEAT LIST OF ALTERNATIVES)

133a. Have you ever made donations or paid cuotas (dues, special assessments) to the leaders of this colonia, or to other persons or groups within the colonia for some purpose? (IF NEEDED:) Perhaps to pay for some type of public building, or to install some public service or improvement (such as water, light or sewers)? (IF YES:) To whom have you made these payments? For what purposes did you make these payments? How many times have you done this?

133b. (IF PAYMENTS MADE FOR PUBLIC SERVICES OR IMPROVEMENTS:) Has this (service/improvement) been installed (provided)?

133c. (IF NO:) What do you think was done with the money you paid?

134. (ALL RESPONDENTS:) Here is a ladder. Suppose the group or person who contributes most to the welfare of the people around here—that is, the person or group which acts most strongly in the interests of you and other residents of this colonia—is at the top of the ladder; and the group or person who does the least or does nothing for the welfare of the people around here is at the bottom. Where would newspapermen be in terms of their contribution to the welfare of the people around here?—Near the top of the ladder, near the one which contributes most, or near the one which contributes least to your welfare? (REPEAT QUESTION FOR EACH PERSON OR GROUP ON LIST)
—The President of the Republic
—Priests
—Politicians
—School Teachers
—The Police
(ALL RESPONDENTS EXCEPT RESIDENTS OF COLONIA TEXCOCO)

—The head of the Department of the Federal District [Mayor of Mexico City], Corona del Rosal
—(ALL RESPONDENTS EXCEPT RESIDENTS OF UNIDAD POPULAR AND ESFUERZO PROPIO:) subdividers or landowners
—(ALL RESPONDENTS EXCEPT RESIDENTS OF COLONIA TEXCOCO)
The head of the Office of Colonias, Félix Ramírez
—(ONLY RESIDENTS OF COLONIA TEXCOCO:) The Municipal President of Ciudad Netzahualcóyotl, Gonzalo Barquín
—(ONLY RESIDENTS OF COLONIA TEXCOCO:) The Governor of the State of Mexico, Hank González

135. What political party do you think contributes the most to solving the problems of this colonia?

136a. Some people feel that the PRI has helped to make their lives better ones; others don't think it has helped. How do you feel about it? (IF NEEDED:) Has the PRI helped to make your life a better one or not?

136b. Where is the nearest office of the PRI? In what colonia and on what street is it located?

136c. (IF ABLE TO LOCATE PRI OFFICE:) Have you ever gone there? (IF YES:) For what purpose?

136d. (IF YES:) How do you think you were treated (attended) there?

136e. (IF NO:) If you did go there some day, how do you think you would be treated (attended)?

136f. (ALL RESPONDENTS:) Have you ever seen any officials or representatives of the government, of the PRI, or of the CNOP, come to this colonia? (IF YES:) When did this happen? Was this during an election campaign? Do you know why this person (these persons) came to the colonia? Did anything happen in the colonia as a result of their visit(s)? (IF YES:) What kinds of things?

137a. (ALL RESPONDENTS:) Have you ever heard of the C.N.O.P.? (IF NEEDED:) CENOP—the Confederación Nacional de Organizaciones Populares?

137b. (IF YES:) Could you tell me something about the work done by this organization? For example, do you think that the CNOP contributes to the welfare of people in this colonia, that it does nothing for the people, or that it is harmful to the welfare of people around here?
(IF "BENEFICIAL" OR "ITS HARMFUL" ASK 137c, 137d AND 137e.)

137c. In what ways does it do this?

137d. Have you or some member of your family benefitted in some way from the activities of the C.N.O.P.? (IF YES:) In what way?

137e. Have you personally ever been in contact with the C.N.O.P.? For example, have you ever visited one of its offices, or talked with any people who work for it? (IF YES:) What was that about? How did it come about? What resulted from this visit (conversation)? (IF NEEDED:) What happened or how did it turn out?

138a. (ALL RESPONDENTS:) Have you ever heard of the C.C.I.--the Central Campesino Independiente?

138b. (IF YES:) Could you tell me something about the work done by this organization? For example, do you think that the CCI contributes to the welfare of the people in this colonia, that it does nothing for the people, or that it is harmful to the welfare of people around here?

(IF "IS BENEFICIAL" OR "IS HARMFUL" ASK 138c, 138d, AND 138e.)

138c. In what ways does it do this?

138d. Have you or some member of your family benefitted in some way from the activities of the C.C.I.? (IF YES:) In what way?

139. (ALL RESPONDENTS:) We are interested in some of the services the government provides the people of this city. Think about your family--that is yourself, your parents, (IF MARRIED:) your wife, (IF CHILDREN:) your children, and your brothers and sisters. Have you or any other member of your family ever: (READ LIST)
--Received medical care at some government hospital or clinic, a public health center, or some Social Security facility?
--Received medical care, vaccination, or other health treatment here in the colonia, from doctors sent by the government or by the PRI?
--Received help in finding a job or a place to live from some government office or from a labor union?
--Received free legal services or aid from some office of the government of the PRI?
--Received or bought food or other products from the CONASUPO or from a "Market on Wheels"?
--Received benefits of any kind from the Social Security administration (other than medical attention)?
--Received any other kinds of benefits or assistance from an office of the government or of the PRI? Or perhaps from some person who works for the government or the PRI, such as a social worker? (IF YES:) What kind of help? From what office or person?

140a. (IF NO SOCIAL SECURITY BENEFITS MENTIONED:) Do you have Social Security in your job?

140b. (ALL RESPONDENTS:) Have you ever visited one of the Centros Sociales Populares? (IF NEEDED:) That is, the Centers of Tepito, Leandro Valle, Miguel Hidalgo, Aquiles Serdán, Pino Suárez, Ignacio Zaragoza, and others like them, built by the Department of the Federal District. (IF YES:) For what purpose?

141a. (ALL RESPONDENTS:) Now I am going to read a list of activities. As I read each type of activity, I would like you to give me your opinion of how well the government is doing in each of these areas. If you don't think the government has any responsibility for doing some of these things, please tell me. For example, providing potable water. Would you say that the government is doing very well, not so well, or poorly in fulfilling its responsibility for providing potable water?
--Providing electricity
--Providing sewers
--Paving streets
--Providing public transportation
--Providing police protection for lives and property
--Providing fire protection
--Providing decent housing for the poor
--Helping people to regularize their land holdings or secure title to their property
--Providing parks and recreation areas
--Building or improving public markets
--Providing enough schools and teachers
--Providing medical care for the poor
--Providing economic help (that is, credit, loans, pension benefits, and other kinds of Social Security benefits) to those in need
--Seeing to it that everyone who needs a job can have one
--Assuring fair treatment of the poor by the police
--Trying to even out differences between the rich and the poor classes in Mexico

141b. In general, how satisfied are you with the performance of the government in providing services for the people? Are you very dissatisfied, somewhat dissatisfied, more or less satisfied, or very satisfied?

142. (ALL RESPONDENTS:) Some people say that one can only wait and accept government programs; others feel that a person can have influence on the government and make the government help people. How do you feel about this? Do you think that one can only wait and accept government programs, or do you think a person can have influence and make the government help?

143a. Thinking again about the problems and needs of (COLONIA IN WHICH RESPONDENT LIVES), which we were discussing before...are you now, or have you been in the last year or so, personally concerned about such problems? (IF YES:) Any particular kind of problem?

143b. Do you ever discuss problems of this sort with other people in this colonia? (IF YES:) How often?

143c. (ALL RESPONDENTS:) Have you ever worked or cooperated with other residents of (COLONIA IN WHICH RESPONDENT LIVES) to try to solve some problem or meet some need of the colonia? (IF YES:) When was this? With what kind of problems or needs were you concerned? What did you try to do about it? What were the results of your efforts?

144. (ALL RESPONDENTS:) In general, which do you think would be more helpful to you and your family in maintaining and improving your economic situation: Working with other families in the colonia for common goals and improvements, or trying to get individual benefits of favors through someone like a friend with "influence," an employer, or a political leader?

145. Now I would like to know how right or wrong you think different kinds of actions are. For example, most people think that something like murder is very wrong, while something like bragging may be considered only a little bit wrong or not wrong at all. Here are some other examples:
--A poor man accepts 20 pesos [U.S. $1.60] from a politician to vote the way the politician wants him to. Would you say that this is not wrong, that it is a little bit wrong, or that it is very wrong?
--And how about this case: A man accuses his neighbor of dumping garbage on his property. Instead of discussing the problem with the neighbor, he challenges him to a fist fight. Would you say there is nothing wrong about this, that it is only a little wrong, or that it is very wrong?
--And how about this case: A man joins in a protest march or demonstration to get public officials to correct an unjust situation. Would you say that this is not wrong, that it is a little bit wrong, or that it is very wrong?
--And finally, how about this case: A man recently arrived from the countryside invades a piece of land when he has trouble finding a place to live in the city. Would you say that this is not wrong, that it is a little bit wrong, or that it is very wrong?

146a. Here is a different kind of question. There are some persons who are so much like you that you can really understand their way of thinking. There may be others who differ from you so much that it is really hard to understand their way of thinking. For example: Suppose you were to meet a person who has just arrived from another part of Mexico a long way off—hundreds of kilometers away—where you had never been. Do you think you could understand his way of thinking?

146b. And a person who occupies an important position in the government—for example, (EVERYWHERE EXCEPT COLONIA TEXCOCO:) the head of the Department of the Federal District (IN COLONIA TEXCOCO: the governor of the State of Mexico). Could you understand his way of thinking?

146c. And a person who lives in Lomas de Chapultepec, here in Mexico City. Could you understand his way of thinking?

147. Think now about the problems of Mexico. In your opinion, what are the most important problems of the country? (IF TWO OR MORE PROBLEMS MENTIONED:) Of all these problems you have mentioned, which do you think is the most important?

148. What do you think are the most important things that make Mexico different from other countries? (IF MORE THAN ONE ATTRIBUTE MENTIONED:) Which of these things you have mentioned is the most important in your opinion?

149a. Our Mexican Revolution is a very important event which is always much discussed. Could you tell me, in your opinion, what are the most important purposes and ideals of the Revolution?

149b. Do you believe that the ideals and purposes of the Revolution have been achieved, that they have not yet been achieved but the government is still working to achieve them, or that they have been forgotten?

149c. How would you feel if a foreigner criticized the Mexican Revolution or the Constitution of 1917?

150. Now I'm going to read a list of famous persons in Mexico's past. Would you tell me, who were these persons? (IF NEEDED, AFTER EACH NAME:) What did he do? (READ LIST)
--Cuauhtémoc
--Father Hidalgo
--Benito Juárez
--Porfirio Díaz
--Emiliano Zapata
--Venustiano Carranza
--Lázaro Cárdenas

151. Of all the persons you know or have heard or read about—dead or alive—whom do you admire most? In your opinion, what is it that makes (made) this person outstanding?

152. What do you think a person ought to do in order to be a good Mexican?

153. Some people say that a person should go along with whatever his country does, even if he disagrees with it. Others feel that a person always has the right to question or criticize, because the government can sometimes be mistaken. How do you feel about this?

Do you think that a person should go along with whatever his country does even if he disagrees with it, or should he question or criticize when he thinks the government is mistaken?

154a. Now here are a few questions of a different sort. How often do you listen to or watch the news or other programs about the things that are happening, on the radio or television?

154b. How often do you read about the news and the things that are happening in the newspapers?

154c. How do you get most of your news and information about politics and public affairs?

154d. (IF RESPONDENT OBTAINS MOST POLITICAL INFORMATION THROUGH NEWS-PAPERS, RADIO OR TELEVISION:) Would you say that the newspapers (radio, television) from which you get your news and information are usually correct and trustworthy, or are they not very correct or trustworthy?

155a. (ALL RESPONDENTS:) In general, how interested are you in what the federal government is doing?--That is, the government of the President of the Republic.

155b. (IF RESIDENT OF COLONIA TEXCOCO:) How interested are you in what the government of the State of Mexico is doing?--That is, the government of Hank González in Toluca.

155c. (IF INTERESTED:) Has anything the state government has done recently in Ciudad Netzahualcóyotl caught your attention? (IF YES:) What, in particular?

155d. (ALL RESPONDENTS EXCEPT RESIDENTS OF COLONIA TEXCOCO:) How interested are you in what the Department of the Federal District is doing?--That is, the Departamento Central, the government of Corona del Rosal.

155e. (IF RESIDENT OF COLONIA TEXCOCO:) How interested are you in what the Municipal Government of Ciudad Netzahualcóyotl is doing? --That is, the government of Gonzalo Barquín.

155f. (IF MIGRANT:) Since you left (PLACE MENTIONED IN RESPONSE TO QUESTION 7a, OR IF RESPONDENT LIVED IN MEXICO CITY AT AGE 15, HIS PLACE OF BIRTH), have you become any more or any less interested in politics and public affairs?

156a. (ALL RESPONDENTS:) We are also interested in knowing how well known are various public officials. Can you tell me the name of the President of the Republic?

156b. Can you tell me the name of the candidate of the PRI for President of the Republic in the current election campaign?

156c. And can you tell me the name of the congressman who represents your district in the federal Congress?

156d. (IF RESIDENT OF COLONIA PERIFÉRICO:) Can you tell me who Ignacio Herrerías is? (IF ABLE TO IDENTIFY:) In general, how would you rate his performance as a political leader? (IF NEEDED:) That is, the way he has done his job during his period in office.

157a. (ALL RESPONDENTS:) How much attention do you pay to what goes on during election campaigns, such as the one now in progress for the elections next July 5?

157b. Do you know if there are any workers, organizers, or leaders of a political party here in (COLONIA IN WHICH RESPONDENT LIVES)?-- That is, people who live here and work part time or full time seeking support for some political party. (IF YES:) Can you tell me their names and for what party they work?

157c. (IF ONE OR MORE PARTY WORKERS IDENTIFIED:) Does this person (do these persons) work at their job all the time or only when there are elections?

157d. (ALL RESPONDENTS:) During the current election campaign--that is, the campaign for elections of July 5--what kinds of things have the political parties done to try to win the support of the people in this colonia for their candidates?

157e. (IF CAMPAIGN ACTIVITY RECALLED:) Which parties have done this (these things)?

157f. (ALL RESPONDENTS:) During an election campaign--the present one or any other in the past--has any political party worker or organizer ever contacted you to ask your support or cooperation in some way? (IF YES:) In what way? How many times has this happened? Who was (were) the party worker(s)? For which party were they working? Was (were) this (these) person(s) from (COLONIA IN WHICH RESPONDENT LIVES), or from outside the colonia?

157g. (IF MIGRANT:) Did this ever happen during an election campaign in the place or places where you lived before coming to Mexico City? (IF YES:) How many times did this happen? In this (these) place(s) where you lived before coming to Mexico City, were there any workers or leaders of any other political parties beside the PRI?

158a. (ALL RESPONDENTS:) Thinking now again about the federal government--that is, the government of the President of the Republic, the Federal Congress, and all the other federal agencies: How much effect do its activities have on your life from day to day?

158b. How much do you think you can trust the federal government to do what is right? Would you say that you can trust the federal

158c. government almost always, most of the time, sometimes, or almost never?

158c. (ALL RESPONDENTS:) Thinking now about the (Municipal Government of Ciudad Netzahualcóyotl--the government of Gonzalo Barrufn/ Department of the Federal District--that is, the Departamento Central, the government of Corona del Rosal): How much effect do its activities have on your life from day to day?

158d. How much do you think you can trust the (Municipal Government/ Department of the Federal District) to do what is right? Would you say you can trust the (Municipal Government/ Federal District) almost always, most of the time, sometimes, or almost never?

158e. How much interest do you think the (Municipal Government/ Department of the Federal District) takes in this colonia? Why do you feel that way?

158f. (IF RESIDENT OF COLONIA TEXCOCO:) Thinking now about the State Government--the government of Hank González in Toluca: How much effect do its activities have on your life from day to day?

158g. (IF RESIDENT OF COLONIA TEXCOCO:) How much do you think you can trust the State Government to do what is right? Would you say you can trust the State Government almost always, most of the time, sometimes, or almost never?

159a. (ALL RESPONDENTS:) Now we would like to know something about your opinions of some political parties. Is there any political party in this country that you think would do more good for the people of the country than any of the others?

159b. Is there any party you would never support--that you feel particularly opposed to? (IF YES:)

159c. Are you currently a member of some political party? (IF YES:) Which one?

159d. (IF NO:) Do you consider yourself a supporter of some particular political party? (IF YES:) Which one?

159e. (IF NO:) If you had to choose, is there any party that you might prefer? (IF YES:) Which one?

160a. (ALL RESPONDENTS:) Think now of your three closest friends. What party do you think they support or prefer?

160b. Do you think that most people living in this colonia support or prefer the same party, or do they prefer different parties? (IF "SAME PARTY":) Which one?

160c. Suppose you were a supporter of some political party or candidate for public office, but most people in this colonia favored another party or candidate. What do you think the supporters of the other candidate or party would do to you? How would they act toward you (IF NEGATIVE ACTION OR BEHAVIOR ANTICIPATED:) What would you do then? Would you decide to support the party or candidate favored by most of your neighbors, or would you go on supporting the party or candidate that you preferred? (IF WOULD SUPPORT PARTY OR CANDIDATE OF MAJORITY:) Why would you do that?

161a. (ALL RESPONDENTS:) Do you try to vote in every national election (that is, elections for President of the Republic, or congressman in the Federal Congress), or do you sometimes miss an election, or do you rarely vote in such elections?

161b. Would you tell me for which party or presidential candidate you voted in the last national election--in 1964?

161c. Would you tell me for which party or presidential candidate you intend to vote in the next national election--on July 5?

161d. (IF INTENDS TO VOTE IN NEXT ELECTION:) Are you registered to vote? (IF NEEDED:) Do you have your voter's credential? (IF NO:) Why are you not registered? (IF NEEDED:) Why do you lack your voter's credential?

161e. (IF DIFFERENCE BETWEEN RESPONDENT'S PARTY PREFERENCE IN 1964 AND 1970 ELECTIONS:) Have you changed your ideas or opinions about politics and parties in the past six years--that is, since the last national election? (IF YES:) In what way? What was the most important reason for the change of opinion?

161f. (IF NO DIFFERENCE BETWEEN RESPONDENT'S PARTY PREFERENCE IN 1964 AND 1970 ELECTIONS:) Could you tell me the main reason why you have always supported the (NAME OF PARTY SUPPORTED IN 1964 AND 1970 ELECTIONS)?

161g. (IF RESPONDENT HAS VOTED IN NATIONAL ELECTIONS:) Which of these statements best describes how you feel when you go to the polls to vote? (READ LIST)
"I take pleasure in doing this"
"I am only complying with my duty"
"I feel bothered--it's a waste of time"
"I don't feel anything in particular"

161h. (IF RESPONDENT HAS NOT VOTED IN NATIONAL ELECTIONS:) Many persons with whom we have spoken say they have not voted. Do you think there is some particular reason for this?

162a. (IF RESIDENT OF COLONIA TEXCOCO:) Thinking now about local elections--that is, for state legislator or Municipal President: Do you try to vote in all of these elections, do you sometimes miss one, or do you rarely vote in these elections?

162b. (IF RESIDENT OF COLONIA TEXCOCO:) Would you tell me for which party or candidate for Municipal President you voted in the last elections--that is, in November of last year?

162c. (ALL RESPONDENTS EXCEPT RESIDENTS OF COLONIA TEXCOCO:) Can you tell me the names of any of the persons who are currently running for congressman in your district?

162d. If there was an election for (IN COLONIA TEXCOCO: Municipal President; ELSEWHERE: Congressman), and you did not happen to know anything about the candidates or the problems of interest in the election, to whom would you go for information and advice?

162e. By the way, where do people vote around here? Where is the nearest polling place?

163. Some people say that it is useless to vote in elections because those who will govern have already been selected by the PRI. Do you think this is true or not?

164. Do you think that the majority of public officials in this country are trying to help the people in general, or are they trying mostly to advance their own personal interests or careers? (IF NEEDED:) Are they mostly trying to help the people or are they mostly working for their own benefit?

165. In your opinion, how much attention do the leaders of this country--that is, the really powerful public officials and politicians--pay to the opinions of the ordinary man like your-self? Would you say that they pay a great deal of attention, some attention, only a little attention, or no attention at all?

166. Which of these statements do you think is most true? (READ LIST)
--However good the politicians sound in their speeches, you can never tell what they will do once elected.
--Most politicians who are elected try to do what they promised to do.

167. What do you think causes a man to become a politician--that is, to have a political career?

168. Would you say that dishonesty and corruption are more prevalent in the government service than in most other careers, less prevalent, or about the same? (IF "MORE PREVALENT":) Much more prevalent or only a little more prevalent?

169. Many people say that some groups have too much power and influence in this country and that other groups have too little power and influence. I'm going to read a list of groups. Please tell me for each of these groups whether you think they should have more power and influence or less power and influence than they have now in politics and public affairs.

--University students
--Priests (The Church)
--Labor union leaders
--Businessmen and industrialists
--The police
--The middle class
--Military officers
--Scientists and technicians
--The poor
--Peasants
--Large landowners

170. Do you think that the way people vote in elections has some effect on what the government does? Would you say it has a lot of effect, only a little effect, or no effect at all?

171a. Do you think that most people in Mexico are getting their fair share or less than their fair share of the good things in life--that is, the things that are needed to live happily and comfortably? (IF "LESS THAN FAIR SHARE":) Much less, or only a little less?

171b. What should be done in order to see that most people get their fair share?

171c. (ALL RESPONDENTS:) In comparison with other people living in Mexico, do you think that you are getting your fair share of the good things in life, more than your fair share, or less than your fair share? (IF "LESS THAN FAIR SHARE":) Much less, or only a little less?

171d. Who or what would you say is principally to blame for your not getting your fair share?

171e. (ALL RESPONDENTS:) In your opinion, what is it that Mexico needs most--a total and immediate change, a total but gradual change, a partial and immediate change, or no change at all?

172. Some people say that, in general, our system of government and politics is good for the country; others feel it is bad for the country. How do you feel about this? Do you think that, in general, the present system of government and politics is good for the country or bad for the country? Why do you feel that way?

173a. Thinking now about the government now in power, that of Díaz Ordaz: Do you believe that this government would ever pass some law or take some other kind of action that would be harmful to people like yourself? How likely is it that this would ever occur? Would you say it is very likely, somewhat likely, or not at all likely?

173b. And how about the government for the new sexenio [six-year period of government], that of Luis Echeverría, if he is elected to the presidency? Do you think that this government would ever pass some law or take some other action that would be harmful to people like yourself? How likely is it that this might happen? Would you say it is very likely, somewhat likely, or not at all likely?

174a. Could you tell me who, in your opinion, was the best President of the Republic?

174b. (IF RESPONDENT HAS PERSONAL PREFERENCE:) Why do you think he was the best President?

174c. (ALL RESPONDENTS:) In terms of their overall performance as President of the Republic--that is, the kind of job they did while in office--how would you rate each of these men: (READ LIST)
--Miguel Alemán
--Adolfo López Mateos
--Gustavo Díaz Ordaz

174d. Could you tell me who Carlos Madrazo was? (IF ABLE TO IDENTIFY MADRAZO:) How would you rate him as a political leader--very good, good, average, not very good, or poor?

175a. (ALL RESPONDENTS:) In general, how often do you discuss politics and public affairs with other persons?

175b. (IF SOMETIMES DISCUSSES POLITICS:) With whom do you discuss these matters?

175c. Do you discuss politics and public affairs in the period between elections, or just at election time?

175d. (ALL RESPONDENTS:) Do you try to keep informed about politics and public affairs?

175e. In the last six months, did you: (READ LIST)
--Attend a political meeting or rally, perhaps a rally held in connection with the current election campaign?
--Do anything to help get people registered to vote?

175f. Have you ever done anything during an election campaign to help elect some candidate?--For example, give money, put up posters, pass out handbills, urge friends or neighbors to vote for some candidate or party, or some similar activity? (IF YES:) In what ways did you help? About how many times have you done that?

175g. (IF MIGRANT AND HAS ENGAGED IN CAMPAIGN ACTIVITY:) Did you do this kind of thing in the place or places where you lived before coming to Mexico City, only in Mexico City, or in both places?

176a. (ALL RESPONDENTS:) We were talking earlier about the needs and problems that you and the other residents of this colonia have. Have you ever personally--either alone or with other residents of the colonia--gone to see some official of (IN COLONIA TEXCOCO: the Municipal Government; ELSEWHERE: the Department of the Federal District), or some other person of influence in the city, about some problem or need? (IF YES:) Who was that? What position did he hold, or in what office did he work? What kind of problem or need were you concerned about? What kind of treatment did you receive? (IF NEEDED:) How were your needs attended to?

176b. (ALL RESPONDENTS:) Has a representative of the government, the PRI, or the CNOP ever come to speak with you? (IF YES:) Who was this person?--Not his name, but what position he held, or what office he worked in. Why did he come to see you? Exactly what matter or problem was he concerned about? What did he want of you? What happened as a result of his visit?

176c. (IF NO CONTACT WITH PUBLIC OFFICIALS:) Many persons we have spoken to say that they have never talked with any government official or representative of the PRI or the CNOP or other influential people. Do you think there is some particular reason for this?

176d. (ALL RESPONDENTS:) Suppose you had to go to one of the offices of the government to discuss some personal problem--for example, a legal matter, or some credential that you needed. How do you think you would be treated there?

176e. If you tried to explain your business to the persons in that office, do you think they would pay a great deal of attention to you, only a little attention, or would they ignore you completely?

176f. And if you were to go to this office as a representative of the colonia, do you think they would pay a great deal of attention to you, only a little attention, or would they ignore you completely?

176g. If you had some problem with the police--say you were accused of a small crime--how do you think you would be treated there, in the station house?

176h. And if you tried to explain your reasons to the police, do you think they would pay much attention to you, only a little attention, or would they ignore you completely?

176i. Have you or any members of your family ever had some experience with the authorities—that is, with some government office or with the police—which caused you pain? (IF YES:) Could you tell me something about this experience? When did this happen? What exactly was the problem?

176j. Suppose a group of people in this city strongly feels that the government is treating them unfairly. I'm going to read a list of some things these people might do to try to get the government to change the situation. Which do you think would be the most effective way? (READ LIST)
—Working through personal connections with public officials
—Sending someone as a representative of the group to try to take care of the matter
—Organizing a protest demonstration
—Working through the PRI or the CNOP
—Organizing public meetings or rallies to get other people interested in the problem
Now I'll read the list again. Please tell me which you think would be the least effective way?

176k. Have you ever gotten so angry about some public issue or problem that you really wanted to do something about it?

176l. (IF YES:) What kind of problem were you concerned about?

176m. Did you do anything about it? (IF YES:) What?

176n. (ALL RESPONDENTS:) Have you ever joined in sending a protest message or complaint to some public official about a problem which concerned you greatly? What kind of problem were you concerned about?

176o. (ALL RESPONDENTS:) Have you ever gone with a group of people to protest or complain to a public official about some problem? (IF YES:) What kind of problem were you concerned about?

177a. (ALL RESPONDENTS:) Do you know of any group or organization of residents which concerns itself with the needs and problems of this colonia in particular? (IF YES:) What is the name of this group or organization? Can you tell me some of the things it does?

177b. During the past six months, did you participate in any of the activities of this group? (IF YES:) In what ways did you participate? (IF NEEDED:) Did you attend meetings of the group, give money, participate in work projects of the group, or did you participate in some other way?

177c. (IF ATTENDED MEETINGS:) During the past six months, how often did you attend the meetings of this group?

177d. Do you ever take part in the discussion during meetings of this group? (IF YES:) How often do you do that?

177e. To what extent do you feel you have to (are obligated to) participate in the meetings and activities of this group?

177f. Suppose this group made a decision which you did not like. Would you feel free to protest, would you feel uneasy about protesting, or do you think it would be better not to protest?

177g. Would you say that the activities of this group tend to improve conditions in this colonia, or would the colonia be better off without these activities?

177h. Do you consider this group to be connected in any way with political or governmental affairs?

177i. (ALL RESPONDENTS:) How would you rate the leaders of this colonia? Would you say they are very able or competent, more or less able, not very able, or very incompetent?

177j. In your opinion, which is the better leader? (READ ALTERNATIVES)
—The man who makes decisions without permitting discussion on the part of the members of the group, or
—The man who makes decisions only after listening to the discussions of members of the group.

177k. Suppose we talk with other residents of this colonia... How much attention should we pay to what the common man says as against what the leaders of the colonia tell us?

178a. Do you know of any other group or association within the colonia that is concerned with some problem or need of the residents? (IF YES:) What kind of group? What are its main activities?

178b. (IF OTHER GROUP OR ORGANIZATION IDENTIFIED:) Do you participate in any of the meetings or activities of this group? (IF YES:) How often?

179. (ALL RESPONDENTS:) In this colonia are there groups of people who came from the same state or town in the countryside who meet together from time to time? (IF NEEDED:) —As a club or organization? (IF YES:) Do you participate in the meetings or activities of a group such as this? (IF YES:) Which group? What is its name? What kinds of things does this group do?
(IF RESIDENT OF COLONIA TEXCOCO: ASK QUESTIONS 180a, 180b, 180c)

180a. Have you ever heard of the Restorative Movement of Residents of Ciudad Netzahualcóyotl? (IF YES:) Have you supported this group in any way?—For example, by attending its meetings or rallies, giving money, or by making your land payments to Nacional Financiera instead of to the subdivider? (IF YES:) In what way?

180b. The principal goal of this group is to secure the expropriation of all the subdivisions of Ciudad Netzahualcóyotl by the President of the Republic, as a means of solving the problems of the municipality. Would you be in favor of this goal, or against it? Why do you feel that way?

180c. How likely do you think it is that this goal will be achieved—that is, the expropriation of all the subdivisions of Ciudad Netzahualcóyotl? (IF "NOT VERY LIKELY" OR "NOT AT ALL LIKELY":) Why do you feel that way? What do you think will prevent it from being achieved?

181a. (ALL RESPONDENTS:) We are also interested in other kinds of groups and organizations to which people belong. For example, do you now belong, or have you ever belonged, to some group or organization connected with your work, such as a labor union? (IF YES:) Which one? What is the name of this union (group)?

181b. (IF DOES NOT OR HAS NOT BELONGED TO WORK-RELATED ORGANIZATION:) Is there a union at the place where you work?

181c. (IF UNION MEMBER:) I'm going to read a list of three things done by labor unions in this country. Please tell me which you think is the most important to you personally. (READ LIST)
--Informing the workers about government programs and activities relating to the workers
--Providing benefits and favors for individual workers on an individual basis
--Bargaining collectively with employers for higher wages

182. Now I'm going to read a list of some other kinds of groups and organizations. Please tell me if you are a member of any of these: (READ LIST)
--A religious association
--A social group or club (for example, one that sponsors social gatherings, fiestas, etc.)
--A sports or recreation club
--An association or club related to school (for example, a parent-teacher association)
--A cooperative
--An association for credit, savings, or loans
--A group or organization that is interested in politics or public affairs
--Any other kind of group or organization

183. (IF MIGRANT AND BELONGS TO GROUP OR ORGANIZATION:) Do you belong to more or fewer groups and organizations now than you did before you came to live in Mexico City?

184a. I would like to ask about a few things to see if you have them. Please tell me, do you now own any of the following things? (READ LIST)
--A radio
--A wristwatch
--A television set
--A gas stove
--A refrigerator
--A blender
--A sewing machine
--An electric iron
--A car or truck
--A house or some land in another place (outside of this colonia)

184b. (IF MIGRANT AND HAS ONE OR MORE POSSESSIONS:) Did you have any of these things mentioned, before coming to live in Mexico City? (IF YES:) Which things?

185. (ALL RESPONDENTS:) Do you and your family receive your income usually by the week, by the quincena, or by the month? (SHOW APPROPRIATE CARD) Using this card, I would like you to show me which of these groups, from "A" to "I," comes closest to the total amount of the income of the members of your family, including the income from all sources, such as wages, rent, or any other source.

186a. Who besides yourself contributes (with money) to the family income?

186b. Do you have any other source of income—besides the wages that you (and other members of your family) earn? (IF NEEDED:) That is, besides the income from your job(s). (IF YES:) What are they?

186c. We would like to be as familiar as possible with the economic problems of people around here. For example, do you owe much money to other persons, stores, or the like? (IF YES:) About how much do you owe altogether at the present time?

186d. For what kinds of things do you owe this money?

186e. (ALL RESPONDENTS:) Thinking of your economic situation in general—that is, the money that you and your family earn and the amount that you have to spend: How adequate is your family income for covering your most pressing needs? Would you say it is very adequate, more or less adequate, inadequate, or very inadequate? (IF "VERY ADEQUATE":) Are you presently saving any money?

186f. (ALL RESPONDENTS:) In order to live as you would like to live, about how much money would you and your family need each month? (IF NEEDED:) More or less—500 pesos, 700, 1000, 2000, or how much?

186g. In comparison with the majority of families in this colonia, would you say that the economic situation of you and your family is better, worse, or about the same as the others? (IF "BETTER" OR "WORSE":) How much better (worse)? Much better (worse), or only a little better (worse)?

186h. (IF MIGRANT:) Do you believe that, in general, the economic situation of you and your family at the present time is better, about the same, or worse than your situation before coming to live in Mexico City? (IF "BETTER" OR "WORSE":) Much better (worse), or only a little better (worse)?

187a. (ALL RESPONDENTS:) Here are a few questions about your house. Please tell me whether you have any of the following things. (READ LIST)
--A bathroom or toilet inside the house
--Electricity (IF YES:) With or without a contract?
--Sewage system connection
--Running water inside the house
--Shower or bathtub

187b. (IF LACKS RUNNING WATER INSIDE THE HOUSE:) How do you get your water?

187c. How far do you have to go to get water?

187d. (IF MIGRANT AND HOUSE EQUIPPED WITH ANY OF THESE THINGS:) Did you have any of these things, such as (INSERT IMPROVEMENT MENTIONED IN QUESTION 187a), in your house before coming to live in Mexico City? (IF YES:) Which things?

(IF INTERVIEWER CANNOT OBSERVE ALL HABITABLE ROOMS IN THE HOUSE, ASK 187e AND 187f.)

187e. How many rooms do you have in your house?

187f. How many bedrooms—or rooms used for sleeping—do you have?

187g. How many persons—including all the children—sleep regularly in this house?

187h. Do you raise any animals or vegetables on your property?

188a. Here are a few final questions. Concerning religious ideas... could you tell me which religion you prefer?

188b. (IF RELIGIOUS PREFERENCE EXPRESSED:) During the last three months, how often did you go to Mass (church, synagogue)?—That is, how many times did you go each month?

188c. (IF MIGRANT:) About how many times a month did you go to Mass (church, synagogue) in the place or places where you lived before moving to Mexico City?

188d. (ALL RESPONDENTS:) How important would you say religion is in your life today?

188e. (IF MIGRANT:) Now, comparing this with your life before coming to Mexico City...how important is religion in your life today? Would you say it is more important now, that it has about the same importance, or that it is less important now? (IF "MORE IMPORTANT" OR "LESS IMPORTANT":) Much (more/less) important, or only a little (more/less) important?

189a. (ALL RESPONDENTS:) What do you do when you are not working—that is, what kinds of things do you do most often in your free time?

189b. If you had another hour of free time during the day, with whom would you prefer to spend it?—With your family, with friends, with neighbors, or alone?

189c. What do you do on September 15 and 16? Are they special days for you?

190. Would you tell me your age?

191a. Before finishing, we would like to ask you just a few things about your family life. For example, how many times have you been married?

191b. (IF MARRIED MORE THAN ONCE:) Were you separated, widowed, divorced, or abandoned?

191c. (ALL RESPONDENTS:) In the life of every family there are times and situations in which decisions have to be made. In some families the decisions are made by the husband; in other families the decisions are made by the wife; in others the husband and the wife make the decisions, but make them separately (individually). Which of these ways of making decisions comes closest to the way in which the most important decisions are made in your family? --For example, if you have to decide where the family should live, or whether a child should continue his studies or quit and go to work.

191d. (IF MIGRANT:) Would you say that you have <u>more</u> or <u>fewer</u> arguments and quarrels with your wife (IF CHILDREN:) and children here in Mexico City than in the place or places where you lived before coming here? Or is it about the same?

192a. (ALL RESPONDENTS:) We would also like to know about your education. Do you know how to read and write?

192b. How far did you get with your education? What was the last year of school you completed?

192c. Have you received any other kind of schooling or training? --For example, training for some trade or job at a government job-training center, or perhaps in some training program at the places where you have worked? (IF YES:) What kind? Where did you receive this training?

192d. And what was the last year of school that your father completed? (IF RESPONDENT DOESN'T KNOW OR CAN'T REMEMBER, ASK ABOUT HIS MOTHER)

192e. Do you speak any other language or dialect besides Spanish-- perhaps an Indian language, or some English? (IF YES:) Which one?

192f. (IF YES:) What language or dialect is usually spoken in your home?

192g. (ALL RESPONDENTS:) Have you ever visited or lived in a foreign country? (IF YES:) What country? For how long were you there? (IF HE HAS VISITED FOREIGN COUNTRY MORE THAN ONCE, ASK ABOUT LONGEST VISIT:) What was the purpose of your stay there?

193a. (ALL RESPONDENTS:) And what about your worries...what kinds of things do you worry about most? (IF NEEDED:) Could you give me an example of what you mean?

193b. In general, how would you say you feel most of the time--in good spirits or in low spirits?

194. And one last question: How many interviews have you had before this one, other than the one for the national census?

Thank you very much for your kind cooperation and your patience.

195. (RESPONDENT'S SOCIO-ECONOMIC LEVEL--BY OBSERVATION)
Lower class
Lower-middle class
Middle class
Upper-middle class
Upper class

196. (RESPONDENT'S "RACE")
White
Mestizo
Indian
Other

197. (RESPONDENT WAS WEARING)
Shoes
Sandals
Barefoot

198a. (TYPE OF HOUSE)
Single room or shack of provisional materials
Room in vecindad or courtyard
Apartment
Independent dwelling of permanent materials
Other

198b. (TYPE OF HOUSING CONSTRUCTION: PERMANENT MATERIAL IN WALLS)
Scrap materials (miscellaneous)
Laminated cardboard
Wood
Rock
Adobe
Low-grade brick (tabique)
Concrete, concrete blocks
High-grade brick (ladrillo)
Other
(PREDOMINANT MATERIAL IN ROOF)
Scrap materials (miscellaneous)
Laminated cardboard
Laminated asbestos
Wood
Concrete
Other
(PREDOMINANT MATERIAL IN FLOOR)
Earth
Wood
Concrete
Tile
Other

198c. (NUMBER OF WINDOWS IN DWELLING)
None
One
Two
Three
Four or more

198d. (IF HOUSE FACES A STREET, IS IT)
Unpaved
Paved

198e. (IF HOUSE FACES A STREET, IS THERE A SIDEWALK IN FRONT OR TO THE SIDE OF THE HOUSE?)
No
Yes

199. (DURATION OF INTERVIEW)
Less than 120 minutes (-2hours)
120-149 minutes (2-2½ hours)
150-179 minutes (2½-3 hours)
180-209 minutes (3-3½ hours)
210-239 minutes (3½-4 hours)
240-269 minutes (4-4½ hours)
270-299 minutes (4½-5 hours)
300 minutes or more (5+ hours)

200. (INTERVIEW WAS COMPLETED)
Without prolonged interruptions
With one or more prolonged interruptions
Was not completed

201. (INTERVIEW TOOK PLACE IN)
Respondent's house
Respondent's place of work
Public place
Other

202. (PERSONS PRESENT DURING THE INTERVIEW BESIDES THE RESPONDENT)
—No one else (or only children under age 16)
—Others present, but took no part in the interview; did not appear to influence respondent's answers
—Others present and did participate in interview or appeared to influence respondent's answers

203. (RESPONDENT'S ATTITUDE DURING THE INTERVIEW)
—Very cooperative (seemed actively interested in helping)
—Generally cooperative (answered cooperatively but did not seem actively interested)
—Somewhat uncooperative (reluctant to answer some questions, suspicious of interviewer intent)
—Very uncooperative (reluctant to answer numerous questions, highly suspicious of interviewer intent, openly hostile)
—Indifferent (preoccupied with something else)

204. (FRANKNESS OR SINCERITY OF RESPONDENT)
—Very sincere (gave frank answers to all or almost all questions)
—Generally sincere (gave frank answers to most questions)
—Insincere (not speaking his true opinions, gave insincere answers to numerous questions)

205. (RESPONDENT'S OVERALL UNDERSTANDING AND SENSITIVITY TO QUESTIONS)
—Good (understood most questions without difficulty, most responses well formulated)
—Fair, average (understood most questions but with some difficulty; occasional difficulty in formulating responses)
—Poor (considerable difficulty in understanding most questions and formulating responses, showed insensitivity to question content)

00I. (SAMPLE STATUS)
Respondent is original sample element
Respondent is substitute for original

00J. (REASONS FOR SAMPLE MORTALITY)
Absence of original after 2 or more callbacks
Refusal of original to grant interview

00K. (NUMBER OF CALLBACKS)
Interview obtained on first visit
One callback
Two callbacks
Three callbacks
Four callbacks
Five or more callbacks

ITEMS ADMINISTERED ONLY AS PART OF SON'S
INTERVIEW SCHEDULE

S43a. To what do you devote most of your time at present? Do you work? Study?

(IF LESS THAN 30 YEARS OLD, ASK S48b TO S48e)

S48b. What kind of job would you like to have when you are 30 years old? In this job, would you work for an employer or boss, or would you be an owner or business partner?

S48c. There are many things which might keep a person from getting the job he would like to have. What are the things you feel might stand in the way of your getting the kind of job you would like? (IF NEEDED:) That is, the job that you would like to have when you are 30 years old.

S48d. Taking account of the things that could really stand in your way, what do you think your chances are of really having this kind of job some day?

S48e. You have mentioned some things which might stand in the way of your getting the kind of job you would like to have. Taking account of things like this, and really being honest about it, what kind of job do you really expect to have when you are 30 years old? In this job, would you work for an employer or boss, or would you be an owner or business partner?

S50b. (IF CURRENTLY EMPLOYED:) How old were you when you started to work full-time?

S63b. (ALL RESPONDENTS:) Suppose the son of a poor man has gone much farther in life than his father. What, in your opinion, must be the most important reason for this?

S65a. In what ways do you want your life to be different from that of your father?

S65b. Do you and your father agree in your ideas and opinions about the things you consider really important in life, or do you disagree? (IF SOME DISAGREEMENT:) On what things do you disagree?

S73b. Some people say that a son should always try to find a better kind of work than his father does. Others say that a son should feel proud to do the same kind of work as his father. How do you feel about it?

S81b. (IF RESPONDENT HAS NO CHILDREN OF HIS OWN AND CURRENTLY ATTENDS SCHOOL:) You can't always tell how things will work out. How much schooling do you really expect to finish? (IF RESPONDENT EXPECTS LESS THAN UNIVERSITY EDUCATION:) What are the most important reasons that might keep you from getting more education?

S84c. (ALL RESPONDENTS:) When you think realistically about your future, how sure are you of: (READ LIST)
--Doing better in life than your parents did?
--Owning your own house and land?
--Being able to provide for a family?

S159f. Is your father a member or supporter of some political party? (IF YES:) Which one? (IF NEEDED:) Does he prefer any particular party? (IF NEEDED:) Is there any party that you think he might prefer, if he had to choose?

S161i. Do you think there are any important differences between the way younger voters think and the way older voters think? Could you give me an example of what you mean?

S165b. Do you think that the political ideas and opinions of young people in this country will have more weight--that is, more influence with the government--now that they can vote as early as age 18? (IF YES:) How much more?--Much more, or only a little more?

S165c. (IF NO:) Why do you feel that way?

S165d. (ALL RESPONDENTS:) Why do you think the government has given young people of 18, 19, and 20 years of age the right to vote?

S191e. Do you think that a man should have the same ideas and opinions as his father in all matters of importance, in the majority of matters, or only in certain matters?

S191f. When you were younger, how often did you disobey your parents and do things contrary to their instructions and wishes?

S191g. When you were younger, did your parents intervene frequently in your affairs, for example, in matters like the friends you associated with, the places you went, how you spent your money, and so on--or were you pretty much on your own in these matters?

S192b. Are you continuing your studies? (IF YES:) In which school? In what year of school are you at present?

S192s. (IF RESPONDENT DID NOT FINISH SECONDARY SCHOOL:) Why did you leave school?

S193c. If you had a personal problem that you were very concerned about, to whom would you go first for advice?

POST-INTERVIEW ITEMS

S198. (WAS THE RESPONDENT PRESENT DURING ANY PORTION OF THE INTERVIEW WITH HIS FATHER?)
Yes, during the entire interview
Yes, during most of the interview
Yes, during a part of the interview
No, not present during any part

Construction of Summative Indexes

Simple Indexes

Most of the variables in the quantitative data analysis for this study have been operationalized through additive indexes constructed from responses to two or more items (or subsections of a single item) in the questionnaire reproduced in Appendix A. To construct each index, a set of items considered *a priori* to be relevant to the variable being operationalized was isolated from the full set of questionnaire items. Responses to each item in this subset were assigned scores of 0 or 1, in the direction suggested by the variable's name. Responses were dichotomized either on logical grounds or, in the case of items with ordinal response categories that indicated intensity of attitude or behavioral predispositions, as closely as possible to the median response. For most items, the responses "don't know" and "not ascertained" (because of the interviewer's error or a respondent's refusal to answer) were given a score of 0. If a respondent failed to answer more than 50 percent of the items included in any index, he was declared a "missing unit," and his score on that index was not included in any subsequent computations.

Correlations between the items were then computed, and any items obviously unrelated to the variable being operationalized were eliminated. A preliminary index was then constructed by summing scores across the remaining items in the index. Item-to-index correlations were then computed, and those failing to correlate with the preliminary summative index at or above the .30 level were eliminated. The remaining items were then factor analyzed according to the principal components technique. Items with loadings of less than .500 on the first unrotated factor extracted were then eliminated. The final index was constructed by summing scores across the remaining items. The index was then tested for internal consistency using the Spearman-Brown split-half technique (see Guilford 1954: Chap. 14). To be considered acceptable, an index was required to have a minimum reliability coefficient of .80.

Overall Indexes

A number of indexes utilized in the analysis (e.g., overall political participation or overall life satisfaction) were constructed from scores on three or more of the finalized simple summative indexes. Since the number of component items varied considerably from one index to another, scores were standardized according to the z-score transformation procedure to ensure that each component index contributed equally to a respondent's score on the overall summative index. The overall index was then constructed by taking the simple sum of the standardized scores on each simple summative index included in it.

Correlational and factor analyses performed to construct the indexes, as well as other statistical procedures employed in the quantitative data analysis for this study, were carried out at the IBM 370/165 computer installation at the Massachusetts Institute of Technology, using programs included in the Statistical Package for the Social Sciences (see Nie et al. 1970).

Item Content of Summative Indexes

The numbering of individual items in the indexes corresponds with their order of appearance in the sample survey questionnaire (Appendix A). For convenient reference, the index names are listed alphabetically rather than by topical category.

(1) *Affect for national political institutions*: 135, 159a (both coded for mention of PRI); 172

(2) *Aspirations for children's socioeconomic mobility*: 76a, 80a

(3) *Attentiveness to electoral compaigns and political content of mass media*: 154a, 154b, 157a, 175d

(4) *Authoritarianism*: 60b, 60g, 60j, 60n, 60r, 60u, 177j, 177k, 191c

(5) *Awareness of community leadership*: 115a (coded for mention of community leader), 122a (coded for number of leaders identified), 177i (coded for ability to make an evaluation)

(6) *Awareness of government outputs affecting community*: 122a–g (coded for mention of political or governmental agency), 158e (coded for mention of governmental actions or programs affecting community)

(7) *Awareness of social injustice*: 67, 68a, 68b, 69a (coded for attribution of blame to social or economic structure, or to governmental performance), 72d (coded for mention of inequalities in distribution of wealth), 141a, 147 (coded for mention of unequal distribution of wealth), 171a, 171c, 171d (coded for attribution of blame to social or economic structure, or to governmental performance), 186g

(8) *Campaign involvement*: 175e, 175f

(9) *Civic-mindedness*: 152 (coded for mention of "civic duty" activities), 161g, 177e

(10) *Cognitive flexibility*: 60b, 60g, 146a, 146b, 146c, 177j

(11) *Commitment to urban life* (migrants only): 18a, 18b, 31, 32, 34a, 34c, 35a, 35b, 39, 40, 41a

(12) *Conflict orientation*: 123, 125b, 128a, 129c, 160c, 177f

(13) *Contact with extended family*: 4, 118d, 118e

(14) *Contacting political and governmental officials* (demand-making): 136c, 143c, 176a, 176m, 176n, 176o

(15) *Deference to authority*: 60j, 60l, 60t, 83b, 153, 177j, 177k

(44) *Mutual aid given and received among relatives*: 118f, 118g
(45) *Need for achievement*: 60i, 60q, 60t
(46) *Negative contact with officials*: 102a, 102h, 102i, 104d, 176a
(47) *Nuclear family cohesion*: 62, 189b, 191c
(48) *Number of political acts engaged in beyond voting*: 136c, 143c, 175e, 175f, 176a, 177b
(49) *Openness to innovation*: 60r, 171e
(50) *Overall achievement orientation*: Composite index constructed from scores on Indexes 2, 23, 26, 28, 45, and 85
(51) *Overall attitudinal modernity*: Composite index constructed from scores on Indexes 2, 18, 20, 26, 28, and 45
(52) *Overall community affect*: Composite index constructed from scores on Indexes 73, 80, 109, and 114
(53) *Overall community involvement*: Composite index constructed from scores on Indexes 36, 98, and 122
(54) *Overall contact with officials*: 136c, 137e, 157f, 176a, 176b
(55) *Overall diffuse support for political system*: Composite index constructed from scores on Indexes 1, 86 (reversed), 128, and 130
(56) *Overall disposition to conformity*: 124, 125a, 125b, 160c, 177f
(57) *Overall life satisfaction*: Composite index constructed from scores on Indexes 107, 108, 109, 115, 121
(58) *Overall membership in voluntary organizations*: 159c, 177b, 181a, 182
(59) *Overall political alienation*: Composite index constructed from Item 68b and scores on Indexes 86, 120, and 130 (reversed)
(60) *Overall political awareness*: Composite index constructed from scores on Indexes 3, 16, 33, 37, 72, and 87
(61) *Overall political involvement*: Composite index constructed from scores on Indexes 60 and 62.
(62) *Overall political participation*: Composite index constructed from scores on Indexes 8, 14, 71, and 133
(63) *Overall political radicalism*: Composite index constructed from scores on Indexes 78, 95, and 126
(64) *Overall political system support*: Composite index constructed from scores on Indexes 1, 19 (reversed), 27, 77, 86 (reversed), 91, 128, and 130
(65) *Overall psychosocial adjustment*: Composite index constructed from scores on Indexes 13, 41, 44, 47, 73, 83, 85, and 131
(66) *Overall psychological involvement in politics*: Composite index constructed from scores in Indexes 3, 16, and 33
(67) *Overall sense of individual progress* (migrants only): 33a, 33b, 54, 64a, 64b, 64d, 64e, 64f, 186h
(68) *Overall socioeconomic mobility* (inter- and intragenerational): 7c, 27c, 43a, 51, 52a, 52b, 52c, 52d, 57, 192b, 192d
(69) *Overall socioeconomic status*: 43a, 185, 192b, 195
(70) *Overall specific support for political system*: Composite index constructed from scores on Indexes 19 (reversed), 27, 77, and 91
(71) *Participation in community problem-solving activity*: 120b, 133a, 143c
(72) *Partisanship*: 159a (coded for ability to specify any party), 159b (coded for ability to specify any party), 159c, 159d, 159e

(94) *Preference for manual work*: 82a, 82b

(95) *Propensity for unconventional political behavior*: 129c, 129e–129h, 145, 176j

(96) *Property accumulation in postmigration period* (migrants only): 93b, 96a, 101a, 101b, 184b

(97) *Protest orientation*: 129e, 129f, 129h, 145 (section pertaining to "joining in a protest march or demonstration to get public officials to correct an unjust situation"), 176j (coded for selection of protest strategy), 176k, 176n, 176o, 176p, 177f

(98) *Psychological integration into the community*: 89a, 90, 113a, 60k, 143a, 176i (coded for mention of community problem)

(99) *Quality of housing*: 187a, 187e, 198b, 198c

(100) *Real property ownership*: 93a, 97a, 184a

(101) *Receipt of personal services*: 139, 140b

(102) *Receipt of urban services*: 187a, 198d, 198e

(103) *Reliance on primary group resources*: 115a, 130a, 162d

(104) *Religiosity*: 62 (coded for mention of "practicing his religion faithfully"), 132 (coded for mention of "God's help"), 134 (section pertaining to "priests"), 169 (section pertaining to "priests" or "the Church"), 188b, 188d

(105) *Residential mobility*: 5, 11a, 22a, 28a, 29a, 30a, 192g

(106) *Risk-taking propensity*: 49, 50

(107) *Satisfaction with current job*: 47a, 47b, 47c, 53

(108) *Satisfaction with economic situation*: 186e, 186f

(109) *Satisfaction with residential environment*: 107a, 107c (coded for no mention of source of dissatisfaction), 110, 111a

(110) *Satisfaction with self-help program* (residents of Colonia Esfuerzo Propio): 100c (coded for mention of advantages and for no mention of disadvantages), 100d, 100e, 100f

(111) *Satisfaction with urban environment* (migrants only): 32, 35a, 35b, 39, 40, 41a

(112) *Satisfaction with urban environment* (natives only): 36a (coded for mention of source of satisfaction), 36b (coded for no mention of source of dissatisfaction), 39

(113) *Self-help orientation*: 131d, 143c, 171b (coded for mention of self-help efforts)

(114) *Sense of community progress*: 108, 114a, 114c

(115) *Sense of individual progress*: 33a, 33b, 54, 64a, 64b, 64d, 64e, 64f, 186h

(116) *Sense of national progress*: 69b, 71b, 149b, 172

(117) *Sense of insecurity of land tenure*: 105a; 131a, 143a (both coded for mention of insecurity of land tenure)

(118) *Sense of openness in society*: 41a, 55, 63, 73, 74, 86b

(119) *Sense of political efficacy*: 60d, 60m, 142, 165, 170

(120) *Sense of political powerlessness*: 60d, 60h, 60m, 60w, 142, 161h, 165, 170, 176c

(121) *Sense of relative deprivation*: 67, 171c, 186g

(122) *Social integration into the community*: 115b, 116a, 117, 118a, 118b, 118d, 119a, 130a, 143b

(123) *Socioeconomic status of respondent's father*: 57, 192d
(124) *Stabilization of urban residence*: 18a, 18b, 34a, 34c
(125) *Strength of ties to place of origin*: 34a, 35c, 35d, 35e, 35f
(126) *Structural blame orientation*: 68b, 69a, 72d, 171b, 171d
(127) *Support for official party*: 159a, 159c, 159d, 159e
(128) *Symbolic commitment to political system*: 62 (coded for mention of "being a good Mexican"), 83a, 83b, 148, 149a, 149b, 149c, 150, 151
(129) *Tolerance for dissent and opposition*: 60b, 60g, 123, 177j
(130) *Trust in government*: 158b, 159a, 173a, 173b
(131) *Trust in people*: 66, 126a, 127a
(132) *Violence orientation*: 129a, 129c, 145 (section pertaining to "challenging one's neighbor to a fistfight")
(133) *Voting participation*: 161a, 161b (coded for voting in election), 161c (coded for intention to vote)
(134) *Want/get ratio*: 64a, 64b, 64c

Sample Survey Design, Administration, and Analysis

Questionnaire Construction

The questionnaire employed in the sample survey phase of the study was developed after several months of participant observation and unstructured interviewing of key informants in each of the research communities. No assumption of literacy was made in questionnaire construction. About one-third of the items included in the final version were open-ended, and the remainder included no forced-choice, agree/disagree (Likert format) items. These aspects of the questionnaire design reflect my concern with minimizing the response set problem (especially acquiescence response set) often encountered among low-income respondents. Numerous internal checks for consistency were built into the instrument, to assist in evaluating the reliability of recall data. Standard demographic and socioeconomic items were placed at the beginning and end of the questionnaire. The most politically sensitive or otherwise tension-laden items were situated about three-quarters of the way through the interview schedule, to take maximum advantage of trust and rapport built up during the course of the interview.

Three different English-to-Spanish translations of the questionnaire were prepared: one by myself, one by a Mexican sociologist, and the third by a professional translator with no social science training. The alternative versions of each item were presented to key informants residing in three of the communities included in the study. The version selected for pretesting was the one considered most appropriate by a majority of the informants. The final step before pretesting involved an oral retranslation of the Spanish language version of the preliminary questionnaire into English; this was done by a bilingual Mexican who had not seen the original English version. A total of 30 pretest interviews were conducted, five in each of the communities included in the study. The questionnaire was then revised in accordance with the pretest results.

Interviewing Staff and Training

The interviewers employed in the sample survey phase of the study were recruited from the permanent staff of International Research Associates de México (México, D.F.). A group of 24 persons, about half male and half female, was assembled for the pretest. All were professional interviewers, 25 years of age or older, who had extensive experience working in low-income sections of the city. Interviewers received approximately 40 hours of training for the present study. The last two days of training were devoted to practice interviews conducted among the interviewers themselves. On the basis of pretest performance, 17 interviewers were selected to participate in the final interviewing. I was fully responsible for day-to-day supervision of interviewers during the final interview phase. Each interviewer reported to me daily to pick up assignments and questionnaires and to discuss any problems of administration he or she had encountered during the previous day. Completed interviews were checked for omissions and systematic administration errors as they were returned to me. In addition, every fifteenth respondent was reinterviewed to ensure that key sections of the questionnaire had been properly administered by the original interviewer.

Sampling

Sampling procedures were tailored to the particular physical conditions encountered in each of the research communities. The aim was to achieve a stratified probability sample of male heads of family in each community, plus a randomly selected subsample of eldest sons in families headed by migrants. The stratification variable was length of residence in Mexico City.

To provide basic data for sampling, which was not available for individual communities from the national census or other public or private sources, a preliminary mapping and census were undertaken. A basic map of each community showing any existing streets, major footpaths, and other physical features was drawn by visual inspection and compared with recent aerial photographs, if these were available. In communities having a more or less regular street layout, blocks were numbered in serpentine fashion and every other block beginning with a randomly selected number was designated for censusing. In Colonia Nueva and Colonia Periférico, squatter settlements with no discrete blocks of housing, areas of each community were delimited on the basis of footpaths and other major topographical features. Complete censuses (i.e. including all sampling areas) were taken in these two communities. A total of 4,293 dwellings were censused in the six communities. Respondents (any adult present at the time of the census) were asked whether the head of the family residing in the dwelling was male or female. If male, his full name, his length of residence in the Mexico City urban area, and the age of his eldest son still living in the same dwelling were also obtained. The exact location of the dwelling within the community was also marked on the master map, to be used by interviewers during the final interview phase, and its street address number was recorded. Dwellings in squatter settlements that had no street addresses were assigned numbers by the census takers, who included myself and seven of the professional interviewers who later participated in the sample survey interviewing. The composite map of one of the research communities resulting from this preliminary census and mapping is reproduced in Figure D.1.

Respondents included in the sample of male family heads drawn from each of the research communities were selected randomly within each of four strata defined in terms of length of residence in the city: migrants with less than 5 years of residence in the city; migrants with 5 to 9 years of residence; migrants with 10 or more years of residence; and nonmigrants (native-born residents of Mexico City).

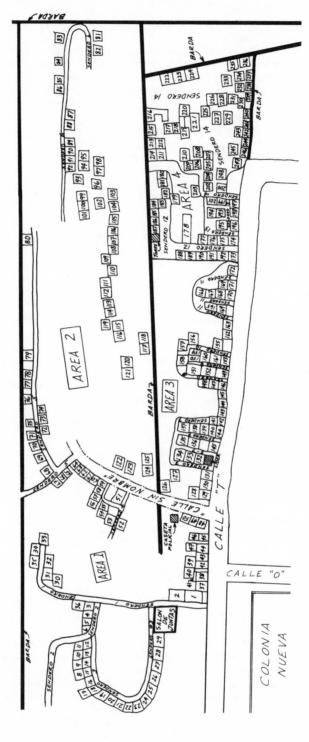

Figure D.1. Map of Colonia Nueva showing individual dwellings, compiled for sampling purposes.

For each interview, the interviewer was provided with the full names and addresses of one "original" element of the sample and two potential "substitutes," as well as the demographic data on all three individuals that had been gathered during the preliminary census. A substitute was to be interviewed only after the original respondent was found to be absent after two visits to his home, or after he had been contacted but had definitely refused the request for an interview. This was the minimum requirement; in numerous cases, three, four, or even five attempts were made to reach the originally selected respondent. In those cases in which a substitute was interviewed, the individual had to reside in the same block (or sampling area) and to have lived in the Mexico City urban area for approximately the same number of years (under 5, 5–9, etc.) as the originally designated respondent. No interviewer discretion was permitted in the selection of original elements of the sample, and his or her selection of a substitute was limited to the two potential substitutes already designated for each original respondent. Interviews were completed with 79 percent of the original respondents. Only 1.7 percent of the sample mortality resulted from the refusal of original respondents to be interviewed.

Administration

The average duration of an interview was 150 to 180 minutes. Interviewers completed 89 percent of the interviews in a single session, with no prolonged interruptions, and 97 percent were conducted in the respondent's home. Eighty-six percent of the respondents were described by interviewers as generally or very cooperative. Comprehension of questions was rated fair or good among 83 percent of the respondents, and 86 percent of the respondents were judged to be "generally sincere" or "very sincere" in their responses to most questions.

In those families in which both a migrant family head and his eldest son were interviewed, interviewers were instructed never to conduct an interview with the family head in the presence of his eldest son, and vice versa; this usually required separate interview sessions on different days.

The high degree of cooperation received from most respondents, despite the considerable length of the interview, reflects the obvious relevance of the vast majority of questionnaire items to the respondents' personal experiences, needs, and community of residence. Special care was taken to include as many items as possible relating to the immediate life space of the respondents, and to minimize items dealing with the city or nation as a whole. Not all items in the questionnaire were asked of every respondent. For example, questions about rural experience and migratory history were asked only of migrants, and questions regarding squatter invasions were asked only of those who had participated in such invasions. In each of the research communities, a separate series of questions was asked about some problem, experience, or condition unique to that community. All of these community-specific questions were derived from my informal, open-ended interviews with residents and community leaders before the sample survey.

Analysis

I myself coded approximately two-thirds of the completed interview schedules for computer analysis. The remainder were coded by three research assistants who underwent lengthy training and worked under my close supervision. The agreement among coders on coding decisions involving open-ended questions was between 85 and 95 percent for most items.

In the sampling procedure adopted for this survey, migrants with 10 or more years of residence in the Mexico City urban area and native-born residents of the Mexico City urban area were deliberately undersampled in order to obtain a greater representation of more recently arrived migrants in the sample. In the analysis of the survey responses, the undersampled strata of respondents were upweighted to correspond with actual population parameters in each of the research communities, as determined by the preliminary census. The total number of interviews actually conducted was 747. There are 1,062 cases in the weighted sample.

To determine the effects of sample weighting upon the findings reported in this study, marginal frequencies for both the weighted and unweighted samples were computed and compared. In addition, several of the most important analyses reported in Chapters 4, 5, and 8 were performed separately on the weighted and unweighted samples. The very slight differences in the results obtained indicate that the use of a weighted sample in the analysis did not bias the research findings in any significant way.

Bibliography

Bibliography

Adams, Richard N. 1967. *The Second Sowing: Power and Secondary Development in Latin America.* San Francisco: Chandler.

Adelman, Irma, and Cynthia T. Morris. 1973. *Economic Growth and Social Equity in Developing Countries.* Stanford, Calif.: Stanford University Press.

Alba, Victor. 1967. *The Mexicans: The Making of a Nation.* New York: Praeger.

Alford, Robert R., and Harry M. Scoble. 1968. "Sources of Local Political Involvement," *Amer. Pol. Sci. Rev.* 62 (4): 1192–1206.

Alisky, Marvin. 1973. "CONASUPO: A Mexican Agency Which Makes Low-Income Workers Feel Their Government Cares," *Inter-Amer. Econ. Affairs* 27 (3): 47–60.

Almond, Gabriel A., and Sidney Verba. 1963. *The Civic Culture.* Princeton, N.J.: Princeton University Press.

Almy, Timothy A. 1973. "Residential Location and Electoral Cohesion: The Pattern of Urban Political Conflict," *Amer. Pol. Sci. Rev.* 67 (3): 914–23.

Ambrecht, Biliana, and Harry Pachon. 1973. "Continuity and Change in a Mexican American Community: East Los Angeles, 1965–1972." Paper presented at the annual meeting of the American Political Science Association (New Orleans).

Ames, Barry. 1970. "Bases of Support for Mexico's Dominant Party," *Amer. Pol. Sci. Rev.* 64 (1): 153–67.

Anderson, Bo, and James D. Cockcroft. 1966. "Control and Cooptation in Mexican Politics," *Int. J. Comp. Sociol.* 7 (1): 16–22.

Andrews, Frank M., and George W. Phillips. 1970. "The Squatters of Lima: Who They Are and What They Want," *J. Developing Areas* 4: 211–24.

Antochiw, Michel. 1974. "Asentamientos habitacionales planificados y no planificados," *Cuadernos Técnicos AURIS* (Gobierno del Estado de México) 9.

Arterton, F. Christopher. 1974. "Political Participation as Attempted Interpersonal Influence: Test of a Theoretical Model Using Data from Rural Mexican Villages." Unpubl. dissertation, MIT.

Astiz, Carlos. 1969. *Pressure Groups and Power Elites in Peruvian Politics.* Ithaca, N.Y.: Cornell University Press.

Aubert, Vilhelm, Burton R. Fisher, and Stein Rokkan. 1954. "A Comparative

Study of Teachers' Attitudes to International Problems and Policies," *J. Soc. Issues* 10 (4): 25–39.

Baker, Marvin W., Jr. 1970. "Land Use Transition in Mexican Cities: A Study in Comparative Urban Geography." Unpubl. dissertation, Syracuse.

Balán, Jorge, Harley L. Browning, and Elizabeth Jelin. 1973a. *Men in a Developing Society: Geographic and Social Mobility in Monterrey, Mexico.* Austin: University of Texas Press.

————— ed. 1973b. *Estudios sobre migración, estructura ocupacional, y movilidad en México.* Mexico City: Instituto de Investigaciones Sociales, Universidad Nacional Autónoma de México.

Bamberger, Michael. 1968. "A Problem of Political Integration in Latin America: The Barrios of Venezuela," *Int. Affairs* 44 (4): 709–19.

Banco de México. 1974. *La distribución del ingreso en México: Encuesta sobre los ingresos y gastos de las familias, 1968.* Mexico City: Fondo de Cultura Económica.

Barkin, David. 1971. "La persistencia de la pobreza en México," *Comercio Exterior* (Mexico City) 21 (8): 667–74.

————— 1975. "Regional Development and Interregional Equity: A Mexican Case Study," in Wayne A. Cornelius and Felicity M. Trueblood, eds., *Urbanization and Inequality: The Political Economy of Urban and Rural Development in Latin America (Latin American Urban Research,* Vol. 5). Beverly Hills: Sage Publications.

Barrows, Walter L. 1974. "Comparative Grassroots Politics in Africa," *World Politics* 26 (2): 283–97.

Bartolomé, L. J. 1971. "Política y redes sociales en una comunidad urbana de indígenas Toba: Un análisis de liderazgo y 'brokerage'," *Anuario Indigenista* 31: 77–98.

Barton, Allen H. 1968. "Bringing Society Back In: Survey Research and Macro-Methodology," *Amer. Behav. Scientist* 12 (2): 1–9.

————— 1970. *Communities in Disaster: A Sociological Analysis of Collective Stress Situations.* Garden City, N.Y.: Doubleday Anchor.

Barton, Allen H., and Robert Hauser. 1970. "Comments on Hauser's 'Context and Consex': Rejoinder," *Amer. J. Sociol.* 76 (3): 514–21.

Bartra, Roger, Eckart Boege, Pilar Calvo, Jorge Gutiérrez, Víctor Martínez Vazquez, and Luisa Paré. 1975. *Caciquismo y poder político en el México rural.* Mexico City: Siglo Veintiuno.

Bataillon, Claude, and Hélène Rivière d'Arc. 1973. *La Ciudad de México.* Mexico City: Sep/Setentas (Secretaría de Educación Pública).

Bayes, Jane H. 1967. "Political Participation and Geographic Mobility." Unpubl. dissertation, Dept. Political Science, UCLA.

Becker, Howard S. 1963. *The Outsiders: Studies in the Sociology of Deviance.* New York: Free Press.

————— 1964. "Personal Change in Adult Life," *Sociometry* 27 (1): 40–53.

Behrman, Lucy C. 1971. "The Convergence of Religious and Political Attitudes and Activities among Workers in Santiago, Chile." Paper presented at the annual meeting of the American Political Science Association (Chicago).

————— 1972. "Political Development and Secularization in Two Chilean Communities," *Comp. Politics* 5 (2) 269–80.

Bell, C. G. 1969. "A New Suburban Politics," *Soc. Forces* 47: 280–88.

Bell, Daniel, and Virginia Held. 1969. "The Community Revolution," *Public Interest* 19: 142–77.

Bell, Wendell. 1965. "Urban Neighborhoods and Individual Behavior," pp. 235–64 in Muzafer Sherif and Carolyn W. Sherif, eds., *Problems of Youth*. Chicago: Aldine.

Bell, Wendell, and Maryanne T. Force. 1956. "Urban Neighborhood Types and Participation in Formal Associations," *Amer. Sociol. Rev*. 21: 25–34.

Benítez, Fernando. 1975. "La destrucción del Valle de México: ¿Estamos ante un desastre poblacional?" *Excélsior* (México City), 10-part series, Mar. 9–18.

Benjamin, Roger W. 1972. *Patterns of Political Development: Japan, India, Israel*. New York: McKay.

Berelson, Bernard R., et al. 1954. *Voting*. Chicago: University of Chicago Press.

Berger, Bennett M. 1960. *Working Class Suburb*. Berkeley: University of California Press.

Betley, Brian J. 1971. "Otomí Juez: An Analysis of a Political Middleman," *Hum. Organiz*. 30 (1): 57–63.

Blalock, H. M. 1967. "Status Inconsistency, Social Mobility, Status Integration, and Structural Effects," *Amer. Sociol. Rev*. 32: 790–801.

Blau, Peter M. 1960. "Structural Effects," *Amer. Sociol. Rev*. 25: 178–93.

Bleiker, A. H. 1972. "The Proximity Model and Urban Social Relations," *Urban Anthrop*. 1: 151–75.

Bonilla, Frank. 1964. "The Urban Worker," pp. 186–205 in John J. Johnson, ed., *Continuity and Change in Latin America*. Stanford, Calif.: Stanford University Press.

———— 1970. *The Failure of Elites*. Cambridge, Mass.: MIT Press.

Bourricaud, François. 1970. *Power and Society in Contemporary Peru*. New York: Praeger.

Brigg, Pamela. 1973. "Some Economic Interpretations of Case Studies of Urban Migration in Developing Countries," Bank Staff Working Paper No. 251, International Bank for Reconstruction and Development, Washington, D.C.

Brim, Orville G., Jr. 1966. "Socialization Through the Life Cycle," in Orville G. Brim and Stanton Wheeler, *Socialization After Childhood*. New York: Wiley.

Brody, Eugene, ed. 1970. *Behavior in New Environments: Adaptation of Migrant Populations*. Beverly Hills, Calif.: Sage Publications.

Brown, Jane Cowan. 1972. *Patterns of Intra-Urban Settlement in Mexico City: An Examination of the Turner Theory*. Latin American Studies Program Dissertation Series No. 40, Cornell University.

Browning, Harley L. 1971. "Migrant Selectivity and the Growth of Large Cities in Developing Societies," pp. 273–314 in National Academy of Sciences, *Rapid Population Growth*, Vol. II. Baltimore: Johns Hopkins Press.

Burstein, Paul. 1972. "Social Structure and Individual Political Participation in Five Countries," *Amer. J. Sociol*. 77 (6): 1087–1110.

Butterworth, Douglas. 1972. "Two Small Groups: A Comparison of Migrants and Non-Migrants in Mexico City," *Urban Anthrop*. 1: 29–50.

———— 1973. "Squatters or Suburbanites?—The Growth of Shantytowns in

Oaxaca, Mexico," pp. 208–32 in Robert E. Scott, ed., *Latin American Modernization Problems*. Urbana: University of Illinois Press.

———— 1974. "Grass Roots Political Organizations in Cuba: The Case of the Committees for the Defense of the Revolution," in Wayne A. Cornelius and Felicity M. Trueblood, eds., *Anthropological Perspectives on Latin American Urbanization* (*Latin American Urban Research*, Vol. 4). Beverly Hills: Sage Publications.

Calderón, Luis. 1963. "Poder retentivo del área local urbana en las relaciones sociales," *Problemas de urbanización en América Latina: Estudios sociológicos Latinoamericanos* 13 (1963): 14–185.

Cameron, David R., J. Stephen Hendricks, and Richard I. Hofferbert. 1972. "Urbanization, Social Structure, and Mass Politics: A Comparison Within Five Nations," *Comp. Pol. Stud.* 5 (3): 259–90.

Campbell, Angus. 1958. "The Political Implications of Community Identification," pp. 318–328 in Roland Young, ed., *Approaches to the Study of Politics*. Evanston: Northwestern University Press.

———— 1962. "The Passive Citizen," *Acta Sociol.* 6 (1–2): 9–21.

Campbell, Angus, et al. 1964. *The American Voter: An Abridgement*. New York: Wiley.

Campbell, Ernest Q., and C. Norman Alexander. 1965. "Structural Effects and Interpersonal Relationships," *Amer. J. Sociol.* 71 (3): 284–89.

Campbell, Howard L. 1972. "Bracero Migration and the Mexican Economy, 1951–1964." Unpubl. dissertation, American University, Washington, D.C.

Cantril, Hadley. 1965. *The Pattern of Human Concerns*. New Brunswick: Rutgers University Press.

Castells, Manuel, et al. 1973. *Revista Latinoamericana de Estudios Urbano Regionales* 3 (7): 9–112 (special issue on low-income urban settlements in Chile).

Cataldo, Everett F., et al. 1968. "The Urban Poor and Community Action in Buffalo." Paper presented at the annual meeting of the Midwest Political Science Association (Chicago).

Cataldo, Everett F., and Lyman Kellstedt. 1968. "Conceptualizing and Measuring Political Involvement Over Time: A Study of Buffalo's Urban Poor," *Proc. Amer. Statist. Assoc.*, Social Statistics Section, pp. 83ff.

CEED (Centro de Estudios Económicos y Demográficos). 1970. *Dinámica de la población de México*. Mexico City: El Colegio de México.

Chalmers, Douglas A. 1972. "Parties and Society in Latin America," *Stud. Comp. Int. Devel.* 7 (2): 102–8.

Chance, John K. 1973. "Parentesco y residencia urbana: Grupo familiar y su organización en un suburbio de Oaxaca, México," *América Indígena* 33 (1): 187–212.

Cleaves, Peter S. 1974. *Bureaucratic Politics and Administration in Chile*. Berkeley: University of California Press.

Cockcroft, James D. 1972. "Coercion and Ideology in Mexican Politics," pp. 245–67 in J. D. Cockcroft, et al., *Dependence and Underdevelopment: Latin America's Political Economy*. Garden City: Doubleday Anchor.

———— 1974. "Misdeveloped Mexico," in Ronald Chilcote and Joel Edelstein (eds.), *Latin America: The Struggle with Dependency and Beyond*. Cambridge, Mass.: Schenkman.

Cohen, Ernesto. 1968. "Marginality: An Explanatory Essay." Paper presented at the Conference on Urban Poverty Leadership Styles in the Americas (Philadelphia).

Cohen, Michael A. 1974. *Urban Policy and Political Conflict in Africa.* Chicago: University of Chicago Press.

Coleman, James S. 1958–59. "Relational Analysis: The Study of Social Organization with Survey Methods," *Hum. Organiz.* 17: 28–36.

——— 1961. "Comment on Three 'Climate of Opinion' Studies," *Pub. Opin. Quart.* 25: 607–10.

Coleman, Kenneth M. 1972. *Public Opinion in Mexico City about the Electoral System.* (James Sprunt Studies in History and Political Science 53). Chapel Hill, North Carolina: University of North Carolina Press.

Collier, David. 1971. "Squatter Settlement Formation and the Politics of Cooptation in Peru." Unpubl. Ph.D. dissertation, U. Chicago.

——— 1973. *"Squatters and Oligarchs: Urbanization and Public Policy in Peru."* Unpubl. book ms., Department of Political Science, Indiana U.

——— 1975. "Squatter Settlements and Policy Innovation in Peru," in Abraham F. Lowenthal, ed., *Continuity and Change in Contemporary Peru.* Princeton, N.J.: Princeton University Press.

Comisión Nacional de los Salarios Mínimos. 1970. *Salarios mínimos que regirán en los años de 1970 y 1971.* Mexico City: Comisión Nacional de los Salarios Mínimos.

Contreras, Enrique. 1972. "Migración interna y oportunidades de empleo en la Ciudad de México," in *El perfil de México en 1980,* Vol. III. Mexico City, Siglo Veintiuno.

Cook, Thomas J., and Frank P. Scioli, Jr. 1972. "A Critique of the Learning Concept in Political Socialization Research," *Soc. Sci. Quart.* 52 (4): 949–62.

Cooper, Kenneth. 1959. "Leadership Role Expectations in Mexican Rural and Urban Environments." Unpubl. dissertation, Stanford.

Corbett, John G. 1974. "The Context of Politics in a Mexican Community: A Study in Constraints on System Capacity." Unpubl. dissertation, Stanford.

Cornelius, Wayne A. 1969. "Urbanization as an Agent in Latin American Political Instability: The Case of Mexico," *Amer. Pol. Sci. Rev.* 63 (3): 833–57.

——— 1971. "The Political Sociology of Cityward Migration in Latin America: Toward Empirical Theory," pp. 95–147 in Francine F. Rabinovitz and Felicity M. Trueblood, eds., *Latin American Urban Research,* Vol. 1. Beverly Hills: Sage Publications.

——— 1973. "Nation Building, Participation, and Distribution: The Politics of Social Reform under Cárdenas," pp. 392–498 in Gabriel A. Almond, et al., eds., *Crisis, Choice, and Change: Historical Studies of Political Development.* Boston: Little, Brown.

Cornelius, Wayne A., and Henry A. Dietz. 1973. "Urbanization, Demand-Making, and Political System 'Overload': Political Participation Among the Migrant Poor in Latin American Cities." Paper presented at the annual meeting of the American Political Science Association (New Orleans). (Forthcoming in Rodney Stiefbold, ed., *Frontiers of Urban Research.* Coral Gables: University of Miami Press.)

Cox, Kevin R. 1969. "The Spatial Structuring of Information Flow and Partisan Attitudes," pp. 157–85 in Mattei Dogan and Stein Rokkan, eds., *Quantitative Ecological Analysis in the Social Sciences.* Cambridge, Mass.: MIT Press.

———— 1970. "Geography, Social Contexts, and Voting Behavior in Wales, 1861–1951," pp. 117–59 in Erik Allardt and Stein Rokkan, eds., *Mass Politics: Studies in Political Sociology.* New York: Free Press.

———— 1973. *Conflict, Power, and Politics in the City: A Geographic View.* New York: McGraw-Hill.

Cox, Kevin R., David R. Reynolds, and Stein Rokkan, eds. 1974. *Locational Approaches to Power and Conflict.* Beverly Hills: Sage Publications.

Crosson, Pierre R. 1974. "Rural-to-Urban Migration in Mexico." Unpubl. paper, Resources for the Future, Inc., Washington, D.C.

Dahl, Robert A. 1961. *Who Governs?* New Haven: Yale University Press.

Daland, Robert T. 1971. "Urbanization Policy and Political Development in Latin America," pp. 235–63 in John Miller and Ralph Gakenheimer, eds., *Latin American Urban Policies and the Social Sciences.* Beverly Hills: Sage Publications.

Davies, J. Clarence. 1966. *Neighborhood Groups and Urban Renewal.* New York: Columbia University Press.

Davis, Charles L. 1974. "Towards an Explanation of Mass Support for Authoritarian Regimes: The Case of Mexico." Unpubl. dissertation. U. Kentucky.

Davis, Charles L., and Kenneth M. Coleman. 1974. "The Regime-Legitimating Function of External Political Efficacy in an Authoritarian Regime: The Case of Mexico." Paper presented at the annual meeting of the American Political Science Association (Chicago).

Davis, James A. 1962. *Great Books and Small Groups.* New York: Free Press.

Davis, James A., Joe L. Spaeth, and Carolyn Huson. 1961. "A Technique for Analyzing the Effects of Group Composition," *Amer. Sociol. Rev.* 26 (2): 215–25.

Deneke, Jorge A. Harth. 1966. "The Colonias Proletarias of Mexico City: Low-Income Settlements of the Urban Fringe." Unpubl. M.A. thesis, Dept. City Planning, MIT.

Dennis, N. 1968. "The Popularity of the Neighborhood Community Idea," pp. 74–92 in R. E. Paul, ed., *Readings in Urban Sociology.* London: Pergamon.

Deutsch, Karl W. 1961. "Social Mobilization and Political Development," *Amer. Pol. Sci. Rev.* 55 (3): 493–514.

Díaz, May N. 1966. *Tonalá: Conservatism, Responsibility, and Authority in a Mexican Village.* Berkeley: University of California Press.

Díaz Díaz, Fernando. 1972. *Caudillos y caciques.* Mexico City: El Colegio de México.

Dietz, Henry A. 1973. "The Office and the Poblador: Perceptions and Manipulations of Housing Authorities by the Lima Urban Poor." Paper presented at the meeting of the American Society for Public Administration (Los Angeles). (Forthcoming in James M. Malloy, ed., *Authoritarianism and Corporatism in Latin America.* Pittsburgh: University of Pittsburgh Press.)

———— 1974. "Becoming a Poblador: Political Adjustment to the Urban Environment in Lima, Peru." Unpubl. dissertation, Stanford.

———— 1975. "Some Modes of Participation in an Authoritarian Regime." Paper presented at the annual meeting of the American Political Science Association (San Francisco).

Di Palma, Giuseppe. 1970. *Apathy and Participation: Mass Politics in Western Societies.* New York: Free Press.

Di Tella, Torcuato. 1965. "Populism and Reform in Latin America," pp. 47–74 in Claudio Véliz, ed., *Obstacles to Change in Latin America.* London: Oxford University Press.

Dogan, Mattei, and Stein Rokkan, eds. 1969. *Quantitative Ecological Analysis in the Social Sciences.* Cambridge, Mass.: MIT Press.

Domínguez, Jorge I. 1971. "Social Mobilization, Traditional Political Participation, and Government Response in Early Nineteenth-Century Spanish America." Unpubl. dissertation, Harvard.

———— 1974. "Political Participation and the Social Mobilization Hypothesis: Chile, Mexico, Venezuela, and Cuba in 1800–1825," *J. Interdisc. Hist.* 5 (2): 237–66.

Drake, Paul W. 1970. "Mexican Regionalism Reconsidered," *J. Inter-Amer. Stud.* 12 (3).

Duff, Ernest A., and John F. McCamant. 1968. "Measuring Social and Political Requirements for System Stability in Latin America," *Amer. Pol. Sci. Rev.* 62 (4): 1125–43.

Duque, Joaquín, and Ernesto Pastrana. 1972. "La movilización reivindicativa urbana de los sectores populares en Chile, 1964–1972," *Rev. Uruguaya Cienc. Soc.* 1 (2).

Easton, David. 1965. *A Systems Analysis of Political Life.* New York: Wiley.

Eckstein, Susan. 1972a. "The Poverty of Revolution: A Study of Social, Economic, and Political Inequality in a Central City Area, A Squatter Settlement, and a Low Cost Housing Project in Mexico City." Unpubl. dissertation, Columbia.

———— 1972b. "Ideological and Intellectual Biases in the Study of Latin American Urban Poverty." Paper presented at the annual meeting of the American Sociological Association.

———— 1973. "The Poverty of Revolution: Social Controls of Mexican Urban Poor." Unpubl. ms., Department of Sociology, Boston U. (Forthcoming from Princeton University Press, Princeton, N.J.)

ECLA (Economic Commission on Latin America). 1972. *Economic Survey of Latin America.* New York: United Nations.

Edelman, Murray. 1965. *The Symbolic Uses of Politics.* Urbana: University of Illinois Press.

———— 1971. *Politics as Symbolic Action.* Chicago: Markham.

Effrat, Marcia P., ed. 1974. *The Community: Approaches and Applications.* New York: Free Press.

Eisenstadt, S. N. 1965. *Essays on Comparative Institutions.* New York: Wiley.

Eisinger, Peter K. 1970. "The Impact of Anti-Poverty Expenditures in New York," pp. 539–60 in J. P. Crecine, ed., *Financing the Metropolis (Urban Affairs Annual Reviews,* Vol. 4). Beverly Hills: Sage Publications.

———— 1971. "Protest Behavior and the Integration of Urban Political Systems," *J. Politics* 33 (4): 980–1007.

———— 1972. "The Pattern of Citizen Contacts with Urban Officials," pp. 43–70 in H. Hahn, ed., *People and Politics in Urban Society (Urban Affairs Annual Reviews*, Vol. 6). Beverly Hills: Sage Publications.

———— 1973. "The Conditions of Protest Behavior in American Cities," *Amer. Pol. Sci. Rev.* 67 (1): 11–28.

Eldersveld, S. J., V. Jagannadham, and A. P. Barnabas. 1968. *The Citizen and the Administrator in a Developing Democracy.* Glenview, Ill.: Scott, Foresman.

Elkins, David J. 1971. "Social Mobilization, Social Structure, and Politics: Evidence and Qualifications." Paper presented at the annual meeting of the American Political Science Association (Chicago).

El-Shakhs, Salah S. 1972. "The Urban Crisis in International Perspective," *Amer. Behav. Scientist* 15 (Mar.-Apr.).

Ennis, Philip H. 1962. "The Contextual Dimensions in Voting," pp. 180–211 in William N. McPhee and Willam A. Glaser, eds., *Public Opinion and Congressional Elections.* Glencoe, Ill.: Free Press.

Epstein, David G., 1973. *Brasília, Plan and Reality: A Study of Planned and Spontaneous Urban Development.* Berkeley, Calif.: University of California Press.

Equipo de Estudios Poblacionales del CIDU. 1972a. "Pobladores y administración de justicia: Informe preliminar de una encuesta," *Rev. Latinoamer. Estudios Urbano Regionales* 2 (5): 135–50.

———— 1972b. "Reivindicación urbana y lucha política: Los campamentos de pobladores en Santiago de Chile," *Rev. Latinoamer. Estudios Urbano Regionales* 2 (6): 55–82.

Erbe, William. 1964. "Social Involvement and Political Activity: A Replication and Elaboration," *Amer. Sociol. Rev.* 29: 198–215.

Eulau, Heinz. 1969. *Micro-Macro Political Analysis.* Chicago: Aldine.

Fagen, Richard R. 1964. "International Politics and Cuba." Paper presented at the annual meeting of the American Political Science Association.

———— 1969. *The Transformation of Political Culture in Cuba.* Stanford, Calif.: Stanford University Press.

Fagen, Richard R., and William S. Tuohy. 1972. *Politics and Privilege in a Mexican City.* Stanford, Calif.: Stanford University Press.

Feldman, Roy E. 1973. "New Directions in Political Psychology." Unpubl. book ms., Department of Political Science, MIT.

Fellin, Phillip, and Eugene Litwak. 1968. "The Neighborhood in Urban American Society," *Social Work* 13: 72–80.

Festinger, Leon, S. Schachter, and Kurt Back. 1950. *Social Pressures in Informal Groups.* New York: Harper.

Field, John O. 1973. "Partisanship in India: A Survey Analysis." Unpubl. dissertation, Stanford.

Figueroa, Alfredo, and Richard Weisskoff. 1974. "Visión de las pirámides sociales: Distribución del ingreso en América Latina," *Ensayos ECIEL* (Rio de Janeiro and Washington, D.C.) 1: 83–154.

Finifter, Ada W. 1972. "Dimensions of Political Alienation," pp. 189–212 in A. W. Finifter, ed., *Alienation and the Social System.* New York: Wiley.

Fischer, Claude S. 1975. "The City and Political Psychology," *Amer. Pol. Sci. Rev.* 69 (2): 559–71.

Flinn, William L. 1970. "Influence of Community Values on Innovativeness," *Amer. J. Sociol.* 75 (6): 983–91.

Flinn, William L., and Alvaro Camacho. 1969. "The Correlates of Voter Participation in a Shantytown Barrio in Bogotá, Colombia," *Inter-Amer. Econ. Affairs* 22 (4): 47–58.

Flores, Edmundo. 1961. *Tratado de Economía Agrícola.* Mexico City: Fondo de Cultura Económica.

Foladare, Irving S. 1968. "The Effect of Neighborhood on Voting Behavior," *Pol. Sci. Quart.* 83 (4): 516–29.

Form, William H., and Joan Huber. 1971. "Income, Race, and the Ideology of Political Efficacy," *J. Politics* 33 (3): 659–88.

Foster, Donald W. 1971. "Tequío in Urban Mexico: A Case from Oaxaca City," *J. Steward Anthrop. Soc.* 2 (2): 148–79.

Foster, George. 1967. *Tzintzuntzan: Mexican Peasants in a Changing World.* Boston: Little, Brown.

Frank, A. G. 1969. *Latin America: Underdevelopment or Revolution.* New York: Monthly Review Press.

Fraser, John. 1970. "The Mistrustful-Efficacious Hypothesis and Political Participation," *J. Politics* 32 (2): 444–49.

Frederickson, George, ed. 1973. *Neighborhood Control in the 1970's.* New York: Chandler.

Frey, Frederick W. 1970a. "Cross-Cultural Survey Research in Political Science," pp. 173–294 in Robert T. Holt and John E. Turner, eds., *The Methodology of Comparative Research.* New York: Free Press.

——— 1970b. "Political Development and Political Participation: 'Lost in the Horse Latitudes'?" Paper presented at the MUCIA Conference on Requirements and Consequences of Political Participation for Development Policies (Chicago).

——— 1973. "A Power-Analytic Approach to Political Socialization." Unpubl. paper, Dept. Political Science, MIT.

Frey, Frederick W., and Leslie L. Roos. 1967. *Social Structure and Community Development in Rural Turkey: Village and Elite Leadership Relations.* Cambridge, Mass.: MIT Center for International Studies, Rural Development Research Project, Rept. 10.

Fried, Marc. 1973. *The World of the Urban Working Class.* Cambridge, Mass.: Harvard University Press.

Fried, Robert C. 1972. "Mexico City," pp. 645–88 in William A. Robson and D. E. Regan, eds., *Great Cities of the World,* 3d ed., 2 vols. Beverly Hills: Sage Publications.

Friedman, Herbert D. 1968. "Squatter Assimilation in Buenos Aires, Argentina." Unpubl. dissertation, MIT.

——— 1969. "Los adolescentes de las villas de emergencia de Buenos Aires," *Rev. Latinoamer. Sociol.* 5 (March).

Friedmann, John. 1972. "The Spatial Organization of Power in the Development of Urban Systems," *Comp. Urban Res.* 1 (2): 5–42.

Friedrich, Paul. 1957. "Cacique: The Recent History and Present Structure of Politics in a Tarascan Village." Unpubl. dissertation, Yale.

———— 1965. "A Mexican Cacicazgo," *Ethnology* 4 (2): 190–209.

———— 1966. "Revolutionary Politics and Communal Ritual," pp. 191–220 in Marc J. Swartz, Victor W. Turner, and Arthur Tuden, eds., *Political Anthropology*. Chicago: Aldine.

———— 1968. "The Legitimacy of a Cacique," pp. 243–69 in Marc J. Swartz, ed., *Local-Level Politics: Social and Cultural Perspectives*. Chicago: Aldine.

———— 1970. *Agrarian Revolt in a Mexican Village*. Englewood Cliffs, N.J.: Prentice-Hall.

Frolic, B. Michael. 1970. "The Soviet Study of Soviet Cities," *J. Politics* 32 (3): 675–95.

Furlong, William L. 1972. "Obstacles to Political Development: Case Studies of Center and Periphery in Northern Mexico." Paper presented at the annual meeting of the American Political Science Association (Washington, D.C.).

Furtak, R. 1969. "El Partido Revolucionario Institucional: Integración nacional y movilización electoral," *Foro Internac.* (Mexico) 9 (2): 339–53.

Gans, Herbert J. 1961a. "Planning and Social Life: Friendship and Neighbor Relations in Sub-Communities," *J. Amer. Inst. Planners* (27): 134–40.

———— 1961b. "The Effect of a Community Upon Its Residents: Some Considerations for Sociological Theory and Planning Politics." Paper presented to the American Sociological Association (St. Louis).

———— 1962. *The Urban Villagers*. New York: Free Press.

———— 1963. "The Effect of the Move from City to Suburb," in Leonard Duhl, ed., *The Urban Condition: People and Policy in the Metropolis*. New York: Basic Books.

———— 1968. *People and Plans: Essays on Urban Problems and Solutions*. New York: Basic Books.

García, F. Chris. 1973. *Political Socialization of Chicano Children: A Comparative Study with Anglos in California Schools*. New York: Praeger Special Studies.

Gauhan, Timothy O. 1974. "Some Important Characteristics of Low-Income Housing in Bogotá, Colombia and Their Economic and Political Implications." Unpubl. paper, Dept. Political Science, Rice.

Germani, Gino. 1962. *Política y sociedad en una época de transición*. Buenos Aires: Paidós.

———— 1967. "The City as an Integrating Mechanism: The Concept of Social Integration," pp. 175–89 in Glenn H. Beyer, ed., *The Urban Explosion in Latin America*, Ithaca: Cornell University Press.

———— 1973. *Modernization, Urbanization, and the Urban Crisis*. Boston: Little, Brown.

Giusti, Jorge. 1971. "Organizational Characteristics of the Latin American Urban Marginal Settler," *Int. J. Politics* 1 (1): 54–89.

Glassberg, A. 1972. "The Linkage Between Urban Policy Outputs and Voting Behavior: New York and London." Paper presented at the annual meeting of the American Political Science Association (Washington, D.C.).

Goel, Madan Lal. 1969. "The Relevance of Education for Political Participation in a Developing Society," *Comp. Pol. Stud.* 3 (3): 333–50.

———— 1971. "Urban-Rural Correlates of Political Participation in India," *Pol. Sci. Rev.* (India) 10 (1–2): 51–64.

Goldkind, Victor. 1966. "Class Conflict and Cacique in Chan Kom," *Sthwest. J. Anthrop.* 22: 325–45.

Goldrich, Daniel M. 1964. "Peasants' Sons in City Schools," *Hum. Organiz.* 23: 328–33.

———— 1965. "Toward the Comparative Study of Politicization in Latin America," pp. 361–77 in Dwight Heath and Richard N. Adams, eds., *Contemporary Cultures and Civilizations of Latin America* (1st ed.). New York: Random House.

———— 1970. "Political Organization and the Politicization of the Poblador," *Comp. Pol. Stud.* 3 (2): 176–202.

Goldrich, Daniel M., Raymond B. Pratt, and C. R. Schuller. 1970. "The Political Integration of Lower-Class Urban Settlements in Chile and Peru," pp. 175–214 in Irving L. Horowitz, ed., *Masses in Latin America.* New York: Oxford University Press.

González Casanova, Pablo. 1968. "Dynamics of the Class Structure," pp. 64–82 in Joseph A. Kahl, ed., *Comparative Perspectives on Stratification: Mexico, Great Britain, Japan.* Boston: Little, Brown.

———— 1970. *Democracy in Mexico.* London: Oxford University Press.

Gosnell, Harold F. 1939. *Machine Politics: Chicago Model.* Chicago: University of Chicago Press.

Gove, Walter, and Herbert Costner. 1969. "Organizing the Poor: An Evaluation of a Strategy," *Soc. Sci. Quart.* 50: 643–56.

Graham, George J., Jr., and Richard A. Pride. 1971. "Styles of Political Participation, Want Conversion, and Political Support Among Adults and Students in a Metropolitan Community." Paper presented at the annual meeting of the American Political Science Association (Chicago).

Graves, Nancy B., and Theodore D. Graves. 1974. "Adaptive Strategies in Urban Migration." Unpubl. paper, Dept. Anthropology, University of Auckland, New Zealand.

Greenberg, Edward S., ed. 1970. *Political Socialization.* New York: Atherton.

Greenstone, J. David, and Paul E. Peterson. 1973. *Race and Authority in Urban Politics: Community Participation and the War on Poverty.* New York: Russell Sage Foundation–Basic Books.

Greer, Scott. 1956. "Urbanism Reconsidered: A Comparative Study of Local Areas in a Metropolis," *Amer. Sociol. Rev.* 21: 19–25.

———— 1970. "The Social Structure and Political Process of Suburbia," pp. 600–616 in Robert Gutman and David Popenoe, eds., *Neighborhood, City, and Metropolis.* New York: Random House.

Greer, Scott, and Ann Lennarson Greer, eds. 1974. *Neighborhood and Ghetto.* New York: Basic Books.

Greer, Scott, and Peter Orleans. 1962. "The Mass Society and the Parapolitical Structure," *Amer. Sociol. Rev.* 27: 634–46.

Grindle, Merilee S. 1975. "Exchange Processes and Public Policy in Mexico." Unpubl. dissertation, MIT.

Gurrieri, Adolfo. 1965. *Situación y perspectivas de la juventud en una población urbana popular.* United Nations Economic Commission for Latin America, Document E/LACCY/BP/L.2, Santiago, Chile.

Gustafsson, Gunnel. 1974. "Environmental Influence on Political Learning," Chapter 8 in Richard G. Niemi, et al., *The Politics of Future Citizens: New*

Directions in the Political Socialization of Children. San Francisco: Jossey-Bass.

Gutkind, Peter C. W. 1973. "From the Energy of Despair to the Anger of Despair: The Transition from Social Circulation to Political Consciousness among the Urban Poor in Africa," *Canad. J. Afric. Stud.* 7 (2): 179–98.

Hallman, Howard W. 1974. *Neighborhood Government in a Metropolitan Setting.* Beverly Hills, Calif.: Sage Publications.

Hamburg, Roger. 1972. "Urbanization, Industrialization, and Modernization in Latin America: Soviet Views," *Stud. Compar. Communism.* 5 (1): 1–20.

Hanna, William J., and Judith L. Hanna. 1967. "The Integrative Role of Urban Africa's Middleplaces and Middlemen," *Civilisations* 17 (1–2): 12–29.

———— 1969. "Influence and Influentials in Two Urban-Centered African Communities," *Comp. Politics* 2 (1): 17–40.

———— 1971. *Urban Dynamics in Black Africa: A Guide to Research and Theory.* Chicago: Aldine.

Hansen, Roger D. 1971. *The Politics of Mexican Development.* Baltimore: Johns Hopkins.

Hardoy, Jorge E. 1972. "Urbanization Policies and Urban Reforms in Latin America," pp. 19–44 in Guillermo Geisse and Jorge Hardoy, eds., *Latin American Urban Research,* Vol. II. Beverly Hills: Sage Publications.

Harris, Louis. 1956. "Government for the People of Mexico City." Unpubl. dissertation, UCLA.

Havens, A. Eugene, and William L. Flinn. 1970. "The Power Structure in a Shantytown," pp. 93–107 in A. Eugene Havens and W. L. Flinn, eds., *Internal Colonialism and Structural Change in Colombia.* New York: Praeger.

Hawkins, Brett W., et al. 1971. "Efficacy, Mistrust, and Political Participation: Findings from Additional Data and Indicators," *J. Politics* 33 (4): 1130–36.

Heffernan, W. Joseph, Jr. 1969. "Research Note on the Conventional Political Behavior of the Poor," *J. Hum. Resources* 4 (2): 253–59.

Hensler, Deborah R. 1973. "The Impact of Suburban Residence on Political Attitudes: A Contextual Analysis." Unpubl. dissertation, MIT.

Hillman, Arthur, and Frank Seever. 1970. "Elements of Neighborhood Organization," pp. 273–88 in Fred M. Cox, et al., eds., *Strategies of Community Organization.* Itasca, Ill.: F. E. Peacock.

Himmelstrand, Ulf. 1960. *Social Pressures, Attitudes, and Democratic Processes.* Stockholm: Almquist Wiksell.

Hirsch, Herbert. 1971. *Poverty and Politicization: Political Socialization in an American Sub-Culture.* New York: Free Press.

Hirschman, Albert O. 1973. "The Changing Tolerance for Income Inequality in the Course of Economic Development," *Quart. J. Econ.* 87 (4): 544–66.

Hobsbawm, E. J. 1967. "Peasants and Rural Migrants in Politics," pp. 43–65 in Claudio Véliz, ed., *The Politics of Conformity in Latin America.* London: Oxford University Press.

Hogan, J. B. 1972. "Social Structure and Public Policy: A Longitudinal Study of Mexico and Canada," *Comp. Politics* 4 (4): 477–509.

Horowitz, Irving L. 1967. "Electoral Politics, Urbanization, and Social Development in Latin America," in Glenn H. Beyer, ed., *The Urban Explosion in Latin America.* Ithaca: Cornell University Press.

———— 1970. "Personality and Structural Dimensions in Comparative International Development," *Soc. Sci. Quart.* 51: 494–513.

Houlihan, Kevin, et al. 1970. "Some Motivational Correlates of Attitudes Toward Political Participation," *Midw. J. Pol. Sci.* 14 (3): 383–91.

Huber, Joan, and William H. Form. 1973. *Income and Ideology: An Analysis of the American Political Formula.* New York: Free Press.

Hunt, Eva. 1974. "Ceremonies of Confrontation and Submission: The Symbolic Dimension of Indian-Mexican Political Interactions." Paper presented at the Burg Wartenstein Symposium No. 64, on Secular Rituals Considered. (Available from Wenner-Gren Foundation for Anthropological Research, New York.)

Hunter, Albert. 1974. *Symbolic Communities: The Persistence and Change of Chicago's Local Communities.* Chicago: University of Chicago Press.

Huntington, Samuel P. 1968. *Political Order in Changing Societies.* New Haven: Yale University Press.

Huntington, Samuel P., and Joan M. Nelson. 1973. "Socio-Economic Change and Political Participation: Report to the Civic Participation Division of the Agency for International Development." Center for International Affairs, Harvard University, Research Agreement AID/csd-2502. (Forthcoming as *Socioeconomic Change and Political Participation*, Cambridge, Mass.: Harvard University Press.)

Inkeles, Alex. 1969. "Participant Citizenship in Six Developing Countries," *Amer. Pol. Sci. Rev.* 63 (4): 1120–41.

Inkeles, Alex, and David H. Smith. 1974. *Becoming Modern: Individual Change in Six Developing Countries.* Cambridge, Mass.: Harvard University Press.

Instituto Nacional de la Vivienda. 1968. *Una ciudad perdida.* Mexico City: Instituto Nacional de la Vivienda.

Jackson, Harold E. 1973. "Intra-Urban Migration of Mexico City's Poor." Unpubl. dissertation, U. Colorado (Boulder).

Jacob, Phillip, et al. 1972. *Values and the Active Community.* New York: Free Press.

Jaguaribe, Helio. 1973. *Political Development: A General Theory and a Latin American Case Study.* New York: Harper & Row.

Janowitz, Morris. 1952. *The Community Press in an Urban Setting.* Glencoe, Ill.: Free Press.

Johnson, John J. 1958. *Political Change in Latin America: The Emergence of the Middle Sectors.* Stanford, Calif.: Stanford University Press.

Johnson, Kenneth F. 1971. *Mexican Democracy: A Critical View.* Boston: Houghton Mifflin.

Johnston, R. J. 1972. *Urban Residential Patterns.* New York: Praeger.

Juppenlatz, Morris. 1971. *Cities in Transformation: The Urban Squatter Problem of the Developing World.* Brisbane: University of Queensland Press.

Kahl, Joseph A. 1968. *The Measurement of Modernism.* Austin: University of Texas Press.

Karpat, Kemal H. 1973. "The Politics of Transition: Political Attitudes and Party Affiliation in Turkish Gecekondu." Unpubl. paper, Dept. History, U. Wisconsin (Madison).

Karst, Kenneth L., Murray L. Schwartz, and Audrey J. Schwartz. 1973. *The*

Evolution of Law in the Barrios of Caracas. Los Angeles: Latin American Center, UCLA.

Katz, Daniel, and Samuel J. Eldersveld. 1961. "The Impact of Local Party Activity Upon the Electorate," *Publ. Opin. Quart.* 25: 12–15.

Kaufman, Clifford. 1966. "Urbanization, Personal Welfare, and Politicization: The Lower Class in Santiago, Chile." Unpubl. dissertation, U. Oregon.

——— 1970. "Latin American Urban Inquiry: Some Substantive and Methodological Inquiry," *Urb. Aff. Quart.* 5: 394–411.

——— 1971. "Urbanization, Material Satisfaction, and Mass Political Involvement: The Poor in Mexico City," *Comp. Pol. Stud.* 4 (3): 295–319.

——— 1972. "Urban Structure and Urban Politics in Latin America," *J. Comp. Admin.* 4 (3): 343–64 (rejoinder on pp. 373–79).

Kaufman, Clifford, Karen Lindenberg, and Bryan Jones. 1973. "Personal Welfare and Political Performance: Testing a Model in Chile and Peru." Paper presented at the annual meeting of the Southwestern Social Science Association (Dallas).

Kazemi, Farhad. 1973. Oral presentation of research findings from Iran, at the Panel on Migration and Politics in Developing Countries, annual meeting of the American Political Science Association (New Orleans).

Keesing, Donald B. 1974. "External Finance and the Requirements of Full Modernization in Mexico." Research Memorandum 54, Center for Development Economics, Williams College, Williamstown, Mass.

Keller, Suzanne. 1968. *The Urban Neighborhood.* New York: Random House.

Kemper, Robert Van. 1971a. "Rural-Urban Migration in Latin America," *Int. Migration Rev.* 5: 36–47.

——— 1971b. "Migration and Adaptation of Tzintzuntzan Peasants in Mexico City." Unpubl. dissertation, U. California (Berkeley).

——— 1974. "Family and Household Organization Among Tzintzuntzan Migrants in Mexico City," pp. 23–46 in Wayne A. Cornelius and Felicity M. Trueblood, eds., *Anthropological Perspectives on Latin American Urbanization (Latin American Urban Research,* Vol. 4). Beverly Hills: Sage Publications.

Kendall, Patricia L., and Paul F. Lazarsfeld. 1950. "Problems of Survey Analysis," in Robert K. Merton and Paul F. Lazarsfeld, eds., *Continuities in Social Research: Studies in the Scope and Method of "The American Soldier."* Glencoe, Ill.: Free Press.

——— 1955. "The Relation Between Individual and Group Characteristics in 'The American Soldier,'" pp. 290–96 in Paul F. Lazarsfeld and Morris Rosenberg, eds., *The Language of Social Research.* New York: Free Press.

Kenski, Henry C., Jr. "Urbanization and Political Change in Latin America, 1950–64." Unpubl. dissertation, Georgetown U.

Kern, Robert, ed. 1973. *The Caciques: Oligarchical Politics and the System of Caciquismo in the Luso-Hispanic World.* Albuquerque: University of New Mexico Press.

Klassen, D. L. 1972. "Political Expectation/Perception Differences as Predictors of Public Trust in Government." Paper presented at the annual meeting of the American Political Science Association (Washington, D.C.).

Klorman, R. 1971. "Contextual Effects of Socio-Political Environment on Political Attitudes and Behavior." Unpubl. dissertation, U. California (Berkeley).

Kornblum, William. 1974. *Blue Collar Community*. Chicago, Ill.: University of Chicago Press.

Kramer, Ralph M. 1969. *Participation of the Poor: Comparative Community Case Studies in the War on Poverty*. Englewood Cliffs, N.J.: Prentice-Hall.

Krauss, Ellis S. 1974. *Japanese Radicals Revisited: Student Protest in Postwar Japan*. Berkeley: University of California Press.

Krickus, Richard J. 1968. "Rapid Urbanization: A Challenge to Political Development." Unpubl. dissertation, Georgetown U.

Kurtz, Donald V. 1973. *The Politics of a Poverty Habitat*. Cambridge, Mass.: Ballinger.

Kurtz, Norman R. 1966. "Gatekeepers in the Process of Acculturation." Unpubl. dissertation, U. Colorado (Boulder).

Lambert, Jacques. 1967. *Latin America: Social Structures and Political Institutions*. Berkeley: University of California Press.

Lane, Robert E. 1959. *Political Life*. New York: Free Press.

Laquian, Aprodicio A. 1972. "Slums and Squatters in South and Southeast Asia," pp. 183–203 in Leo Jakobson and Ved Prakash, eds., *Urbanization and National Development* (*South and Southeast Asia Urban Affairs*, Vol. I). Beverly Hills: Sage Publications.

Lazarsfeld, Paul F., and Herbert Menzel. 1961. "On the Relation between Individual and Collective Properties," pp. 422–40 in Amatai Etzioni, ed., *Complex Organizations*. New York: Holt, Rinehart, & Winston.

Lee, Chae-Jin. 1971. "Urban Political Competition in a Developing Nation: The Case of Korea," *Comp. Pol. Stud.* 4 (1): 107–16.

Lee, Terrence. 1968. "Urban Neighborhood as a Socio-Spatial Schema," *Hum. Relations* 21: 241–67.

Leeds, Anthony. 1968. "The Anthropology of Cities: Some Methodological Issues," pp. 31–47 in Elizabeth M. Eddy, ed., *Urban Anthropology: Research Perspectives and Strategies* (*Sthern. Anthrop. Soc. Proc. 2*). Athens, Ga.: University of Georgia Press.

———— 1969. "The Significant Variables Determining the Character of Squatter Settlements," *Amér. Latina* 12 (3): 44–86.

———— 1973. "Political, Economic, and Social Effects of Producer and Consumer Orientations Toward Housing in Brazil and Peru: A Systems Analysis," in Francine F. Rabinovitz and F. M. Trueblood, eds., *Latin American Urban Research*, Vol. III. Beverly Hills: Sage Publications.

———— 1974. "Housing-Settlement Types, Arrangements for Living, Proletarianization, and the Social Structure of the City," in Wayne A. Cornelius and Felicity M. Trueblood, eds., *Anthropological Perspectives on Latin American Urbanization* (*Latin American Urban Research*, Vol. 4). Beverly Hills: Sage Publications.

Leeds, Elizabeth R. 1972. "Forms of 'Squatment' Political Organization: The Politics of Control in Brazil." Unpubl. M.A. thesis, U. Texas (Austin).

Lenz-Romeiss, Felizitas. 1973. *The City: New Town or Home Town?* New York: Praeger.

Lerner, Daniel. 1958. *The Passing of Traditional Society*. New York: Free Press.

Levenson, George B. 1971. "The Behavioral Relevance of the Obligation to Participate." Paper presented at the annual meeting of the American Political Science Association (Chicago).

Levin, Martin L. 1961. "Social Climates and Political Socialization," *Pub. Opin. Quart.* 25 (4): 596–606.

Lewis, Oscar. 1961. *The Children of Sánchez: Autobiography of a Mexican Family.* New York: Random House.

————— 1965. "Further Observations on the Folk-Urban Continuum and Urbanization, with Special Reference to Mexico City," pp. 491–503 in P. Hauser and L. F. Schnore, eds., *The Study of Urbanization.* New York: Wiley.

Lindenberg, K. E. M. 1970. "The Effect of Negative Sanctions on Politicization among Lower-Class Sectors in Santiago, Chile, and Lima, Peru." Unpubl. dissertation, U. Oregon.

Lipset, S. M. 1960. *Political Man.* New York: Doubleday.

Lipset, S. M., Martin A. Trow, and James S. Coleman. 1956. *Union Democracy.* Glencoe, Ill.: Free Press.

Lipsky, Michael. 1970. *Protest in City Politics.* Chicago: Rand McNally.

Lipsky, Michael, and M. Levi. 1972. "Community Organization as a Political Resource," pp. 175–99 in H. Hahn, ed., *People and Politics in Urban Society (Urban Affairs Annual Reviews*, Vol. 6). Beverly Hills: Sage Publications.

Litwak, Eugene. 1970. "Voluntary Associations and Neighborhood Cohesion," pp. 583–600 in Robert Gutman and David Popenoe, eds., *Neighborhood, City, and Metropolis.* New York: Random House.

Lomnitz, Larissa. 1974. "The Social and Economic Organization of a Mexican Shantytown," in Wayne A. Cornelius and Felicity M. Trueblood, eds., *Anthropological Perspectives on Latin American Urbanization (Latin American Urban Research,* Vol. 4). Beverly Hills: Sage Publications.

————— 1975. *Como sobreviven los marginados.* Mexico City: Siglo Veintiuno.

Lopes, Juárez Rubens Brandão. 1970. "Some Basic Developments in Brazilian Politics and Society," pp. 162–66 in Richard R. Fagen and Wayne A. Cornelius, eds., *Political Power in Latin America: Seven Confrontations.* Englewood Cliffs, N.J.: Prentice-Hall.

López Rosado, Diego. 1975. *El costo de la vida en la Ciudad de México.* Mexico City: Departamento del Distrito Federal.

Lozier, John D. 1971. "Political Organization and Cooperative Work in a Mexican Village." Unpubl. dissertation, U. Minnesota.

Lutz, Thomas M. 1967. "Some Aspects of Community Organization and Activity in the Squatter Settlements of Panama City." Unpubl. paper, Georgetown U.

————— 1970. "Self-Help Neighborhood Organizations, Political Socialization, and the Developing Political Orientations of Urban Squatters in Latin America: Contrasting Patterns from Case Studies in Panama City, Guayaquil, and Lima." Unpubl. dissertation, Georgetown U.

Lynch, Thomas D., et al. 1972. "Symposium: Neighborhoods and Citizen Involvement," *Publ. Admin. Rev.* 32 (3): 189–223.

Mabry, Donald J. 1973. *Mexico's Acción Nacional: A Catholic Alternative to Revolution.* Syracuse, N.Y.: Syracuse University Press.

McClosky, Herbert. 1968. "Political Participation," pp. 252–65 in David L. Sills, ed., *International Encyclopedia of the Social Sciences,* Vol. 12. New York: Macmillan–Free Press.

McDonald, Ronald H. 1969. "National Urban Voting Behavior: The Politics of Dissent in Latin America," *Inter-Amer. Econ. Affairs* 23 (1): 3–20.

MacEwen, Allison M. 1971. "Marginalidad y movilidad en una villa miseria," *Rev. Latinoamer. Sociol.* 7 (1): 37–53.

———— 1972. "Stability and Change in a Shantytown: A Summary of Some Research Findings," *Sociology* 6 (1): 41–57.

McKenney, James W. 1969. "Voluntary Associations and Political Integration: An Exploratory Study of the Role of Voluntary Association Membership in the Political Socialization of Urban Lower-Class Residents of Santiago, Chile, and Lima, Peru." Unpubl. dissertation, U. Oregon.

McKenzie, Roderick Duncan. 1972. "The Neighborhood," pp. 42–44 in Robert K. Yin, ed., *The City in the Seventies.* Itasca, Ill.: Peacock.

Maguire, Kevin. 1969. "Political Resocialization: A Theoretical and Empirical Analysis." Unpubl. dissertation, U. Colorado (Boulder).

Main, Eleanor C. 1966. "The Impact of Urbanization: A Comparative Study of Urban and Non-Urban Political Attitudes and Behavior." Unpubl. dissertation, U. North Carolina (Chapel Hill).

Mangin, William. 1967. "Latin American Squatter Settlements: A Problem and a Solution," *Lat. Amer. Res. Rev.* 2 (3): 65–98.

———— ed. 1970. *Peasants in Cities.* Boston: Houghton Mifflin.

Mann, Peter H. 1970. "The Neighborhood," pp. 568–83 in Robert Gutman and David Popenoe, eds., *Neighborhood, City, and Metropolis.* New York: Random House.

Marshall, Dale R. 1968. "Who Participates in What? A Bibliographic Essay on Individual Participation in Urban Areas," *Urb. Aff. Quart.* 4 (2): 201–24.

———— 1971. *The Politics of Participation in Poverty.* Berkeley: University of California Press.

Martínez Ríos, Jorge. 1972. "Los campesinos mexicanos: Perspectivas en el proceso de marginalización," *El perfil de México en 1980,* Vol. III. Mexico City: Siglo Veintiuno.

Martinussen, Willy. 1972. "The Development of Civic Competence: Socialization or Task Generalization?" *Acta Sociol.* 15 (3): 213–27.

Maruska, Donald L. 1972. "Government Policy and Neighborhood Organizations in the Squatter Settlements of Lima." Unpubl. honors thesis, Dept. Government, Harvard.

Mathiason, John R. 1972. "Patterns of Powerlessness among Urban Poor: Toward the Use of Mass Communications for Rapid Social Change," *Stud. Comp. Int. Devel.* 7 (1): 64–84.

Mathiason, John R., and John D. Powell. 1972. "Participation and Efficacy: Aspects of Peasant Involvement in Political Mobilization," *Comp. Politics* 4 (3): 303–29.

Medler, Jerry F. 1966. "Negative Sanctions: Their Perception and Effect in the Political System." Unpubl. dissertation, U. Oregon.

Mercado Villar, Olga, et al. 1970. *La marginalidad urbana: Orígen, proceso, y modo.* Buenos Aires: Troquel.

Merelman, Richard. 1966. "Learning and Legitimacy," *Amer. Pol. Sci. Rev.* 60: 548–61.

Michelson, William. 1970. *Man and His Urban Environment: A Sociological Approach.* Reading, Mass.: Addison-Wesley.

Michl, Sara. 1973. "Urban Squatter Organization as a National Government Tool: The Case of Lima, Peru," in Francine F. Rabinovitz and Felicity M. Trueblood, eds., *Latin American Urban Research*, Vol. III. Beverly Hills: Sage Publications.

Milbrath, Lester. 1965. *Political Participation*. Chicago: Rand McNally.

Miller, George A., and L. Wesley Wager. 1971. "Adult Socialization, Organizational Structure, and Role Orientations," *Admin. Sci. Quart.* 16 (2): 151–63.

Miller, John, and Ralph A. Gakenheimer, eds. 1971. *Latin American Urban Policies and the Social Sciences*. Beverly Hills: Sage Publications.

Miller, Warren E. 1956. "One-Party Politics and the Voter," *Amer. Pol. Sci. Rev.* 50 (3): 707–25.

Moinat, Sheryl M., et al. 1972. "Black Ghetto Residents as Rioters," *J. Soc. Issues* 28 (4): 45–62.

Moiron, Sara. 1975. "El desempleo: Un problema creciente y poco estudiado." *Diorama de la Cultura, Excélsior*, 18 May: 6–7.

Mollenkopf, John H. 1973. "Causes and Consequences of Neighborhood Political Mobilization." Paper presented at the annual meeting of the American Political Science Association (New Orleans).

Montaño, Jorge. 1974. "Political Attitudes of the Urban Poor in Mexico." Unpubl. dissertation, U. London.

Moreno, José A. 1970. *Barrios in Arms: Revolution in Santo Domingo*. Pittsburgh: University of Pittsburgh Press.

Morse, Richard M. 1965. "Recent Research on Latin American Urbanization: A Selective Survey with Commentary," *Lat. Amer. Res. Rev.* 1 (1): 35–74.

——— 1971. "Trends and Issues in Latin American Urban Research, 1965–1970," *Lat. Amer. Res. Rev.* 6 (1): 3–52; 6 (2): 19–75.

Muñoz, Humberto, and Orlandina de Oliveira. 1973. "Migración interna y movilidad ocupacional en la Ciudad de México," *Demografía y Econ.* (Mexico) 7 (2): 135–48.

Muñoz, Humberto, Orlandina de Oliveira, and Claudio Stern. 1972: "Migración y marginalidad ocupacional en la Ciudad de México," pp. 325–53 in *El perfil de México en 1980*, Vol. III. Mexico City: Siglo Veintiuno.

——— 1973. "Categorías de migrantes y nativos y algunas de sus características socioeconómicas: Comparación entre las ciudades de Monterrey y México," in Balán, Browning & Jelin, 1973b.

Navarrete, Ifigenia M. de. 1970. "La distribución del ingreso en México: Tendencias y perspectivas," pp. 15–72 in David Ibarra, et al., *El perfil de México en 1980*, Vol. 1. Mexico City: Siglo Veintiuno.

Needler, Martin C. 1971. *Politics and Society in Mexico*. Albuquerque: University of New Mexico Press.

Nelson, Joan M. 1969. *Migrants, Urban Poverty, and Instability in Developing Nations*. Cambridge, Mass.: Center for International Affairs, Harvard University.

——— 1972. "The Search for Useful Hypotheses," *J. Comp. Admin.* 4 (3): 365–71.

——— 1974. *Politics and the Urban Poor in Developing Nations*. Unpubl. book ms., Johns Hopkins School of Advanced International Studies, Washington, D.C.

———— 1975. *Sojourners vs. New Urbanites: Causes and Consequences of Temporary Versus Permanent Migration.* Cambridge, Mass.: MIT Center for International Studies, Migration and Development Study Group, Working papers.

Nie, Norman H., G. Bingham Powell, and Kenneth Prewitt. 1969. "Social Structure and Political Participation: Developmental Relationships," *Amer. Pol. Sci. Rev.* 63 (2, 3): 361–78, 808–32.

Nie, Norman H., D. Bent, and H. Hull. 1970. *Statistical Package for the Social Sciences.* New York: McGraw-Hill.

Nowak, Thomas, and Kay Snyder. 1970. "Urbanization and Clientelist Systems in the Philippines," *Philippine J. Publ. Admin.* 14 (3): 259–75.

Nun, José. 1969. "Sobrepoblación relativa, ejército industrial de reserva, y masa marginal," *Rev. Latinoamer. Sociol.* 5 (2): 178–236.

Nuñez, Theron A., Jr. 1963. "Cultural Discontinuity and Conflict in a Mexican Village." Unpubl. dissertation, U. California (Berkeley).

O'Brien, David J. 1974. "The Public Goods Dilemma and the 'Apathy' of the Poor toward Neighborhood Organization," *Soc. Service Rev.* 48 (2): 229–44.

———— 1975. *Neighborhood Organization and Interest Group Processes.* Princeton, N.J.: Princeton University Press.

Oldman, Oliver, et al. 1967. *Financing Urban Development in Mexico City.* Cambridge, Mass.: Harvard University Press.

Olsen, Marvin E. 1972. "A Model of Political Participation Strata." Paper presented at the annual meeting of the American Sociological Association (New Orleans).

Orbell, John M. 1970. "The Impact of Metropolitan Residence on Social and Political Orientations," *Soc. Sci. Quart.* 51 (3): 634–48.

Orbell, John M., and Kenneth S. Sherrill. 1969. "Racial Attitudes and the Metropolitan Context: A Structural Analysis," *Publ. Opin. Quart.* 33 (1): 46–54.

Orbell, John M., and Toru Uno. 1972. "A Theory of Neighborhood Problem Solving: Political Action vs. Residential Mobility," *Amer. Pol. Sci. Rev.* 66 (2): 471–89.

Ornelas, Charles. 1973. "Land Tenure, Sanctions, and Politicization in Mexico, D.F." Unpubl. dissertation, U. California (Riverside).

Ozbuden, Ergun. 1973. "Political Participation in Turkey." Unpubl. book ms., Center for International Affairs, Harvard.

Padgett, L. Vincent. 1966. *The Mexican Political System.* Boston: Houghton Mifflin.

Paré, Luisa. 1972. "Diseño teórico para el estudio del caciquismo actual en México," *Rev. Mex. Sociol.* 34 (2): 335–54.

Parenti, Michael. 1970. "Power and Pluralism: A View from the Bottom," *J. Politics* 32 (3): 501–30.

Park, Robert E. 1952. *Human Communities.* New York: Free Press.

Park, Robert E., Ernest W. Burgess, and Roderick D. McKenzie. 1925. *The City.* Chicago: University of Chicago Press.

Patch, Richard W. 1961. "Life in a Callejón: A Study of Urban Disorganization," *American Universities Field Staff Reports,* West Coast South America Series 8 (6).

———— 1968. "La Parada, Lima's Market," pp. 177–223 in Associates of the American Universities Field Staff, *City and Nation in the Developing World: AUFS Readings*, Vol. II. New York: American Universities Field Staff.

Peattie, Lisa R. 1968. *The View from the Barrio*. Ann Arbor: University of Michigan Press.

———— 1974. "The Concept of 'Marginality' as Applied to Squatter Settlements," in Wayne A. Cornelius and Felicity M. Trueblood, eds., *Anthropological Perspectives on Latin American Urbanization* (*Latin American Urban Research*, Vol. 4). Beverly Hills: Sage Publications.

Perlman, Janice E. 1971. "The Fate of Migrants in Rio's Favelas." Unpubl. dissertation, MIT.

Petras, Elizabeth M. 1973. *Social Organization of the Urban Housing Movement in Chile*. Buffalo: Council on International Studies, State University of New York at Buffalo. Special Studies Series 39.

Petras, James F. 1970. *Politics and Social Structure in Latin America*. New York: Monthly Review Press.

Pizzorno, Alessandro. 1970. "An Introduction to the Theory of Political Participation," *Soc. Sci. Information* 9: 29–61.

Portes, Alejandro. 1969. *Cuatro poblaciones: Informe preliminar sobre situación y aspiraciones de grupos marginados en el gran Santiago*. Santiago, Chile: Programa en Sociología del Desarrollo de la Universidad de Wisconsin y Centro de Estudios Socio-Económicos de la Universidad de Chile.

———— 1971a. "The Urban Slum in Chile: Types and Correlates," *Land Economics* 47 (3): 235–48.

———— 1971b. "Political Primitivism, Differential Socialization, and Lower-Class Leftist Radicalism," *American Sociol. Rev.* 36 (5): 820–35.

———— 1971c. "Urbanization and Politics in Latin America," *Soc. Sci. Quart.* 52: 697–720.

———— 1972. "Rationality in the Slum: An Essay in Interpretive Sociology," *Comp. Stud. Soc. Hist.* 14 (3): 268–86.

Portes, Alejandro, and John Walton. 1975. *Urban Latin America: The Political Condition from Above and Below*. Austin: University of Texas Press.

Powell, John Duncan. 1970. "Peasant Society and Clientelist Politics," *Amer. Pol. Sci. Rev.* 64 (2): 411–25.

Powell, Sandra. 1969. "Political Participation in the Barriadas: A Case Study," *Comp. Pol. Stud.* 2 (2): 195–215.

Pratt, Raymond B. 1968. "Organizational Participation, Politicization, and Development: A Study of Political Consequences of Participation in Community Associations in Four Lower Class Urban Settlements in Chile and Peru." Unpubl. dissertation, U. Oregon.

———— 1971a. "Community Political Organizations and Lower Class Politicization in Two Latin American Cities," *J. Developing Areas* 5: 523–42.

———— 1971b. "Parties, Neighborhood Associations, and the Politicization of the Urban Poor in Latin America: An Exploratory Analysis," *Midwest J. Pol. Sci.* 15 (3): 495–524.

PRI (Partido Revolucionario Institucional). 1970. *Memoria de la reunión para el estudio de los problemas del Distrito Federal.* 2 vols. Mexico City: Instituto de Estudios Políticos, Económicos, y Sociales del PRI.

Prysby, Charles. 1973. "Social Mobilization, Economic Development, and Left Voting: Chile, 1958–1964." Unpubl. dissertation, Michigan State U.

Purcell, Susan K., and John F. H. Purcell. 1973. "Community Power and Benefits from the Nation: The Case of Mexico," pp. 49–76 in Francine F. Rabinovitz and Felicity M. Trueblood, eds., *Latin American Urban Research*, Vol. 3. Beverly Hills: Sage Publications.

———— 1975a. "Machine Politics and Socio-Economic Change in Mexico," in James W. Wilkie, Michael C. Meyer, and Edna Monzón de Wilkie, eds., *Contemporary Mexico: Papers of the IV International Congress of Mexican History*. Berkeley and Mexico City: University of California Press and El Colegio de México.

———— 1975b. "Mexican Business and Public Policy," in James M. Malloy, ed., *Authoritarianism and Corporatism in Latin America*. Pittsburgh: University of Pittsburgh Press.

Putnam, Robert D. 1966. "Political Attitudes and the Local Community," *Amer. Pol. Sci. Rev.* 60 (3): 640–54.

Quijano, Aníbal. 1972. "La constitución del 'mundo' de la marginalidad urbana," *Rev. Latinoamer. Estudios Urbano Regionales*, 2 (5): 89–106.

Rabinovitz, Francine F. 1965. "Urban Development Decision-Making in the Mexican Federal District," in *Programs for Urban Development in Latin America*. Washington, D.C.: U.S. Agency for International Development.

———— 1969a. "Urban Development and Political Development in Latin America," pp. 86–123 in Robert T. Daland, ed., *Comparative Urban Research*. Beverly Hills: Sage Publications.

———— 1969b. "Political Correlates of Urbanization in Latin America: Is There a Micro/Macro Dilemma?" Unpubl. paper, Dept. Political Science, UCLA.

Rabushka, Alvin. 1970. "A Note on Overseas Chinese Political Participation in Urban Malaya," *Amer. Pol. Sci. Rev.* 64 (1): 177–78.

Ray, Talton F. 1969. *The Politics of the Barrios of Venezuela*. Berkeley: University of California Press.

Reyes Heroles, Jesús. 1972. "Cuando se combaten los cacicazgos, el pueblo vota con entusiasmo: Texto íntegro del discurso del Presidente del PRI pronunciado en Aguascalientes," *El Día*, Dec. 7, p. 9.

Reyna, José Luis. 1971. *An Empirical Analysis of Political Mobilization: The Case of Mexico*. Latin American Studies Program Dissertation Series (Cornell U.) No. 26.

———— 1974. "Control político, estabilidad y desarrollo en México," *Cuadernos del Centro de Estudios Sociológicos* (El Colegio de México) No. 3.

Richardson, Bradley M. 1973. "Urbanization and Political Participation: The Case of Japan," *Amer. Pol. Sci. Rev.* 67 (2): 433–52.

Riordan, William L. 1963. *Plunkitt of Tammany Hall*. New York: Dutton. (First publ. 1905.)

Ríos, José Arthur. 1960. "El pueblo y el político," *Política* (Caracas) 6: 11–36.

Roberts, Bryan R. 1970a. "The Social Organization of Low-Income Families," pp. 345–82 in Irving L. Horowitz, ed., *Masses in Latin America*. London: Oxford University Press.

———— 1970b. "Urban Poverty and Political Behavior in Guatemala," *Hum. Organiz.* 29 (1): 20–28.

———— 1973. *Organizing Strangers: Poor Families in Guatemala City.* Austin: University of Texas Press.

———— 1974. "The Interrelationships of City and Provinces in Peru and Guatemala," pp. 207–35 in Wayne A. Cornelius and Felicity M. Trueblood, eds., *Anthropological Perspectives on Latin American Urbanization (Latin American Urban Research,* Vol. 4). Beverly Hills: Sage Publications.

Roberts, J. M., and T. Gregor. 1971. "Privacy: A Cultural View," in J. R. Pennock and J. W. Chapman, eds., *Privacy.* New York: Atherton.

Robles Quintero, Salvador. 1975. "Análisis de la economía mexicana," *El Día,* 9 June: 18; 10 June: 15.

Robson, B. T. 1969. *Urban Analysis.* London: Cambridge University Press.

Rodríguez, Alfredo, Gustavo Riofrío, and Eileen Welsh. 1972. "De invasores a invadidos," *Rev. Latinoamer. Estudios Urbano Regionales* 2 (6): 101–42.

Rogler, Lloyd. 1967. "Slum Neighborhoods in Latin America," *J. Inter-Amer. Stud.* 9: 507–28.

———— 1974. "The Changing Role of a Political Boss in a Puerto Rican Migrant Community," *Amer. Sociol. Rev.* 39 (1): 57–67.

Rohter, Ira S. 1970. "A Social-Learning Theory Approach to the Study of Political Socialization." Paper presented at the annual meeting of the American Political Science Association (Los Angeles).

Rokkan, Stein. 1955. "Party Preferences and Opinion Patterns in Western Europe: A Comparative Analysis," *Int. Soc. Sci. Bull.* 7 (4): 575–96.

Rollwagen, Jack R. 1974. "Mediation and Rural-Urban Migration in Mexico: A Proposal and a Case Study," pp. 47–63 in Wayne A. Cornelius and Felicity M. Trueblood, eds., *Anthropological Perspectives on Latin American Urbanization (Latin American Urban Research,* Vol. 4). Beverly Hills: Sage Publications.

Ronfeldt, David. 1972. *Atencingo: The Politics of Agrarian Struggle in a Mexican Ejido.* Stanford, Calif.: Stanford University Press.

Rosa, Martín de la. 1975. *Netzahualcóyotl: Un fenómeno.* Mexico City: Fondo de Cultura Económica, "Testimonios del Fondo."

Rosenbaum, Allan. 1973. "Machine Politics, Class Interest, and the Urban Poor." Paper presented at the annual meeting of the American Political Science Association (New Orleans).

Ross, H. Laurence. 1970. "The Local Community: A Survey Approach," pp. 557–68 in Robert Gutman and David Popenoe, eds., *Neighborhood, City, and Metropolis.* New York: Random House.

Ross, Marc H. 1973a. "Two Styles of Political Participation in an African City," *Amer. J. Pol. Sci.* (formerly *Midwest J. Pol. Sci.*) 17 (1): 1–22.

———— 1973b. *The Political Integration of Urban Squatters.* Evanston, Ill.: Northwestern University Press.

———— 1973c. "Community Formation in an Urban Squatter Settlement," *Comp. Pol. Stud.* 6 (3): 293–328.

Rossi, Peter H., Richard A. Berk, and B. Eidson. 1974. *The Roots of Urban Discontent.* New York: Wiley.

Roth, Barbara. In progress. "Adult Political Socialization: The Study of American Immigrants in Israel." Dissertation, Rutgers.

Salaff, Janet. 1971. "Urban Residential Communities in the Wake of the Cultural Revolution," pp. 289–323 in John W. Lewis, ed., *The City in Communist China*. Stanford, Calif.: Stanford University Press.

Salamon, Lester M., and Steven Van Evera. 1973. "Fear, Apathy, and Discrimination: A Test of Three Explanations of Political Participation," *Amer. Pol. Sci. Rev.* 67 (4): 1288–1306.

Sallach, David L., Nicholas Babchuk, and Alan Booth. 1972. "Social Involvement and Political Activity: Another View," *Soc. Sci. Quar.* 52 (4): 879–92.

Savitch, Harold V. 1972. "Powerlessness in an Urban Ghetto," *Polity* 5 (1): 19–56.

Schers, David. 1972. *The Popular Sector of the Partido Revolucionario Institucional in Mexico*. Tel Aviv: The David Horowitz Institute for the Research of Developing Countries, Tel Aviv University, Res. Rpt. 1. (Submitted as a Ph.D. dissertation in Political Science, U. New Mexico, 1972.)

Scheuch, Erwin K. 1969. "Social Context and Individual Behavior," pp. 133–55 in Dogan and Rokkan, 1969.

Schneider, Peter R., and Anne L. Schneider. 1971. "Social Mobilization, Political Institutions, and Political Violence: A Cross-National Analysis," *Comp. Pol. Stud.* 4 (1): 69–90.

Schorr, Alvin L. 1970. "Housing and Its Effects," pp. 709–25 in Robert Gutman and David Popenoe, eds., *Neighborhood, City, and Metropolis*. New York: Random House.

Schoultz, Lars. 1972a. "Urbanization and Changing Voting Patterns: Colombia, 1946–1970," *Political Science Quarterly*, Vol. 87, No. 1 (March).

———— 1972b. "Urbanization and Political Change in Latin America," *Midwest. J. Pol. Sci.* 16 (3): 367–87.

Schuman, Howard, and Barry Gruenberg. 1972. "Dissatisfaction with City Services: Is Race an Important Factor?", pp. 369–92 in Harlan Hahn, ed., *People and Politics in Urban Society* (*Urban Affairs Annual Reviews*, Vol. 6). Beverly Hills: Sage Publications.

Schwartz, David C. 1973. *Political Alienation and Political Behavior*. Chicago: Aldine.

Scott, James C. 1969. "Corruption, Machine Politics, and Political Change," *Amer. Pol. Sci. Rev.* 63 (4): 1142–58.

———— 1972. "Patron-Client Politics and Political Change in Southeast Asia," *Amer. Pol. Sci. Rev.* 66 (1): 91–113.

Scott, John Finley. 1971. *Internalization of Norms: A Sociological Theory of Moral Commitment*. Englewood Cliffs, N.J.: Prentice-Hall.

Scott, Robert E. 1964. *Mexican Government in Transition*, 2d ed. Urbana: University of Illinois Press.

———— 1965. "Mexico: The Established Revolution," pp. 330–95 in Lucian W. Pye and Sidney Verba, eds., *Political Culture and Political Development*. Princeton: Princeton University Press.

———— 1973. "National Integration Problems and Military Regimes in Latin America," pp. 285–356 in R. E. Scott, ed., *Latin American Modernization Problems*. Urbana: University of Illinois Press.

———— 1974. "Politics in Mexico," in Gabriel A. Almond, ed., *Comparative Politics Today*. Boston: Little, Brown.

———— Forthcoming. *Politics in Mexico*. Boston: Little, Brown.

Searing, Donald D., Joel J. Schwartz, and Alden E. Lind. 1973. "The Structuring Principle: Political Socialization and Belief Systems," *Amer. Pol. Sci. Rev.* 67 (2): 415–32.

Segal, David R., and Marshall W. Meyer. 1969. "The Social Context of Political Partisanship," pp. 217–32 in Dogan & Rokkan, 1969.

Segal, David R., and S. H. Wildstrom. 1970. "Community Effects on Political Attitudes: Partisanship and Efficacy," *Sociol. Quar.* 11: 67–86.

Segovia, Rafael. 1974. "La reforma política: El ejecutivo federal, el PRI y las elecciones de 1973," *Foro Internacional* (Mexico) 14 (3): 51–67.

——— 1975. *La politización del niño mexicano.* Mexico City: El Colegio de México.

Sennett, Richard. 1970. *The Uses of Disorder: Personal Identity and City Life.* New York: Knopf.

Sewell, William H., and J. Michael Armer. 1966. "Neighborhood Context and College Plans," *Amer. Sociol. Rev.* 31 (2): 159–68.

Shannon, Lyle W. 1965. "Urban Adjustment and Its Relationship to the Social Antecedents of Immigrant Workers," *Int. Rev. Comm. Devel.* 13–14: 177–88.

Shannon, Lyle W., and Magdaline Shannon. 1968. "The Assimilation of Migrants to Cities: Anthropological and Sociological Contributions," pp. 49–76 in Leo F. Schnore, ed., *Social Science and the City: A Survey of Urban Research.* New York: Praeger.

Sherif, Musafer, and Carolyn W. Sherif. 1964. *Reference Groups.* New York: Harper & Row.

Sills, D. L., et al. 1961. "Three 'Climate of Opinion' Studies," *Publ. Opin. Quart.* 25: 571–610.

Silverman, Sydel F. 1965. "Patronage and Community-Nation Relationships in Central Italy," *Ethnology* 4 (2): 172–89.

Simpson, Lesley Byrd. 1967. *Many Mexicos*, 4th ed. Berkeley: University of California Press.

Sinding, Steven W. 1972. "The Evolution of Chilean Voting Patterns: A Reexamination of Some Old Assumptions," *J. Politics* 34 (3): 774–96.

Smith, Robert B. 1972. "Neighborhood Context and College Plans: An Ordinal Path Analysis," *Social Forces* 51 (2): 199–217.

Snyder, Peter Z. 1972. "Indigenous Neighborhood Gatekeepers in the Process of Urban Adaptation." Paper presented at the annual meeting of the American Anthropological Association (Toronto).

Soares, Gláucio Ary Dillon. 1973. "Notas sôbre as consequências políticas da migração." Unpubl. paper, Dept. Sociology, Cornell. Abridged version in Spanish published in Jorge Balán et al., *Migración y desarrollo: Consideraciones teóricas y aspectos socioeconómicos y políticos.* Buenos Aires: Consejo Latinoamericano de Ciencias Sociales, 1973.

Solís, Leopoldo. 1971. "Mexican Economic Policy in the Post-War Period: The Views of Mexican Economists," *Amer. Econ. Rev.* 61: 28–46.

——— 1972. *Controversias sobre el crecimiento y la distribución: Las opiniones de economistas mexicanos acerca de la política económica.* Mexico City: Fondo de Cultura Económica.

Stavenhagen, Rodolfo. 1970. "Social Aspects of Agrarian Structure in Mexico," pp. 225–70 in Rodolfo Stavenhagen, ed., *Agrarian Problems and*

Peasant Movements in Latin America. Garden City, N.Y.: Doubleday Anchor Books.

Stea, David. 1966. "Urban Images in Mexico: A Study of the Conceptual Forms of Three Mexican Cities, As Seen By Their Inhabitants." Unpubl. paper, Dept. Geography, Clark U., Worcester, Mass.

———— 1968. "La conducta humana y el diseño urbano," *Rev. Soc. Interamer. Planificación* 2: 12–16.

Stevens, Evelyn P. 1974. *Protest and Response in Mexico.* Cambridge, Mass.: MIT Press.

Stokes, Charles J. 1962. "A Theory of Slums," *Land Econ.* 38: 187–97.

Stouffer, Samuel A., et al. 1949. *The American Soldier, I.* Princeton, N.J.: Princeton University Press.

Suttles, Gerald D. 1968. *The Social Order of the Slum.* Chicago: University of Chicago Press.

———— 1972. *The Social Construction of Communities.* Chicago: University of Chicago Press.

Swanson, B. E. 1970. *The Concern for Community in Urban America.* New York: Odyssey.

Tannenbaum, Arnold S., and Jerald G. Bachman. 1964. "Structural Versus Individual Effects," *Amer. J. Sociol.* 69 (6): 585–95.

Tate, C. Neal. 1974. "Individual and Contextual Variables in British Voting Behavior: An Exploratory Note," *Amer. Pol. Sci. Rev.* 68 (4): 1656–62.

Tello, Carlos. 1971. "Notas para el análisis de la distribución del ingreso en México," *Trimestre Econ.* (Mexico) 150.

Temple, Nelle R. In progress. "Urban Commitment and Political Demand-Making in Kenya." Ph.D. dissertation, Dept. Political Science, MIT.

Tessler, Mark A. 1972. "The Application of Western Theories and Measures of Political Participation to a Single-Party North African State," *Comp. Pol. Stud.* 5 (2): 175–91.

Tilly, Charles. 1974. "Do Communities Act?," pp. 209–40 in Effrat 1974.

Timms, Duncan. 1971. *The Urban Mosaic: Towards a Theory of Residential Differentiation.* London: Cambridge University Press.

Tingsten, Herbert. 1937. *Political Behavior.* London: P. S. King.

Tomeh, Aida K. 1969. "Empirical Considerations in the Problem of Social Integration," *Sociol. Inquiry* 39: 65–76.

Toness, Odin A., Jr. 1967. "Power Relations of a Central American Slum." Unpubl. M.A. Thesis, U. Texas (Austin).

Torres Trueba, Henry E. 1969. "Factionalism in a Mexican Municipio," *Sociologus* (Berlin) n.s. 19 (2): 134–52.

Touraine, Alaine, and Daniel Pécaut. 1967–68. "Working-Class Consciousness and Economic Development in Latin America," *Stud. Comp. Int. Devel.* 3 (4): 71–84.

Townsend, James R. 1967. *Political Participation in Communist China.* Berkeley: University of California Press.

Tuohy, William S. 1969. "Centralism and Political Elite Behavior in Mexico." Unpubl. paper, Dept. Political Science, U. California (Davis). (Original version of Tuohy 1973.)

———— 1973. "Centralism and Political Elite Behavior in Mexico," pp. 260–80 in Clarence E. Thurber and Lawrence S. Graham, eds., *Development*

Administration in Latin America. Durham, N.C.: Duke University Press.

Turner, Frederick C. 1973. "Mexican Politics: The Direction of Development," pp. 151–81 in William P. Glade and Stanley R. Ross, eds., *Críticas constructivas del sistema político Mexicano.* Austin: Institute of Latin American Studies, University of Texas.

Turner, John F. C. 1968a. "Uncontrolled Urban Settlement: Problems and Policies," *Int. Soc. Devel. Rev.* (United Nations), 1: 107–28.

———— 1968b. "Housing Priorities, Settlement Patterns, and Urban Development in Modernizing Countries," *J. Amer. Inst. Planners* 34 (6): 354–63.

———— 1970. "Barriers and Channels for Housing Development in Modernizing Countries," pp. 1–19 in William Mangin, ed., *Peasants in Cities: Readings in the Anthropology of Urbanization.* Boston: Houghton Mifflin.

———— 1971. "The Squatter Revolution: Autonomous Urban Settlement and Social Change in Transitional Economies." Unpubl. book ms., Dept. Urban Studies and Planning, MIT.

———— 1974. Housing Priorities and Policies in Mexico: Report to the International Bank for Reconstruction and Development." Unpubl. paper, Dept. Urban Studies and Planning, MIT.

Turner, John F. C., and Robert Fichter. 1972. *Freedom to Build.* New York: Free Press.

Ugalde, Antonio. 1970. *Power and Conflict in a Mexican Community.* Albuquerque: University of New Mexico Press.

———— 1973. "Contemporary Mexico: From Hacienda to PRI, Political Leadership in a Zapotec Village," pp. 119–34 in Kern 1973.

Ugalde, Antonio, Leslie Olson, David Schers, and Miguel Von Hoegen. 1974. *The Urbanization Process of a Poor Mexican Neighborhood: The Case of San Felipe del Real Adicional, Juárez.* Austin: Institute of Latin American Studies, University of Texas.

Unikel, Luis. 1972. *La dinámica del crecimiento de la Ciudad de México.* Mexico City: Fundación para Estudios de la Población, A.C.

———— 1973. "El proceso de urbanización en México," in *El perfil de México en 1980,* Vol. III. Mexico City: Siglo Veintiuno.

Unikel, Luis, et al. 1973. "Factores de rechazo en la migración rural en México, 1950–1960," *Demografía y Econ.* 7 (1): 24–57.

Unikel, Luis, with Gustavo Garza and Crescencio Ruiz Chiapetti. 1975. *El desarrollo urbano de México: Diagnóstico e implicaciones futuras.* Mexico City: El Colegio de México.

Uno, Toru. 1972. "The Discontinuity of Political Socialization: Toward a Dynamic Model of Social Change." Unpubl. dissertation, U. Oregon.

Usandizaga, Elsa, and A. Eugene Havens. 1966. *Tres barrios de invasión.* Bogotá: Tercer Mundo.

Uzzell, Douglas. 1972. "Bound for Places I'm Not Known To: Adaptation of Migrants and Residence in Four Irregular Settlements in Lima, Peru." Unpubl. dissertation, U. Texas (Austin).

———— 1973. "Bureaus and the Urban Poor in Lima." Paper presented at the annual meeting of the American Anthropological Association (New Orleans).

———— 1974. "The Interaction of Population and Locality in the Development of Squatter Settlements in Lima," pp. 113–34 in Wayne A. Cornelius and Felicity M. Trueblood, eds., *Anthropological Perspectives on Latin American Urbanization* (*Latin American Urban Research*, Vol. 4). Beverly Hills: Sage Publications.

Valdés, Luis. 1968. "Voting Patterns in Rural and Urban São Paulo: Socio-logical-Economic-Demographic Correlates of Voting Behavior in Brazil, 1952–1963." Unpubl. dissertation, U. Wisconsin, Madison.

Vanderschueren, Franz. 1973. "Political Significance of Neighborhood Committees in the Settlements of Santiago," pp. 256–83 in Dale L. Johnson, ed., *The Chilean Road to Socialism*. Garden City, N.Y.: Doubleday Anchor Books.

van Sauer, Franz A. 1974. *The Alienated "Loyal" Opposition: Mexico's Partido Acción Nacional*. Albuquerque: University of New Mexico Press.

Vaughan, Denton R. 1968. "Links Between Peripheral Lower-Income Residential Areas and Political Parties in a Latin American City." Unpubl. paper, Dept. Anthropology, U. Texas (Austin).

Vaughan, Denton R., and Waltraut Feindt. 1973. "Initial Settlement and Intracity Movement of Migrants in Monterrey, Mexico," *J. Amer. Inst. Planners* 39 (6): 388–401.

Vekemans, Roger, and Jorge Giusti. 1969–70. "Marginality and Ideology in Latin American Development," *Stud. Comp. Int. Devel.* 5 (11).

Verba, Sidney. 1967. "Some Dilemmas in Comparative Research," *World Politics* 20 (1): 111–27.

———— 1969. "The Uses of Survey Research in the Study of Comparative Politics," in Stein Rokkan, et al., *Comparative Survey Analysis*. The Hague: Mouton.

———— 1971. "Cross-National Survey Research: The Problem of Credibility," pp. 309–56 in Ivan Vallier, ed., *Comparative Methods in Sociology*. Berkeley: University of California Press.

Verba, Sidney, Bashir Ahmed, and Anil Bhatt. 1971. *Caste, Race, and Politics: A Comparative Study of India and the United States*. Beverly Hills: Sage Publications.

Verba, Sidney, and Norman H. Nie. 1972. *Participation in America: Political Democracy and Social Equality*. New York: Harper & Row.

Verba, Sidney, Norman H. Nie, and Jae-On Kim. 1971. *The Modes of Democratic Participation: A Cross-National Comparison* (*Sage Professional Papers in Comparative Politics*, No. 01–013). Beverly Hills: Sage Publications.

Vernez, Georges. 1973. "The Residential Movements of Low-Income Families: The Case of Bogotá, Colombia." Santa Monica, Calif.: Rand Corp. Report P-5102.

Walton, John. 1973. "Standardized Case Comparison: Observations on Method in Comparative Sociology," pp. 173–91 in Michael Armer and Allen D. Grimshaw, eds., *Comparative Social Research: Methodological Problems and Strategies*. New York: Wiley.

Walton, John, and Joyce A. Sween. 1971. "Urbanization, Industrialization, and Voting in Mexico: A Longitudinal Analysis of Official and Opposition Party Support," *Soc. Sci. Quart.* 52: 721–45.

Ward, Peter M. 1975. "Intra-City Migration to Squatter Settlements in Mexico City." Unpubl. paper, Dept. Geography, University College, London.

Warren, Donald I., and Jesse F. McClure. 1973. "Toward a Theory of Black Community Structure: The Linkage Between Neighborhood and Voluntary Association Patterns." Paper presented at the annual meeting of the American Sociological Association (New York).

Weiner, Myron. 1971. "Political Participation: The Crisis of the Political Process," pp. 159–204 in Leonard Binder, et al., *Crises and Sequences in Political Development*. Princeton, N.J.: Princeton University Press.

———— 1973a. "When Migrants Succeed and Natives Fail," pp. 315–29 in *International Population Conference, Liège, 1973: Proceedings*, Vol. I. Liège: International Union for the Scientific Study of Population.

———— 1973b. "Socio-Political Consequences of Interstate Migration in India," pp. 190–228 in W. Howard Wriggins and James F. Guyot, eds., *Population, Politics, and the Future of Southern Asia*. New York: Columbia University Press.

Weiner, Myron, and John O. Field. 1973. *India's Urban Constituencies*. Cambridge, Mass.: Center for International Studies, MIT.

White, James W. 1973. *Political Implications of Cityward Migration: Japan as an Exploratory Test Case* (*Sage Professional Papers in Comparative Politics*, No. 01–038). Beverly Hills: Sage Publications.

Wilken, Paul H. 1971. "Size of Organizations and Member Participation in Church Congregations," *Admin. Sci. Quart.* 16 (2): 173–79.

Wilkie, James W. 1970. "Mexico City as a Magnet for Mexico's Economically Active Population," pp. 379–95 in Bernardo García, et al., eds., *Historia y sociedad en el mundo de habla española: Homenaje a José Miranda*. Mexico City: El Colegio de México.

———— 1971. "New Hypotheses for Statistical Research in Recent Mexican History," *Lat. Amer. Res. Rev.* 6 (2): 3–18.

———— 1974. "Recentralization: The Budgetary Dilemma in the Economic Development of Mexico, Bolivia, and Costa Rica," in David T. Geithman, ed., *Fiscal Policy for Industrialization in Latin America*. Gainesville: University of Florida Press.

Wilkie, Richard W. 1975. "Urban Growth and the Transformation of the Settlement Landscape of Mexico: 1910–1970," in James W. Wilkie, Michael C. Meyer, and Edna Monzón de Wilkie, eds., *Contemporary Mexico: Papers of the IV International Congress of Mexican History* Berkeley and Mexico City: University of California Press and El Colegio de México.

Wilson, Robert A. 1971a. "Anomia and Militancy Among Urban Negroes: A Study of Neighborhood and Individual Effects," *Sociol. Quart.* 12: 369–86.

———— 1971b. "Anomie in the Ghetto: A Study of Neighborhood Type, Race, and Anomie," *Amer. J. Sociol.* 77 (1): 66–88.

Wolf, Eric R. 1965. "Aspects of Group Relations in a Complex Society: Mexico," pp. 85–101 in Dwight B. Heath and Richard N. Adams, eds., *Contemporary Cultures and Societies of Latin America*. New York: Random House.

Wolf, Eric R., and Edward C. Hansen. 1967. "Caudillo Politics: A Structural Analysis," *Comp. Stud. Soc. & Hist.* 9: 168–79.

Wolpert, J. 1965. "Behavioral Aspects of the Decision to Migrate," *Paps. Reg. Sci. Assoc.* 15: 159–69.

World Bank. 1972. *Urbanization Sector Working Paper.* Washington, D.C.: World Bank.

Wriggins, W. Howard, and James F. Guyot. 1973. "Demographic Change and Politics," in W. Howard Wriggins and James F. Guyot, eds., *Population, Politics, and the Future of Southern Asia.* New York: Columbia University Press.

Yates, Douglas T., Jr. 1973. *Neighborhood Democracy: The Politics and Impacts of Decentralization.* Lexington, Mass.: Heath-Lexington.

Young, Michael, and Peter Wilmott. 1957. *Family and Kinship in East London.* London: Routledge & Kegan Paul.

Zimmerman, Joseph F. 1971. "The Politics of Neighborhood Government," *Stud. Comp. Loc. Govt.* 5 (1): 28–39.

———— 1972. "Community Building in Large Cities," *Administration* 20 (2): 71–82.

Index

Index

Abstentionism, 163–64
Adams, Richard, 148n
Africa, cities in, 141, 181, 231
Age: and political learning, 9, 11–12; upon migration, 19; and political involvement, 122f, 134
Agriculture, in Mexico, 17, 19
Alienation, political, 61–63, 163–64, 221, 232
Allende, President Salvador, 198f
Almond, Gabriel, 54, 77, 82n, 107n
Ames, Barry, 64n
Argentina, 78
Arterton, F. Christopher, 175
Asia, cities in, 196–97
Assimilation, socioeconomic, 21–26
Asunción, Paraguay, 232
Attitudes, political, *see* Political attitudes
Austria, 91, 133

Barros, Ademar de, 153n
Barton, Allen, 5, 112, 117
Becker, Howard, 12, 128, 228
Berkowitz, Leonard, 224
Bonilla, Frank, 36n
Bracero program, 17
Brazil, 132n, 153, 176, 179, 183n. *See also* Rio de Janeiro
Brokerage, political, 158–59, 162, 178
Bureaucracy, government, 184, 192, 217–20 *passim*

Cacicazgo, see Caciques
Caciques: and political participation, 76, 85, 96; defined, 139–44; in rural Mexico, 140–42, 163f; relations with

supralocal authorities, 141–42, 147–50, 159–60; motivations of, 143; bases of influence, 144–53; performance of, 150–59 *passim*; origins and durability of, 160–63; and political reform, 163–64. *See also* Leadership, community
Cali, Colombia, 197n
Campaigns, electoral: participation in, 81–88 *passim*, 92–106 *passim*; and political system performance, 215–17
Campamentos, 198–99
Cantril, Hadley, 25
Caudillo, 140, 143
Centralism, political, 189, 202
Chile, 78, 132n, 176f, 179, 198–99, 227. *See also* Santiago, Chile
China, People's Republic of, 227
Church, Catholic, 62, 175. *See also* Religiosity
Citizen-government interaction, 8, 10, 157–58, 201, 203–13, 224; in research communities, 38, 48–52 *passim*. *See also* Demand-making, political
Ciudad perdida, 26, 35–36
Civic duties, perceived, 84–86, 105–6
Ciudad Guayana, Venezuela, 183n
Ciudad Juárez, Mexico, 81n
Ciudad Netzahualcóyotl, *see* Netzahualcóyotl, municipio of
Civic-mindedness, 113f
Class, social, *see* Socioeconomic status
CNOP (Confederación Nacional de Organizaciones Populares), 207, 211
Collective stress, 104
Collective work orientation, 95–96, 122, 124, 127
Colonia Esfuerzo Propio: history and